The Music of
Johann Sebastian Bach

The Music of Johann Sebastian Bach

THE SOURCES, THE STYLE, THE SIGNIFICANCE

ROBERT L. MARSHALL

SCHIRMER BOOKS
A Division of Macmillan, Inc.
NEW YORK

Schirmer Books
A Division of Macmillan, Inc.
866 Third Avenue, New York, N.Y. 10022

Collier Macmillan Canada, Inc.

Library of Congress Catalog Card Number: 88-23921

Printed in the United States of America
First Schirmer Books paperback edition, 1990

printing number
  2 3 4 5 6 7 8 9 10

Library of Congress Cataloging in Publication Data

Marshall, Robert Lewis.
  The music of Johann Sebastian Bach.

  Bibliography: p.
  1. Bach, Johann Sebastian, 1685–1750—Criticism and interpretation. I. Title.
ML410.B13M28 1989   780'.92'4   88-23921
ISBN 0-02-871781-3 (hc)
ISBN 0-02-871782-1 (pb)

This book is dedicated
to my wife
Traute
with deepest gratitude
for a quarter century
of unflagging patience
and unfailing wisdom

Contents

Introduction

I

The Historical Significance

II

On the Compositional Process

III

Questions of Authenticity and Chronology

IV

Aspects of Performance Practice

Plates

Preface

The sixteen essays collected here were written over the course of some twenty years. They share a common objective—to help refine our understanding and appreciation of the muscial phenomenon Johann Sebastian Bach—but do so by approaching the music and, to a lesser extent, the composer himself, from several points of view. Most broadly, the essays are of two kinds: stylistic and historical inquiries, and studies of the original sources. The latter are divided by topic into three sections devoted in turn to the compositional process, matters of authenticity and chronology, and issues of performance practice. Accordingly, this volume, after an introductory chapter, is organized into four parts. But the divisions are by no means hard and fast. In fact, it is particularly the interconnections between essays and sections—and the way some studies pick up on ideas first advanced in another—that lend the collection as a whole its unity.

The first item in the volume is by design an introduction: it is meant to provide basic biographical and historical information pertaining to "Bach, Johann Sebastian" in a reasonably concise and objective form. It is in fact an encyclopedia entry, written originally by Walter Emery, which I had occasion to revise for the 15th edition of the *Encyclopaedia Britannica*. For the present publication it has been updated yet again, especially with respect to the concluding bibliography. The introduction is also intended to serve as a point of departure for Part I, "The Historical Significance," consisting of studies devoted to a reassessment of Bach's position in Western musical history and reflecting on the larger cultural significance of his artistic achievement.

Part I begins with "Bach the Progressive," a challenge to the conventional view of Bach as a traditionalistic, even a reactionary composer. The essay argues specifically that Bach's dissatisfaction with his situation in Leipzig during the 1730s and early 1740s, fed by his keen awareness of the superior musical establishment flourishing in Dresden, provided the impetus for him to expand his own artistic horizons in many directions, most notably that of the latest Italian, "pre-classic" style. We find elements of this new style in a number of compositions including two of his greatest masterpieces dating from this period: the B-minor Mass and the "Goldberg" Variations. In a Postscript, printed here for the first time, I address the principal arguments that have been recently advanced in response to this thesis.

"Bach's *Orchestre*," despite its title, is more of a biographical contribution than anything else, although it is also something of a whimsical epilogue to the argument of "Bach the Progressive." It demonstrates, on the basis of a terminological investigation, that when Bach offered to write "music for the *orchestre*" for the Dresden court, he meant music for the orchestra pit, i.e., theatrical music—in the first instance, opera. Needless to say, this does not conform to the prevailing notions regarding Bach's understanding of his mission as a composer. The main contribution of this brief article, however, is one of method. The study is meant to demonstrate the relatively neglected potential of terminological studies to illuminate music-historical questions—a resource that is exploited later on in the volume.

"On Bach's Universality" was written as a public lecture, presented on Bach's 300th birthday—March 21, 1985—at the Library of Congress. In many ways it pursues the implications of the line of thought begun in "Bach the Progressive," this time contemplating in what respects Bach's music can be regarded as universal. It attempts to view the question from two perspectives, Bach's own and that of history, in the first case documenting the intimate connection between Bach's roles as a teacher and as a composer and suggesting that Bach, among other things, conceived his works as pedagogical demonstrations of the operation of universal and eternally valid *laws* governing the nature of "true" music. From the perspective of history, I argue that Bach—knowingly or intuitively—was attempting to create a universal music that would unite diverse geographical, historical, and formal principles of composition, and that by doing so he was prophetically transcending the tendency of his own time to separate and isolate musical styles and genres.

Part II, "On the Compositional Process," is the first of three sections devoted to studies of the sources—primarily Bach's autograph manuscripts. The six essays in Part II develop in various ways the approaches and observations presented in my book, *The Compositional Process of J. S. Bach*, as well as probe their implications and limits. Initial impressions to the contrary, attempting to reconstruct the act of composition by examining clues left behind in the original sources is less an exercise in positivist musicology than it is a biographical, even a psychological, inquiry asking of the great composer eminently personal questions directed to the core of his artistic life: how he actually went about creating music.

The studies in Part II proceed more or less from the general to the particular and happen to form three pairs of essays. "'Composing Scores' and 'Fair Copies'" describes the basic types of Bach autograph score and illustrates what information one can learn from each: encompassing handwriting style and performance practice, as well as the process of composition. The manuscripts considered—all preserved in American collections—span a thirty-year period and represent virtually the entirety of Bach's career as a cantata composer. Taken together, the discussions reveal how Bach typically proceeded to compose a church cantata, while the examination of a number of specific corrections, and even omissions, in the manuscripts helps shed light on how Bach confronted a variety of compositional choices.

The article on "The Sketches," similarly, is something of an introduction. In addition to creating definitions and classifications for the 150-odd marginal jottings and fragmentary drafts preserved in the Bach sources, it seeks above all to comprehend the several formative functions and stages represented by this material in the generation and elaboration of musical ideas.

Following upon these initial surveys are two essays devoted to a single work. As noted in the "The Autograph Score of *Herr, gehe nicht ins Gericht,* BWV 105/3," the manuscript of this remarkable cantata is unusually illuminating with respect to the shaping and refinement of melodic ideas, the formulation of larger tonal and formal designs, and, most strikingly, to the gradually emerging symbolic conceit that informs the entire composition.

"The Genesis of an Aria Ritornello," the most technical and analytical essay in the volume, carries the previous discussion considerably further and represents something of an experiment: an attempt, figuratively, to "become the composer composing" by trying to uncover the compositional rationale and "internal dialogue" underlying *every* anomaly and correction visible in the composer's original notation: to follow him every step of the way. Since this is by design a highly detailed and intensive investigation, only the opening ritornello section of a single aria could be examined, but examined from as many points of view as I was able to divine.

The next pair of studies is devoted to two of Bach's most celebrated works: the *Magnificat* and the Mass in B minor. The approaches, however, are altogether different. "The Origin of the *Magnificat:* A Lutheran Composer's Challenge" is another experiment, but the diametric opposite of that pursued in "The Genesis of an Aria Ritornello." The idea here is not to analyze every visible correction but rather to see what can be learned from those aspects of the work that underwent no changes in the composing score. That is, the focus here is on "negative" evidence that seems to testify to fundamental decisions that the composer must have reached before he had set down any notes in a score and that must constitute the earliest stage in the evolution of the work: the stage "before genesis." This inquiry entails for us (as it must have for Bach) a survey of the prevailing musical and liturgical conventions—i.e., compositional constraints—surrounding the tradition of *Magnificat* setting in Bach's historical milieu. The essay also attempts to account for the existence of two versions of the *Magnificat,* suggesting that they bear witness to a delicate aesthetic and theological problem that had confronted Bach, one which he ultimately resolved.

The essay on the B-minor Mass, finally, explores the relationship between the Mass and some of the earlier compositions it is based on. But it concentrates mainly on the formal and even theological consequences flowing from some of the most substantial changes observable in the autograph: the insertion (virtually at the last moment) of the adagio introduction at the beginning of the *Kyrie,* and the equally belated decision to set the words "Et incarnatus est" as a separate movement.

Part III, "Questions of Authenticity and Chronology," consists of just two essays, both concerned with these traditional issues of musical scholarship. The Fantasia in C minor, BWV 906, one of the most famous of Bach's independent keyboard compositions, is also one of only two known cases in which Bach himself took the trouble of writing out two fair copies. The present study attempts to provide an explanation for this curious double labor and in the process proposes datings for each of the copies that reverse the common assumption about them. At the same time the new datings suggest connections between the Fantasia and two of Bach's most ambitious projects of the 1730s: the composition of the Keyboard Partitas of the *Clavier-Übung* and his work on Volume II of the *Well-Tempered Clavier.*

By combining studies of the manuscripts with a consideration of some little-noticed biographical material (again involving Dresden, by the way), the essay on Bach's flute compositions concludes that the argument advanced in recent years that Bach was not the composer of two of them does not hold. Since that position has been based almost entirely on a limited conception of the range of Bach's style, the discussion returns to the central issue dealt with at the outset of this volume, now trained on a specific body of works. The study also challenges the longstanding assumption that Bach's instrumental chamber music was largely composed during his Köthen years, 1717–1723, suggesting that the flute sonatas, at all events, were probably written over a time span of some twenty-five years. More generally, the essay argues that new research tools are necessary to investigate the perennial but basic questions of authenticity and chronology, now that the potential of the prevailing ones—most notably, paper and handwriting analysis—seems to be reaching its limits. A Postscript has been appended to consider some of the dissenting views that the original publication of this essay has provoked.

Part IV is devoted to the ever-lively issue of "authentic" performance practice. The approach, again, is through the original sources.

The first essay (based on a review of the first volumes of the Harnoncourt-Leonhardt complete recording of the Bach cantatas), addresses problems surrounding the musical text, performing forces, and performance style.

The issue of the reliability of the musical text, particularly with respect to slurring and articulation, is considered further in "Editore traditore," an essay communicating some deeply unsettling findings regarding the authenticity of certain articulation markings not only in the venerable *Bach-Gesellschaft* edition, but also in the ultimate arbiter of all authenticity claims, the original manuscripts themselves. This is a cautionary tale revealing that even the original sources may not accurately reflect the composer's intentions. A short Postscript reports on recent research that promises to help determine the origin of questionable entries in the original Bach sources.

The final essays of the volume, "Tempo and Dynamics" and "Organ or 'Klavier?'", both exploit the virtually untapped potential of terminological investigations to illuminate very practical questions of performance. The animating question informing both studies is: what can we learn from those instances where Bach was obliged to resort to words to indicate his musical intentions?

"Tempo and Dynamics," a progress report of sorts, outlines the growth over time of Bach's vocabulary related to these topics and establishes what must have been his understanding both of the specific meaning of particular terms and of the relationships between them. "Organ or 'Klavier'?" establishes, first of all, that Bach's own prescriptions in this regard are more numerous, more specific, and hence more informative than is commonly assumed. It proceeds to question the prevailing view that any keyboard work by Bach without a pedal part must have been intended for the harpsichord. The evidence advanced here should have immediate practical consequences: affecting, for example, the choice of instrument for the performance of the so-called harpsichord toccatas and concertos.

This volume is not a simple reprint of previously published material. Virtually every essay has been revised to some degree, in order both to avoid redundancy and to enhance the unity and continuity among the individual pieces. I have also tried to take cognizance of the most significant and pertinent research that has appeared since the original publications. To this end, Postscripts have been appended to three items: "Bach the Progressive" (Chapter 2), "The Compositions for Solo Flute" (Chapter 12), and "'Editore traditore'" (Chapter 14). Two essays have been substantially rewritten (and expanded) for this publication; both, incidentally, have previously appeared only in German: "The Mass in B minor" (Chapter 10) and "'Editore traditore'" (Chapter 14.)

For the most part changes and additions have been worked into, and restricted to, the endnotes. I have tried to make it possible for the reader to recognize at once what has been changed or added vis-à-vis the original publication by putting all such material in square brackets. At the same time, however, the original footnote (or endnote) numbering has been retained, as far as possible. (Only in "The Sketches" (Chapter 6) has it been necessary, owing to several substantial deletions in the text, to renumber the notes entirely.) Completely new notes have been interpolated between existing notes, placed in square brackets, and given a letter superscript. For example, a note added between old numbers "43" and "44" will have the number: "[43a]." Where the original content of an existing note has been entirely replaced, but the original number retained, the number (along with the new material) appears in square brackets, e.g.:

> [20.Dreyfus 1987 is precisely the study called for.]

Where new material has been added to an existing note, only the new material (usually appearing at the end of the entry) appears in brackets, e.g.:

> 28.Early versions . . . appear in Bach's hand. . . . See Breckoff 1965 . . . [Also Brokaw 1985.]

Facsimile plates, tables, and musical examples, however, have been renumbered here for uniformity within the volume. Plates have been numbered consecutively in a single series for the whole volume. For tables and musical examples the principle of numbering is to use the essay number followed by the consecutive number of the item within the essay, e.g.: "Example 5.2," "Table 12.2."

Throughout the volume bibliographical citations in the notes appear in the form of surname-plus-date of publication (When necessary, a first name initial is included as well, e.g.: F. Neumann 1964, W. Neumann 1969.) The complete citation appears in the Bibliography section.

Finally, since references in the existing scholarly literature to specific passages in these essays are invariably to the page numbers of the original publications, the original pagination has been indicated here with bracketed numbers placed in the "gutter," or inner, margins of the running head at the top of each page. This should make it an easy matter to locate such citations in this volume.

It remains only to express my gratitude to the following individuals for helpful comments and information of various sorts: Paul Badura-Skoda, Howard Schott, George B. Stauffer, and Russell Stinson; to Maribeth Payne and Schirmer Books for their interest and encouragement for this publication; to Karen Komar for preparing the index; to Roberta Marvin for her invaluable assistance in the preparation of the final manuscript.

CREDITS

The essays included in this volume, all reprinted here with permission, were originally published as follows:

1. "Bach, Johann Sebastian." With Walter Emery. In *Encyclopaedia Britannica*, 15th edition, II, 556–61. Chicago: Encylopaedia Britannica, 1974. Reprinted with permission from *Encyclopaedia Britannica*, 15th edition, © 1974 by Encyclopaedia Britannica, Inc.

2. "Bach the Progressive: Observations on his Later Works." *The Musical Quarterly*, 62 (1976): 313–57.

3. "Bach's *Orchestre*." *Early Music*, 13 (1985): 176–79. Copyright Oxford University Press.

4. "On Bach's Universality." In *The Universal Bach. Lectures Celebrating the Tercentenary of Bach's Birthday, Fall 1985*, 50–66. Philadelphia: American Philosophical Society, Special Publication No. 43 (1986).

5. "Introduction." *Johann Sebastian Bach: Cantata Autographs in American Collections. A Facsimile Edition*, edited and with a preface by Robert L. Marshall, *Music in Facsimile*, 2, vii–xv. New York and London: Garland Publishing, Inc., 1985.

6. "Musical Sketches in J. S. Bach's Cantata Autographs." In *Studies in Music History: Essays for Oliver Strunk*, edited by Harold S. Powers, 405–27. Princeton: Princeton University Press, 1986. Reprinted by permission of Princeton University Press.

7. "Commentary." *Johann Sebastian Bach: Herr, gehe nicht ins Gericht (BWV 105)*. Faksimile nach dem Partiturautograph der Deutschen Staatsbibliothek Berlin mit einem Nachwort von Robert L. Marshall. *Bibliothek Seltener Bücher: Neudrucke herausgegeben von der Deutschen Staatsbibliothek zu Berlin, 5)*, 5–7. Leipzig: Zentralantiquariat der Deutschen Demokratischen Republik, 1983.

8. "The Genesis of an Aria Ritornello: Observations on the Autograph Score of 'Wie zittern und wanken,' BWV 105/3." In *Studies in Renaissance and Baroque Music in Honor of Arthur Mendel*, edited by Robert L. Marshall, 165–82. Kassel: Bärenreiter and Hackensack: Joseph N. Boonin, 1974.

9. "On the Origin of Bach's *Magnificat:* A Lutheran Composer's Challenge." In *New Bach Studies*, edited by Don Franklin, 3-17. Cambridge: Cambridge University Press, 1988. Copyright © 1988, Cambridge University Press.

10. "Beobachtungen am Autograph der h-moll-Messe: Zum Kompositionsprozess J. S. Bachs." *Musik und Kirche*, 50 (1980): 230–39.

11. "Introduction." *Johann Sebastian Bach: Fantasia per il Cembalo, BWV 906*. Facsimile edition with an introduction by Robert L. Marshall, [2]–[7]. Leipzig: Neue Bach-Gesellschaft, 1976.

12. "J. S. Bach's Compositions for Solo Flute: A Reconsideration of their Authenticity and Chronology." *Journal of the American Musicological Society*, 32 (1979): 463–98.
13. "Reviews of Records. Johann Sebastian Bach: The Complete Cantatas." [Volumes 1 and 2 of the Telefunken Series, Nikolaus Harnoncourt and Gustav Leonhardt, conductors.] *The Musical Quarterly*, 59 (1973): 145–59.
14. "*Editore traditore*: Ein weiterer 'Fall Rust'?" In *Bachiana et alia Musicologica: Alfred Dürr zum 65. Geburtstag,* edited by Wolfgang Rehm, 183–91. Kassel: Bärenreiter, 1983.
15. "Tempo and Dynamic Indications in the Bach Sources: A Review of the Terminology." In *Bach, Handel, Scarlatti: Tercentenary Essays,* edited by Peter Williams, 259–75. Cambridge: Cambridge University Press, 1985. Copyright © 1985, Cambridge University Press.
16. "Organ or '*Klavier*'?—Instrumental Prescriptions in the Sources of Bach's Keyboard Works." In *Bach as Organist,* edited by George B. Stauffer and Ernest May, 212–39. Bloomington: Indiana University Press, 1986.

The following individuals and institutions kindly granted permission to reproduce pages from the priceless manuscripts in their possession:

Deutsche Staatsbibliothek, Berlin/DDR: Musikabteilung (Plates 1–3, 25–30, 39).

Private collection, New York (Plates 6–8).

The Library of Congress, Washington, D.C.: Music Division, The Gertrude Clarke Whittall Foundation Collection (Plates 9–10).

Collection of William H. Scheide, Princeton, N.J. (Plates 11–13, 20–21).

Robert Owen Lehman Collection, on deposit in The Pierpont Morgan Library, New York (Plate 14).

Mary Flagler Cary Music Collection in The Pierpont Morgan Library, New York (Plate 15).

The New York Public Library at Lincoln Center, Astor, Lenox and Tilden Foundations: Music Division (Plates 16–18).

The Library of Congress, Washington, D.C.: Music Division (Plate 19).

Staatsbibliothek Preussicher Kulturbesitz, Berlin: Musikabteilung (Plates 22–24, 31).

The Bach Choir of Bethlehem, Bethlehem, PA (Plates 32–33).

Sächsische Landesbibliothek, Dresden/DDR: Musikabteilung (Plate 34).

Hochschule der Künste, Berlin, Hochschulbibliothek Abteilung 2 (Plates 36–38).

Bach-Archiv, Nationale Forschungs- und Gedenkstätten Johann Sebastian Bach der DDR, Leipzig/DDR (Plate 40).

Abbreviations

BG	*Johann Sebastian Bach's Werke.* Complete edition of the Bach-Gesellschaft. 46 volumes. Leipzig: Breitkopf & Härtel, 1851–1900. Reprint edition. Ann Arbor: J. W. Edwards, 1947.
BJ	*Bach-Jahrbuch.* Leipzig and Berlin, 1904–.
BR	Hans T. David and Arthur Mendel. *The Bach Reader: A Life of Johann Sebastian Bach in Letters and Documents.* Revised edition. New York: Norton, 1966.
BWV	Wolfgang Schmieder. *Thematisch-systematisches Verzeichnis der musikalischen Werke von Johann Sebastian Bach. Bach-Werke-Verzeichnis (BWV). Leipzig: Breitkopf & Härtel, 1950.*
f . . .^{r}	folio . . . recto
f . . .^{v}	folio . . . verso
m., mm.	measure, measures
NBA	*Johann Sebastian Bach. Neue Ausgabe sämtlicher Werke. (Neue Bach-Ausgabe).* Edited by the Johann-Sebastian-Bach-Institut, Göttingen, and the Bach-Archiv, Leipzig. Kassel: Bärenreiter and Leipzig: Deutscher Verlag für Musik, 1954–.
NBA . . . KB	*Neue Bach-Ausgabe . . . Kritische Berichte.*

Library identifications: Bach manuscripts originally belonging to the former Preussische Staatsbibliothek, Berlin (and now divided between the Deutsche Staatsbibibliothek in East Berlin and the Staatsbibliothek Stiftung Preussischer Kulturbesitz in West Berlin) carry the designations *Mus. ms. Bach P. . .* (=*Partitur,* i.e., score) or *Mus. ms. Bach St. . .* (=*Stimme(n),* i.e., part(s)). Manuscripts from this collection presently located in East Berlin are cited here as "P . . ." (or "St . . ."), those in West Berlin as "SPK P . . ." (or "SPK St . . .").

The Music of
Johann Sebastian Bach

Introduction

1

BACH, JOHANN SEBASTIAN

Although he was admired by his contemporaries primarily as an outstanding harpsichordist, organist, and expert on organ building, Johann Sebastian Bach is now generally regarded as one of the greatest composers of all time and is celebrated as the creator of the Brandenburg Concertos, the *Well-Tempered Clavier,* the Mass in B minor, and numerous other masterpieces of church and instrumental music. Appearing at a propitious moment in the history of music, Bach was able to survey and bring together the principal styles, forms, and national traditions that had developed during preceding generations and, by virtue of his synthesis, enrich them all.

He was a member of a remarkable family of musicians who were proud of their achievements, and about 1735 he drafted a genealogy, *Ursprung der musicalisch-Bachischen Familie* ("Origin of the Musical Bach Family"), in which he traced his ancestry back to his great-great-grandfather Veit Bach, a Lutheran baker (or miller), who was driven from Hungary to Wechmar in Thuringia, a historic region of Germany, by religious persecution late in the sixteenth century and died in 1619. There were Bachs in the area before that, and it may be that, when Veit moved to Wechmar, he was returning to his birthplace. He used to take his cittern to the mill and play it while grinding was going on. Johann Sebastian remarked, "A pretty noise they must have made together! However, he learnt to keep time, and this apparently was the beginning of music in our family."

Until the birth of Johann Sebastian, his was the least distinguished branch of the family; its members had been competent practical musicians, but not composers such as Johann Christoph, Johann Michael, and Johann Ludwig. In later days the most important musicians in the family were Johann Sebastian's sons, Wilhelm Friedemann, Carl Philipp Emanuel, and Johann Christian (the "English Bach").

EARLY YEARS

J.S. Bach was born at Eisenach, Thuringia (now in East Germany), on March 21, 1685, the youngest child of Johann Ambrosius Bach and Elisabeth Lämmerhirt. Ambrosius was a string player, employed by the town council and the ducal court of Eisenach. Johann Sebastian started school in 1692 or 1693 and did well in spite of frequent absences. Of his musical education at this time, nothing definite is known; but he may have picked up the rudiments of string playing from his father, and no doubt he attended the Georgenkirche, where Johann Christoph Bach was organist until 1703.

By 1695 both his parents were dead, and he was looked after by his eldest brother, also named Johann Christoph (1671-1721), organist at Ohrdruf. This Christoph had been a pupil of the influential keyboard composer Johann Pachelbel, and he apparently gave Johann Sebastian his first formal keyboard lessons. The young Bach again did well at school, until in 1700 his voice secured him a place in a select choir of poor boys at the school at the Michaeliskirche, Lüneburg (now in West Germany).

His voice must have broken soon after this, but he remained at Lüneburg for a time, making himself generally useful. No doubt he studied in the school library, which had a large and up-to-date collection of church music; he probably heard Georg Böhm, organist of the Johanniskirche; and he visited Hamburg to hear the renowned organist and composer Johann Adam Reinken at the Catharinenkirche, contriving also to hear the French orchestra maintained by the Duke of Celle.

He seems to have returned to Thuringia in the late summer of 1702, for, at some time between July and November, he applied for the post of organist at Sangerhausen (in modern East Germany). But for ducal interference, he would have obtained it; and, when every allowance is made for the low technical standards of that area, this means that he must already have been a reasonably proficient organist. His experience at Lüneburg, if not at Ohrdruf, had turned him away from the secular string-playing tradition of his immediate ancestors; thenceforth, he was, chiefly, though not exclusively, a composer and performer of keyboard and sacred music. The next few months are wrapped in mystery, but, by March 4, 1703, he was a member of the orchestra employed by Johann Ernst, Herzog von Weimar (brother of Wilhelm Ernst, whose service Bach entered in 1708). This post was a mere stopgap; he probably already had his eye on the organ then being

built at the Neukirche in Arnstadt; for, when it was finished, he helped
to test it, and in August 1703 he was appointed organist—all this at
the age of eighteen. Arnstadt documents imply that he had been court
organist at Weimar; this is incredible, though it is likely enough that he
had occasionally played there.

THE ARNSTADT PERIOD

At Arnstadt, on the northern edge of the Thuringian forest, where he remained until 1707, Bach devoted himself to keyboard music, the organ
in particular. While at Lüneburg, he had apparently had no opportunity of becoming directly acquainted with the spectacular, flamboyant
playing and compositions of Dietrich Buxtehude, the most significant
exponent of the north German school of organ music. In October 1705
he repaired this gap in his knowledge by obtaining a month's leave
and walking to Lübeck (over two hundred miles [three hundred kilo-
meters]). His visit must have been profitable, for he did not return
until about the middle of January 1706. In February his employers complained about his absence and about other things as well: he had harmonized the hymn tunes so freely that the congregation could not sing
to his accompaniment, and, above all, he had produced no cantatas.
Perhaps the real reasons for his neglect were that he was temporarily
obsessed with the organ and was on bad terms with the local singers
and instrumentalists, who were not under his control and did not come
up to his standards. In the summer of 1705 he had made some offen-
sive remark about a bassoon player, which led to an unseemly scuffle
in the street. His replies to these complaints were neither satisfactory
nor even accommodating; and the fact that he was not dismissed out of
hand suggests that his employers were as well aware of his exceptional
ability as he was himself and were reluctant to lose him.

During these early years, Bach inherited the musical culture of the
Thuringian area, a thorough familiarity with the traditional forms and
hymns (chorales) of the orthodox Lutheran serivce, and, in keyboard
music, perhaps (through his brother, Johann Christoph) a bias toward
the formalistic styles of the south. But he also learned eagerly from the
northern rhapsodists, [Reinken and] Buxtehude above all. By 1708 he
had probably learned all that his German predecessors could teach him
and arrived at a first synthesis of northern and southern German styles.
He had also studied, on his own and during his presumed excursions
to Celle, some French organ and instrumental music.

Among the few works that can be ascribed to these early years
with anything more than a show of plausibility are the *Capriccio sopra
la lontananza del suo fratello dilettissimo* (*Capriccio on the Departure of His
Most Beloved Brother*, 1704, BWV 992); the chorale prelude on *Wie schön*

leuchtet (*How Brightly Shines* ca. 1705, BWV 739); the fragmentary early version of the organ *Prelude and Fugue in G minor* (before 1707, BWV 535a). The "BWV" numbers provided are the standard catalog numbers of Bach's works as established in the *Bach-Werke-Verzeichnis,* prepared by the German musicologist Wolfgang Schmieder.) [In addition, 33 organ chorales (recently discovered at Yale University), perhaps representing an early stage in the history of the *Orgel-Büchlein* (*Little Organ Book*) were presumably composed at this time.]

THE MÜHLHAUSEN PERIOD

In June 1707 Bach obtained a post at the Blasiuskirche in Mühlhausen in Thuringia. He moved there soon after and married his cousin Maria Barbara Bach at Dornheim on October 17. At Mühlhausen things seem, for a time, to have gone more smoothly. He produced several church cantatas at this time; all of these works are cast in a conservative mold, based on biblical and chorale texts and displaying no influence of the "modern" Italian operatic forms that were to appear in Bach's later cantatas. The famous organ Toccata and Fugue in D minor (BWV 565), written in the rhapsodic northern style, and the Prelude and Fugue in D major (BWV 532) may also have been composed during the Mühlhausen period, as well as the organ Passacaglia in C minor (BWV 582), an early example of Bach's instinct for large-scale organization. Cantata No. 71, *Gott ist mein König (God is my King),* of February 4, 1708, was printed at the expense of the city council and was the first of Bach's compositions to be published. While at Mühlhausen, Bach copied music to enlarge the choir library, tried to encourage music in the surrounding villages, and was in sufficient favor to be able to interest his employers in a proposal for rebuilding the organ (February 1708). His real reason for resigning on June 25, 1708, is not known. He himself said that his plans for a "well-regulated [concerted] church music" had been hindered by conditions in Mühlhausen and that his salary was inadequate. It is generally supposed that he had become involved in a theological controversy between his own pastor Frohne and Archdeacon Eilmar of the Marienkirche. Certainly, he was friendly with Eilmar, who provided him with librettos and became godfather to Bach's first child; and it is likely enough that he was not in sympathy with Frohne, who, as a Pietist, would have frowned on elaborate church music. It is just as possible, however, that it was the dismal state of musical life in Mühlhausen that prompted Bach to seek employment elsewhere. At all events, his resignation was accepted, and shortly afterward he moved to Weimar, some miles west of Jena on the Ilm River. He continued, nevertheless, to be on good terms with Mühlhausen personalities, for he supervised the rebuilding of the organ, is supposed to have inaugurated it on October 31, 1709, and composed a cantata for February 4, 1709, which was printed but has disappeared. [Other important cantatas from the Mühlhausen period include *Aus der Tiefen* (*From the Depths*), BWV 131—evidently Bach's first cantata (1707?); *Christ lag in Todesbanden* (*Christ Lay in the Bonds of Death*), BWV 4; and *Gottes Zeit ist die allerbeste Zeit* (*God's Time is the Best of TImes*), BWV 106.]

THE WEIMAR PERIOD

Bach was, from the outset, court organist at Weimar and a member of the orchestra. Encouraged by Wilhelm Ernst, he concentrated on the organ during the first few years of his tenure. From Weimar, Bach occasionally visited Weissenfels; in February 1713 he took part in a court celebration there that included a performance of his first secular cantata, *Was mir behagt,* or the "Hunt" Cantata (BWV 208).

Late in 1713 Bach had the opportunity of succeeding Friedrich Wilhelm Zachow at the Liebfrauenkirche, Halle; but the Herzog raised his salary, and he stayed on at Weimar, becoming Konzertmeister on March 2, 1714, with the duty of composing a cantata every month. He became friendly with a relative, Johann Gottfried Walther, a music lexicographer and composer who was organist of the town church, and, like Walther, Bach took part in the musical activities at the Gelbes Schloss (Yellow Castle), then occupied by Herzog Wilhelm's two nephews, Ernst August and Johann Ernst. The latter was a talented composer who wrote concertos in the Italian manner, some of which Bach arranged for keyboard instruments; the boy died in 1715, in his nineteenth year.

Unfortunately, Bach's development cannot be traced in detail during the vital years 1708-14, when his style underwent a profound change. There are too few datable works. From the series of cantatas written in 1714-16, however, it is obvious that he had been decisively influenced by the new styles and forms of the contemporary Italian opera and by the innovations of such Italian concerto composers as Antonio Vivaldi. The results of this encounter can be seen in such cantatas as Nos. 182, 199, and 61 in 1714; 31 and 161 in 1715; and 70 and 147 in 1716. His favorite forms appropriated from the Italians were those based on refrain (ritornello) or da-capo schemes in which wholesale repetition—literal or with modifications—of entire sections of a piece permitted him to create coherent musical forms with much larger dimensions than had hitherto been possible. These newly acquired techniques henceforth governed a host of Bach's arias and concerto movements, as well as many of his larger fugues (especially the mature ones for organ) and profoundly affected his treatment of chorales.

Among other works almost certainly composed at Weimar are most of the *Orgel-Büchlein;* all but the last of the so-called eighteen "Great" chorale preludes; the earliest organ trios; and most of the organ preludes and fugues. The "Great" Prelude and Fugue in G major for organ (BWV 541) was finally revised about 1715, and the Toccata and Fugue in F major (BWV 540) may have been played at Weissenfels.

On December 1, 1716, Johann Samuel Drese, musical director at Weimar, died. He was then succeeded by his son, who was rather a nonentity. Bach presumably resented being thus passed over; and in due course he accepted an appointment as musical director to Prince Leopold of Köthen, which was confirmed in August 1717. Herzog Wilhelm, however, refused to accept his resignation—partly, perhaps, because of Bach's friendship with the Herzog's nephews, with whom the Herzog was on the worst of terms. About September a contest between Bach and the famous French organist Louis Marchand was arranged at Dresden. The exact circumstances are not known; but Marchand avoided the contest by leaving Dresden a few hours before it should have taken place. By implication, Bach won. Perhaps this emboldened him to renew his request for permission to leave Weimar; at all events he did so but in such terms that the duke imprisoned him for a month (November 6–December 2). A few days after his release, Bach moved to Köthen (in modern East Germany), some thirty miles (fifty kilometers) north of Halle.

THE KÖTHEN PERIOD

There, as musical director, he was concerned chiefly with chamber and orchestral music. Even though some of the works may have been composed earlier and revised later, it was at Köthen that the sonatas for violin and clavier, viola da gamba and clavier, and the works for unaccompanied violin and cello were put into something like their present form. The Brandenburg Concertos were finished by March 24, 1721; in the Sixth concerto—so it has been suggested—Bach bore in mind the technical limitations of the Prince, who played the gamba. Bach played the viola by choice; he liked to be "in the middle of the harmony." He also wrote a few cantatas for the Prince's birthday and other such occasions; most of these seem to have survived only in later versions, adapted to more generally useful words. And he found time to compile pedagogical keyboard works: the *Clavier-Büchlein* for W.F. Bach (begun January 22, 1720); some of the French Suites; the Inventions (1723); and the first book (1722) of *Das Wohltemperierte Clavier* (The *Well-Tempered Clavier*, eventually consisting of two books, each of twenty-four preludes and fugues in all keys and known as the Forty-eight). This remarkable collection systematically explores both the potentials of a newly established tuning procedure, which, for the first time in the history of keyboard music, made all the keys equally usable, and the possibilities for musical organization afforded by the system of "functional tonality," a kind of musical syntax consolidated in the music of the Italian concerto composers of the preceding generation and a system that was to prevail for the next 200 years. At the same time the *Well-Tempered Clavier* is a compendium of the most popular forms and styles of the era: dance types, arias, motets, concertos, etc., presented within the unified aspect of a single compositional technique: the rigorously logical and venerable fugue.

Maria Barbara Bach died unexpectedly and was buried on July 7, 1720. About November, Bach visited Hamburg; his wife's death may have unsettled him and led him to inquire after a vacant post at the Jacobikirche. Nothing came of this, but he played at the Catharinenkirche in the presence of Reinken. After hearing Bach improvise variations on a chorale tune, the old man said, "I thought this art was dead; but I see it still lives in you."

On December 3, 1721, Bach married Anna Magdalena Wilcken, daughter of a trumpeter at Weissenfels. Apart from his first wife's death, these first four years at Köthen were probably the happiest of Bach's life. He was on the best terms with the Prince, who was genuinely musical; and in 1730 Bach said that he had expected to end his days there. But the Prince married on December 11, 1721, and conditions deteriorated. The Princess—described by Bach as "an *amusa*" (that is to say, opposed to the muses)—required so much of her husband's attention that Bach began to feel neglected. He also had to think of the education of his elder sons, born in 1710 and 1714, and he probably began to think of moving to Leipzig as soon as the cantorate fell vacant with the death of Johann Kuhnau on June 5, 1722. Bach applied in December, but the post—already turned down by Bach's friend, Georg Philipp Telemann—was offered to another prominent composer of the day, Christoph Graupner, the musical director at Darmstadt. As the latter was not sure that he would be able to accept, Bach gave a trial performance (Cantata No. 22, *Jesu nahm zu sich die Zwölfe* [(*Jesus took to Himself the Twelve*) and No. 23, *Du wahrer Gott und Davids Sohn* (*Thou very God and David's Son*),] on February 7, 1723; and, when Graupner withdrew (April 9), Bach was so deeply committed to Leipzig that, although the Princess had died on April 4, he applied for permission to leave Köthen. This he obtained on April 13, and on May 13 he was sworn in at Leipzig.

He was appointed honorary musical director to Köthen, and both he and Anna were employed there from time to time until the Prince died, on November 19, 1728.

YEARS AT LEIPZIG

As Director of Church Music for the city of Leipzig, Bach had to supply performers for four churches. At the Peterskirche the choir merely led the hymns. At the Neukirche, Nikolaikirche, and Thomaskirche, part singing was required; but Bach himself conducted, and his own church music was performed, only at the last two. His first official performance was on May 30, 1723, the First Sunday after Trinity Sunday, with Cantata No. 75, *Die Elenden sollen essen.* New works produced during this year include many cantatas and the *Magnificat* in its first version. The first half of 1724 saw the production of the St. John Passion, which was subsequently revised. The total number of cantatas produced during this ecclesiastical year was about sixty-two, of which about thirty-nine were new works.

On June 11, 1724, the First Sunday after Trinity, Bach began a fresh cycle of cantatas, and within the year he wrote fifty-two of the so-called chorale cantatas, formerly supposed to have been composed over the nine-year period 1735–44. The *Sanctus* of the Mass in B minor was produced at Christmas. [A third cycle was composed over the years 1725–27.]

During his first three years at Leipzig, then, Bach had produced a large number of new cantatas, sometimes, as recent research has revealed, at the rate of one a week. This phenomenal pace raises the question of Bach's approach to composition. Bach and his contemporaries, subject to the hectic pace of production, had to invent or discover their ideas quickly and could not rely on the unpredictable arrival of "inspiration." Nor did the musical conventions and techniques or the generally rationalistic outlook of the time necessitate this reliance, as long as the composer was willing to accept them. The baroque composer who submitted to the regimen inevitably had to be a traditionalist who willingly embraced the conventions.

Symbolism

A repertory of melody types existed, for example, that was generated by an explicit "doctrine of figures" that created musical equivalents for the figures of speech in the art of rhetoric. Closely related to these "figures" are such examples of pictorial symbolism in which the composer writes, say, a rising scale to match words that speak of rising from the dead or a descending chromatic scale (depicting a howl of pain) to sorrowful words. Pictorial symbolism of this kind occurs only in connection with words—in vocal music and in chorale preludes, where the words of the chorale are in the listener's mind. There is no point in looking for resurrection motifs in the *Well-Tempered Clavier.* Pictorialism, even when not codified into a doctrine, seems to be a fundamental musical instinct and essentially an expressive device. It can, however, become more abstract, as in the case of number symbolism, a phenomenon observed too often in the works of Bach to be dismissed out of hand. Number symbolism is sometimes pictorial; in the St. Matthew Passion it is reasonable that the question "Lord, is it I?" should be asked eleven times, once by each of the faithful disciples. But the deliberate search for such symbolism in Bach's music can be taken too far. Almost any number may be called "symbolic" (three, six, seven, ten, eleven, twelve, fourteen, and forty-one are only a few examples); any multiple of such a number is itself symbolic; and the number of sharps in a key signature, notes in a melody, measures in a piece, and so on may all be considered significant. As a result, it is easy to find symbolic numbers anywhere, but ridiculous to suppose that such discoveries invariably have a meaning.

Besides the melody types, the baroque composer also had at his disposal similar stereotypes regarding the further elaboration of these themes into complete compositions, so that the arias and choruses of a cantata almost seem to have been spun out "automatically." One is reminded of Bach's delightfully innocent remark "I have had to work hard; anyone who works just as hard will get just as far," with its implication that everything in the "craft" of music is teachable and learnable. The fact that no other composer of the period, with the arguable exception of Handel, even remotely approached Bach's achievement indicates clearly enough that the application of the "mechanical" procedures was not literally "automatic" but was controlled throughout by something else—artistic discrimination, or taste. "Taste," a most respected attribute in the culture of the eighteenth century, is an utterly individual compound of raw talent, imagination, psychological disposition, judgment, skill, and experience. It is unteachable and unlearnable.

As a result of his intense activity in cantata production during his first three years in Leipzig, Bach had created a supply of church music to meet his future needs for the regular Sunday and feast-day services. After 1726, therefore, he turned his attention [increasingly to other projects. Whether he in fact completed two further cycles of church cantatas, as asserted in the obituary published soon after his death, has been a matter of controversy. Bach did, however, produce the St. Matthew Passion in 1727, a work that prefigured] a renewed interest in the 1730s for vocal works on a larger scale than the cantata: the now-lost St. Mark Passion (1731), the Christmas Oratorio, BWV 248 (1734–35), and the Ascension Oratorio (Cantata No. 11, *Lobet Gott in seinen Reichen*, 1735). [Like other major works of the period, notably the Mass in B minor, these all make use of previously composed (largely secular) material.]

Nonmusical Duties

In addition to his responsibilities as musical director, Bach also had various nonmusical duties in his capacity as the cantor of the school at the Thomaskirche. Since he resented these latter obligations, Bach frequently absented himself without leave, playing or examining organs, taking his son Friedemann to hear the "pretty tunes," as he called them, at the Dresden opera and fulfilling the duties of the honorary court posts that he contrived to hold all his life. To some extent, no doubt, he accepted engagements because he needed money; he complained in 1730 that his income was less than he had been led to expect (he re-marked that there were not enough funerals); but, obviously, his routine work must have suffered. Friction between Bach and his employers thus developed almost at once. On the one hand, Bach's initial understand-ing of the fees and prerogatives accruing to his position—particularly regarding his responsibility for musical activities in the University of Leipzig's Paulinerkirche—differed from that of the town council and the university organist, Johann Gottlieb Görner. On the other hand, Bach remained, in the eyes of his employers, their third (and unen-thusiastic) choice for the post, behind Telemann and Graupner. Fur-thermore, the authorities insisted on admitting unmusical boys to the school, thus making it difficult for Bach to keep his churches supplied with competent singers; they also refused to spend enough money to keep a decent orchestra together. The resulting ill-feeling had become serious by 1730. It was temporarily dispelled by the tact of the new rec-tor, Johann Matthias Gesner, who admired Bach and had known him at Weimar; but Gesner stayed only until 1734 and was succeeded by Johann August Ernesti, a young man with "progressive" ideas on edu-cation, one of which was that music was not one of the humanities but a time-wasting sideline. Trouble flared up again in July 1736; it then took the form of a dispute over Bach's right to appoint prefects and became a public scandal. Fortunately for Bach, he became court com-poser to the Elector of Saxony in November 1736. As such, after some delay, he was able to induce his friends at court to hold an official in-quiry, and his dispute with Ernesti was settled in 1738. The exact terms of the settlement are not known; but, thereafter, Bach did as he liked.

Instrumental Works

In 1726, after he had completed the bulk of his cantata production, Bach began to publish the clavier partitas singly, with a collected edition in 1731, perhaps with the intention of attracting recognition beyond Leipzig and thus securing a more amenable appointment elsewhere. The Second Part of the *Clavier-Übung*, containing the Concerto in the Italian Style and the French Overture (Partita) in B minor appeared in 1735. The Third Part, consisting of the Organ Mass with the Prelude and Fugue ["St. Anne"] in E Flat major (BWV 552), appeared in 1739. From ca. 1729–36 Bach was honorary musical director to Weissenfels; and, from 1729 to 1737 and again from 1739 for a year or two, he directed the Leipzig Collegium Musicum. For these concerts he adapted some of his earlier concertos as harpsichord concertos, thus becoming one of the first composers in history—if not the very first—of concertos for keyboard instrument and orchestra, just as he was one of the first to use the harpsichordist's right hand as a true melodic part in chamber music. These are just two of several respects in which the basically conservative and traditional Bach, as is becoming increasingly recognized, was a significant innovator as well.

About 1733 Bach began to produce cantatas in honor of the Elector of Saxony and his family, evidently with a view to the court appointment he secured in 1736; many of these secular movements were adapted to sacred words and reused in the Christmas Oratorio. The *Kyrie* and *Gloria* of the Mass in B minor, written in 1733, were also dedicated to the Elector, but the rest of the Mass was not put together until Bach's last years. On his visits to Dresden, Bach had won the regard of Graf Hermann Karl von Keyserlingk, the Russian envoy, who commissioned the so-called "Goldberg" Variations; these were published as [the last part of the *Clavier-Übung* about 1741 or 1742]. Book Two of the *Well-Tempered Clavier* seems to have been compiled at about the same time [(or a few years earlier) as were the first stages in the composition of the *Art of the Fugue.*]

Last Years

In May 1747 Bach visited his son Emanuel at Potsdam and played before Frederick II the Great of Prussia; in July his improvisations, on a theme proposed by the King, took shape as the *Musical Offering*. In June 1747 he joined a Sozietät der Musikalischen Wissenschaften (Society of the Musical Sciences) that had been founded by his former pupil Lorenz Christoph Mizler; he presented the canonic variations on the chorale "Von Himmel hoch da komm' ich her" ("From Heaven Above to Earth I come") to the society, in manuscript, and afterward published them. [He wrote a few further cantatas in his later years as well as revised some of his Weimar organ works. In addition, he published the so-called "Schübler" Chorale Preludes in or after 1748.]

Of Bach's last illness little is known, except that it lasted several months and prevented him from finishing the *Art of the Fugue*. [(Unfinished as it was, it was published in 1751.)] His constitution was undermined by two unsuccessful cataract operations performed by one John Taylor (an itinerant English quack who numbered Handel among his other failures); and he died [after a stroke] on July 28, 1750, at Leipzig. His employers proceeded with relief to appoint a successor; Burgomaster Stieglitz remarked, "The school needs a cantor, not a musical director—though certainly he ought to understand music." Anna Magdalena was left badly off. For some reason, her stepsons did nothing to help her, and her own sons were too young to do so. She died on February 27, 1760, and was given a pauper's funeral.

Emanuel Bach and the organist-composer Johann Friedrich Agricola (a pupil of Sebastian's) wrote an obituary; Mizler added a few closing words and published the result in the journal of his society (1754). There is an English translation of it in *The Bach Reader*. Though incomplete and inaccurate, the obituary is of very great importance as a firsthand source of information.

Bach appears to have been a good husband and father. Indeed, he was the father of twenty children, only [nine] of whom survived to maturity. There is amusing evidence of a certain thriftiness, a necessary virtue; for he was never more than moderately well off, and he delighted in hospitality. Living as he did at a time when music was beginning to be regarded as no occupation for a gentleman, he occasionally had to stand up for his rights both as a man and as a musician; he was then obstinate in the extreme. But no sympathetic employer had any trouble with Bach, and with his professional brethren he was modest and friendly. He was also a good teacher and from his Mühlhausen days onward was never without pupils.

REPUTATION AND INFLUENCE

For about 50 years after Bach's death, his music was neglected. This was only natural; in the days of Haydn and Mozart, no one could be expected to take much interest in a composer who had been considered old-fashioned even in his lifetime—especially since his music was not readily available, and half of it (the church cantatas) was fast becoming useless as a result of changes in religious thought.

At the same time, musicians of the late eighteenth century were neither so ignorant of Bach's music nor so insensitive to its influence as some modern authors have suggested. Emanuel Bach's debt to his father was considerable and Bach exercised a profound and acknowledged influence directly on Haydn, Mozart, and Beethoven.

After 1800 the revival of Bach's music gained momentum. The German writer Johann Nikolaus Forkel published a *Life, Genius and Works* in 1802 and acted as adviser to the publishers Hoffmeister and Kühnel, whose collected edition, begun in 1801, was cut short by the activities of Napoleon. By 1829 a representative selection of keyboard music was nonetheless available, although very few of the vocal works were published. But in that year the German musician Eduard Devrient and the German composer Felix Mendelssohn took the next step with the centenary performance of the St. Matthew Passion. It and the St.

John Passion were both published in 1830; the Mass in B minor followed (1832–45). The Leipzig publisher Peters began a collected edition of "piano" and instrumental works in 1837; the organ works followed in 1844–52.

Encouraged by Robert Schumann, the Bach-Gesellschaft (BG) was founded in the centenary year 1850, with the purpose of publishing the complete works. By 1900 all the known works had been printed, and the BG was succeeded by the Neue Bach-Gesellschaft (NBG), which exists still, organizing festivals and publishing popular editions. Its chief publication is its research journal, the *Bach-Jahrbuch* (from 1904). By 1950 the deficiencies of the BG edition had become painfully obvious, and the Bach-Institut was founded with headquarters at Göttingen (West Germany) and Leipzig, to produce a new standard edition (the *Neue Bach-Ausgabe* or NBA) expected to comprise 84 volumes.

In retrospect, the Bach revival, reaching back to 1800, can be recognized as the first conspicuous example of the deliberate exhumation of old music, accompanied by biographical and critical studies; and it served as an inspiration and a model for subsequent work of that kind.

Among the biographical and critical works on Bach, the most important was the monumental study *Johann Sebastian Bach* (2 vols., Leipzig, 1873–80), by the German musicologist Philipp Spitta, covering not only Bach's life and works but also a good deal of the historical background. Although wrong in many details, the book is still indispensable to the Bach student.

EDITIONS OF BACH'S WORKS

The word *Urtext* (original text) may lead the uninitiated to suppose that they are being offered an exact reproduction of what Bach wrote. It must be understood that the autographs of many important works no longer exist. Therefore, Bach's intentions often have to be pieced together from anything up to twenty sources, all different. Even first editions and facsimiles of autograph manuscripts are not infallible guides to Bach's intentions. In fact, they are often dangerously misleading, and practical musicians should take expert advice before consulting them. Editions published between 1752 and ca. 1840 are little more than curiosities, chiefly interesting for the light they throw on the progress of the revival.

No comprehensive edition is trustworthy throughout: neither Peters nor the BG nor even the NBA. Nevertheless, it is advisable to begin by finding out whether the music desired has been published by the NBA.

MAJOR WORKS

Vocal Music (Sacred)

MASSES: Mass in B minor, BWV 232 (1724–48); 4 Lutheran masses (i.e., containing only settings of the *Kyrie* and the *Gloria*).

ORATORIOS: Christmas Oratorio, BWV 248 (1734); Easter Oratorio (*Kommt, eilet und laufet*, BWV 249; 1725); Ascension Oratorio (1735).

PASSIONS: *Passion According to St. John*, BWV 245 (1724); *Passion According to St. Matthew*, BWV 244 (1727?).

CANTATAS: About 200 for different Sundays in the church year (1707–after 1735; mainly 1714–16, 1723–27), mostly for soloist(s), chorus, and orchestra.

OTHER WORKS: *Magnificat*, BWV 243; 7 motets; 2 *Sanctus* settings (3 others based on works by other composers); 186 independent chorale harmonizations [(many possibly belonging to lost cantatas or Passion settings)].

Vocal Music (Secular)

CANTATAS: 24, mostly for soloists, chorus, and orchestra—all on German texts, except two Italian. They include the "Coffee" Cantata (*Schweigt stille, plaudert nicht*, BWV 211; ca. 1732) and the "Peasant" Cantata (*Mer hahn en neue Oberkeet*, BWV 212; 1742).

OTHER WORKS: 5 songs for voice and continuo and 1 quodlibet for four voices and continuo.

Orchestral Music

CONCERTOS: 6 Brandenburg Concertos (pre-1721); 2 concertos for violin and orchestra and one for two violins (1717–23); 7 for one harpsichord, 3 for two harpsichords, 2 for three and 1 for four harpsichords; 1 concerto for harpsichord, flute, and violin.

OTHER ORCHESTRAL WORKS: 4 overtures (suites); Sinfonia in D major (incomplete).

Chamber Music

SONATAS: 2 for violin and continuo; 3 for flute and continuo; 1 for two flutes and harpsichord; 2 for flute, violin and continuo; 3 for harpsichord and flute; 3 for harpsichord and viola da gamba; 6 for harpsichord and violin.

OTHER CHAMBER MUSIC: *Musicalisches Opfer* (1747) for strings, flute, and continuo; 6 unaccompanied sonatas (partitas) for violin (ca. 1720); 6 unaccompanied suites for cello (ca. 1720).

Organ Music

CHORALE PRELUDES: 140 chorale preludes including the *Orgel-Büchlein* (mainly 1714–16); *Clavier-Übung,* vol. 3 (1739), and "Schübler" Chorale Preludes (1748).

FUGUES: 18 preludes and fugues (1708–17, 1729–39), including the "St. Anne" in E flat major and the "Wedge" in E minor; 5 toccatas and fugues (1700–17), including the "Dorian" in D minor; 3 fantasies and fugues; 4 other fugues.

OTHER ORGAN COMPOSITIONS: Variations on the chorale "Vom Himmel hoch" (1747); Passacaglia in C minor, BWV 582 (1708–17); 4 concertos; 7 fantasies; 4 preludes; 6 sonatas (trios); 3 trios.

Harpsichord Music

COLLECTION: *Clavier-Übung:* vol. 1 (1726–31), 6 partitas; vol. 2 (1735), French Overture in B minor and Concerto in the Italian Style; vol. 4 (1741), "Goldberg" Variations; also 6 French Suites and 6 English Suites.

OTHER HARPSICHORD WORKS: *Aria variata* in A minor; Chromatic Fantasy and Fugue; [numerous capriccios, fantasies, preludes, fughettas, fugues, sonatas, suites, and arrangements].

[OTHER CLAVIER (KEYBOARD) MUSIC]:   The *Well-Tempered Clavier,* 2 vols. (1722 and 1742), containing 48 preludes and fugues, one in each key in each book; *Clavier-Büchlein* (1720) for Wilhelm Friedemann Bach, containing 15 two-part and 15 three-part inventions, 20 preludes, 2 allemandes, 4 minuets, a fugue, and an "applicatio;" *Clavier-Büchlein* (1722) and *Notenbuch* (1725) both for Anna Magdalena Bach, containing marches, minuets, a musette, polonaises, etc.; [various] fantasies and toccatas [mostly not by J. S. Bach].

For Unspecified Instrument(s)

Die Kunst der Fuge [posth.]; 16 fugues and 4 canons.

BIBLIOGRAPHY

Catalogues

Wolfgang Schmieder, *Thematisch-systematisches Verzeichnis der musikalischen Werke von Johann Sebastian Bach. Bach-Werke-Verzeichnis (BWV).*

Leipzig: Breitkopf & Härtel, 1950. The standard catalogue of Bach's music, including a comprehensive bibliography (up to 1950) for each work. [Hans-Joachim Schulze and Christoph Wolff, *Bach-Compendium: Analytisch-bibliographisches Repertorium der Werke Johann Sebastian Bachs* (*BC*). Leipzig and Frankfurt: Edition Peters, 1985–. A reference work with factual information bearing on each individual composition (five volumes projected).]

Collections of Correspondence, Sketches, and Reminiscences

Bach-Dokumente I: Schriftstücke von der Hand Johann Sebastian Bachs. Kassel: Bärenreiter, 1963. A critical edition of all surviving nonmusical documents, such as letters and receipts, in Bach's hand. *Bach-Dokumente II: Fremdschriftliche und gedruckte Dokumente zur Lebensgeschichte Johann Sebastian Bachs 1685–1750.* Kassel: Bärenreiter, 1969. A critical edition of all known printed and handwritten discussions of and references to Bach dating from his lifetime. [*Bach-Dokumente III: Dokumente zum Nachwirken Johann Sebastian Bachs 1750–1800.* Kassel: Bärenreiter, 1972. A critical edition of all known printed and handwritten discussions of and references to Bach dating from 1750 to 1800. Vols. 1 and 2 of the *Dokumente* are edited by Werner Neumann and Hans-Joachim Schulze; vol. 3 is edited by Hans-Joachim Schulze. All three volumes are published as supplements to the *Neue Bach-Ausgabe*. Hans David and Arthur Mendel, eds., *The Bach Reader: A Life of Johann Sebastian Bach in Letters and Documents*, revised edition. New York: Norton, 1966. Robert L. Marshall, *The Compositional Process of J. S. Bach*, 2 vols. Princeton: Princeton University Press, 1972, with transcriptions of all surviving musical sketches and drafts included in vol. 2.

Biography and Criticism

Philipp Spitta, *Johann Sebastian Bach*, 2 vols. Leipzig: Breitkopf & Härtel, 1883–85. English translation reprinted New York: Dover, 1951. Spitta's monumental study is still the standard biography, although no longer valid in many particulars. Further important full-length studies are: Albert Schweitzer, *J. S. Bach*, 2 vols., Leipzig: Breitkopf & Härtel, 1908. English translation reprinted London: A & C. Black, 1966. An influential, if highly subjective and personal interpretation; Charles Sanford Terry, *Bach: A Biography*. London: Oxford University Press, 1928. A useful supplement (based on new archival researches) to the biographical portions of Spitta's work. Karl Geiringer, *Johann Sebastian Bach: The Culmination of an Era*. New York: Oxford University Press, 1966. The [first] full-length account of the life and works to make use of the far-reaching results of research in the 1950s by Alfred Dürr and Georg von Dadelsen bearing on the chronology of Bach's works. [Christoph Wolff, *The New Grove Bach Family.* New York: Norton, 1983. A revision of the highly informative and reliable essay originally published in *The New Grove Dictionary of Music and Musicians* (London: Macmillan, 1980), including the most accurate available list of works.]

On the Vocal Music

Alfred Dürr, *Die Kantaten von Johann Sebastian Bach,* 2 vols. Kassel: Bärenreiter, 1971. A general survey plus individual essays on each cantata by one of the principal editors of the *Neue Bach-Ausgabe.* Werner Neumann, *Handbuch der Kantaten Joh. Seb. Bachs,* 3rd edition. Leipzig: Breitkopf & Härtel, 1966. A handbook of useful factual data and schematic analyses of all the cantatas. W. Neumann, [*Sämtliche von Johann Sebastian Bach vertonte Texte.* Leipzig: Deutscher Verlag für Musik, 1974. A complete critical edition of all vocal texts set by Bach.] W. G. Whittaker, *The Cantatas of Johann Sebastian Bach, Sacred and Secular,* 2 vols. London: Oxford University Press, 1959. A stimulating appreciation, but needs to be used with caution. [Eric Chafe, *Tonal Allegory in the Vocal Music of J. S. Bach.* Berkeley: University of California Press, 1989. A far-reaching interpretation based on the theological and music-theoretical outlook of Bach's time.]

On the Instrumental Music

Hermann Keller, *Die Orgelwerke Bachs.* Leipzig: Peters, 1948, English translation New York: Peters, 1967, and *Die Klavierwerke Bachs.* Leipzig, Peters, 1950. The historical context of Bach's organ and keyboard works, and individual analyses of the compositions. [Peter Williams, *The Organ Music of J. S. Bach,* 3 vols. New York: Cambridge University Press, 1980–84. A comprehensive survey of the repertoire. D. F. Tovey, *A Companion to "The Art of Fugue."* London: Oxford University Press, 1931. An analysis. Hans T. David, *J. S. Bach's Musical Offering: History, Interpretation and Analysis.* New York: G. Schirmer, 1945.

On Performance

Erwin Bodky, *The Interpretation of Bach's Keyboard Works.* Cambridge: Harvard University Press, 1960. A controversial but stimulating approach. Walter Emery, *Bach's Ornaments.* London: Novello, 1953. A discussion of the problems and suggested solutions. Arthur Mendel, the preface to his edition of the vocal score of J. S. Bach, *The Passion According to St. John*. New York: G. Schirmer, 1951. [Frederick Neumann, *Ornamentation in Baroque and Post-Baroque Music: With Special Emphasis on J. S. Bach*. Princeton: Princeton University Press, 1978. An unorthodox and controversial reinterpretation.]

I

The Historical
Significance

2

BACH THE PROGRESSIVE
Observations on His Later Works

In 1730 Johann Sebastian Bach was forty-five years old, and he was not content. There is really no doubt about this; it is documented for us by Bach himself in two remarkable letters he wrote in that year which are uncharacteristically revealing about his life, personality, and outlook. In 1730 Bach had been Cantor of Saint Thomas's Church and Director of Church Music for the city of Leipzig for seven years and, as we now know, had already achieved the self-proclaimed goal of his youth of creating "a well-regulated church music to the glory of God."[1] In fact, Bach had achieved that goal almost immediately upon his arrival in Leipzig in the spring of 1723, having systematically produced within the first four years of his tenure three complete annual cycles of church cantatas for the Lutheran liturgical year (many of them composed at the rate of one per week), the St. John Passion, and very probably the St. Matthew Passion as well—an outburst of creative energy that continues to astonish us, despite our not wholly unsuccessful efforts to account for it analytically and historically.[2]

But in 1728 there was a falling-off of compositional activity that is as striking in every way as the productivity of the preceding years. The year 1728 may indeed have been the least productive of Bach's maturity.[3] For besides the publication of the fourth partita of the *Clavier-Übung,* Part I (BWV 828)—a work very likely composed at an earlier time[4]—we know with certainty of only one new work from his pen that year: the wedding cantata *Vergnügte Pleissenstadt,* BWV 216, written for the February 1728 wedding of a Leipzig merchant. And we know that even this work was at most only in part newly composed at this time, at least two of the arias being parodies of arias from earlier cantatas.[5] This circumstance is especially curious in view of the fact that in that very year Bach's favorite Leipzig librettist, Christian Friedrich Henrici (alias Picander), published a collection of cantata texts for the church year containing a foreword dated June 24, 1728, in which the poet expresses the hope that "perhaps the lack of poetic charm may be compensated for by the loveliness of the music of the incomparable Kapellmeister Bach."[6] Bach evidently set at least nine of Picander's seventy-one cantata texts in the course of 1728 and 1729.[7] And it is not inconceivable, of course, that he composed music for other texts from this collection and that they have all disappeared without a trace; but it is surely at least as reasonable to assume that for some reason—and lack of commitment to the project is as good an explanation as any—Bach discontinued his work on the cycle after setting more or less the portion that has survived.

Indeed, a consideration of Bach's activities in the year 1729 provides further impetus for such speculation, for they seem to testify to his growing disengagement from his regular church duties. Bach himself reports in an important letter of March 20, 1729, to a former student, Christoph Gottlob Wecker, that he has just returned from a three-week (unexplained) absence from Leipzig, and, most significantly, mentions in the same letter that he is about to assume the direction of the Collegium Musicum, a reputable amateur music-making society founded long since by Georg Philipp Telemann and consisting mainly of students from the University of Leipzig.[8] By March 23, three days after his letter to Wecker, Back was in Köthen to conduct the funeral music for his former patron, Prince Leopold, performing as the main work the cantata *Klagt, Kinder, klagt es aller Welt*, BWV 244a. This composition, it now seems certain, was for the most part not an original work but a parody of movements from the St. Matthew Passion, which for its part evidently was not composed in 1729 but, as mentioned above, two years earlier.[9]

Finally, in addition to taking on the direction of the Collegium Musicum, Bach expanded his activities in the spring of 1729 in a different sphere, becoming in effect a book distributor and functioning as the Leipzig sales representative for the important musical treatise *Der Generalbass in der Composition* by the Kapellmeister of the Dresden court, Johann David Heinichen, and for the *Musicalisches Lexicon* by his Weimar colleague and cousin, Johann Gottfried Walther.[10] Nor should we forget that it was sometime before the end of June of that year that Bach attempted (unsuccessfully and not for the first time) to make the personal acquaintance of George Frideric Handel, dispatching his son Wilhelm Friedemann to Halle in the vain hope of inducing Handel to accept an invitation to Leipzig (Bach was sick at the time).[11]

The impending crisis, however—surely the most painful of Bach's life—did not reach its climax until the summer of 1730. On August 2, 1730, Bach was criticized at a meeting of the Leipzig town council for neglecting his teaching duties, and on August 25 the Vice-Chancellor and Burgomeister, Dr. Jacob Born, reported at a meeting that "he has spoken with the Cantor, Bach, but he shows little inclination to work. . . ."[12]

Just two days before Dr. Born gave his report to the town council, Bach had written the first of the two letters referred to at the outset of this essay. It is the often quoted and analyzed memorandum to the same town council bearing the title "Short but Most Necessary Draft for a Well-Appointed Church Music, with Certain Modest Reflections on the Decline of the Same." The memorandum was a plea to the council to reinstate and increase the honoraria traditionally paid to the supplementary musicians Bach was obliged to employ for his regular Sunday performances, but its real importance—as has always been recognized—is the light it sheds on Bach's performance practice in Leipzig through its precise descriptions of the remarkably modest forces at his disposal and his views on their quality and adequacy.

Yet in the closing portion of the memorandum Bach offers some observations on the larger musical scene. He writes:

> . . . The state of music is quite different from what it was, since our artistry has increased very much, and the *gusto* has changed astonishingly, and accordingly the former style of music no longer seems to please our ears. . . .

And later:

> It is, anyhow, somewhat strange that German musicians are expected to be capable of performing at once and *ex tempore* all kinds of music, whether it come from Italy or France, England or Poland. . . . To illustrate this statement with an example one need only go to Dresden and see how the musicians there are paid by his Royal Majesty, it cannot fail, since the musicians are relieved of all concern for their living, free from *chagrin*, and obliged each to master but a single instrument: it must be something choice and excellent to hear. . . .[13]

There is certainly more than one way of understanding these remarks, but it seems clear that Bach, among other things, is making three points: (1) that musical style and taste have changed—for the better, with the obvious implication that Bach associates himself with the latest developments; (2) that German musicians are uniquely expected to be at home in all the principal national musical idioms of the time; and (3) that the state of music at the court of Dresden is particularly enviable.

Dresden at this time was the operatic capital of Germany. It was also Catholic, modish, the center of Italian taste, and in every way represented the opposite cultural pole to traditionalistic, conservative, orthodox Lutheran Leipzig. And while the quality of musical life was in decline in Leipzig in 1730—we have just presented Bach's testimony on the decline of church music; the moribund Leipzig German opera had been closed in 1720 and the opera house razed in 1729[14]—while musical life, then, was in decline in 1730 in Leipzig, it was approaching its zenith in Dresden. The reorganization of the Italian opera there had begun in the mid-1720s. In 1724 the Saxon ambassador to Venice was charged with locating three young Italian female singers and four castratos, and having them trained for six years by the finest voice teachers in Italy, whereupon they would come to Dresden to join the opera company. They finally arrived—by June 1730.[15] The climax, though, was to come the following year with the arrival on July 7, 1731, of the totally Italianized and immensely successful composer Johann Adolph Hasse and his wife Faustina, the leading prima donna of her age.

Now Bach, back in 1717, had enjoyed in Dresden one of the greatest triumphs of his life in the legendary nonconfrontation with the French organist Louis Marchand; Bach's organ recital in the Dresden Sophienkirche in 1725 was a great success; Bach was the Leipzig sales representative for the Dresden Royal Kapellmeister Heinichen; Bach frequently went with his son Wilhelm Friedemann to hear "the lovely Dresden ditties" at the Dresden opera; and, finally, in the "Short but Most Necessary Draft" of August 1730, Bach wrote that music in Dresden "must be something choice and excellent to hear." In short, Bach must have been well aware of musical developments in Dresden and able to compare them to the deteriorating situation in Leipzig.[16]

By October Bach was actively looking for another position. In a letter of October 28, 1730, to his childhood friend and classmate Georg Erdmann, who was now the Imperial Russian Resident Agent in Danzig (this is the second letter alluded to at the beginning and the most personal document to survive from his hand), Bach includes among the reasons for his dissatisfaction the fact that "the authorities are odd and little interested in music, so that I must live amid almost continual vexation, envy and persecution," and he continues: "accordingly I shall be forced . . . to seek my fortune elsewhere. Should Your Honor know or find a suitable post in your city for an old and faithful servant, I beg you most humbly to put in a most gracious word of recommendation for me. . . ."[17] Bach of course was never to leave Leipzig.

II

Between the "Short but Most Necessary Draft" of August 23 and the letter to Erdmann of October 28, it seems (according to our present knowledge) that Bach composed only two new works—apparently the only compositions he wrote at all during the second half of the year.[18] The first was the obligatory annual cantata (now lost) celebrating, ironically enough, the formal installation of the new town council on August 28—three days after Dr. Born reported to that body on Bach's disinclination to work.[19] The second composition, which has been tentatively dated September 17, 1730, was Cantata No. 51, *Jauchzet Gott in allen Landen,* the famous cantata for solo soprano and obbligato trumpet.

This cantata is unique and remarkable in just about every respect. It is Bach's only cantata for this combination (a combination, incidentally, found in the works of Italian composers of the period, for example, Alessandro Scarlatti's well-known cantata *Su le sponde del Tebro*),[20] and, more significantly, it is written in an unabashedly—and, for Bach, unprecedentedly—flamboyant style.

Who in Leipzig would have performed the solo parts of this cantata? The trumpet obbligato could have been intended for Gottfried Reiche, Bach's regular, brilliant, and proven first trumpeter. But the soprano part, requiring the most highly skilled and accomplished singer, was surely well beyond the powers of the young boys of the Thomaskirche. (The most difficult solo arias in the church cantatas of the Leipzig period are overwhelmingly given to altos—that is, falsettists—tenors, and basses.)

Before speculating about the intended soprano—and speculation is all that can be offered here—a few observations on the original sources of this piece are in order. Like the music it contains, Bach's autograph score is remarkable. It was penned with such care that it is at times difficult to say whether the manuscript is Bach's first notation of the cantata—a composing score—or a fair copy. (See Plates 1 and 2.)[21] It is certainly the most attractive manuscript (from the standpoint of penmanship) of any of Bach's regular Sunday cantatas from the Leipzig period, the manuscripts and music of which were for his personal use only. The autograph of Cantata No. 51, however, could pass for a presentation copy, although it does not seem that Bach ever actually presented it to anyone.

The autograph poses another problem. The original wrapper, which contained both the score and the performing parts, bears a heading in Bach's hand which begins: "Dominica 15 post Trinitatis. / et / In ogni Tempo." (See Plate 3.) Now, it is largely on the basis of that heading that current Bach research has dated the cantata specifically to September 17, 1730, which was the Fifteenth Sunday after Trinity that year. (The assignment to 1730, which, again, is somewhat tentative, is based on the usual examination of copyists' handwriting, watermarks, and other similar external evidence.)[22] But, as Alfred Dürr has pointed out, the text of the cantata has practically nothing in common with the Epistle and Gospel readings for the Fifteenth Sunday after Trinity—thus, presumably, the additional designation *et in ogni tempo.*[23]

The uncharacteristically handsome appearance of the manuscript, then, the puzzling heading, the uncertain date, and, most of all, the virtuoso nature of the soprano part raise some doubts as to whether this cantata was really composed—exclusively or even primarily—for

PLATE 1. Autograph score, P 104, f. 1ʳ: BWV 51/1, mm. 1–13.

the regular Sunday service in one of Bach's usual Leipzig churches, especially when one further recalls Bach's state of mind in the summer and autumn of 1730 and his general lack of creative productivity at the time.

PLATE 2.   P 104, f. 8ʳ: BWV 51/5, mm. 59b–83

Now *Jauchzet Gott* is not only difficult; it is an outright showpiece, a *nec plus ultra* of coloratura fireworks—virtuosity, really, for its own sake. And it has an immediacy of appeal, owing not only to its difficulty but

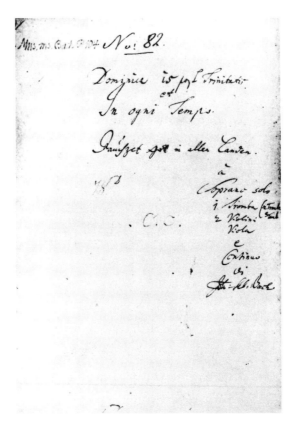

PLATE 3.   P 104: BWV 51, Title page

also to such factors as the fanfare melodies in the first movement and the snappy syncopations in the alleluia theme, which, I submit, represents in this context, a new fresh element in Bach's music—a stylistic trait, then, and a manner of vocal writing one would surely have associated at the time with nothing so much as the Italian opera—of the kind cultivated in Dresden.[24] It is therefore an irresistible temptation to suggest that Bach wrote Cantata No. 51 for a singer at the Dresden court, perhaps one of the five sopranos who finally arrived, amid much eager anticipation, in the summer of 1730 after six years of training in Italy. Perhaps, more specifically, the soprano part was intended for the castrato Giovanni Bindi, one of the newcomers, who rapidly became a favorite of the Dresdeners and for whom Hasse liked to write up to high c''', the highest note, incidentally, in our cantata.[25] Bach could have had occasion to hear Bindi in the three months between the singer's arrival and the presumed date of the cantata, and familiarized himself with his voice at that time.

It is even conceivable that Bach wrote the cantata exactly one year later—a possibility not excluded by the external evidence[26]—for none other than the divine Faustina Bordoni Hasse herself. She made her Dresden debut on September 13, 1731, in Hasse's opera *Cleofide* at a performance that Bach undoubtedly heard, since on the following afternoon, in the presence of "the assembled musicians and virtuosi of the court,"[27] he gave an organ recital in the Sophienkirche. Bach would surely have known in advance about Faustina's arrival, would have been familiar with her reputation as a brilliant virtuosa, and could have prepared the handsome autograph to present to her as a welcoming gift upon her debut in Dresden. Only after hearing her for himself in *Cleofide,* this speculation continues, would Bach have realized that her voice was not at all suitable for *Jauchzet Gott,* since it had an absolute top of a" and a general tessitura around a fifth lower than Bach's cantata, and he would then have taken the cantata back to Leipzig with him.

But the Bindi hypothesis is rather more plausible: the year fits the evidence somewhat better; the sex of the singer suits the circumstances much better (since it is unlikely that women sang in a Leipzig Protestant church service[28]—and the cantata remains a Lutheran work, which, it must be assumed, was to be sung at some time in one of the Leipzig churches);[29] and Bindi's range was perfect, presumably, for the vocal requirements of the composition. On the other hand, well-trained falsettists at the time were reportedly able to sing in the soprano range; and the possibility cannot be eliminated that one of the advanced students of the Thomasschule or the university—Carl Philipp Emanuel Bach has been suggested—may have been equipped for the part.[30] But if there had been a singer of this caliber regularly available in Leipzig at the time, then one wonders why Bach evidently wrote no further music of this nature for him.[30a]

It would be futile and unnecessary to indulge in further speculation here about Cantata No. 51 and its possible connections with Dresden. This discussion of the cantata was in any event mainly an attempt to juxtapose, rather dramatically and provocatively, two facts that are beyond mere conjecture. First, from about 1730 on, the time of the "Short but Most Necessary Draft" and the letter to Erdmann, Bach began to expand his professional activities (the Collegium Musicum, the book dealership) and also (and this is infinitely more significant), within his creative work, to expand his stylistic horizons—in all geographic and historical directions, really—including the direction of the most recent developments emanating from Italy and permeating not only opera and instrumental music but sacred music as well. Second, one of the primary sources—I would submit, *the* primary source—for Bach's increased stylistic awareness (and stylistic tolerance) at this time was the excellent, enviable, and vigorous musical establishment at Dresden.

Bach's ties with Dresden were to grow considerably, most particularly during the years from 1733 to about 1742. This period is marked at the beginning by Bach's presentation (on July 27, 1733) of the dedication copy of the *Kyrie* and *Gloria* of the B-minor Mass to Frederick Augustus II, the new elector of Saxony, and it is marked at the end by the publication (probably in 1742) of the Fourth Part of the *Clavier-Übung*, the "Goldberg" Variations, a work commissioned in the early 1740s by the Baron Hermann Carl von Keyserlingk (1696–1746), one of Bach's principal supporters and patrons.[30b] Keyserlingk was present in the audience and presumably first made Bach's acquaintance—in Dresden—on December 1, 1736, when he was the Russian ambassador to the Dresden court and Bach was giving one of his Dresden organ recitals, this time on the new Silbermann organ of the Frauenkirche, in formal acceptance (or so one assumes) of the title of Dresden Court Kapellmeister.[31] This title, for its part, had been conferred the previous November as the outcome of a process initiated in 1733 with the dedication of the B-minor Mass.

Finally, we should recall the testimony of C. P. E. Bach in a famous letter of January 13, 1775, to Johann Nikolaus Forkel:

> In his last years [Bach] esteemed highly: Fux, Caldara, Händel, Kayser, Hasse, both Grauns, Telemann, Zelenka, Benda, and in general everything that was worthy of esteem in Berlin and Dresden. Except for the first four, he knew the rest personally. . . .[32]

The "Dresden connection" in Bach's career has always been acknowledged yet never comprehensively explored in all its biographical and artistic ramifications. But our information about it has been accumulating, especially in the past ten or fifteen years, and the time for such an investigation seems ripe.[33]

III

Now the point is that Bach's new activities pursued in the course of the 1730s—his connections with Dresden *and* his association with the Leipzig Collegium Musicum—reinforced one another in shaping similar tendencies in his development as a composer, since Bach found himself in both activities engaged to a large extent in related, indeed, often identical, compositional projects such as the production of secular cantatas for birthdays, name days, weddings, commemorations, and similar celebrations in honor of the royal family in Dresden or of notable professors or middle-class burghers in Leipzig. For the most part these works were to be performed by the Collegium Musicum.[34] The conventions observed in music written for such secular purposes encouraged a lighter, more *galant*, that is, more modern, style. And, if other conventions permitted the large-scale importation of secular music and the stylistic elements associated with it, into church music (the well-known practice of parody), then they only assured further, in Bach's case, that these elements inevitably found their way increasingly into his sacred music as well. And in the 1730s this is represented by many of Bach's most ambitious large-scale works: the Christmas and Ascension Oratorios and the *Kyrie* and *Gloria* of the B-minor Mass, the latter, again, intended for Dresden.

The extent to which Bach incorporated elements of the modern style into the music he was writing during the 1730s and '40s—either as part of his duties as director of the Collegium Musicum or presumably with a view towards making a favorable impression on the Dresden audience—has not been sufficiently recognized in the Bach literature. There are at least two likely reasons for this. Either the works exhibiting the light, *galant* traits that are characteristic of the new style (the "Peasant" and "Coffee" Cantatas, for example) contain them abundantly and obviously and are accordingly dismissed (not quite unjustifiably, but not quite justifiably either) as relatively marginal and inconsequential products of his pen, or the new elements are so naturally integrated and assimilated into Bach's mature and peculiarly individual style, with its uncompromising commitment to technical sophistication and expressive subtlety and depth, that they have attracted almost no attention to themselves at all—a testimony itself to the success of Bach's effort. Cantata No. 51, in addition to everything else just said about it, and most important of all, is an example of such a synthesis.

It would be helpful at this point to sketch some of the well-known hallmarks of what is usually designated the "pre-classical" or *galant* style in music. First it should be recalled that this style, which began to become prominent in Italian opera in the 1720s and to prevail not only in Italy but throughout much of Europe in the 1730s and '40s, was not really all that new. It has been traced back at least to the 1690s—when Bach was a young boy.[35] Receiving continued and increasing moral support from the aesthetic outlook of the Enlightenment and Age of Reason, particularly its naturalistic tendencies, the "new" style was effecting a fundamental simplification and clarification, with consequences for all musical elements:

1. Melodies were modeled on or even borrowed from folk song and folk dance to assure immediate and popular appeal; the more difficult (and poignant) melodic intervals were increasingly eliminated, while rhythmic patterns, often adopted from dance types, were enlivened with snappy syncopations or more frequent mixtures of longer and shorter note-values.

2. The rich harmonic vocabulary of the late-baroque style was substantially reduced, relieved especially of its most intense and expressive combinations, while at the same time the rate of harmonic change—the harmonic rhythm—was slowed down.

3. More complex polyphonic and imitative textures were discarded in favor of a melody-dominated setting in which the bass part relinquished independent melodic interest and contented itself with the most unassuming thumping of repeated notes and similar patterns; and the middle parts often became totally inconsequential or disappeared altogether.

4. Finally, the long, freely spun-out, and seemingly irrational melodic arches and arabesques characteristic of the late-baroque style (a product of the recent development of instrumental and vocal virtuosity and the old art of improvisation) were replaced by clearly articulated and almost arithmetically balanced phrases—a method of organization imported mainly from the dance genres. This was only secondarily a revision of melodic style; it was mainly a redefinition of the principles of musical form itself.

The mechanics by which a composition was to unfold and take shape were put into the service of the Enlightenment ideology of rationality, simplicity, clarity, and naturalness. It was not hard for musical theorists and aestheticians to find in the symmetrically balanced phrases and periods indigenous to dance music, and in their tendency to form similar patterns on higher levels of organization, analogies with the hierarchical organization of language: words and parts of speech forming phrases which form sentences which form paragraphs which form chapters. In musical terms: melodic motives join to form phrases which form periods which form sections and so on. And this method of formal construction, as it became more and more prevalent (which was all but inevitable, since it realized the prevailing aesthetic values so well), had its effect on the other important determinant of musical form: on tonality.

Like melody, the tonal organization of a composition was not simply to unfold, with the music almost imperceptibly slipping from one key to another and back again, while the harmonic stations along the way were perhaps—but also perhaps not—accorded some formal recognition through the presence of a more or less noticeable cadence. On the contrary. The changes of key, the modulations, in the pre-classical style were to be perceptible indeed, experienced as significant formal and even dramatic events and points of arrival by such means as long, expectant, often suspenseful harmonic preparations, strongly articulated cadences, and perhaps even the introduction of a new melody to reinforce the introduction of the new key. Such concern with formal clarity was underlined and insured often and understandably enough by the employment of strong contrasts throughout the musical fabric: contrasts (frequently in immediate juxtaposition) of motives, themes, rhythms, and key. And it resulted finally in the breakdown of the main aesthetic underpinning of the musical baroque—the aesthetic of the

Unity of Affect, the notion that a single composition should represent and explore just one basic emotional state. Such an aesthetic had been obviously well served by the devices of the period emphasizing a relatively undifferentiated continuity: the unfolding, say, by sequential repetition or polyphonic imitation of an initial thematic idea over one basic underlying pulse and at one basic tempo, while quite unobtrusively passing through a number of keys along the way. This ideal of unity was replaced in the new style by an aesthetic of a rather dramatic dualism. The exploration of a single affect was replaced by the juxtaposition of two, or more; continuity of procedure was replaced by differentiation and balanced contrast of parts, while these were to be unified again at a higher level of the musical structure.

Now, nothing in this brief and oversimplified description of the pre-classical style is new.[36] The question is: to what extent, if any, is it really pertinent for the music of Bach? Again, at the risk of becoming repetitive, the contention here is that for around a decade and a half, and always within the context of his basically unshakable late-baroque idiom, it is increasingly so.

It has long been assumed that Bach's first substantial and deliberate appropriation of the *galant* style for his own music takes place in Cantata No. 201, *Geschwinde, geschwinde, ihr wirbelnden Winde,* better known as "The Contest between Phoebus and Pan."[37] This work is now thought to have been written around 1729 or '30, that is, at the beginning of Bach's association with the Collegium Musicum—perhaps indeed serving as his inaugural composition with that organization and evidently proclaiming, via the mythological singing contest between Phoebus Apollo and the demigod Pan, Bach's own aesthetic credo: his unwavering commitment to solid musical craftsmanship and his emphatic repudiation of the easy, light, and merely pleasing in music.[38] His portrayal, then, of Pan's contest piece, the aria "Zu Tanze, zu Sprunge," is normally taken as a parodistic caricature of the *galant* mode, and Apollo's entry, "Mit Verlangen," as the representative of Bach's traditionalistic values of high quality.

It is not necessary to disagree here with the common and really compelling interpretation of the allegory. Indeed, it is important to notice that Bach's attitude at this time towards the musical style represented by Pan's aria *was* one of amused contempt. But it is important to notice also that the cantata as a whole is by no means written in a complex or austerely contrapuntal idiom. Quite the contrary. While the texture on the whole is rich, the music seems really to be permeated more by elements of the dance than by systematic polyphony. Indeed, Apollo's "Meistergesang" is itself based on the meter of the rather new-fashioned minuet; and an underlying periodic phrase structure of the kind just described is never very heavily disguised. Consider the ritornello theme itself, shown in Ex. 2.1.[39]

Example 2.1.   BWV 201/5, "Mit Verlangen," mm. 1–12 (after NBA I/40)

On the other hand, the closest approach to an academic, imitative counterpoint is found in the ritornello of Pan's aria (see Ex. 2.2).

Example 2.2.   BWV 201/7, "Zu Tanze, zu Sprunge," mm. 1–8 (after NBA I/40)

Example 2.2.   (Continued)

It would seem, then, that Bach here is mocking pretentiousness in art at least as much as "simplicity."[40] (One wonders indeed whether the *style galant* was Bach's target here at all.) And of course the ridiculous setting of the word "wackelt" ("shake" or "stir") can be understood as Bach's demand for the same naturalness in text declamation that was often leveled by critics against him (Ex. 2.3).

Example 2.3   BWV 201/7, "Zu Tanze, zu Sprunge," mm. 40–44 (after NBA I/40)

so   wack-ack - ack - ack - ack - ack - ak - kelt___ das___   Herz,

In the problematic Italian cantata, No. 209, *Non sa che sia dolore*, for soprano, flute, and strings, which may have been written about the same time as Cantata No. 201, the juxtaposition of a thoroughly Bachian late-baroque style in the opening sinfonia and first aria with a quite pure example of the Italian *galant* in the final aria has led to strong doubts about the authenticity of the work.[41] Indeed the dance meter, the triadic melody (with its—for Bach—uncharacteristically sweet emphasis on the sixth degree), the regular four-measure phrases and the often thumping bass line of the last aria "Ricetti gramezza e pavento," make it quite suspect (see Ex. 2.4). It is therefore not difficult to under-

Example 2.4.   BWV 209/5, "Ricetti gramezza e pavento," mm. 1–16 (after BG 29)

Example 2.4.   (Continued)

stand why Bach's authorship of this cantata has been doubted. But it is hard to imagine who else would have written the well-crafted and elaborate opening movements, although even here—in the first measures of the sinfonia—the start–stop rhythms and the sighing grace-note figures remind one of the new Italian manner (see Ex. 2.5).

Example 2.5.   BWV 209/1, Opening Sinfonia, mm. 1–4 (after BG 29)

Perhaps some of the problems surrounding this cantata—the poor source transmission, the unknown date and occasion of the work, the impossible Italian (with its puzzling references to persons and places)—could be clarified, again, by considering Dresden. This time the range d' to a" does fit Faustina's precisely; and the choice of flute for the obbligato instrument suggests that the work could have been intended for Pierre Gabriel Buffardin, the great French flute virtuoso at the Dresden court, whom Bach may have had in mind (or so it has been suggested) for the B-minor Orchestral Suite, a work with many resemblances to the sinfonia of this cantata.[42] On the whole it would be rather premature to strike this cantata from the Bach canon.[43]

But, on the other hand, it would be ill-advised to rest much of the case on a work which may in the end prove to be spurious; and there is no need to do so. Sometime in late 1734 or early 1735 Bach composed the "Coffee" Cantata to be performed certainly by the Collegium Musicum in its regular surroundings: Zimmermann's coffee house in Leipzig. It is not necessary to elaborate at length here on the modernity of this highly popular composition. For its similarities to the world of the young opera buffa have long been recognized: the choice of contemporary middle-class characters, plot, and milieu, the scoring basically for just two roles sung by soprano and bass, the rapid parlando style of Bach's vocal writing, as in Father Schlendrian's opening aria, "Hat man nicht mit seinen Kindern" (Ex. 2.6).

Example 2.6.   BWV 211/2, "Hat man nicht," mm. 11–13 (after NBA I/40)

Consider, too, the modern jaunty rhythm of "Heute noch" and the strictly chordal setting in which, significantly, the soprano is often doubled by the first violin, a characteristic common in pre-classical scoring (see Ex. 2.7).[44]

Example 2.7.   BWV 211/8, "Heute noch," mm. 12–16 (after NBA I/40)

All these features are reminiscent of, say, Pergolesi's *La serva padrona*, which was written at just about the same time,[45] and have, together with Bach's convincing musical characterization, prompted expressions of regret that Bach never composed an opera.[46] (Apropos the bourgeois element in the "Coffee" Cantata: it was at about this time—1736, to be precise—that the Leipzig poet Sperontes published the best-selling song collection *Singende Muse an der Pleisse,* a volume which helped prepare the emergence of the modern German lied in the second half of the eighteenth century and which fulfilled a felt need among the new German middle classes with a deliberately unpretentious poetry that affirms middle-class values and depicts everyday activities. Bach is thought to have contributed the music to at least two songs in this collection: BWV Anhang 40 and 41.)[47]

It is hardly possible to mention the "Coffee" Cantata without simultaneously bringing to mind the "Peasant" Cantata—a work, however, which was written considerably later. In fact it is Bach's last datable cantata, written for a performance on August 30, 1742, just at the end of the period of concern here.[48] The "Peasant" Cantata is Bach's ultimate and, surely, undeniably sympathetic tribute to folk dance and folk song, whose elements appear here—sometimes literally, sometimes skillfully imitated—shorn of all disguise and elaboration. Even Pan's aria "Zu Tanze, zu Sprunge" from Cantata No. 201 reappears (now with the text "Dein Wachstum sei feste"), no longer a symbol of artistic mediocrity but rather, or so it seems to me, of a kind of aesthetic tolerance and universality. After the twelve or thirteen years separating the "Contest between Phoebus and Pan" from the "Peasant" Cantata, Bach no longer feels defensive about his own artistic credo and, accordingly, obliged to condemn the naive style, but is prepared to accommodate it—with good, uninhibited humor, and really without the patronizing, mocking posture he assumed in 1729 and 1730. But surely the most significant fact about both the "Coffee" and "Peasant" Cantatas is that Bach composed them at all, that he obviously enjoyed doing so, that he knew so well what stylistic conventions were entailed, and that he succeeded so well—and naturally—in applying them.[49]

IV

We are approaching the main point (one which was touched upon in passing before), namely, that the most recent stylistic trends which engaged Bach's attention and interest and which he assimilated more and more willingly and comfortably in his secular vocal music of the 1730s and '40s left strong imprints as well in his most serious and ambitious compositions of that period—unmistakably and, in my opinion, most successfully in the two monumental masterpieces described above as marking in a sense the formal beginning and end of the Dresden experience: the Mass in B minor and the "Goldberg" Variations.

It is known that Bach modeled the very form of the B-minor Mass on the cantata Masses of the Neapolitan school as practiced by his

Dresden contemporaries Zelenka and Hasse,[50] adopting from that tradition, for example, the idea of rounding off the large cyclical work
by setting the concluding "Dona nobis pacem" to the music of an earlier section of the Mass—in Bach's case from the "gratias agimus tibi."
More recently, Christoph Wolff has demonstrated that one of the principal formal considerations at work in the B-minor Mass is the deliberate opposition and balance of choruses written in the contrasting idioms of the so-called *stile antico* and *stile moderno;* the former constituting
the eighteenth-century approximation of the contrapuntal style of the
sixteenth-century masters, notably Palestrina, and the *stile moderno* being basically the common concertante fugal style of the late baroque.[51]
(Indeed, Wolff was particularly interested in showing that Bach was a
diligent student of the *stile antico,* that he personally copied out a Mass
by Palestrina and the scores of his own contemporaries written in the
archaic manner, and that his prime source for this repertoire was, again,
Dresden.)

But the solo arias and duets enclosed within the structural pillars of the large choral numbers, especially in the *Kyrie* and *Gloria*
sections—that is, precisely those portions of the Mass prepared in 1733
for Dresden—frequently suggest yet another style: that of the modern Italianate *galant.* Consider the "Christe eleison," a duet for two sopranos (the higher of which remains within Faustina's range, incidentally) with unison violins and continuo and placed between the
late-baroque *stile moderno* of the first *Kyrie* and the pseudo-Palestrinian
Kyrie II.

The tender mood prevailing in the "Christe" duet was surely
deemed by Bach to be most appropriate for the text. But, as it turns
out, it was precisely the *affetti amorosi,* or "gentle affections," which were
explicitly preferred during the *galant* period[52] and which testified to a
fundamentally new understanding of what was proper musical expression. Accordingly, no factor was as decisive in determining how fashionable, or modern, a composer was perceived by his contemporaries
to be, as was his personal vocabulary of affections. This meant, ironically enough, that the bold harmonies and dissonances such as are to be
found in the works of Bach's early maturity—the Chromatic Fantasy, for
example, or the opening measures of the Weimar cantata *Widerstehe doch
der Sünde,* with their stunning dominant seventh chords repeated over
a tonic pedal[53]—for all their acknowledged "originality," were "counter-
progressive" when measured according to the aesthetic values of the
galant style, which consciously eschewed the violent and extreme affections (along with their stylistic resources) that had been the favorite
subjects of baroque composers since the time of Monteverdi.

The means Bach uses to portray the "gentle affections" in the
"Christe eleison" of the B-minor Mass all belong to the vocabulary of
the *galant* style: the unison violins, the frequent, sweet parallel thirds or

sixths between the two voices (emphasized here by the long, drawn-out first note), then the mixtures of rhythms in the vocal theme (especially the mixture of duplets and triplets) and the feminine cadence with its subdivided downbeat and appoggiatura embellishment (Ex. 2.8).

Example 2.8.   BWV 232/2, "Christe eleison," mm. 10–12: Sopranos I and II (after NBA II/1)

Of course, the "Christe eleison" is not a *galant* piece. The harmony and counterpoint are both too rich. Indeed the fascination of the number derives in part from the delicate balance and almost systematic alternation of *galant* homophony and late-baroque imitative counterpoint practically from one phrase to the next.

The first aria of the *Gloria*, the "Laudamus te," seems to be (as Arthur Mendel once suggested)[54] a coloratura showpiece for Faustina, employing just the kind of agile and ornate passage work, set in a rather low tessitura and studded with trills, for which she was famous (Ex. 2.9).

Example 2.9.   BWV 232/6, "Laudamus te," mm. 12–26: Soprano II (after NBA II/1)

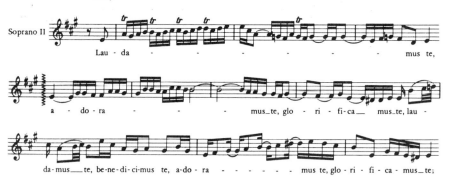

And it has been shown most recently that the flute theme of the "Domine Deus" (Ex. 2.10a) was almost certainly meant to be rendered in the popular "Lombard" rhythm of the *style galant* (Ex. 2.10b).[55]

Example 2.10.   BWV 232/8, "Domine Deus," mm. 1–2: Flauto traverso

The duet between the soprano and the tenor in the "Domine Deus" reveals, by the way, the same alternation of canonic imitation (here a symbol of the identity of Father and Son and of the issuance of the Son from the Father) with the sweetness of parallel thirds and sixths found in the "Christe"; and we find once again the *galant* mannerism of the mixed rhythms, the subdivided downbeat, and the lingering half-cadence (see Ex. 2.11).

Example 2.11.   BWV 232/8, "Domine Deus," mm. 17–22: Soprano I, Tenore
(after NBA II/1)

But it is important not to overstate the case. The B-minor Mass is not a *galant* piece by any means, but neither is it a very typical product of the late baroque. Its enormous dimensions alone make that clear. By the time Bach had composed and compiled the remaining sections of the work and organized them into a complete Mass Ordinary, sometime in the late 1740s,[56] the B-minor Mass had become—surely by design—an encyclopedic, universal compendium of just about all the styles and forms available to the composer: *Stile antico, stile moderno, style galant,* fugue, concerto, passacaglia, pastorale, *aria di bravura,* and so on. It shares this encyclopedic ambition with the *Well-Tempered Clavier* and, to some extent, with the "Goldberg" Variations as well. The B-minor Mass in its ultimate form is a work whose constituent parts were written over a period of thirty years, extending from Bach's Weimar period to the end of his life, and should be understood, perhaps, as representing, among other things, Bach's *summa* of sacred vocal music.

V

We must retrace our steps to the early 1740s to consider the "Keyboard Practice Consisting of an Aria with 30 Variations for the Harpsichord with Two Manuals Prepared for the Enjoyment of Music Lovers"[57]—the so-called "Goldberg" Variations commissioned by Baron von Keyserlingk for his own harpsichordist, the former Bach pupil Johann Gottlieb Goldberg (1727–56), and published most probably in the year [1741].[58] Although the "Goldberg" Variations were characterized above as marking something of a formal conclusion to Bach's Dresden episode, there are good reasons to consider them rather as a new departure. Indeed they have usually been regarded as standing at the threshold of Bach's last creative period, beginning the series of formidable and increasingly severe instrumental cycles: the *Musical Offering,* the *Canonic Variations on the Christmas Chorale "Vom Himmel hoch,"* and, finally, the unfinished *Art of Fugue*—those retrospective, monumental surveys of the venerable skills of strict counterpoint, canon, and fugue.[58a]

There is even some reason to believe that Bach, too, may have looked upon the "Goldberg" Variations as the beginning of a new venture. For while it is customary and understandable to count the "Goldbergs" as the "Fourth Part" of the *Clavier-Übung,* it just may be significant that this designation does not appear on the original title page—in contrast to the French Overture and Italian Concerto and the organ pieces which are duly counted as the "Zweyter Theil" and the "Dritter Theil der Clavier Ubung," respectively. The title page of the "Goldberg" Variations begins simply "Clavier Ubung bestehend in einer Aria" and so forth. (Compare Plates 4 and 5.) Can we infer from this that Bach intended to separate this work at least to some degree from the preceding parts?[58b] It did, after all, apparently unlike the first three parts, receive a specific outside impetus—Keyserlingk's commission[58c]—and therefore was not purely a product of Bach's own initiative. Furthermore, the circumstances surrounding the appearance of the "Goldberg" Variations are somewhat peculiar. First of all, the date of its publication is not altogether certain, while there is no doubt about the dates of the other parts. Moreover, it was not published by Bach himself, as were the First and Third Parts, nor was it, like the Second Part, published by a firm with no substantial reputation as a music publisher, namely, Christoph Weigel of Nuremberg. (This turned out to be a disappointing experience; the edition is blemished by an intolerably high number of misprints.)[59]

For the "Goldberg" Variations Bach engaged the well-known Nuremberg printer and publisher Balthasar Schmid, to serve this time not only as the printer and engraver, as he had for the Third Part of the *Clavier-Übung* in 1739, but as its publisher as well.[60] In the year

Zweyter Theil
Der
Clavier Ubung
bestehend in
einem Concerto nach Italienischen Gusto
und
einer Ouverture nach Französischer Art.
vor ein
Clavicymbel mit zweyen
Manualen.
Denen Liebhabern zur Gemüths-Ergötzung verfertiget
von
Johann Sebastian Bach
Hochfürstl. Sæchss. Weißenfelss. Capellmeistern
und
Directore Chori Musici Lipsiensis.
in Verlegung
Christoph Weigel Junioris.

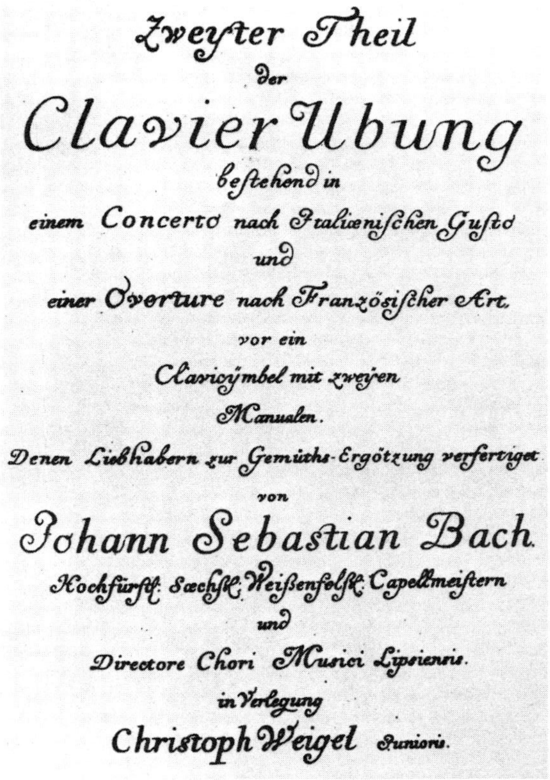

PLATE 5. Original edition of the Second Part of the *Clavier-Übung*: Title page

Clavier Ubung
bestehend
in einer
A R I A
mit verschiedenen Veraenderungen
vors Clavicimbal
mit 2 Manualen.
Denen Liebhabern zur Gemüths-
Ergetzung verfertiget von
Johann Sebastian Bach
Königl. Pohl. u. Churfl. Sæchss. Hof
Compositeur, Capellmeister, u. Directore
Chori Musici in Leipzig.
Nürnberg in Verlegung
Balthasar Schmids.

PLATE 4. Original edition of the "Goldberg" Variations: Title page

45

1742, presumably shortly after the "Goldberg" Variations, Schmid was to publish Carl Philipp Emanuel Bach's so-called "Prussian" Sonatas, long considered a watershed in the development of the pre-classical sonata form.

Now the implications of Bach's interest during the 1730s in establishing contacts with the publishing world of Nuremberg must be fully understood. The music publishers of Nuremberg, particularly the houses of Johann Ulrich Haffner and Balthasar Schmid, played a crucial role in the early flowering and dissemination of the solo keyboard sonata and therewith in the dissemination of the pre-classical style.[61] While Dresden, then, in the 1730s and '40s served evidently as Bach's principal stimulus and source of knowledge about the latest stylistic trends, the composer, it seems, at the same time regarded the Nuremberg publishers as potentially providing the principal outlet and opportunity for him to make his own contribution to the new and rapidly expanding mainstream.

The "Goldberg" Variations obviously have almost nothing in common with the modish trifles aimed at the growing market of middle-class amateur players which Schmid's previous publications had addressed. On the contrary, they form the largest-scaled single keyboard work published at any time during the eighteenth century, indeed until the publication of Beethoven's Hammerklavier Sonata and the Diabelli Variations. And, like the B-minor Mass and the *Well-Tempered Clavier*, the "Goldberg" Variations, too, constitute an encyclopedic compendium, which this time, as Manfred Bukofzer had suggested, "sums up the entire history of Baroque variation."[62]

It is surely not necessary to point out here that all of the thirty variations are built upon the same thirty-two-measure ground bass, that nine are cast in the form of strict canons, each appearing (as every third number) at a different interval of imitation and systematically proceeding from the unison to the ninth, that among the remaining variations we find an overture, a fugue, a trio sonata, several different dances, a quodlibet, and so on. We find also, in addition to the virtuoso display of compositional technique, another element not present either in Bach's previous "encyclopedic" essays or in those yet to come: namely, the dazzling virtuoso display of keyboard writing—the devilish hand-crossings, passages in thirds, trills in inner parts, rapid arpeggios and runs, etc. There is nothing like these extroverted acrobatics in any of Bach's other keyboard music. In fact, demanding and idiomatic keyboard writing at this level of difficulty can be found in the works of only one other composer of the time: Domenico Scarlatti.

Now it used to be assumed that the keyboard technique of the "Goldberg" Variations and other late keyboard works of Bach in fact reflected Scarlatti's influence,[63] until it was pointed out by Ralph Kirkpatrick that most of the surviving music by Domenico Scarlatti was probably written late in his life, much of it indeed probably after Bach had died.[63a] Moreover, Scarlatti's music does not seem to have become known in most of Europe until much later. To quote Kirkpatrick:

> In Germany a few sonatas were reprinted . . . and brief biographical notes were devoted to Scarlatti by theorists and lexicographers such as Heinichen, Walther, Quantz, Mizler, Marpurg, and Gerber. . . . Moreover, the date of publication of the *Essercizi* (1738), the first of Scarlatti's harpsichord music to become at all widely known, effectively discredits the oft-repeated statement that in certain of his harpsichord works Johann Sebastian Bach was influenced by Scarlatti.[64]

But is that necessarily so? It was mentioned above that Bach was the sales representative for the publications of Heinichen and Walther from the late 1720s and '30s which contain the references to Scarlatti. Lorenz Mizler was a pupil of Bach's, as was Heinrich Nicolaus Gerber, the father of the Ernst Ludwig Gerber whose lexicon also refers to Scarlatti. Bach knew Marpurg personally, and undoubtedly Quantz, too.

Moreover, Bach's good friend of the 1730s, Johann Hasse, had studied in Naples around 1724 with Alessandro Scarlatti and would surely have heard about Domenico, whom indeed he seems to have met in Naples that year.[65] It is difficult to imagine that he would never have found an occasion to speak to the great German keyboard virtuoso Bach about the Italian virtuoso at one of their frequent encounters. Or perhaps his wife, Faustina, who had sung in London during the seasons of 1726, '27 and '28 in five operas of Handel, may have heard then, if not during her years in Italy, about the famous contest between Handel and Scarlatti that had taken place in Rome in 1708 or '09. She, too, could have brought Scarlatti to Bach's attention. The point is that there were a number of possible intermediaries and mutual acquaintances who could have made Bach aware of Domenico Scarlatti's existence and perhaps of his music as well.

Finally in this regard, it does not seem altogether inconceivable that a copy of Scarlatti's *Essercizi,* published in London in 1738 or '39, may have found its way to Bach in Leipzig by, say, 1741, perhaps via the book and music trade of either Nuremberg or Leipzig, which was even then host to one of the leading book fairs in Europe, or perhaps through the agency of someone like Johann Mattheson, who maintained close contacts with the musical scene in London. In general, musical commerce was apparently more efficient at that time than we customarily assume. If a copy of Bach's *Musical Offering* could reach Padre Martini in Bologna during Bach's lifetime—and we know that one did[66]—surely a copy of Scarlatti's *Essercizi* could have reached Bach in Leipzig within three years of its publication.

Historical and geographical conditions, then, by no means preclude Bach's having had an opportunity to know Scarlatti's music, particularly the *Essercizi*. Indeed there are striking similarities between the title of Scarlatti's *Essercizi per gravicembalo* consisting of thirty virtuoso sonatas[67] and that of Bach's synonymous *Clavier Ubung . . . vors Clavicimbal* consisting of thirty virtuoso variations. And there is also a similarity besides mere technical difficulty between the keyboard writing of Scarlatti and that found in some of the numbers of the "Goldberg" Variations. I am referring to the very sudden, capricious shifts of ideas and patterns.

In variation 14, for example, a long trilled note in various registers is followed by running arpeggio patterns in eighths and sixteenths. These in turn are followed by an outburst of mordents alternating between the hands. There is then a rush of thirty-second-notes combined with a crossing of hands, and the section ends with a flurry of thirty-second-note mordents for both hands together. Similar antic, Scarlattian goings-on occur elsewhere—for instance, in the first section of variation 23, aptly characterized by Tovey as a "madcap frolic."[68]

Does it not seem that Bach, in conceiving variations such as these and then placing them alongside others constructed as the strictest canons, must have known, and been responding to, Scarlatti, who in the first sentence of the preface to his *Essercizi* had written: "In these compositions do not expect any profound learning, but rather an ingenious Jesting with Art"?[69] We find in the "Goldberg" Variations *both* profound learning and an ingenious jesting with art to a degree unsurpassed anywhere in the musical literature.[70]

Now such sudden and drastic changes and contrasts of thematic patterns and of rhythmic motion in many of the individual numbers were made possible only by the fact that the theme and thus *almost* inevitably, all the variations of the "Goldbergs" are constructed throughout according to just that formal principle which was deliberately emphasized earlier as being perhaps the single most important characteristic of pre-classical music: its organization into clearly articulated and balanced phrases. Indeed, it is hard to imagine a more symmetrical and architectonically constructed composition than the theme of the "Goldberg" Variations: a binary division into two sixteen-measure halves, which in turn are each divided into two eight-measure periods. These are further divided into two four-measure phrases, which, finally, are divided into two two-measure motives. Furthermore, the actual theme of the "Goldberg" Variations, as is well known, is not the right-hand melody but the bass line, which proceeds in its slow tread of one note per measure with each note supporting its own harmony. The result is a rather slow—and typically pre-classical—rate of harmonic change of one chord per measure. The theme of the "Goldberg" Variations, then, manifests in a veritably clinical or textbook form two of the main characteristics of the pre-classical style: thoroughgoing periodicity of phrase structure and, in combination with this, a slow harmonic rhythm. (A symmetrical design of this type, as mentioned before, can be projected just as well by replication, that is, by the immediate and literal repetition of a phrase unit or by juxtaposing to the first idea another—perhaps completely contrasting—idea of equal length. In variations 14 and 23 Bach was delighted to exploit the second possibility.)

It is true that periodic phrase structure was in existence for a very long time in dance music, and it is found elsewhere in Bach's music, particularly but not exclusively, in his dance pieces. The sixteen-measure ritornello theme of the aria "Wie zittern und wanken" from Cantata No. 105, for example, composed in 1723, is as regular in its structure as the "Goldberg" theme: $16 = 8 + 8 = (4 + 4) + (4 + 4) = (2 + 2) + (2 + 2) + (2 + 2) + (2 + 2) = 16 \times 1$, consisting of antecedent–consequent related motive or phrase pairings on each level of the hierarchy.[71] Moreover, a typically late-baroque, and asymmetrical, *Fortspinnungsthema* in which an opening motif is followed by a freely spun-out, sequential continuation to the cadence, often discloses, upon closer scrutiny, a latent or superimposed eight-measure organization on higher levels of the structure. An instance is the ritornello theme of the aria "Blute nur" from the St. Matthew Passion, whose phrase structure, proceeding from the lower to the higher levels, can be represented as follows (in measures): $(\frac{1}{2} + \frac{3}{4}) + (\frac{1}{2} + \frac{3}{4}) + (4 \times \frac{1}{2}) + (4 \times \frac{1}{2}) = (2 + 2) + (2 + 2) = 4 + 4 = 8$. Even such a complex and tightly unified theme as the eight-measure fugue subject of the Chromatic Fantasy and Fugue, BWV 903, reveals from one point of view a regular symmetry, the pivot tone b'-flat in m. 5 serving to bisect the theme, and the regular alternation between measures with exclusive quarter-note motion and measures with eighths creating two-measure groups thus: $2 + 2 + 2 + 2 = 4 + 4 = 8$ (see Ex. 2.12).

Example 2.12.   BWV 903: Rhythmic design of the fugue subject

(From another point of view, the subject is quite irregular; the temporal distance between the successive pitches of the structural melody—a diatonically descending fifth from the dominant to the tonic—becoming progressively shorter [see Ex. 2.13].)[72]

Example 2.13.   BWV 903: Linear structure of the fugue subject (based on Schenker)

Now the theme of the "Goldberg" Variations is itself a dance—a sarabande. But baroque composers from Monteverdi to Purcell to Bach, when writing variations on a regular ground bass, which as a rule was taken from a dance, typically sought to make their variations slightly shorter or longer than the bass pattern and thus create often exquisite and delicate tensions by means of the constantly changing relationship between the regularly recurring four- or eight-measure theme and the unpredictable and asymmetrical figurations being spun out above it. What is unique about the "Goldberg" Variations is that Bach not only retains the underlying balanced phrase structure throughout the work but even reinforces it with his variation patterns and figurations. Even more than the keyboard virtuosity, this thoroughgoing periodicity constitutes the true "modern" or "classical" element in the "Goldberg" Variations.

If a new idea is introduced or repeated in a variation, it will normally be so at the beginning of a four-measure unit. In the first section of the first variation, for instance, the pattern of the first four bars is repeated in the next four, with the right and left hands exchanging their parts. Then a new four-measure pattern is introduced at the beginning of the second eight-measure period. This, too, is repeated after four measures, again with the parts of the right and left hands exchanged. This persistent four-measure phrase organization is maintained even in the tenth variation, the "Fughetta." The four-measure subject (actually the ground bass in disguise) is answered immediately, that is, after four measures, in the tenor; then after another four measures in the soprano; and finally after yet another four measures in the alto (Ex. 2.14).

Example 2.14.   BWV 988, variation 10: "Fughetta" (after Kirkpatrick)

The pattern is inverted in the second half of the variation with entrances every four measures in the order: soprano, alto, bass, tenor.[73]

In his essay, "On Mozart's Rhythm," Edward Lowinsky writes:

> When Mozart encountered Bach's music for the first time in his life at
> Baron van Swieten's, he wrote, under the impact of this event, a fugue
> in C major (K. 394, 1782). It shows a marvelous command of fugal
> technique. . . . What a paradox this fugue presents: it has all of Bach's
> technique and none of his style! The reason for this paradox is that
> there are features of musical expression that lie so deep below the sur-
> face of musical consciousness that the composer, remaining unaware
> of them, cannot change them. Rhythm, meter, phrase structure—these
> are elements as natural, and therefore ordinarily as withdrawn from
> consciousness, as are breathing, speaking, and walking.
>   The frequent shift of meter and accent, the natural irregularity
> of phrasing in a Bach fugue are replaced in Mozart's fugue by a
> regularity of metrical design and a periodicity of phrasing that are
> utterly un-Bachian. . . .
>   The subject is two measures long, it enters at intervals of two
> measures . . . Nothing of the subtle polyrhythmic and polymetric
> design that are essential elements in the continuity and flow of Bach's
> music. Periodicity, symmetry of phrase structure, regular recurrence
> of stress are so much a part of Mozart's musical thinking that it is
> superfluous to illustrate them.[74]

I do not mean to be altogether facetious now when I claim that what
Bach has done in the "Fughetta" from the "Goldberg" Variations is clear:
he has composed a fugue in the style of Mozart.

Some time in the early 1740s Bach prepared a German sacred
parody of the *Stabat Mater* by Giovanni Battista Pergolesi, setting it
to a paraphrase of the Fifty-first Psalm.[75] Bach's is the earliest known
performance of the Pergolesi work in Germany—a work which in part
could and does serve as a textbook example of the *galant* style. Bach's
arrangement manages to remain quite faithful to Pergolesi's original and
yet at the same time to refashion it in his own artistic image. The texture
is increased from Pergolesi's two- or three-part to a four-part norm;
complementary rhythms between voices are introduced; polyphonic
implications are realized; and harmonies are enriched. At the same
time, though, Bach has introduced into his arrangement not only more
dynamic indications than one finds in his own compositions but indeed
more than are contained in Pergolesi's original[76]—a sign, it would seem,
of Bach's understanding and acceptance of the organization in short
motivic units, repetitions, and contrasts characteristic of the *galant* style.
    And one should also mention here the elements of *galant* and
empfindsam style that Christoph Wolff has been able to identify in
the three-voice ricercar and trio sonata of the *Musical Offering*—Bach's
tribute to the taste prevailing in that other leading center of musical
fashion which, as mentioned earlier, in addition to Dresden had held

Bach's admiration and for which he composed the *Musical Offering:* Berlin.[77]

VI

The controversy about Bach's position in the history of music had already begun in Bach's day; it has continued to the present (indeed it has been rekindled in the past few decades) and does not promise ever to be resolved. The concern here was not really to join that controversy but rather to present biographical and musical evidence—some of it admittedly circumstantial or inferential—in support of a limited thesis which has been briefly, but fragmentarily presented in the course of the present discussion. It could be stated in summary as follows:

For around a decade and a half, from 1730 to the mid-1740s and prompted by his disaffection with Leipzig and his heightened awareness of the excellent and varied musical life being cultivated in nearby Dresden, Bach increasingly expanded his own artistic horizons, and that as a result of this experience much of his music written during this period, including some of his most important works, absorbed the elements of the latest Italian pre-classical style.[78] At first Bach was willing to appropriate only relatively superficial details: a melodic or rhythmic cliché, a cadential formula. But by the early 1740s he was able to incorporate even the most fundamental structural principle of the new style—regular, periodic phrase organization—into his personal idiom.

To the extent, then, that Bach allowed himself to be influenced by the latest developments in musical fashion, it seems justified to characterize him as "progressive." And it is clear, not only from the musical evidence adduced here but from reports of his contemporaries as well, that Bach was prepared to do this. To quote from one of the most important of Bach's early defenders, Lorenz Mizler:

> If Mr. Bach at times writes inner parts more fully than other composers, he has taken as his model the music of 20 or 25 years ago. He can write otherwise, however, when he wishes to. Anyone who has heard the music that was performed . . . at the Easter Fair in Leipzig last year, in the Most High Presence of his Royal Majesty in Poland, must admit that it was written entirely in accordance with the latest taste and was approved by everyone. So well does the Kapellmeister know how to suit himself to his listeners.[79]

The argument here is quite different from that put forth in the early 1950s by Heinrich Besseler in his provocative essay "Bach als Wegbereiter,"[80] for the "progressive" in art is anything but a trailblazer or innovator. He follows the latest fashion; he does not normally lead it. He does not, like the radical or individualist, strike out in isolation on bold new paths. (The paradox was already pointed out above that the bolder Bach was, the less he was "progressive;" see p. 41, above.) Indeed, it has always been rather easy, even before Besseler but in a more superficial way, to make a case for Bach as an innovator: as the creator (perhaps) of new genres (the chorale-paraphrase cantata, the harpsichord concerto, the trio sonata with obbligato harpsichord), of new compositional techniques and devices (the permutation fugue, the written-out cadenza [in the fifth Brandenburg Concerto], the keyboard recitative [in the Chromatic Fantasy], the "second theme" [in the G-minor Gamba Sonata, BWV 1029, third movement]), and of new musical instruments (the "viola pomposa," the lute harpsichord).

Besseler, for his part, was attempting to demonstrate that during the Weimar and Köthen years Bach had developed many of the stylistic elements characteristic of the *empfindsam* school of the 1740s and '50s (which was in fact established mainly by Bach's immediate pupils) and that he thus directly influenced the immediate historical course. But it is quite questionable, of course, whether the German *empfindsam* style was much more than a local, rather manneristic denouement to the baroque era in Germany, for the most part running parallel to the mainstream pre-classical style emanating from Italy. Moreover, just as convincing a case could be (and has been) made for Bach's direct and critical influence on the formulation of the High Classic style of Mozart and Haydn, as well as on the major composers of the nineteenth and twentieth centuries. The rather obvious point is that the concepts *progressive, innovator, influence, originality,* and so on are by no means synonymous, and that the assessment of an artist's historical position and significance in each instance reflects the application of substantially different criteria.

The attempt here has been in effect to understand one aspect of the relationship between the artist, Bach, and his historical situation at a particular moment not from the perspective of history but from that of the individual. And in order to do this, it is necessary now to recall that Bach, in his early career, had also realized, in addition to his announced goal of a "regulated church music," an unstated goal of the greatest significance.

While in Mühlhausen, Weimar, and Köthen, that is, during the fifteen years or so from around 1707 to 1723, Bach had succeeded in creating a synthesis of the leading national traditions of his age: the organ and church music of Germany, the concerted instrumental music of Italy, and the keyboard music of France. This is all well known. Now Bach's assimilation of the "latest taste" (in Mizler's words) in the 1730s and '40s was actually one aspect of a second, larger and more complex, synthesis in the composer's career, extending this time much further afield historically and culturally. It is almost as if the composer was attracted now to anything "exotic," that is, remote in time, place, or tradition, maintaining, as it were, a Janus-like involvement with both the remote past and the newest trends, juxtaposing Palestrina[81] and Pergolesi, the technical virtuosity of a Domenico Scarlatti or a Dresden opera star and the simple directness of the opera buffa, the high art of canon and the low art of the rowdy quodlibet, not to mention the peasant idioms of German—and even Polish[82]—folk music: all this, as the phenomena of the B-minor Mass and the "Goldberg" Variations reveal—in the ultimate service of a truly universal *réunion des goûts*.[83]

Postscript

In "Bach the Progressive" I question the conventional view of Bach as the quintessential musical conservative—the "culmination of an era," "the terminal point"—a view that portrays the composer as so exclusively devoted to the sublime and timeless in his art as to be virtually "beyond" history: unaffected by, and if concerned at all, merely disdainful of the music of his contemporaries—especially that of his younger contemporaries, and, even more especially, that of his younger Italian contemporaries. This traditional understanding of the phenomenon Johann Sebastian Bach is clearly the product, in equal measure, of nineteenth-century German romanticism and nineteenth-century German nationalism, with its propensity to regard the artistic genius as a hero of mythological proportions suited to serve as a symbol of national pride and a model worthy of emulation.[1]

The trouble with this orthodox, and almost touchingly naive, interpretation is not that it is wrong but that it is incomplete. As I maintain in Chapter 4, "On Bach's Universality," "it does not really do full justice to the magnitude of Bach's achievement."

In calling attention, in "Bach the Progressive," to several hitherto neglected biographical and stylistic issues that seemed to challenge the conventional wisdom about the composer, and in proposing an unorthodox thesis to account for them, I had of course expected to provoke some controversy. Indeed I had looked forward to it and was rather disappointed that no formal, published response was forthcoming for some ten years—until the publication of Frederick Neumann's "Bach: Progressive or Conservative and the Authorship of the Goldberg Aria" in the Bach year 1985 (F. Neumann 1985). Neumann declares at the outset of his article that he intends to take issue with my "provocative reevaluation of Bach's style." Indeed, one of his stated objectives is to "try to show that Marshall did not succeed in demonstrating his point and that the earlier picture of Bach's conservatism remains valid" (p. 281). (The other is to "give reasons why the Aria of the *Goldberg*

Variations that plays a prominent role in Marshall's argument is quite certainly not by Bach, but by a so far unknown Frenchman.")

To be provocative is to run the risk not only of provoking disagreement but, even more, of seeing one's views misconstrued. This turns out, alas, to be the case here. The thesis with which Neumann takes issue is not mine but rather a caricature of it. The consequence is that it is necessary for me here not so much to defend or augment my argument as to point out distortions and issue denials.

Let me state for the record, then, that I never assert (or even imply) that the "salient features" of the *galant* style—folk-like melodies, chordal texture, regular phrase structure, immediacy of appeal, fanfare melodies, syncopations, unison violins, parallel thirds and sixths, feminine cadences, subdivided downbeats, mixed rhythms, and so on—were "limited" to the *galant* style (p. 282), that they were "introduced with the *galant* style" (p. 288) or that they were "*galant* innovations" (p. 285). But it does seem that a musical style is to a large extent the simple sum of the accumulation of such features—at least once a critical mass of them has been achieved—and I continue to maintain that when these particular features appear in concentration on the musical scene in geographical and chronological proximity to the late baroque, then they certainly stand out as the hallmarks of the pre-classical style. (Neumann, for his part, while ridiculing the "saliency" of these features as criteria for describing the new style, fails to provide a more adequate description, or indeed any at all.)

At one point (p. 294) Neumann cites, but nonetheless apparently fails to grasp, the thrust of my argument: namely, that "for around a decade and a half, *and always within the context of his basically unshakable late-baroque idiom* (p. 35, emphasis added), Bach increasingly made use of the elements of the new pre-classical style. This development was part of a profound expansion of Bach's artistic horizons. To quote from the conclusion of my essay (pp. 53–54):

> Bach's assimilation of the "latest taste" . . . in the 1730s and '40s was actually one aspect of a second, larger and more complex, synthesis in the composer's career, extending this time much further afield historically and culturally . . . juxtaposing Palestrina and Pergolesi, . . . the high art of canon and the low art of the rowdy quodlibet . . . in the ultimate service of a truly universal *réunion des goûts*.

My principal concern is with that Second Synthesis—first, in establishing its existence, then in defining its nature, and, finally, in understanding its significance.

In short, it is not my intention to claim that Bach was ever a *galant* composer or even that he showed "a strong inclination to follow the modern *galant* orientation." Bach was not a *galant* composer. I am only willing to argue that "to the extent . . . that Bach *allowed himself* to be influenced by the latest developments in musical fashion, it seems justified [to that extent—no more, no less] to characterize him as 'progressive' " (p. 52, emphasis added).

For his part Neumann is willing to argue that the style Bach had developed "by the age of thirty, so fully satisfied his artistic aspirations that he felt no urge to depart from it. . ." (p. 282). I do not presume to know anything about the urges Bach may have felt and am equally unable to gauge how fully satisfied he may have been at any point in his artistic aspirations. But I am uneasy with the notion of Johann Sebastian Bach ever entertaining a sense of "full satisfaction" in any aspect of his art—especially not by the age of thirty. An old platitude has it that the difference between genius and mere talent is that genius continues to grow. Musical genius of this order—virtually by definition—is never fully satisfied and does not cease to develop, certainly not this early on. (That is another lesson, incidentally, of Bach's Second Synthesis.)

It is Neumann, then, perhaps—not I—who claims insight into the state of Bach's artistic soul. I emphatically plead innocent to the imputation of even remotely suggesting that there is "a close connection between his life's events, his joys or sorrows, and the type of art he produces" (p. 284)—certainly not in the sense that his music carries autobiographical meaning and that one can find in it "reflections of . . . heartbreaking tragedies" such as the death of his wife and children. No one needs to be told that Bach did not compose *Kindertotenlieder.* This is a red herring. Bach's amply documented disaffection with Leipzig around 1730—including his state of mind ("Cantor Bach . . . shows little inclination to work")—and his equally well-documented admiration of Dresden were responses to musical conditions. The point of my discussion of these issues in "Bach the Progressive"—clearly enough, I would have thought—was to try to understand the professional situation Bach perceived himself to be in in order to understand the consequences for the future course of his career that he evidently drew from that perception.

One of these consequences, without question, was the decision to strengthen his connections with Dresden, and to see if he could secure employment—or at least a title—there. In order to do this he would have to demonstrate, of course, that he was capable of producing the kind of music the Dresden court appreciated. (In this regard see Chapter 3, "Bach's *Orchestre,*"). Now, in suggesting that Bach, like any composer of the time, was able (and willing) to write in different styles, including the most fashionable, on the appropriate occasion, I am asserting nothing controversial but rather stating an incontrovertible fact—a fact testified to not only by Bach's contemporary and advocate, Lorenz Mizler, and cited in my essay (p. 52) but by Bach himself (his famous comment that German musicians are expected to be capable of performing "all kinds of music"). Indeed, the idea that there was a style for every purpose—a proper music for the church, the chamber, and the theater, for example—lay at the root of early eighteenth-century musical aesthetics. (Bach's profound understanding of this doctrine and his profoundly original confrontation and transcendence of it are explored in Chapter 4, "On Bach's Universality.")

Finally, we read in Neumann's essay: "Finally Marshall summons the Aria from the *Goldberg Variations* as, perhaps, the main pillar of his thesis. . . . The Aria is a *galant* piece, but is quite certainly not by Bach" (p. 290). There follows an argument against the authenticity of the "Goldberg" theme based on its "un-Bachian" features: its "un-Bachian" flavor and, most of all, its "un-Bachian" ornamentation. In fact, the question of the authorship of the "Goldberg" theme never arises in my essay, simply because it is irrelevant to the point I am making. I am not particularly concerned about whether *Bach* has managed to produce a thoroughly symmetrical and architectonic theme.[2] My point is rather this: "What is unique about the 'Goldberg' Variations is that Bach not only retains the underlying balanced phrase structure throughout the work but even reinforces it with his variation patterns and figurations. Even more than the keyboard virtuosity, this thoroughgoing periodicity constitutes the true 'modern' or 'classical' element in the 'Goldberg' Variations" (p. 50).

As for the authorship of the "Goldberg" theme: It is well known that the bass line makes use of a traditional model that can be traced back to the early seventeenth century—although, as Christoph Wolff points out, there is no known precedent for the thirty-two-measure form used by Bach.[3] There is no reason to think, however, that the original author of this model was French rather than, say, Italian. (Actually, an Italian origin seems far more likely, in light of the pattern's similarities with the other familiar Italian basses cited by Neumann—the Ruggiero, Romanesca, passamezzo—and, especially, the use of the Italian designation "aria" to describe them (p. 291).

The real object of Neumann's charge, "un-Bachian," however, is the right-hand melody. One is free of course to like the melody (as I do) or not, as one will. It is obviously invalid, though, to decide the question of Bach's authorship on that basis. And it is equally invalid to deny its authorship on the ground that it is "un-Bachian." Style criticism is a notoriously unreliable tool for the resolution of authenticity questions. (This issue is treated extensively in Chapter 12, "The Compositions for Solo Flute.") The "Peasant" and "Coffee" Cantatas, after all, are admittedly peripheral, even mediocre works—"un-Bachian," if one insists—but, as even Neumann concedes, they are indisputably by Bach.

There is in fact a strong indication that the melody was composed—in the latest French style, why not?—by Bach. For Bach rarely failed to supply attributions when copying works by other composers or, indeed, even when borrowing themes for variation and elaboration. The "Menuet fait par Mons. Böhm," for example, is the only work by another composer copied into the Anna Magdalena notebooks by J. S. Bach.[4] It is worth noting that, unlike his wife, Sebastian was quite scrupulous about adding an attribution.[5] And the best surviving sources of his fugues, variations, sonatas, and concertos based on themes and compositions by Albinoni, Corelli, Legrenzi, Reinken, and "Vivaldi" as a rule prominently mention the composer (or presumed composer) of the borrowed material in the heading or on the title page. In light of this, is it at all credible that Bach would have failed to provide the name of the composer of the "Goldberg" aria when he submitted his colossal set of variations for publication, if it had been anyone other than himself?

3

BACH'S *ORCHESTRE*

On 27 July 1733, while on a visit to Dresden, Bach delivered a handsomely prepared set of performing parts for the *Kyrie* and *Gloria* of the Mass in B minor to Frederick Augustus II, the Elector of Saxony and, as Augustus III, crowned King of Poland. Bach accompanied the tribute with a letter in which he asked the monarch to confer upon him a court title. In return for this distinction the composer offered to demonstrate his "unermüdeten Fleiss (untiring zeal) . . . in *Componir*ung der Kirchen *Musique* sowohl als zum *Orchestre*."[1] It is not surprising that *The Bach Reader* renders this seemingly unproblematic phrase as "in the composition of music for the church and orchestra."[2] But there is reason to doubt whether Bach could really have been offering to compose "music for the orchestra," that is, orchestral music, in the modern sense.

First of all, in the surviving Bach sources, both literary and musical, the word *orchestre* appears nowhere but in the letter to Frederick Augustus. Indeed, Bach seems to avoid the term precisely where he would have been expected to use it—assuming its meaning was the same then as now. It is strikingly absent, for example, from the famous "Short but Most Necessary Draft for a Well-Appointed Church Music." In this document, dated 23 August 1730, Bach, as is well known, describes the constitution of the vocal and instrumental resources that he considered necessary for the proper performance of church music.[3] For the benefit of his addressees, the members of the town council of Leipzig, he essentially "takes nothing for granted." He thus begins by pointing out that the musicians consist of *Vocalisten* and *Instrumentisten*, and explains that the *Discantisten*, *Altisten*, *Tenoristen*, und *Bassisten* who comprise the *Chöre* must be further divided into *Concertisten* and *Ripienisten*. He notes in this connection that "zu iedweden *musicalischen Chor* gehören

59

wenigstens 3 *Sopranisten*, 3 *Altisten* . . . " (every musical choir should
contain at least 3 sopranos, 3 altos), and so on. (Precisely how Bach's
arithmetic here is to be understood has been a matter of controversy.)[4]
In discussing the *Instrumentisten*, Bach similarly begins by mentioning
that they are divided into *Violisten*, *Hautboisten*, etc., before going on to
calculate the total number of players as follows: "Die *Instrumental Music* bestehet aus folgenden Stimmen; als: 2 auch wohl 3 zur *Violino* 1., 2
biss 3 zur *Violino* 2" (the Instrumental Music consists of the following
parts, namely: 2 or even 3 for the Violino 1., 2 or 3 for the Violino 2),
and so on, ultimately concluding that he requires "*summa* 18. Persohnen
wenigstens zur *Instrumental-Music*" (a total of 18 persons at least, for the
instrumental music). The significance of these passages for the present
purpose is this: they reveal that while Bach ordinarily referred to the
(vocal) chorus or choir as *Chor* (or *musicalischer Chor*), his designation
for its instrumental counterpart evidently was not *Orchester* (or *Orchestra*, or *Orchestre*), but rather *Instrumental(-)Music*. What, then, could Bach
have had in mind when he introduced the unusual French term in his
letter to the Elector?

The most reliable guide to Bach's use—and, presumably, to his
understanding—of musical terminology at this time is surely Johann
Gottfried Walther's *Musicalisches Lexicon*, published in Leipzig in 1732.
The pertinent entry here reads: "*Orchestra* (ital.) *Orchestre* (gall.) ist
heutiges Tages ein Theil des *Theatri*, wo die Instrumentisten sich
befinden" (*Orchestra* [Ital.] *Orchestre* [French] nowadays is that part of
the theater where the instrumentalists are located), in other words, the
orchestra pit.[5] Can it be that Johann Sebastian Bach, with his reference
to the *orchestre* was offering to compose music for the *theater*—that is, in
the first instance, opera (and perhaps ballet as well) for the royal court
at Dresden?

This notion is perhaps not so implausible as would at first appear. Opera, after all, was apparently the Saxon royalty's particular
passion, and Dresden was the operatic capital of Germany at this
time—particularly since the recent revitalization of its company with
the recruitment of a number of outstanding Italian singers and especially with the engagement, in 1731, of Johann Adolph Hasse and his
wife Faustina Bordoni Hasse.[6] In short, the possibility that Bach was
offering himself not only as a composer of church music—the *métier*
in which his reputation and experience were beyond dispute (and his
uncommon mastery confirmed anew by the new Mass setting)—but
also as a composer of opera—the musical entertainment about which
the monarch was known to be most intensely enthusiastic—this possibility, bizarre though it may seem today (given our deeply-rooted
convictions about Bach's personality and about his art), should not be
dismissed lightly.

On the other hand, if Bach was proposing to write music for the theater, why did he not say just that? At that time, after all, musical activity was typically organized into functional (and stylistic) categories associated with the church, the chamber, and the theater, which were so described and designated. It is inconceivable that Bach was unfamiliar with this system of classification since it was central to the writings of musical commentators of the baroque era from Marco Scacchi to Johann Mattheson and Johann David Heinichen.

Heinichen, for example, in his monumental treatise, *Der General-Bass in der Composition* (Dresden, 1728), expounds at great length on the characteristics of the *Stylus Theatralis*. Indeed the subtitle of the volume reads (in part): "Wie Ein *Music*-Liebender . . . die *Principia der Composition* . . . im Kirchen- Cammer- und Theatralischen *Stylo* vollkommen . . . erlernen . . . könne" (how a music lover . . . can acquire complete proficiency in the principles of composition . . . in the church, chamber, and theatrical styles). At the same time, the book's index has no entry for *orchestre* (or its equivalent in translation), and a perusal of the volume has uncovered no appearance of the term, certainly not in the sense of a larger instrumental ensemble (or its location in the opera house). In the famous discussion of the *loci topici* contained in the introductory chapter, for example, where Heinichen prints a variety of aria settings, each intended to represent the same text as interpreted in the light of a different "affect," the author refers to the "*Vocal*-Stimme" on the one hand and to the "*Accompagnement*" on the other, or he simply indicates the required instruments by name (for example, "*Violinen und Violetten all'Ottava*").[7]

Johann Mattheson conspicuously and almost defiantly emblazoned the term *orchestre* in the titles of no fewer than three of his treatises: *Das Neu-Eröffnete Orchestre* (Hamburg, 1713), *Das Beschützte Orchestre* (Hamburg, 1717), and *Das forschende Orchestre* (Hamburg, 1721). These titles constitute the best-known and, at least in Germany, some of the earliest uses of the term from the first half of the eighteenth century. But Mattheson otherwise seems to make no use of it in his discussion of practical musical matters, and in his major work, *Der vollkommene Capellmeister* (Hamburg, 1739), the word appears only in title references to the author's three earlier volumes. Mattheson, too, adopts the church-chamber-theater framework for his discussion of musical styles and genres and manages to do without the term *orchestre* even in his remarks on "Der Instrument-Styl," within the discussion entitled "Vom Theatralischen Styl besonders" (On the Theatrical Style in Particular).[8] He mentions that in "theatralischen Sachen" there can be "manches Vorspiel mit Instrumenten,"[9] and in general gets by with references only to "Instrumente," "Instrumental-Stücke," and the like, even when discussing such genres as the concerto grosso and the sinfonia.[10]

But Mattheson had a reason for featuring the word *orchestre* so prominently in the titles of his three early treatises, and in the first of the series, *Das Neu-Eröffnete Orchestre* (1713), the subtitle of which reads: *Oder Universelle und gründliche Anleitung. Wie ein Galant Homme einen vollkommen Begriff von der Hoheit und Würde der edlen MUSIC erlangen . . . möge* (or universal and thorough instruction in how a *galant* gentleman can attain a perfect understanding of the nobility and dignity of music . . .) he offers the following explanation:[11]

> *Da denn, was den Titul des neu-eröffneten* Orchestres *betrifft, zu wünschen hätte sein können, dass ein* generalers Wort, *welches beides Kirchen- und Theatral-so wol* Vocal- *als* Instrumental-Music *begreiffen möchte, sich hätte wollen finden lassen; Allein so habe ich Abgang dessen, das* Orchestre *oder* Orqvestre *als eine noch nicht sehr gemeine und dabey* galante Expression *lieber setzen wollen . . .*

As for the title of the newly founded *orchestra*: it would have been preferable if a more general word could have been found which would have encompassed both church and theatrical music, vocal as well as instrumental music. However, in the absence of such, I chose *Orchestre* or *Orqvestre* as a not yet very common and yet *galante* expression.

In the same passage Mattheson relates that the ancient Greek and Roman meaning of the term referred to the section of the theater reserved for the most respected citizens but that it now designated the place where the "Herren *Symphonisten*" were located. He also speculates that the meaning of the word changed for two reasons: first, the *orchestre* was the place whence "die *force* und das *tutti*" of the "*Symphonie* oder *Instrumental-Music*" emanated; second, and more important, it was where "das Haupt des gantzen Wesens . . . der Capelmeister . . . seinen beständigen und gar honorablen Platz einnimmt" (the leader of the entire enterprise . . . the Kapellmeister . . . took his regular and indeed honorable place).[12]

As Beekman Cannon argues in his study of Mattheson's writings: "The use of this word and the explanation of it would not hitherto have been countenanced because instrumental and dramatic music had not been recognized as part of the customary calling of the average musician. In fact the theoretical precepts of church music were alone thought worthy of serious discussion. Hence 'Orchestre,' with its suggestions of the opera, as the cognomen for a 'universelle' introduction to music, implies a critical realism new to musical books at that time."[13] That is, Mattheson chose the term not least on account of its polemical connotations in his battle with the traditionalists among the musical intelligentsia.

But Mattheson's immediate—and explicit—purpose in choosing *orchestre* was his need for a general word that embraced "both church and theatrical music, vocal as well as instrumental music." Such a universal meaning, however, could not have been shared by Bach, for the phrase

"*Componir*ung der Kirchen *Musique* sowohl als zum *Orchestre*" makes it clear that Bach regarded the church and the *orchestre* as two quite separate, though evidently complementary, realms, best defined perhaps as the sacred and the secular; taken together the two would have encompassed virtually all the duties expected of a contemporary Kapellmeister. All of this suggests, in turn, that in his choice of the term (in order perhaps to assure the king of his modern outlook on things musical) Bach had in fact appropriated Mattheson's "*galante* expression" but, deliberately or not, had modified its meaning by restricting its claim to "universality" in applying it only to the secular sphere. In short, Bach seems to have construed *orchestre* neither as narrowly as Walther nor as broadly as Mattheson, regarding it apparently as a partial, and modish, synonym for the relatively prosaic Kapelle, and using it here to refer to the secular arm of the musical establishment responsible for both chamber and theatrical music at court.

In doing so, Bach may well have been hoping to demonstrate his familiarity with what he deemed to be the linguistic usage prevailing at the Dresden court; for while the official designation for the musical establishment there since the end of the seventeenth century was *die Königlich Polnische und Churfürstlich Sächsische Kapelle,* also referred to, simply, as *die Kammermusik,*[14] there is evidence that the Saxon royalty, at least, would have preferred a French term. Fürstenau relates that at the time of the original founding of an Italian opera at Dresden, in 1717, the king (Frederick Augustus I) was concerned that the arrival of a substantial number of Italian musicians—both singers and instrumentalists—seemed to be upsetting the regular members of the Kapelle such as the Kapellmeister, Johann Christoph Schmidt, and the Konzertmeister, Jean Baptiste Volumier. He declared, accordingly, that he would approve the new appointments only on condition "que cela ne dérangera rien dans l'orchestre."[15]

Unfortunately, the king's remark, made in the context of a discussion of the establishment of the Italian opera, is not entirely unambiguous. Was the monarch referring to his Kapelle in general, or, more specifically, to the musicians in the pit at the opera house? The answer becomes particularly elusive when one recognizes that he would have had the same musicians in mind in either case. We seem, then, to have come full circle—or at least to have closed a semantic circle of some kind insofar as in Dresden, at least, a principal task of the Kapelle would have been to play in the *orchestre* for the opera. Bach was no doubt aware of this and, in his letter to Frederick Augustus, indicated that he was eager to compose for such an ensemble—even in such a place.

4

ON BACH'S UNIVERSALITY*

A number of years ago I was asked to revise the article on "Bach, Johann Sebastian" for the fifteenth edition of the *Encyclopaedia Britannica*. One of the guidelines was to begin not with the conventional "J. S. Bach was born at Eisenach in Thuringia on March 21, 1685" and so on but with a "Statement of Significance." I decided to put it this way:

> Although he was admired by his contemporaries primarily as an outstanding harpsichordist, organist, and expert on organ building, Johann Sebastian Bach is now generally regarded as one of the greatest composers of all time and is celebrated as the creator of the Brandenburg Concertos, the *Well-Tempered Clavier*, the Mass in B minor, and numerous other masterpieces of church and instrumental music. Appearing at a propitious moment in the history of music, Bach was able to survey and bring together the principal styles, forms and national traditions that had developed during preceding generations and, by virtue of his synthesis, enrich them all.[1]

There is nothing particularly original about this assessment, nor—I'm relieved to say—is it in any way incorrect. But I do believe now that it does not really do full justice to the magnitude of Bach's achievement. It subscribes, first of all, to the traditional view that Bach was "the culmination of an era"—to cite the subtitle of Karl Geiringer's well-known study of the composer[2]—or, in Albert Schweitzer's famous comment: "Bach is a . . . terminal point. Nothing comes from him; everything merely leads up to him."[3]

*A lecture presented at the Library of Congress on the 300th anniversary of Bach's birth: 21 March 1985.

Now, about ten years ago, in an essay entitled "Bach the Progressive,"[4] I tried to demonstrate that Bach's "synthesis" was, if anything, even more extensive than was commonly appreciated—that his music constituted not only a "culmination" or a "terminal point" but often enough reflected the most advanced stylistic currents of his time. Two of Bach's most monumental and serious works in particular—the Mass in B minor and the so-called "Goldberg" Variations—both written relatively late in the composer's career, could be shown to be indebted almost as much to the new, light, "pre-classical" or *galant* style associated with the generation of Bach's sons—and normally taken to be the very antithesis of Bach's personal style—as they were to the venerable contrapuntal traditions of the preceding century. I was arguing, in effect, that Bach's synthesis did not only extend historically into the *past* and geographically to embrace the great European national traditions of France, Italy, and Germany, but that it also sought to encompass the most recent stylistic developments—to look *forward* as much as in any other artistic direction. In other words, Bach's music seemed at times to aspire to, and to achieve, a *universality* of style and idiom that was considerably more far-reaching—and in fact more deliberate—than had hitherto been recognized.

I wish at this time to pursue the notion of Bach's "universality" more fully and to explore its specific implications for our understanding of his art.

I should emphasize that I am not primarily concerned here with the question of the universality of Bach's *appeal*. But it might be good to begin by asking whether the appeal of Bach's music is in fact really all that general. With a few notable exceptions, his music is certainly not as *popular* as that of, say, Beethoven or Mozart, not to mention Tschaikovsky—although that situation might have changed by the end of 1985. But if it did, I would expect it to be a temporary, and most easily explainable, phenomenon. For the fact is that Bach's music by and large is considerably less accessible to the typical music lover than is that of the other major composers of history; nor was it ever intended or expected to appeal to a concert audience in the modern sense, that is, to a large, and, musically considered, minimally educated, assembly of essentially passive listeners. It is important to remember that commercial concert life for the general public was only in its infancy by the end of Bach's life, and that Bach accordingly had little occasion—although there was some—to write what we may call "public" music.

It is possible, in fact, and rather profitable in many ways, to consider Bach's music in terms of its function, or, what is to a great extent the same thing, in terms of its intended audience. In fact, such a functional classification of music was common at Bach's time—but I hasten to add that contemporary commentators did not recognize such a category as "public" music but rather divided musical activity into three principal realms or institutions: the church, the chamber, and the theater. In the eyes of his own contemporaries, accordingly, Bach could hardly have been regarded as a "universal" composer by any means, since, strictly speaking, he wrote no music at all for the theater, that is, operas or ballets—although the argument certainly could be made that there is more genuine musical drama in many of his church compositions than in any opera of his time.

I should like to pursue the notion of "public" music a little further, though, and suggest that Bach's most generally appealing, that is, his most popular music today, falls into one or the other of two categories, both belonging to that sphere: on the one hand, the free toccata or fantasia for the organ or some other keyboard instrument (which his contemporaries would quite properly have considered a species of church music); on the other hand, the instrumental concerto, regarded at the time as music for the chamber. Common to both forms, however, is an emphasis not only on virtuosity and exuberant technical display—that is, on a readily appreciated sort of artistic prowess—and individualism—but also, often enough, on an intensity and immediacy of expression that strikes a sympathetic listener as "personal" in tone and feeling. I am thinking of course of such works as the famous Toccata and Fugue in D minor for organ and the Brandenburg Concertos.

Needless to say, I do not in any way wish to disparage these genuinely grandiose works. They are not only supremely successful but in fact represent the epitome of compositions of their kind. And they are all quintessentially and unmistakably "Bachian" in the vigor and vitality of their rhythms, the boldness and originality of their harmonies, the richness and complexity of their colors and textures. And nowhere is Bach's music more searingly intense, more deeply "personal," if you will, than in the slow movement, say, of the First Brandenburg Concerto, or just about any other slow movement from a Bach concerto, for that matter.

There is surely no need to remind you how the Toccata in D minor goes; and I am confident that you can call to mind the brilliance and excitement, and also the poignant expressivity, of a Bach concerto. Virtually any movement from any Bach concerto, indeed, is music eminently well designed to excite and exhilarate or to move and grip the attentive and responsive listener who would have heard it in Bach's day, as today, as a member of an audience—no matter whether as an invited and privileged guest in the aristocratic salon or "chamber" of, say, the Margrave of Brandenburg or in the less exclusive surroundings of Herr Zimmermann's Coffee House in Leipzig where the members of the local Collegium Musicum would have performed such music under the direction of the composer. That is, the music would have been performed, then, as now, for an audience, and as part of a concert.

But barely two dozen concertos by Bach have survived, and—even if one adds the four orchestral suites (or overtures) which are in many

ways similar and almost as popular—this would still obviously constitute a very small fraction of the close to eleven hundred compositions
from his pen that have come down to us. As for the Toccata in D minor:
its immense popularity is not only quite unique among Bach's organ
works but, sorry to say, probably owes more to the extravagant arrangements of Leopold Stokowski and others and to Hollywood's exploitation of it in such movies as Walt Disney's *Fantasia* and *20,000 Leagues
under the Sea* than it does to its own considerable, inherent interest. And
much the same is true for Bach's other "great hits": the so-called "Air for
the G-String," the aria "Sheep may safely graze," or the chorale "Jesu,
joy of man's desiring": they are typically lifted from their original contexts and often enough outfitted for an entirely different medium from
the one prescribed by the composer.

   Of Bach's close to two hundred church cantatas, on the other hand,
which represent the largest single body of compositions in his out-
put, I doubt whether more than a handful have established themselves
securely in today's musical life. But this is, really, quite understandable. For these works, for all their superb technical craftsmanship and
profound expressivity, are not at all "public music" as I have just defined that term. Moreover, they were clearly designed to have anything
other than a "universal" appeal. Indeed, they are, if you will, Bach's
most "parochial" works, written for a completely circumscribed audience: not only, in the first instance, for an orthodox Lutheran congregation but specifically for one thoroughly familiar with the particular repertory of hymns, local liturgical traditions, and theological
outlook prevailing in early-eighteenth-century Leipzig. It is inevitable,
I should think, that the modern listener has difficulty with this, quite
frankly, rather alien repertoire: difficulty not only with the theological content, and especially, the rather drastic imagery of the texts, but
also with some of the basic *musical* conventions of the genre—which
(as it happens) were largely imported from the even more alien world
of early-eighteenth-century opera: the fairly regular succession and alternation of recitatives and arias, for example, and the apparently relentless repetition schemes associated with the all-pervasive da-capo
principle of aria construction—a device which often renders the individual arias—for all their intrinsic beauty and effectiveness if heard
separately—simply too long and, to our taste, too static in the context
of a complete church cantata. In short, such compositions were not intended primarily for the "delectation" of a concert *public*, but rather for
the "edification" of a church *congregation*. Indeed, from the composer's
own point of view, they may have been conceived for and dedicated
to the ultimately exclusive audience; for almost every one of Bach's
cantata manuscripts closes with the inscription: *SDGl* (*Soli Deo Gloria*),
"to God alone the glory." Bach's cantatas, in fact, were conceived and
should be regarded not as concert pieces at all but as musical sermons;

and they were incorporated as such in the regular Sunday church services. I am reminded at this point of a remark by the Swiss theologian
(and passionate Mozart enthusiast) Karl Barth which goes as follows:
"It may or may not be the case that when the angels make music in
praise of God they play Bach; but I am sure that when they are by
themselves they play Mozart—and then God, too, is especially eager to
listen in."[5]

In contrast to the regular Sunday cantatas, Bach's most monumental, and inspired, church compositions (the St. John and St. Matthew
Passions, the Christmas Oratorio, the Mass in B minor) are not only recognized and appreciated as towering masterpieces but are performed
regularly and frequently. In the case of the Passions and the Oratorio, I suspect it is not only the power of Bach's settings but also the
inherent—and genuinely universal—drama of the biblical narratives at
their core—in addition of course to their association with the major religious holidays, that have eased their way into our musical life. But even
here I can't quite erase the suspicion that their frequent performance
during the holidays may in fact be as much an act of musical piety as
a sign of popular audience appeal. With the B-minor Mass, however, I
believe the explanation is not the same; for it is not only immediately
accessible but positively thrilling with its brilliant and utterly majestic choruses, the grace and straightforward lyricism of its solos and
duets, and its unusually colorful and varied orchestral palette. Above
all, the Mass is entirely free of those problematic baroque conventions
of text and form that I mentioned before. The Mass in B minor is indeed a *catholic* work in every sense of the word, and as such occupies
a unique place in Bach's *oeuvre,* one that gives it special significance in
any consideration of the composer's universality.

I imagine that it is unnecessary for me to say that I have no doubt
at all that even the few works of Bach for which I have just conceded
broad popular "audience" appeal—the concertos, Passions, the Christmas Oratorio and the B-minor Mass—provide ample testimony of his
genius and would guarantee a prominent place for him in the pan-
theon even if no other compositions of his had survived. But it seems
to me that the actual source of Bach's supreme stature at the pinnacle
of Western culture lies elsewhere. It is to be found in those works that,
quite obviously, I'm sure, I have deliberately avoided mentioning up
to now—the awesome collections of instrumental music: the compositions for unaccompanied violin or cello, the various chamber sonatas
for flute, or violin, or viola da gamba and harpsichord; and, of course,
the keyboard masterpieces: the French and English suites, the partitas,
the "Goldberg" Variations, the miniature gems of the *Orgel-Büchlein* as
well as the grander chorale preludes and fantasies, and above all the
sublime preludes and fugues that reach a veritable apotheosis in the
two volumes of the *Well-Tempered Clavier.*

I did not mention these works before because, with the possible exception of the "Goldberg" Variations, they are *not* "public" works aimed at a *listening* "audience." Unlike the fundamentally *dramatic* conception that underlies the concerto (and, to some extent, the toccata and fantasia) which is based on a *dualistic* principle emphasizing and exploiting contrasts and juxtapositions of all kinds—first of all, the inherently dramatic opposition of solo and tutti which brings in its wake sharp contrasts of dynamics, rhythms, melodic ideas, instrumental textures, harmonies, and even keys—most of Bach's instrumental music is governed by an aesthetic principle that was known at the time as the "Unity of Affect," according to which a composition was to be governed and unified by a single emotion or mood. This premise led, in Bach's case, to a veritably breathtaking logic and consistency in the development of musical ideas that has never been surpassed or perhaps even equaled since. The dualistic principle of composition was to reach its culmination in the classical era: in the sonata forms of Haydn, Mozart, and Beethoven. The *dramatically* conceived masterpieces of these composers—the string quartets of Haydn, the operas of Mozart, the sonatas and symphonies of Beethoven—epitomize, if you will, music as an art of personal *communication;* the *logically* conceived preludes and fugues of Bach, it seems to me, are, by contrast, in the first instance an art of *revelation*. Accordingly, they belong, primarily, not in a recital hall—or even in an eighteenth-century salon or "chamber"—but on one's own music stand. They are not so much meant to be merely "listened" to, but to be played—and studied. In this, Bach's position in our musical life is absolutely unique. His most profound appeal is not to the "general" or even "sophisticated" *public* but to the *initiated*—by which I mean, quite frankly, to fellow musicians. This does not mean that one literally has to earn one's living as a professional musician in order to appreciate, and love, Bach's music. But I would venture the guess that almost all of Bach's most devoted admirers today, as in the past, developed their admiration—indeed their almost physical need—for his music not by hearing it performed (on records or at concerts—no matter) but by playing it, or perhaps singing it, themselves and thereby entering actively into an aesthetic realm of a particularly sublime, transcendental, sort. This is a quite different experience from that of allowing oneself to be emotionally moved, be it ever so deeply, by more—shall we call them—worldly, or "human" sentiments transmitted, that is "communicated," by intermediaries: by professional "interpreters."

The sense of actively participating in something transcendental, when we play or intensively listen to Bach's music, I maintain, is central to understanding his position in our culture. Pablo Casals once said:

> For the past eighty years I have started each day in the same manner.
> It is not a mechanical routine but something essential to my daily life.

I go to the piano, and I play two preludes and fugues of Bach. I cannot think of doing otherwise. It is a sort of benediction on the house. But that is not its only meaning for me. It is a rediscovery of the world of which I have the joy of being a part. It fills me with awareness of the wonder of life, with a feeling of the incredible marvel of being a human being. The music is never the same for me, never. Each day it is something new, fantastic and unbelievable. That is Bach, like nature, a miracle.[6]

But I think Goethe came even closer to the essence when he wrote in a letter to a friend after having heard the preludes and fugues of the *Well-Tempered Clavier* for the first time: "I expressed it to myself as if the eternal harmony were communing with itself, as might have happened in God's bosom shortly before the creation of the world."[7]

Perhaps it would be fair to say—in any case, it is the main point of this essay—that the notion of the universality of Bach's music acquires its profoundest meaning when it is understood, once again, not in terms of the universality of its appeal, its popularity, since, as I think I have made clear, such a claim could be credibly challenged, but when it is understood with reference to a kind of universal validity. And there is some evidence that Bach in fact conceived of his art, and also his artistic mission, in much this way. Of course, he would have put it far more modestly himself, and in fact did so, for example, on the title page of the *Well-Tempered Clavier*, which he declared was "for the Use and Profit of the Musical Youth Desirous of Learning as well as for the Pastime of those Already Skilled in this Study." In a similar, if more playful, mode, he ended the title of his *Orgel-Büchlein* with an ingenuous couplet that has been translated as "In Praise of the Almighty's Will / And for my Neighbor's Greater Skill."[8]

That is, it is quite clear that while Bach may not have thought of himself as a musical prophet, he certainly did very much think of himself as a teacher; and not only the title pages and prefaces of the *Well-Tempered Clavier*, and the *Orgel-Büchlein* but those of the Two- and Three-part Inventions, and *Musical Offering*, and the *Art of Fugue* as well, all provide explicit testimony as to the didactic function of these monumental works. It would certainly not be difficult to argue, in fact, that Bach was the most self-consciously pedagogical of the great composers. An important implication of this is that Bach evidently regarded the pieces contained in these collections in the first instance as "exemplary" in the most literal sense: as *models*—to be studied and emulated—rather than, say, as divinely inspired and profoundly individual poetic or visionary statements that were intended to move his fellow man and perhaps even contribute to his spiritual or moral salvation. Unlike Beethoven, Bach did not claim to be a Bacchus who, for the sake of mankind, pressed immortal wine out of the grapes of art—even if he in fact did so.

Now just what did Bach think he was imparting in those didactic compositions? The title page of the Two- and Three-part Inventions reads as follows:

> Upright Instruction / wherein the lovers of the clavier, and especially those desirous of learning, are shown a clear way not alone (1) to learn to play clearly in two voices, but also, after further progress, (2) to deal correctly and well with three obbligato parts; furthermore, at the same time not alone to have good inventions [i.e., ideas] but to develop the same well, and above all to arrive at a singing style in playing and at the same time to acquire a strong foretaste of composition.[9]

Evidently Bach was convinced that virtually everything in the "craft" of music was teachable and learnable. He is supposed to have remarked on one occasion: "I have had to work hard; anyone who works just as hard will get just as far."[10] For music, even first-class music, was not so much the product of divine inspiration granted to the rare genius, but was rather the product of the proper application of certain fundamental principles—principles that Bach seems to have regarded as eternal, that is, as God-given, verities. He once expressed his sentiments on the thorough bass, for example, as follows:

> The thorough bass is the most perfect foundation of music, being played with both hands in such manner that the left hand plays the notes written down while the right adds consonances and dissonances, in order to make a well-sounding harmony to the Glory of God and the permissible delectation of the spirit; and the aim and final reason, as of all music, so of the thorough bass should be none else but the Glory of God and the recreation of the mind. Where this is not observed there will be no real music but only a devilish [wailing and whining].[11]

It seems to me that such phrases as "the most perfect foundation of music," "a well-sounding harmony to the Glory of God," "the aim and final reason of all music," "otherwise no real music but a devilish [wailing and whining"] all document Bach's conviction that music—real music, at all events—is constructed according to God-given, that is, eternally and *universally* valid, principles, call them "laws"; and with his systematically organized collections of keyboard music and their explicitly didactic prefaces, Bach's main, but certainly not sole, purpose, apparently, was to demonstrate these universal musical laws in operation. The *Well-Tempered Clavier,* for example, explores both the potentials of an innovation in tuning which, for the first time in the history of keyboard music, made all the keys equally usable, and, more significantly, the possibilities for musical organization afforded by the newly established system of "functional tonality."[. . .]The basic principle of this "tonal" system has been described as the creation of a sense of key-feeling by means of "sequences of chords that gravitated toward a tonal center. The degree of attraction depended on the distance of the chords from the tonic—that is, the home key—and this distance was measured and determined by the circle of fifths."[12][. . .]

[It is surely significant that] it evolved at just about the same time—in the 1680s, mainly in Italy in the music of Corelli and his contemporaries—that Isaac Newton was giving final form to his theories of gravitation based on precise, and universal, laws and measurements of distance and motion. Both Newton's laws of the universe and the principles of musical tonality were obviously the product of the same Age of Reason into which Bach, like Newton, was born.

When I mentioned in the encyclopedia article which I quoted at the outset of this talk that Bach appeared at a propitious moment in the history of music, what I had in mind was his advent at the completely unique moment when the age-old traditions of counterpoint and polyphony intersected with the newly-established system of tonal harmony. Bach, more than any other composer of his time, or since, not only thoroughly perfected and advanced the techniques of both but fully realized the implications and the potential of their fusion. If I may pursue my analogy with natural science a bit further, I think it may be fair to say that Bach's unification of linear counterpoint and tonal harmony represents an accomplishment in the art of music hardly less impressive than that which would be achieved if a physicist someday would realize Albert Einstein's hope of formulating a theory—a unified field theory—in which the nature of the relationships obtaining among the various forces at work in the cosmos—gravitation, magnetism, electricity, and so on—were precisely defined and established once and for all. But I suspect that I may be rushing in where angels properly fear to tread.

At all events, from the perspective of musical history, synthesis and fusion are the hallmarks of Bach's achievement. Not only did he unify and reconcile the structural principles of harmony and polyphony but, as I remarked at the beginning, he also effected a synthesis of the most important national schools and traditions of Europe; and in this respect as well Bach's music betrays a "universal" ambition in its range and scope.

I have already mentioned that musical commentators of the early eighteenth century, like all writers of the Enlightenment age, were typically fond of categories, and I referred specifically to their division of music into the stylistic realms associated with the church, the chamber, and the theater. They had also developed a system of classification based on national distinctions, particularly those that were to be observed between the dominant French and Italian styles: French instrumental music, for example, was characterized, among other things, by the dance and the dance suite and by profuse and delicate ornamentation; the instrumental music of Italy by the expansive formal designs of the sonata and the concerto and by the propensity for elaborate and extravagant improvisation. Critics were equally sensitive to the differences between Italian and French opera and their vocal styles: between the unabashedly sensuous melody and pyrotechnical display of the Italian aria, on the one hand, and the infinitely more serious, restrained, declamatory airs to be heard in the French *tragédie lyrique,* on the other. And we often find among the composers of the time rather self-conscious efforts to juxtapose and contrast these styles in their music. François Couperin, for example, published a collection of instrumental pieces which he called *Réunion des goûts*—a title awkward to translate but readily understood as the union, or unification of national tastes—and which included, among other things, minuets written in the contrasting styles of the Frenchman Jean-Baptiste Lully and the Italian Arcangelo Corelli.

As for Germany, it not only was exposed to and absorbed the stylistic and cultural influences emanating from France and Italy, and elsewhere, but was deeply conscious of that fact and concerned about how it affected its own cultural "identity," if you will. Bach, it will be recalled, once remarked: "It is . . . somewhat strange that German musicians are expected to be capable of performing at once and *ex tempore* all kinds of music, whether it came from Italy or France, England or Poland. . . ."[13]

Now Bach's mastery of the various national styles went far beyond mere cosmopolitan versatility: the ability to write French suites, Italian concertos, German fugues, or Polish polonaises. Such skills—and we can add to them his familiarity with and command of an impressive array of historical styles encompassing the medieval *cantus-firmus* setting, the vocal motet of the Renaissance (referred to in Bach's day as the *stile antico*), and so on, on to the simple but modish *galant* manner of the younger generation—all of this "encyclopedic competence" represented for Bach little more than a point of departure. For Bach's unique accomplishment was not that he had cultivated and totally mastered each of these forms and conventions but that he succeeded in galvanizing them into a single, coherent whole. That is, in an age that had conceived of music in terms of individual national traditions, and discrete stylistic, functional categories, Bach had managed to create a genuine synthesis: to forge a genuinely *universal* style. The "universality" of the *Well-Tempered Clavier,* for example, consists not only in its fusion of tonal and harmonic forces but also in that it constitutes a virtual compendium of the most important forms and styles of the era: dance types of all nations, Italianate arias, archaic motets, modernistic concertos, etc.,—all developed in accordance with a single compositional principle: that of the venerable, and rigorous, fugue.

Or consider the finale of the Fifth Brandenburg Concerto, (Ex. 4.1). It is, of course, a concerto movement, or more strictly speaking, a concerto grosso movement, since it employs a group of soloists—

Example 4.1.   BWV 1050/3, Brandenburg Concerto No. 5, mm. 1–11

a flute, a violin, and a harpsichord—in alternation and combination with an accompanying tutti ensemble. But the movement is not only a manifestation of the (Italian) concerto principle. It is, at literally the same time, a (German) fugue—in its texture; a (French) dance (a gigue)—in its rhythm, meter and tempo; and a da-capo aria (and thus indebted to the vocal as well as to the instrumental realm)—in its form.

But I can think of no more spectacular demonstration of Bach's powers of synthesis, his unparalleled combinatorial genius—all in the service, I submit, of a "universal" vision unprecedented in the history of Western music—than in one of his church compositions: specifically, in the opening chorus of the cantata *Jesu, der du meine Seele,* Cantata No. 78. Cantata No. 78 is "just another" Sunday cantata, part of a series that Bach had composed at the rate of about one per week over a period of approximately three years that had begun with his arrival in Leipzig in May of 1723. Cantata No. 78 was written in 1724 for the Fourteenth Sunday after Trinity, a day that fell on September 10. Since Bach had composed a new cantata the previous week (Cantata No. 33, first performed on the Thirteenth Sunday after Trinity, September 3, 1724), he most likely wrote Cantata No. 78 in the week beginning on Monday, September 4. I imagine that Bach spent at most three or four days engaged in the composition of the entire work, for he would have had to leave a couple of days for the writing out of parts and for at least one rehearsal, I should think, before the performance on September 10. In short, I doubt whether Bach could have devoted more than one day—it must have been Monday, September 4—to the composition of the chorus I am about to discuss.

The movement is normally described as a chorale-fantasy chorus because it is an elaborate setting, for chorus, of a German "chorale," that is, a congregational hymn—in this instance the chorale *Jesu, der du meine Seele* (Jesus, Thou my weary spirit), by the seventeenth-century poet, Johann Rist. Bach's approach to the movement is a conventional one in that he presents the traditional melody of the chorale—in the soprano part—as a *cantus firmus,* that is, set distinctly apart from the surrounding voices and instruments. In adopting the melody of the chorale Bach also adopts its form: the so-called *Barform,* consisting of a pair of lines or phrases that are repeated (the *Stollen*) and then followed by new material (the *Abgesang*). The form can be represented schematically as AAB. The melody of the chorale goes as shown in Ex. 4.2 (as notated by Bach in the final movement of BWV 78).

Example 4.2.   Chorale melody: Jesu, der du meine Seele

Both the *Barform* and the *cantus-firmus* technique can be traced back to the Middle Ages: the *Barform* is found in the courtly love

songs of the German *Minnesänger* as early as the twelfth century; the *cantus-firmus* technique formed the basis of the earliest examples of Western polyphony dating from the eleventh century or even earlier.

The lower voices of the chorus, for their part, offer a polyphonic commentary, in imitative texture, as in a fugue, on each line of the text preceding its entrance, along with the official hymn melody, in the soprano *cantus firmus*. This is a compositional principle associated with the Renaissance motet of the sixteenth century, specifically, with that of the so-called *cantus-firmus* motet. (The imitation preceding the first line of the chorale goes as shown in Ex. 4.3.)

Example 4.3.   BWV 78/1, mm. 15–23

Now these vocal episodes, each consisting of the *cantus-firmus* melody in the soprano and its polyphonic preview in the lower voices, are separated from one another by a refrain of sorts in the orchestra. This refrain, or ritornello, also appears at the beginning and end of the movement and thus provides a frame for the choral sections. The ritornello principle, in which a relatively constant theme or melody recurs in alternation with a succession of contrasting and changing episodes (such as the chorale phrases here), is the controlling formal idea of the mature baroque concerto of the early eighteenth century, as it was developed by Bach's slightly older Italian contemporaries, in particular Giuseppe Torelli and Antonio Vivaldi. The ritornello melody of our chorus, as it is presented at the outset of the movement, goes as shown in Ex. 4.4.

Example 4.4.   BWV 78/1, mm. 1–7

A most striking feature of this melody is its rhythm, as depicted in Ex. 4.5.

Example 4.5.   BWV 78/1, mm. 1–4: Rhythm

and also its regular phrase structure. Every phrase is exactly the same length; they are all four measures long. In short, the ritornello melody has the phrase structure of a dance and the rhythmic character, specifically, of the sarabande—one of the standard items in the contemporary French dance suite.

There is one further, crucial, structural element in this movement, one that pervades it virtually without interrruption from beginning to end: the ever-recurrent phrase first presented in the bass but later appearing in other parts as well (see Ex. 4.6).

Example 4.6.   BWV 78/1, mm. 1–4: Continuo

This is a *basso ostinato*—a relatively short phrase whose relentless repetitions provide the basis for the passacaglia or chaconne; essentially a set of variations on a dance pattern whose origins can be traced back to early seventeenth-century Spain. The particular *basso ostinato* Bach uses here with its rather mournful half-step descent from the tonic to the dominant is the so-called *lamento* bass frequently encountered in dirges and elegies in seventeenth-century opera. (The most well-known example today, no doubt—although it is inconceivable that Bach would have known it—is the lament "When I am laid in earth" from Henry Purcell's opera *Dido and Aeneas*.)

In sum, *Jesu, der du meine Seele* is one of Bach's most complex creations—a compositional *tour de force* that simultaneously observes or fulfills no fewer than five distinct principles of organization, some of which, one would have thought, were mutually exclusive—such as the combination of the repetitive *basso ostinato* with the ongoing *cantus-firmus* melody. At one and the same time the movement is a

modern Italian concerto—but based on a ritornello in the style of a sarabande from a modern French dance suite; it is a seventeenth-century
passacaglia, that is, a set of variations; but it is also a polyphonic motet
constructed both on "points of imitation" reminiscent of Renaissance
church music of the sixteenth century as well as on a *cantus firmus* according to compositional principles extending back to the Middle Ages;
on yet another level the movement is a German Lutheran chorale in
Barform: AAB—writ very large indeed.

It is virtually impossible to imagine a grander, more comprehensive,
more "universal" synthesis of historical and national styles than Bach
has achieved in this movement—incorporating as it does elements
of the secular as well as the sacred, the instrumental as well as the
vocal; a movement whose frame of reference embraces both the Roman
Catholic motet of the sixteenth century and the Lutheran chorale and
whose procedures are indebted to the medieval *cantus-firmus* setting,
the variation technique of the seventeenth-century passacaglia, and the
modern Italian concerto and the French dance suite.

But Bach's achievement here is not only prodigious, it is in fact
prophetic in its objective of transcending the cultural limitations of
geography and history, of place and time, in order to create—once
again—a "universal" artwork. For the outlook of his contemporaries,
you will recall, was confined by their predilection to conceive of and di-
vide musical practices and traditions along national and other lines. The
idea of a universal musical style—of music as a universal language—was
not to emerge for another half-century: during the classical period, in
the 1770s and 1780s. The composer Christoph Willibald Gluck spoke in
1773 of his wish to write a music that "would appeal to all peoples"
and "wipe out the ridiculous differences in national music." And he
would have been gratified to read, a dozen years later, that his music
represented "the universal language of our continent." Joseph Haydn
once remarked, "My language is understood in the whole world."[14] The
ultimate form of this universal musical language, admittedly, was not
that pursued by Bach. It was rooted rather in the formal conventions
and procedures of the basically Italian sonata colored by folk music
idioms imported from many national and ethnic traditions and enriched with sophisticated harmonic and contrapuntal techniques inherited from the Germans—above all from Bach. The new, more popular-
istic, more democratic aesthetic ideal demanded a lightness, simplicity,
and immediacy of appeal far removed from Bach's clearly contrapun-
tally inspired notion of a musical universality that was universal by
virtue of being all-inclusive and all-encompassing: not so much a universal musical language as a musical "universe"—as Goethe had said:
"as if the eternal harmony were communing with itself as might have
happened in God's bosom shortly before the creation of the world."

II

On the Compositional Process

5

"COMPOSING SCORES" AND "FAIR COPIES"

[In 1985 Garland Publishing, Inc., issued a facsimile edition in honor of the Bach tercentenary consisting of the autograph scores of eight sacred works preserved in American collections, both public and private. The following is the commentary to that edition, together with representative facsimile reproductions.]

Seven of these manuscripts, all dating from Bach's Leipzig years, may be appropriately described as "composing" scores, although they span a considerable range of creative activity: in some cases recording the composer's first thoughts and jottings, in others documenting a more advanced stage of the compositional process. The core of the volume consists of the autograph composing scores of five "chorale cantatas." Two of them—*Meine Seel erhebt den Herren*, BWV 10, for the feast of the Visitation of Mary, and *Allein zu dir, Herr Jesu Christ*, BWV 33, for the Thirteenth Sunday after Trinity—were composed in the summer of the year 1724, specifically in the weeks preceding 2 July and 3 September, respectively. That is, both compositions are part of the so-called second Leipzig cantata *Jahrgang*, the twelve-month period extending from mid-1724 to mid-1725 during which Bach cultivated the "chorale (or "chorale-paraphrase") cantata"—a genre essentially of his own creation—with almost unbroken intensity. The chorale cantatas *Der Herr ist mein getreuer Hirt*, BWV 112; *In allen meinen Taten*, BWV 97; and *Es ist das Heil uns kommen her*, BWV 9, however, all date from the first half of the 1730s and apparently testify to Bach's interest at that time in completing the chorale-cantata *Jahrgang* by filling the occasional gaps that for one reason or another had arisen in the original series of

1724–25. Each of the three remaining compositions is of special interest. *Aus der Tiefen rufe ich, Herr, zu dir,* BWV 131, is evidently Bach's earliest cantata, composed in Mühlhausen in 1707; Cantata No. 171, *Gott, wie dein Name, so ist auch dein Ruhm,* is one of the few surviving cantatas from the so-called "Picander *Jahrgang*" of 1728–29; and, finally, the first version of the late funeral motet *O Jesu Christ, meins Lebens Licht,* BWV 118 (formerly, if inappropriately, counted among the cantatas), dating from ca. 1736–37, is remarkable not least because of its curious scoring for chorus and brass instruments (one cornetto, three trombones, and two obbligato "litui").

The eight manuscripts not only enable the observer to trace the development of Bach's script over a thirty-year period, but also illustrate the range and variety of both his writing habits and his working methods. The early autograph of Cantata No. 131, for instance, is a particularly fine example of a Bach fair copy at its most elegant and most meticulous. And, while four of the seven Leipzig autographs (BWV 9, 10, 33, and 118) are clearly "composing scores" throughout—that is, obviously written down in haste and relatively heavily corrected in all movements—striking handwriting changes in the manuscripts of Cantata Nos. 97, 112, and 171 indicate that these works are partially based on earlier material.

The following essay is arranged in chronological order with separate discussion of selected points of interest raised or illuminated by each manuscript or by the compositions themselves.

AUS DER TIEFEN RUFE ICH, HERR, ZU DIR, BWV 131

The unusual postscript on the final page of the manuscript of Cantata No. 131 reads as follows:

> Auff begehren Tit: Herrn D: Georg: Christ:
> Eilmars in die / Music gebracht von / Joh: Seb:
> Bach / Org: Molhusino

The work, then, was written during the twelve-month period (June/July 1707 to June 1708) that Bach served as organist of the Blasiuskirche in Mühlhausen. Stylistic evidence suggests, moreover, that it is probably the earliest of the surviving cantatas. It surely antedates not only *Gott ist mein König,* BWV 71, composed for the installation of the Mühlhausen town council on 4 February 1708, but also such well-known cantatas generally assumed to date from Bach's Mühlhausen period as *Christ lag in Todesbanden,* BWV 4, and *Gottes Zeit ist die allerbeste Zeit,* BWV 106, and no doubt the fragmentarily preserved "Hochzeitsquodlibet," BWV 524, as well. And since, as Alfred Dürr has noted, Bach is unlikely to have composed any cantatas at all before his arrival in Mühlhausen, *Aus der Tiefen* may well be the first cantata Bach ever composed.[1] Gerhard Herz has suggested that the work was probably composed shortly after Bach's arrival in Mühlhausen and that it would have been performed in the Marienkirche (of which the orthodox minister Georg Christian Eilmar was pastor) as part of a mourning service commemorating the recent fire that, on 30 May 1707, reportedly had destroyed about a fourth of the town.[2]

But *Aus der Tiefen* is not the earliest composition by Bach to survive in autograph. Earlier musical manuscripts from his pen exist. The incomplete autograph of the Prelude and Fugue in G minor, BWV 535a, apparently dates from the late Arnstadt period, ca. 1706–07, and the autograph of the chorale preludes on "Wie schön leuchtet der Morgenstern," BWV 739 and 764, is probably earlier still.[3]

In all events, the score of Cantata No. 131 holds the distinction of being "the earliest autograph of a complete major work by Bach that has come down to us."[4] It is a fine example of Bach's early calligraphic style, written throughout in the small, delicate hand that is typical of the composer's pre-Weimar manuscripts, as are such features as half-notes with curved stems and "bird's-head"-shaped noteheads, and the two different C-clefs: an ornate form for the vocal staves and a simpler one, resembling the numeral 3, for the instrumental parts (f. 1^r: Plate 6).[5] Another early hallmark is the organization of the manuscript into gatherings of double bifolia (biniones) rather than as a loose succession of single sheets, while the ruled bar lines testify to the composer's concern at this time with calligraphy.[6] Indeed, by marking off the same number of measures in all the systems on most of the pages, Bach has not only succeeded in penning a score that rivals a printed edition in the regularity and the clarity of its layout, but surely has succeeded in surpassing any print in elegance and character.

The early date of this manuscript is evident not only from its script and layout but also from certain features of its notation: most notably, its "double" tonality. In contrast to Bach's Leipzig practice of notating a score (with the traditional exception of trumpets, horns, and timpani) entirely in *Kammerton* (i.e., the lower or "chamber" pitch and the normal tuning of the fixed-pitch woodwind instruments), here only the two woodwind instruments themselves, the oboe and bassoon, are so notated, specifically in the key of A minor. All of the other parts—the strings, voices, and the continuo—are notated in the higher *Chorton* ("choir" pitch) calling for a lower notation, here G minor. (During Bach's Leipzig period *Chorton* notation was largely restricted to the organ and the trombones.) The practical consequence of this (as Alfred Dürr has pointed out) is that the proper key of *Aus der Tiefen* should not be G minor—the key in which it usually appears in modern editions—but rather A minor.[7] Another notational curiosity of this score is a strictly conservative use of flats to cancel sharps that contrasts with a "cautiously modern" approach to the minor mode, notating both G

PLATE 6.   Autograph score, Private Possession (PP), f. 1ʳ: BWV 131/(1), mm. 1–33

minor and C minor (in the aria "Meine Seele wartet auf den Herren") with two flats (f. 5ᵛ: Plate 7). Bach was to abandon the practice of canceling sharps with flats about 1713/14 but continued to use Dorian signatures sporadically—at least for the flat keys—at least into the early Leipzig years.

While the calligraphic beauty of this early score suggests that Bach may have intended it as a gift—to Eilmar, possibly, or perhaps to some unknown recipient—it is also possible that Bach primarily had a quite practical purpose in mind in preparing the score so meticulously. This assumption is supported by the unusually complete array of performance indications: tempo and dynamic markings,[8] trills, continuo figures. The presence of figures suggests that Bach, the "Organista Molhusinus," performed the work from the organ, conducting the ensemble from this score and realizing the figured bass at the same time.

For all Bach's evident care, however, the autograph does contain several corrections—minor corrections of detail but interesting ones nonetheless. Changes in the independent bassoon line (the mere presence of which is itself notable) reveal, for example, that Bach was copying this *Kammerton* part from a source notated in *Chorton*, either from a lost draft or, far more likely, from the continuo staff of this same score. More instructive is a correction in the final chorus—at the words "und viel Erlösung," mm. 307–308 (f. 6ᵛ: Plate 8)—where the rhythm that now appears (as a complement to the oboe) in the violin part was originally in the bassoon. The bassoon reading was changed to a continuous sixteenth-note pattern presumably in order to help coordinate the execution of the alternating rhythmic figures of the oboe and violin parts in these measures. That is, the correction seems primarily to serve a practical purpose. Nonetheless, although admittedly modest in scope and consequence, it offers a glimpse of the young Bach engaged in the act of composition—the act of composition, to be sure, in its very final stages.

MEINE SEEL ERHEBT DEN HERREN, BWV 10

Like the vast majority of cantata scores surviving from Bach's early Leipzig period, the autograph of Cantata No. 10 is a "composing score" and was evidently written down in great haste. The work is a chorale cantata based on the text of the German *Magnificat* and was composed for the feast of the Visitation of Mary, Sunday, 2 July 1724. It is the fifth in the series of chorale cantatas belonging to the second Leipzig *Jahrgang*, which had begun on the First Sunday after Trinity, 11 June 1724.

In contrast to such fair copies as the autograph of *Aus der Tiefen*, Bach's Leipzig composing scores contain numerous corrections, rejected passages, and, on occasion, marginal sketches of a tentative

PLATE 7.   PP, f. 5ᵛ: BWV 131/(4), mm. 208–67

PLATE 8.   PP, f. 6ᵛ: BWV 131/(5), mm. 295–310

nature.[9] Performance indications, on the other hand, are rare, and instrumental designations frequently incomplete. Bach in Leipzig, apparently, normally had time to notate only the "essential structure" of a work—little more than the pitches and rhythms—during the formative stages represented by the composing score and would carry out the "final stage" of composition—the addition of tempo and dynamic markings, ornaments, continuo figures, and even the final specification of the instrumentation (particularly regarding the use of doubling instruments)—only when proofreading the performing parts prepared by apprentice copyists from the autograph score. It is therefore not particularly surprising that the autograph of Cantata No. 10 contains no instrumental designations at all, not even for the instrumental *cantus firmus* in the fifth movement, much less separate staves for doubling instruments such as the trumpet (actually a *tromba da tirarsi*) to reinforce the chorale *cantus firmus* in Movement 1 or the doubling oboes in Movement 2. (The full instrumentarium, however, is listed on the title page of the original wrapper in the hand of Bach's principal Leipzig copyist at this time, Johann Andreas Kuhnau.)

The autograph of *Meine Seel*, like most of the composing scores from the main Leipzig period of cantata composition, 1723–27, consists of a succession of single bifolia, suggesting that Bach may have been reluctant to commit more than one sheet at a time to a composition whose dimensions were not yet altogether clear and preferred rather to take a new sheet only after having completely filled the preceding one. The movements of the work follow in the score in direct succession, and there is no reason to think that they were not composed in that sequence. (It is just conceivable that Bach began composition with Movement 2, "Herr, der du stark und mächtig bist," since it begins at the top of a bifolio, and that he went on to write the following movements through the final chorale before composing the opening chorus. But in that case one would have to assume that it is sheer coincidence that the opening chorus happens to fill precisely eight full pages, that is, the first two bifolia of the manuscript.)

It seems, then, that Bach, here as elsewhere, "began at the beginning," specifically by entering the principal theme in the opening measures in the oboe part. (This is clear from the irregular and broken bar lines that had apparently been drawn at first through only the top two staves and then extended through the remaining staves of the system.) After filling the first page (f. 1ʳ: Plate 9) with the first nine measures of the opening movement, Bach had to interrupt composition in order to wait for the ink to dry. He took the occasion to jot a "continuation sketch" on the bottom two staves that leads the two principal parts—the Oboe/Violin 1 and the continuo—to the next important cadence, m. 12.[10]

The score reveals that by the time Bach began to set pen to paper he had a clear conception not only of the general design of the

PLATE 9.   Autograph score, Library of Congress (LC), ML30.8b.B2M4case, f.
1ʳ: BWV 10/1, mm. 1–9

work—the succession of styles, textures, and tonalities of the individual movements, for example—but also of most of the thematic material. Bach's conscious concern, then, was with the refinement of detail.
This is usually the case, as is also the fact that there are nonetheless
a number of illuminating corrections. A revision of the *ostinato* theme

PLATE 10.   LC, f. 8ʳ: BWV 10/4, mm. 47–50; 10/5

Example 5.1
a. BWV 10/5, mm. 1–5: Continuo ostinato *theme, original reading. LC, f. 8ʳ*

b. BWV 10/5, mm. 1–5: Continuo ostinato *theme, final reading. LC, f. 8ʳ*

of Movement 5, better known in its organ arrangement as the fourth "Schübler" Chorale, BWV 648 (f.8ʳ: Plate 10), is particularly fascinating, for it is one of the few instances where essential chromaticism was added to a theme as an afterthought. As a result of the correction, the final form of the melody consists of two descending chromatic lines interwoven into a latent polyphony: d', c'♯, c'♮, b♮, b♭, and a in the upper tones answered by g, f♯, f♮, e, and d at the fifth below (see Ex 5.1a and 5.1b).

ALLEIN ZU DIR, HERR JESU CHRIST, BWV 33

Cantata No. 33 was composed for the Thirteenth Sunday after Trinity, 3 September 1724, that is, two months after Cantata No. 10. It, too, is a chorale cantata from the Second *Jahrgang,* based this time on a hymn by Konrad Hubert (1540). The autograph, once again, is a composing score. The score is still kept in the original wrapper whose title page this time is in Bach's hand. Again, as in Cantata No. 10, there is a paucity of performance indications: only in the heading for Movement 5, the duet "Gott, der du die Liebe heisst," are any instruments mentioned at all (2 *Hautb.*). For the rest, Bach evidently considered the instrumentation to be obvious from the score layout and from the succession of clefs on the staves. Nor did he bother to write the whole text in the final chorale. Bach's fragmentary text indications were later completed—entered into the autograph in red ink (and not altogether reliably)—by Carl Friedrich Zelter.[11]

Of the many corrections in the score a few apparently minor changes shed light on substantial compositional decisions. In the opening chorale chorus, for example, the first two phrases of the *Abgesang,* lines 5 and 6 of the hymn, were at first identical in rhythmic and melodic form, as they are in the original *cantus-firmus* melody (mm. 98–111). Bach then added passing tones to the soprano in mm. 108–109 (f. 4ʳ: Plate 11). This apparently modest melodic refinement would seem to be not just in the service of the simple aesthetic principle of varied repetition but

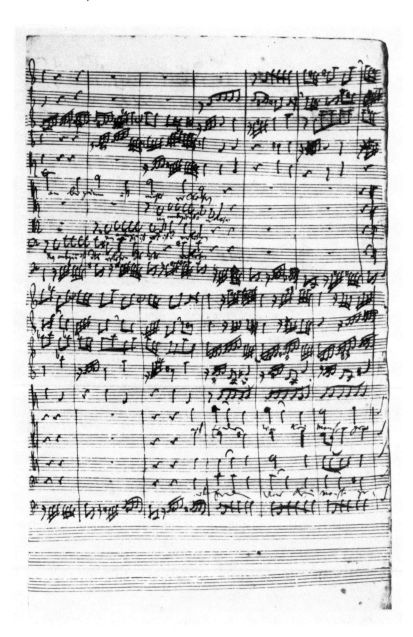

PLATE 11.   Autograph score, Scheide Collection, f. 4ʳ: BWV 33/1, mm. 99–110

also to reflect a sudden and considerably more fundamental decision of Bach's to set the two adjacent chorale phrases quite differently: line 5 ("Von Anbeginn ist nichts erkorn," "Since time began was naught ordained") as an excited stretto imitation in the lower voices, line 6

PLATE 12.   Scheide, f. 6ᵛ: BWV 33/3, mm. 1–19

("Auf Erden war kein Mensch geborn," "On earth there came no man to birth") in a more neutral, more chordal texture.

There is a similar correction in the opening theme of the aria "Wie

PLATE 13.   Scheide, f. 8ʳ: BWV 33/3, mm. 58b–66; 33/4

furchtsam wankten meine Schritte," Movement 3 (f. 6ᵛ: Plate 12). The first measure originally ended with an eighth-note c'. This was changed to a sixteenth-note mordent mainly, it would seem, to avoid a simple parallelism between the upbeat figures of the two short phrases with which the theme begins. But again the consequence is not only greater variety: the additional rhythmic activity in the second member of the melodic sequence introduces a measure of growth and development resulting in the creation of the sense of a larger unity in the unfolding of the phrase.

The autograph, finally, presents an unusual—and puzzling— instance of a substantial tonal change. The recitative "Mein Gott, ver-wirf mich nicht" (f. 8ʳ: Plate 13), which follows upon the C-major aria, "Wie furchtsam," originally began in G major. After four measures the key was changed to A minor essentially by mechanical transposition, by simply enlarging the noteheads. Since the new tonal relationship between the recitative and the preceding aria, namely, tonic-relative minor, is the most usual one found in the Bach cantatas, it is hard to imagine what may have led Bach ever to have considered G major as the opening tonality for this recitative at all.

GOTT, WIE DEIN NAME, SO IST AUCH DEIN RUHM, BWV 171

The New Year's cantata *Gott, wie dein Name*, BWV 171, is set to one of the texts of Bach's principal Leipzig librettist, Picander (Christian Friedrich Henrici), published in the so-called "Picander *Jahrgang*" of 1728/29. The work, accordingly, is thought to have been composed for 1 January 1729, although the dating is not completely certain.[12]

The score is remarkable in several respects. First of all, in its dis-position: the second movement appears not after but under the first. This obviously allows for the most economical use of the available space. Bach entered the heavily scored opening movement on a sin-gle fourteen-stave system at the top of the first seven pages of the manuscript and the second movement directly below it on the remain-ing seven ruled staves, dividing these into two systems of three or four staves each (f. 1ʳ: Plate 14). In addition, the manuscript is written on two different kinds of paper: one in the first two sheets, another in the third and fourth. The entire second half of the cantata, Movements 4 through 6, are notated on the second paper type (beginning on f.5ʳ), with the aria "Jesus soll mein erstes Wort." This movement is a reworking [or "parody,"] of an earlier composition, the aria "Angenehmer Zephyrus," from the 1725 secular cantata *Zerreisset, zersprenget*, BWV 205. The final chorale, Movement 6, is also borrowed from an earlier work, the New

PLATE 14.   Autograph score, Pierpont Morgan Library, f. 1^r: BWV 171/1, mm. 1–10; 171/2, mm. 1–9a

Year's cantata *Jesu, nun sei gepreiset*, BWV 41, composed for 1 January 1725. This time the movement was lifted without change beyond the transposition from C to D major. Both the facts that Bach took different paper for the second half of the cantata and that these movements are largely based on earlier material suggest that the work may have been composed in two separate chronological phases, but this must remain conjecture.[13]

The demonstrable reuse of earlier music in Movements 4 and 6 does reveal of course that in the case of these movements the autograph is not the "composing score" but rather a copy: the aria a fairly hastily penned "revision copy," the chorale virtually a fair copy.[14] The score of the aria, incidentally, illustrates the perils of attempting to reconstruct the details of a lost original from a later rearrangement, for although there are a few corrections in the revision copy, there is no visible clue that m. 24 of the parody is an interpolation into the fabric of the secular model, where m. 25 (of the new version) follows directly upon m. 23. This could be determined only by comparing the readings of the two movements, both fortunately extant in this case.

On the other hand, the appearance of the handwriting in the opening chorus—which was later to serve as the (direct or indirect) model for a far more famous movement, the "Patrem omnipotentem" chorus from the Mass in B minor—strongly suggests that the movement is not an original composition. Not only are there remarkably few corrections for a movement of this size and complexity, but it would be completely uncharacteristic for Bach in his Leipzig composing scores to allocate separate staves for purely doubling instrumental parts—such as the oboes and strings here—much less to rule the bar lines in such a manuscript. Werner Neumann's hypothesis, therefore (buttressed with reference to symptomatic clef corrections in the vocal parts), that the movement is based on a lost instrumental composition is altogether plausible.[15] It would seem, then, that the only newly composed movements in Cantata No. 171 are the aria, "Herr, so weit die Wolken" (Movement 2) and the two recitatives.

DER HERR IST MEIN GETREUER HIRT, BWV 112

Cantata No. 112, a chorale cantata, was apparently composed (or at least completed) in 1731 and, according to a surviving Leipzig libretto from that year, was intended for performance on Misericordias Domini Sunday, April 8. As in the case of BWV 171, the autograph is partly a composing score and partly a revision copy. The first movement, in contrast to the others, is carefully penned, containing only minor corrections of a "grammatical" nature. It is both significant that Bach began to enter continuo figures into the score and puzzling that he

PLATE 15.　Autograph score, Pierpont Morgan Library, f. 1ʳ: BWV 112/1, mm. 1–14a

stopped doing so after the first page. At all events, the movement must have been composed earlier than the others—whether substantially or only slightly earlier, however, cannot be determined.[16] Since all three bifolia of the manuscript contain the same watermark found in a letter of recommendation written by Bach on 4 April 1731, it is evident that the entire manuscript must have been penned shortly before the performance on 8 April.

Undoubtedly the most striking correction in the first movement is found not in the music but in the heading of the work, where the words *d'Amour* were crowded in after the word *Hautb.* It is possible that Bach had in fact intended at first to use regular oboes to double the violins in this movement. But a necessary voice-leading correction as early as the fifth full measure (f. 1ʳ: Plate 15)—f'♯ changed to b in the Violin I and Oboe I staves to avoid unisons with the viola—extended the range below the register of the oboe. Bach may well have corrected the heading only at the moment he made this necessary grammatical change.

IN ALLEN MEINEN TATEN, BWV 97

As the rare autograph date on the final page of the manuscript attests, the score of the chorale cantata *In allen meinen Taten,* BWV 97, was written down in the year 1734. But while the date is secure, the occasion for which the work was written is unknown. Here again we encounter from movement to movement contrasting handwriting types, reflecting different stages in the genesis of the work. The numerous corrections throughout the opening chorus suggest that this is a composing score, although penned with unusual care and clarity. The same is true for the second movement, as the melodic and rhythmic refinements of the ritornello theme—not only in the opening measures, but during its later recurrences as well—attest.

The following secco recitative, Movement 3, however (f. 5ʳ: Plate 16), seems to be a fair copy. The only corrections observable are the enlarged notes in the tenor part of mm. 2–3. Moreover, in sharp contrast to Bach's usual practice of first writing down the entire text when composing a recitative, it seems that in this instance the music was written down before the text. In consequence, words and syllables are often crowded in order to obtain a proper alignment of text and music. But it is difficult to imagine that Bach would have bothered to copy such a short and simple recitative from an earlier source.

It is virtually certain, however, that the fourth movement, the tenor aria "Ich traue seiner Gnaden," [which follows directly below the recitative on the same page,] is based on an earlier composition, at least in the A section and perhaps the first part of the B section as

PLATE 16.   Autograph score, New York Public Library (NYPL), f. 5ʳ: BWV 97/1,
mm. 71–96; 97/3; 97/4, mm. 1–9a

PLATE 17.   NYPL, f. 6ʳ: BWV 97/4, mm. 28b–47

PLATE 18.   NYPL, f. 6ᵛ: BWV 97/4, mm. 48–50a; 97/5

well. The presence of extensive performance indications in the violin part—dynamic markings, slurs, and trills—is a rather reliable hallmark of a Bach fair copy, while the elaborate and virtuosic character of the part may provide a clue as to the movement's origins. Only mm. 36–49, from the second vocal exposition of the B section, are clearly newly composed (f. 6ʳ: Plate 17).

The following recitativo accompagnato, Movement 5, provides an example of the two handwriting types coexisting in a single movement (f. 6ᵛ: Plate 18). Whereas in Movement 4 one section seems to be a fair copy and another a composing score, here the division is "vertical" rather than "horizontal," that is, the accompanying string parts are obviously newly composed and added to what is an essentially fair copy of the voice and continuo lines. The movement conceivably may have existed at one time as a secco recitative.

The mixture and combination of autograph types continue throughout the remainder of this problematic work; the sixth and seventh movements are evidently composing scores—as is, no doubt, the final chorale, as well—while the clean, if hastily written, Movement 8 may well derive from a lost model.

ES IST DAS HEIL UNS KOMMEN HER, BWV 9

Cantata No. 9 is a chorale cantata for the Sixth Sunday after Trinity, written sometime between 1732 and 1735. (Gerhard Herz suggests that it was most likely written for 1 August 1734).[17] The work, then, is a later addition to the chorale-cantata cycle and fills a gap that arose in July 1724 when Bach was away from Leipzig on this liturgical Sunday.

The autograph this time is a composing score throughout, indeed an unusually informative one. A correction on the first page of the score (f. 1ʳ: Plate 19), for example, sheds light on the order in which the parts were composed. In mm. 11–16 the leading melodic part, the flute, was originally written one tone lower than in the final version. Since there is no similar transposition in the remaining parts, they could only have been entered after the flute part had been changed. More significantly, the correction reveals that Bach's original idea was to treat the second phrase of the ritornello as a "real" answer to the modulating I–V progression of the first phrase (mm. 1–10), simply transposing it to the subdominant level and allowing it—by means of the same modulation up a fifth—to return "automatically" to the tonic. Bach then recast the consequent phrase as a "tonal" answer. That is, the underlying harmonic plan of the ritornello was no longer based on the "mechanical" sequence I–V, IV–I, but rather on the more symmetrical, tonally more compelling, progression: I–V, V–I.

PLATE 19.   Autograph score, Library of Congress, ML96.B186case, f. 1r: BWV
9/1, mm. 1–24

   The characteristic economy of a Bachian change is also exemplified
by the "ornamental" correction in the oboe part of m. 3, which originally
was an exact repetition of the opening motif in m. 1 of the same part.
The change was introduced not only for the sake of obvious melodic
variety but also, surely, to continue the sixteenth-note motion begun in
the flute and Violin 1 parts in the preceding measure. (It is worth noting
as well that in drafting the three opening measures of the ritornello,
Bach had to bear in mind as he set them down that they would serve
as the accompaniment for the entrance of the chorus and the chorale
cantus firmus in mm. 25–27.)

   The most fundamental revisions in this manuscript, however, in-
volve two of the three recitatives. The vocal part for Movement 2, the
recitative "Gott gab uns ein Gesetz," is notated entirely in the alto clef.
Directly following the conclusion of the opening chorus, however, on
the same page, Bach wrote the instruction *"Recit seqtr/und muss in die
Bass-/stimme transpo-/niret werden."* As Gerhard Herz observes, the change
documents a revised conception of the layout—and perhaps of the theological significance, as well—of the entire cantata. Bach's original scoring plan for the first part of the work was based on a simple rotation
of the vocal parts: soprano *cantus firmus* (Movement 1), alto (Movement
2), tenor (Movement 3), bass (Movement 4). In the final version, and
as a result of the vocal change in Movement 2, all three recitatives are
sung by the bass. It seems clear that this has symbolic meaning and is
connected to the concerns with the issues of divine law and justification by faith alone that inform the entire cantata text and are indeed
the central concern of the Gospel reading for this feast.[18]

   The third recitative, "Wenn wir die Sünd" (Movement 6), was so
heavily corrected that Bach crossed it out completely.[19] He probably
did not do so until after he had composed the concluding chorale, that
is, had finished composing the entire cantata. It seems likely that when
Bach reviewed the recitative (perhaps in the course of proofreading the
complete work) he discovered that m. 16 contained only two beats.
This anomaly, together with the generally chaotic barring throughout
the movement, obliged the composer to rewrite it on a new page after
Movement 7. He not only normalized the barring but took the occasion
to rework a number of details as well, particularly in mm. 8–11 of the
voice part.[20][. . .]

O Jesu Christ, meins Lebens
Licht, BWV 118, first version

According to the original heading on the autograph, Bach considered
this composition, consisting of a single choral movement, to be a motet.
The heading also informs us as to its curious instrumentation: two

"litui," one cornetto, and three trombones. The watermark suggests a
date of ca. 1736/37 for this version of the work. A later version, scored for
"2 Litui, 2 Violini, Viola, 3 Oboe e bassono se piace e Continuo," seems

PLATE 20.   Autograph score, Scheide Collection, f. 1ʳ: BWV 118¹, mm. 1–18

PLATE 21. Scheide, f. 1^v: BWV 118[1], mm. 19–37

to date from the last decade of Bach's life.[21] Even in its first version, it would seem to be Bach's last extant motet. Like the others—with the single exception of *Singet dem Herrn ein neues Lied,* BWV 225—it was presumably composed for a funeral. Indeed, the absence of any continuo designation or continuo line from the present score—along with the other peculiarities of its scoring—suggests that this version was performed outdoors, no doubt at a grave site. The instrumental bass is provided by the third trombone. (The isolated "continuo" figures in this part, in mm. 55, 69–70, and 75, surely were introduced only in order to clarify corrections.)

The autograph, a composing score, is fairly heavily corrected throughout, although the clean appearance of the opening measures indicates that Bach had worked out the shape and texture of the principal thematic material before setting pen to paper (f. 1^r: Plate 20). On the other hand, the presence of rests "beneath" the first two notes of the soprano line in mm. 19–20 reveals that he originally planned to have at least a three-measure choral pre-imitation in the lower voices before the entrance of the *cantus firmus* (f. 1^v: Plate 21); the characteristically dense, stretto-like contrapuntal treatment of the opening chorale line was an afterthought.

As in other motet-style movements by Bach, the score contains a large number of "diminution" corrections. That is, a passage was first notated in long notes (halves or whole-notes) and the rhythms subsequently subdivided or sharpened. A particularly striking example of this procedure occurs in the first choral entrance (mm. 19–26) where both the soprano *cantus firmus* and the lower parts originally had simpler rhythmic forms consisting largely of even half-notes. The object of such changes is not merely to embellish the long notes, but rather to enhance the text declamation, provide greater rhythmic continuity, and create a more flowing and intricate counterpoint.

The most intriguing aspect of this work is surely its instrumentation, particularly its prescription of "litui." Although there has been general agreement for some time that this must be a reference to horns—specifically to high horns in B-flat—it is just as possible that Bach had trumpets in mind, since the term was applied to both instruments in the eighteenth century. Another peculiarity of this work has largely escaped notice, however: all the vocal and instrumental parts, except for the *"litui,"* are notated in B-flat. Since the trombones in Bach's Leipzig manuscripts are invariably pitched in *Chorton,* it would seem that the "actual" key of the composition is B-flat *Chorton,* that is, C *Kammerton,* and that the *"litui,"* in fact, are pitched here in C, not B-flat.[22] In effect, Bach seems to have reverted here, apparently for the only time in his Leipzig period and surely owing to extraordinary circumstances, to the *Chorton*-based notation characteristic of his earliest scores, as in *Aus der Tiefen,* the autograph with which this essay began.[23]

6

THE SKETCHES

When one considers that present-day Bach research has subjected the available source material to an intensive philological scrutiny epitomized by a new edition of the complete works and the establishment of a new chronology of the vocal compositions, it seems particularly surprising that there has been no study of J. S. Bach's musical sketches and drafts for over thirty years.[1] Georg Schünemann's essay, "Bachs Verbesserungen und Entwürfe,"[2] though managing to provide an idea of the nature of this material, is marred by generality, incorrect identifications, and inaccurate transcriptions (all perhaps inevitable in an initial attempt), making it evident that a new comprehensive and systematic investigation, taking advantage of the latest philological and style-critical research, is in order. The following essay is intended to serve as an outline for such a study.[3]

The sketches present on the whole few problems of identification. The great majority seem to be memory aids written at the bottom of a recto to record the immediate continuation of the music on the next page while the ink was drying. Similarly, tentative marginal notations of the opening themes for later movements of the same work, and more rarely, for works to be composed in the near future, usually resemble the final versions enough to be recognized easily. Rejected drafts for the beginnings of movements and sections (also to be considered here) are hardly problematic when found directly before or above the final version. If the draft began a new sheet, however, Bach often turned the sheet around and started writing again, or he temporarily laid it aside, so that a rejected version for a movement can appear in a much later portion of the same manuscript (as is the case of Plate 22) or even in the manuscript of another work.[4] In the latter case the drafts can usually be readily identified either through an autograph title or the

PLATE 22.　Autograph score, SPK N. Mus. ms. 34, f. 10ᵛ: BWV 117/1, Draft

presence of a text, and sometimes they provide traces of otherwise
lost or presumably lost compositions. It is clear, for example, from the

PLATE 23.   Autograph score, SPK P 36/1, f. 8ᵛ: BWV Anhang 2

title above the draft, BWV Anhang 2 (Plate 23), on the last page of the
autograph score to the motet *Der Geist hilft unsrer Schwachheit auf* that
Bach at least planned to write a new cantata for the Nineteenth Sunday
after Trinity, 1729,[5] and Alfred Dürr demonstrated that Bach probably
composed the cantata *Ich bin ein Pilgrim auf der Welt* by identifying the
text in a copyist's sketch, found in the autograph score to Cantata No.
120a, *Herr Gott, Beherrscher aller Dinge.*[6] The Bach manuscripts, however,
have already been finely combed many times, and it is not likely that
there will be many more discoveries of this kind.

Identification of handwriting creates in general a less troublesome
problem than would at first appear. Although many sketches are so
short and written so hastily that it is impossible to state with absolute
certainty whether or not they are autograph, the musical nature of
these sketches usually enables a reasonably probable attribution. There
is hardly reason to assume, for example, that anyone other than Bach
would have troubled to write preliminary sketches for later movements
or for the following measures in an autograph score, and it is almost
exclusively in such cases that there is really any uncertainty about
the hand. A number of sketch-like entries written to clarify illegible
passages are almost always easily recognizable as nonautograph and
can often be positively identified as being in Zelter's or Philipp Emanuel
Bach's hand. This encourages the assumption that other sketches of this
type written in an ambiguous hand are likewise nonautograph.

A unique combination of problems concerning the identity of both
the handwriting and the musical passage is posed by a pencil sketch,
presumably of a fugue subject, written on the back of a cello part
bound together with the autograph score to Cantata No. 49 (P 111).
While the cello part is in the hand of Anna Magdalena Bach, the sketch
may be autograph.[7] A certain identification of the hand is not possible,
however, since the notation is quite faded. (This unfortunately also

made it impossible to obtain a legible photograph of the sketch to reproduce here.) But the general features of the text script and the form of the C-clefs recall J. S. Bach's handwriting, even though the pencil and ink script of the same person can vary considerably. The theme, given here in Ex. 6.1 in its presumably final reading, *post correcturam,* and the text, Psalm 121, 2, could not be located among the extant cantatas, so that, if the sketch is autograph, we apparently have a trace of another lost or planned composition.[8]

Example 6.1.   Sketch for a fugue subject? Final reading. P 111, f. 13ʳ

The value of the sketches, of course, is not primarily the evidence they may occasionally afford of lost compositions, but what they reveal about Bach's composing practices.[9] Before turning to an analysis of individual sketches, however, a few words about the character of the autograph manuscripts are necessary.

Almost all extant sketches and drafts are found in the "composing" scores of the Leipzig cantatas. Through the often large number of formative corrections, the character of the handwriting, and the presence of sketches and drafts for opening themes, the manuscripts reveal that Bach wrote down these compositions while he composed them.[10] It is therefore doubtful that he kept many, if any, separate sketch books or sheets at this stage of his career. This is easily understandable when we recall that Bach not only wrote the great majority of the Leipzig vocal compositions at the rate of one cantata per week during his first three years as Thomaskantor, but also that the later festival cantatas for state visits of the Saxon royalty and funeral music often had to be prepared on a few days' notice.[11]

In the manuscripts of the pre-Leipzig cantatas, on the other hand, the complete absence of sketches, the comparatively few, mostly minor or technical corrections (e.g., of voice-leading), and the normally relaxed appearance of the handwriting strongly suggest that at this time Bach worked a great deal from preliminary drafts which probably were subsequently destroyed. The autographs of most Weimar church cantatas can perhaps best be described as "revision copies"—an intermediate stage between the "composing scores" of the Leipzig cantatas and the famous fair copies of many instrumental works.[12] The invention of themes and the overall design of the formal movements were presumably worked out in advance, the final touches then added in the revision copy. In at least two instances—Cantata No. 61 (P 45/6) and 185 (SPK P 59)—the preliminary drafts were apparently so complete that Bach had a copyist write out large portions of the final manuscripts. Bach's slower production tempo in Weimar—the church cantatas were mostly written at four-week intervals between 1714 and 1716—presumably encouraged this more leisurely routine.[13]

Single-voiced sketches for the beginnings of movements testify that Bach first wrote down a melodic idea—a motif, phrase, or complete ritornello theme.[14] But this first written gesture was surely preceded by a careful "precompositional" analysis of the given material—for vocal music, the text, sometimes also a chorale *cantus firmus.*

The text must have been analyzed from two points of view: its structure and its "affect." The form and the prosody of the poem clearly influenced not only the composer's choice of form and meter, but also more specific decisions regarding the rhythm of the theme and the placement of tonic accents, that is, the choice of pitches. It is well known also that the *Affektenlehre* played an enormous role in baroque musical aesthetics, and Bach's endorsement of this doctrine is documented.[15] The composer's understanding of the affect influenced his choice of mode (perhaps of tonality as well), tempo, orchestration, texture, style, and the employment of rhetorical "figures."[16] Of course, external circumstances—the singers and instrumentalists at his disposal, and their abilities—also played a significant role in Bach's preliminary considerations. The extant tentative marginal sketches for opening themes can often be regarded as first, rough translations of the text into musical terms which had then to be refined into more idiomatic, convincing musical statements. In comparing these sketches with the final versions it is possible, by observing the elements retained and those reworked or rejected, to determine what the constants were and what the variables in Bach's conception, and in turn what was probably the generating idea of the theme. [See the discussion of the thematic sketch for the aria "Kann ich nur Jesum mir zum Freunde machen," from Cantata No. 105, p. 137.]

Bach's first draft of the "Pleni" theme for the *Sanctus* of the B-minor Mass, written on the bottom of the first page of the autograph (P 13/1, f. 1r),[17] indicates that here the primary consideration was to achieve a proper declamation and representation of the text. The words "coeli" and "terra" suggested an upward octave leap followed by a descending seventh, while "gloria" inspired a melisma. The dactylic structure of the text was directly translated into a straightforward triple meter. Bach wrote down the complete subject to the cadence with no apparent concern at the moment about contrapuntal problems. The conception was exclusively text-engendered and purely melodic (Ex. 6.2).[18]

Example 6.2. BWV 232/21, B-minor Mass: *First sketch for "Pleni" theme.*
P 13/1, f. 1^r

pleni sunt coeli & terra glo ———— ria

While retaining the essential melodic and rhythmic contour elicited from the text in the first sketch for the "Pleni" theme, Bach turned his attention in a second preliminary draft (f. 4^v) again to purely musical problems. [They are discussed below, pp. 186–88.]

Although, as the preceding example indicates, the rhythm and meter originally suggested by the text structure were often generating and constant factors in Bach's conception of the theme, he did on occasion recast the musical realization of the text meter. A rejected draft (Ex. 6.3) found upside down on the last page of the autograph

Example 6.3. BWV 29: *Rejected draft for Movement 3?.* P 166, f. 9^v

score to Cantata No. 29, *Wir danken dir, Gott, wir danken dir* (P 166, f. 9^v) is presumably the first version of Movement 3 of the cantata—"Halleluia, Stärk' und Macht"—which like the draft is a tenor aria in A major and begins a new sheet in the manuscript (f. 6^r).[19] Apparently, Bach originally intended a basically agogic treatment of the trochaic text in triple meter. If the ritornello theme was conceived as a setting for the first line of the text, the planned underlaying may have been as shown in Ex. 6.4.

Example 6.4.   BWV 29/3: Draft, hypothetical text-underlay

Hal - le - lu - ia   or   Stärk' und Macht

The final alla breve setting (Ex. 6.5) relies primarily on dynamic and tonic accentuation to insure a convincing musical declamation of the text.

Example 6.5.   BWV 29/3, mm. 20–24: Tenore, final version

Hal -   - le - lu - ia   Stärk' und___ Macht

Similar reconsiderations probably motivated the abandonment of the first draft (Plate 24) of Movement 31, "Schliesse, mein Herze" of the Christmas Oratorio (SPK P 32, f. 31ᵛ).[20] Here too the ritornello theme was probably text-engendered and designed to declaim the dactylic text in a strict and straightforward syllabic style (Ex. 6.6), but then

Example 6.6.   BWV 248/31: Draft for mm. 1–4, theme with hypothetical text-underlay. SPK P 32, f. 31ᵛ

Schlie - sse, mein Her - ze, dies se - li - ge Wun - der

Bach decided on a heavily emphasized agogic declamation in duple meter (Ex. 6.7):

Example 6.7.   BWV 248/31, mm. 25–28: Alto, final version

Schlie - sse, mein Her - ze, dies se - li - ge Wun - der

The original conception of the affect was retained, however, in the tonality, voice (alto), and phrase structure (2 + 2 measures). A number of characteristic melodic formulae are also common to both versions. Compare m. 2 of the first with m. 1 of the final version, m. 1 of the first with m. 2 of the final reading, and m. 3–4 in both versions.

The sketches and drafts testify overwhelmingly, as do the composing scores in general, that Bach's initial melodic ideas were normally completely formed by the time he set them to paper, although he often corrected or rejected them subsequently. There is no evidence that he

PLATE 24. Autograph score, SPK P 32, f. 31ᵛ: BWV 248/31, Draft for "Schliesse, mein Herze"

ever *deliberately* first wrote down preconceived contrapuntal, melodic, or numerical schemes which were to be elaborated afterwards. The following rejected draft for Cantata No. 183, *Sie werden euch in den Bann thun* (Ex. 6.8)[21] reveals no traces of the two-voiced contrary motion model from which it is presumably derived (Ex. 6.9).[22]

Example 6.8.   BWV 183/1: First draft. P 89, f. 10ᵛ

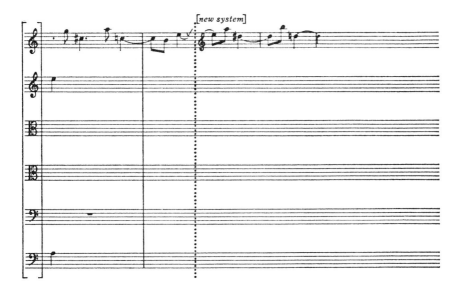

Example 6.9.   Two-voice contrary motion model

In countless instances, however, Bach later added figuration to the original melody. When writing movements in motet style, he often composed to some extent in half-note values, "dissolving" the individual lines subsequently. A similar technique can be observed in the following draft for an unfinished chorale-prelude in the *Orgel-Büchlein* (P 283, f. 18ʳ) (Ex. 6.10).[24]

Example 6.10.   Orgel-Büchlein. P 283, f. 18ʳ

As mentioned earlier, the greatest number of sketches, found almost exclusively on rectos, record the continuation of the music to be written, after the ink dried, on the following verso. One can consider such sketches extended *custodes*, usually found on the bottom of the page on any spare stave or staves. If no staves were available, the sketches were entered below the score in tablature notation. Reaching the end of a recto probably caused a considerable interruption, for the composer had not only to wait until the ink dried, but also to write down the brackets, clefs, signatures—perhaps even rule the staves—on the new page before being able to begin composing again.[25]

Since there are only about a hundred continuation sketches in the Bach autographs, they are obviously not found on every recto page of every composing score. They were usually necessary only when Bach was interrupted at the page-turn *during the free invention of new musical material.* Therefore, they do not occur in recitatives or in simple four-part chorales. In the chorale settings the melodic material, rhythm, and texture were predetermined, while the recitatives are so completely bound to the text that there was hardly a danger of a musical thought being lost during the interruption. The absence of continuation sketches in recitatives suggests that they were not thought out at all in any detail in advance, but composed note by note, or rather syllable for syllable, governed only by the affective and prosodic character of the text, and presumably by a general conception of the tonal design of the movement. But even in the freer forms—choruses and arias—there are relatively few continuation sketches. If a page ended during a major repetition of an earlier passage, usually a quotation of ritornello material, they were rarely necessary, for one can hardly speak here of "free" invention. Such passages for the most part involved literal copying, or perhaps mechanical or nearly mechanical transposition of "preexistent," that is, earlier material. The manuscripts here then cease to be *composing* scores in any real sense and take on a much cleaner appearance reminiscent of the autographs of "parody" compositions and arrangements of earlier works. Similarly, the tight organization of choral fugues, their use of permutation and combination of a limited number of musical elements, reduces the role of free invention even more than the techniques of ritornello repetition in the arias and free choruses and explains the rarity of such memory supports in these movements.[26]

The continuation sketches when present, however, reveal significantly not only what part or parts in a particular musical genre and situation were conceived, that is, written down, first, but also how far in advance they were thought out. They confirm, particularly in arias, the impression gained from observation of opening drafts that Bach usually wrote down the principal melodic part first in a given context. The great majority of these marginal notations, varying in length from two notes to fourteen measures, lead a new melodic unit, begun shortly before the end of the page to the next significant cadence or caesura. Bach rarely sketched the beginning of a completely new passage when the page ended together with a major articulation, suggesting strongly that he normally thought in complete melodic phrases, one at a time.

The sketches occur, as one would conclude from the preceding remarks, predominantly for the leading instrumental part of opening ritornelli or for the voice part of later freely composed passages, that is, sections essentially independent of major quotations of earlier material. Vocal sketches usually include the text, but otherwise carefully notate the beaming, testifying once more to Bach's meticulous concern with problems of declamation and to the text-engendered character of his melodic invention. The passage in Ex. 6.11 from the aria, "Höchster, was ich habe" from Cantata No. 39, *Brich dem Hungrigen dein Brot,* may serve as a typical example. The sketch concludes the final vocal episode of the movement before the closing ritornello.[27]

Occasionally, Bach did not complete the melodic phrase but sketched only the essential contour, the conclusion presumably regarded then as inevitable. There are numerous sketches, for example, in which the sketched phrase is complete except for the last few cadential tones. Similarly, in the continuation sketch (Ex. 6.12) for the bass

Example 6.11.   *BWV 39/5, mm. 56–59: Continuation sketch for Soprano. P 62,*
        f. 10ʳ

    doch kein Opfer wil - tu doch   wiltu   doch kein Opfer   n[icht]

Example 6.12.   *BWV 215/5, mm. 134–35: Continuation sketch for Basso. P 139,*
        f. 15ʳ

part (mm. 134–35) of the aria "Rase nur, verweg'ner Schwarm" from the
cantata *Preise dein Glücke* (BWV 215) Bach was content to note only two
of the remaining four measures of the phrase begun in m. 133, probably since the third measure is a literal repetition of the second and
the final measure an "inevitable" stepwise fall to the cadence tone (Ex.
6.13).

Example 6.13.   *BWV 215/5, mm. 133–37: Basso, final version*

     Weil   das   Gift und der   Grimm   von   dei - nem   Nei - de

At times continuation sketches reveal that the harmonic progression represented by the continuo part was initially drafted. In such
passages the upper parts embellish the harmonic framework defined
by the continuo rather than develop an individual melodic character.
This technique is especially typical of Bach's homophonic choruses and
elaborately orchestrated movements, wherein the upper parts can usually be regarded as written-out thoroughbass realizations characterized
by scale and arpeggio figures, broken chords, and similar rhythmic and
melodic diminutions of the fundamental chord tones. The sketch for
the concluding measures of the *Sanctus* of the B-minor Mass preceding
the "Pleni" section illustrates this technique (see Ex. 10.10).
    In arias, on the other hand, the principal melodic parts rarely
relinquish their primacy in freely composed passages. The few extant
marginal sketches for the continuo line in aria movements are confined
to passages based on ritornello material. The sketches here usually
indicate any modifications of the harmonic structure of the ritornello
that may be necessary for the immediate tonal development of the
music. In the autograph (P 41/1) to the funeral ode *Lass Fürstin, lass noch
einen Strahl* (BWV 198), Bach wrote the following tablature sketch for the

continuo part of m. 30a of the aria "Wie starb die Heldin so vergnügt"
(f. 12^r)

A   a   G   F   E

apparently to remind himself that this measure of the instrumental
interlude was to have the same harmonic and melodic function as the
original statement in m. 5—transposed down a fourth—in contrast to m.
21, where the harmonic rhythm had been retarded (Ex. 6.14). It is clear,
though, that the continuo part is also melodically the most significant,
for the two gambas have held chord tones.

Example 6.14.   BWV 198/5: Continuo

On occasion, Bach sketched a purely melodic part on the bottom
of a recto within a literal repetition of earlier material which entailed,
properly speaking, no "free" invention. Here too, it is usually possible to
reconstruct his deliberations. Emil Platen[28] has demonstrated that the
instrumental interludes in many of Bach's chorale fantasias for chorus
and orchestra are comprised exclusively of elements extracted literally
from the opening orchestral ritornello, but shortened and spliced into
new configurations as well as transposed if necessary to prepare the
entrance of the next line of the chorale strophe. The tablature sketch
shown in Ex. 6.15 appears on the bottom of f. 2^r of the autograph (P
1215) of Cantata No. 133, *Ich freue mich in dir,* noting presumably the
continuation of the Violin 1 part for m. 52 of the first movement.

Example 6.15.   BWV 133/1, m. 52: Original plan

The final version, however, written directly on the new page without any traces of correction, reads as shown in Ex. 6.16.

Example 6.16.   BWV 133/1, m. 52: Violino I, final version. P 1215, f. 2ᵛ

The measure belongs to the fourth interlude of the movement and is constructed from the following measures of the opening ritornello (the exponent $^{-3}$ refers to the interval of transposition—down a minor third; the absence of an exponent indicates a nontransposed repetition of the corresponding measure of the ritornello):

Fourth interlude : m. 47ᵇ 48 49 50 51 52 53 54 55 56 57
Opening ritornello: m. 0^{-3} 1^{-3} 2^{-3} 3^{-3} 4^{-3} 6   7   9   10 11 12.

The tonal function of the interlude, beginning in B minor, is to prepare the entrance of the fifth line of the chorale in A major. According to the sketch, Bach had initially planned to continue the interlude after m. 51 by joining mm. 15–17 of the opening ritornello, rather than mm. 6–7 + 9–12 onto the first four transposed measures of the interlude. The original combination would have effected the desired harmonic progression through E to A major more quickly (Ex. 6.17), but would

Example 6.17.   BWV 133/1, mm. 48ff.: Violino I, fourth interlude, original plan

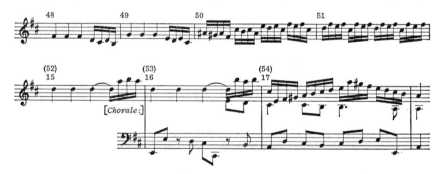

not have permitted a natural *Einbau* of the chorale into the subsequent measures of the ritornello (mm. 57–58 = mm. 12–13a) and was consequently abandoned (Ex. 6.18).

Example 6.18.   BWV 133/1, mm. 51–57: Violino I

Example 6.18.   (Continued)

The various stages of incompleteness represented in the forty-five extant drafts and sketches for the beginnings of movements invite an attempt to reconstruct the sequence of steps in which Bach set down the individual parts in a specific musical context. The available evidence, while admittedly sparse, is sufficient to indicate that Bach composed, even within one musical style, in different ways on different occasions. One is tempted to maintain from one chain of evidence that Bach composed homophonic ritornelli as follows:

1. wrote down the melody for the first phrase;
2. composed the continuo part to this phrase (Ex. 6.3);
3. filled in the inner parts for the first phrase (Plate 23);
4. drafted the melody for the following phrase (Ex. 6.8);
5. wrote the continuo for the second phrase (Plate 22);

and so on until the ritornello was completed.

This hypothesis, considered from the point of view of musical logic, is quite appealing. But as early as the second stage it rests on an assumption—from the fact that there are no extant single-voiced opening sketches of accompanimental continuo parts above which the upper melodic part was later composed[29]—that the melody in this particular instance was also written down before the continuo part. By the third stage the number of different possibilities has further increased, for it is now also possible that Bach composed the continuo in BWV Anhang 2 (Plate 23), for example, after having written down all the upper homophonic parts. Indeed, there are sketches that show that Bach did occasionally write down the middle parts of a homophonic texture before the continuo when his interest in textural detail apparently took precedence over the establishment of the outer-voice harmonic structure. Consider the two-voiced unidentified sketch (Ex. 6.19) appearing on the same page with the draft of BWV 183 (P 89, f. 10ᵛ).

By the fourth stage, we must also reckon with the possibility that Bach first wrote down the two melodic phrases of the ritornello before returning to the beginning to compose the continuo—or the inner parts—for the first phrase.[30] The diagram in Fig. 6.1 attempts to illustrate a few of the various possible combinations of stages:

Example 6.19.   Unidentified sketch. P 89, f. 10ᵛ

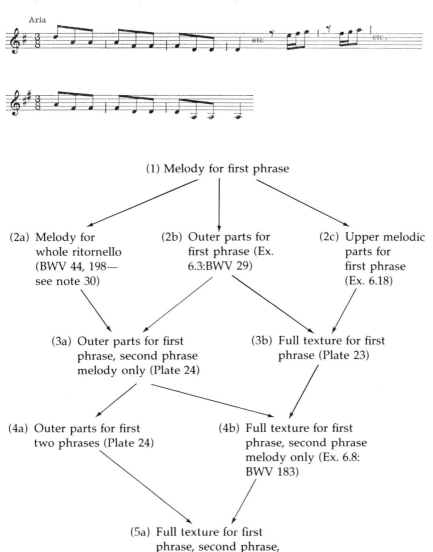

FIGURE 6.1   The Genesis of Homophonic Aria Ritornelli

A careful examination of the manuscripts may help at times to eliminate some of these possibilities in a particular instance. One can regard [the following]:

1. The position of the barlines: (a) what part or parts are most naturally accommodated by the barline, (b) what parts or parts are obviously uncomfortably squeezed into the available resultant space or even

go over the barline, (c) what parts have "too much" room (see, for example, the facsimile of BWV Anh. 2, Plate 23).

2. The vertical alignment of the parts: (a) the alignment of notes to be sounded together within the measure, (b) the evidence of notes placed to avoid clashing with another part which had been previously written down (for example, a note on a leger line above the stave may have been set to avoid clashing with a low note on the stave above. See the facsimile of BWV 117 [Plate 22]. The position of m. 9, note 6 of the flute part in relation to m. 2, note 1 of the continuo implies that the continuo for the first phrase was composed before the melody of the second phrase.).

3. Variations in the color of the ink; this, however, is rarely a reliable index.

An analysis, finally, of any corrections present may yield valuable clues concerning the order in which the parts were composed.[31]

The extant sketches and drafts for choral fugues allow a rather more certain reconstruction of Bach's usual procedures in this form. After deriving from the text a satisfactory subject, Bach apparently then wrote in the statements of answers and subjects in the remaining voices, thereby establishing the order of successive voice entries as well as the pitch and time intervals between them. Thereupon he worked out the shape of the countersubject in the first voice and entered it afterwards in the other parts, and so on. There is no evidence that Bach *in fact* composed choral-fugue expositions in homophonic "blocks" to work out the details of the necessary invertible counterpoint in advance.[32] His procedures, after inventing the subject, accord with traditional notions about how one goes about writing a fugue. The foregoing remarks can be illustrated with a facsimile (Plate 25) of two drafts for mm. 19-23 of the first movement of Cantata No. 65, *Sie werden aus Saba alle kommen* (P 120, f. 7ʳ).[33]

It is possible, by separating the individual layers of corrections, to distinguish at least ten stages in the evolution of this fugue exposition. While considerations of space prohibit a complete analysis, a number of observations are relevant here.[34] The original one-measure subject (Ex. 6.20) had been written down in all voices before the countersubject was entered in any part. This is evident from the vertical alignment of the voices in mm. 2 and 3, and from the low swing of the abbreviation hook of "werden" in m. 4.

Example 6.20.   BWV 65/1, m. 19: Basso, original fugue subject. P 120, f. 7ʳ

paper damage

bringen sie   werden aus Saba alle   ko____

PLATE 25.   Autograph score, P 120, f. 7ʳ: BWV 65/1, Drafts for mm. 19–23a

(In the second draft on staves 17 and 18 the space left in m. 3 of the bass part illustrates the point quite emphatically.) Thereafter, Bach wrote in the first version of the countersubject in the bass and tenor lines. The opening motif of the subject was now altered to the present reading in all four voices (as in Ex. 6.21b), perhaps to obtain a closer melodic relationship with the opening theme of the movement (as in Ex. 6.21a).

Example 6.21.   BWV 65/1

a) m. 9, Bass

Sie   werden aus Sa - ba al - le   kommen aus

b) P 120, f. 7ʳ: m. 19, Bass — second version

bringen. Sie   werden aus Saba alle   ko_____

Perhaps simultaneously, Bach revised the countersubject—before the original reading had been entered in the alto—evidently to shift the tonal orientation of the exposition from G to C major.

Bach decided now to increase the length of the subject from one to two measures, and this obliged him to begin a new system. This fundamental change presumably had a twofold purpose: to offer a contrast to the stretto-like entrances of the first theme (m. 9), and to lend a formal symmetry to the movement which in its final reading has the following proportions:[35]

	A	B	A'	
mm.	1–18(19)	19–45	45–53	or
	18 +	27 +	9	measures
		27		

The remaining strata of corrections are devoted to relatively minor details and need not concern us here.

There has been no attempt here to consider any of the broader questions implicit in this kind of study, regarding, for example, the psychology of the creative process or the relevance of biographical knowledge for an understanding of works of art. This study has been limited rather to the more immediate problems posed by the extant musical sketches of J. S. Bach. However, it is hoped that the examples selected for consideration have succeeded in illustrating not only the questions this material raises but also the kinds of questions it helps to answer.[36]

7

THE AUTOGRAPH SCORE
OF *HERR, GEHE NICHT*
INS GERICHT, BWV 105

Johann Sebastian Bach's *Herr, gehe nicht ins Gericht,* BWV 105, belongs to
the composer's first *Jahrgang* of Leipzig church cantatas. It was written
specifically for the Ninth Sunday after Trinity which, in the year 1723,
fell on 25 July. The only surviving primary source of the work is the
autograph score; the original performing parts are lost. The appearance
of the autograph—the hasty, relatively disorderly script, the numerous
corrections, and even the presence of a marginal thematic sketch—
reveals that it is a "composing score": Bach's first written notation of the
work. We may assume that the manuscript was penned in great haste.
Indeed, since Bach apparently had composed a new cantata (or revised
a preexistent Weimar cantata) for every Sunday service beginning on
30 May 1723, in accordance with his duties as Thomaskantor, and had
certainly composed a new work, *Erforsche mich, Gott,* BWV 136, for the
preceding Sunday, 18 July, it would seem that the score for BWV 105
must have been written within the week preceding its performance.
The composer, in fact, could hardly have had more than a few days to
conceive and write down the new work: if he began composition on,
say, Monday, 19 July, then he surely would have had to be done with
the score by midweek in order to allow one or two days for the copying
of the performing parts and another day (or two) for rehearsals.

The autograph of *Herr, gehe nicht ins Gericht* is representative of
Bach's composing scores of the early Leipzig period and reflects his

typical working procedures in the cantata genre. But, owing to the presence of a particularly large number of substantive musical corrections, often of a formative nature, the manuscript is untypically informative as to the genesis of this, one of Bach's most outstanding church cantatas.

The score enables us, first of all, to trace Bach's composing methods—or, more modestly put, his music-writing procedures—back to the very beginning: to the *tabula rasa* represented by the totally blank sheet of paper. Since Bach did not often use manuscript paper with printed staves but ruled the staves himself (or had them ruled) with a staff-liner, or *Rastral*, the music-writing process can be said to begin with the ruling of the staves on the blank page. As a general practice, Bach prepared a supply of paper in advance, ruling arbitrarily as many staves as could be comfortably fitted on a page, without regard for the musical layout of the score. Thus we find that most of the leaves of our autograph have twenty-one or twenty-two staves (with nineteen on ff. 7^r, 8^v, and twenty on ff. 7^v, and 8^r), and that this number often provides too many or too few staves for the musical requirements of the score. As a consequence there are several pages with unused staves (ff. 1^v–2^r, 3^v–4^r, 5^r–6^v, 9^r–10^v) and others where lack of space necessitated the drawing of freehand staves (ff. 7^r, 8^v). Incidentally, the peculiar stave-ruling on the fourth bifolio of the manuscript (ff. 7^r–8^v) reveals the manner in which the ruling procedure took place. Bach (or whoever ruled the paper for him) first spread out flat the two leaves of the folded sheet and then ruled the two outer leaves from the outer edge of the paper to the center fold and then the two inner leaves in the same manner. Since the ruling of one page served as an optical guide for the ruling of the facing page there is usually an agreement in the number of staves on each of the outer pages of a bifolio as well as an agreement in the (occasionally slightly different) number of staves on the inner pages.

The autograph's fascicle structure, too, testifies to its function as a composing score. As we have seen in chapter 5, during the Leipzig period of cantata production, Bach generally did not collect bifolia into gatherings when writing down new works. Accordingly, the score of BWV 105 consists of five successive single bifolia. In fact, while the first surviving autograph score consisting exclusively of single bifolia is the composing score of the Köthen New Year's cantata, *Die Zeit, die Tag und Jahre macht,* BWV 134a (Paris Bibliothèque du Conservatoire de Musique, Ms. 2), the available evidence suggests that Bach only adopted single-sheet structure on a regular basis in July 1723: with the composition of Cantata No. 105. Single-sheet structure was then used almost exclusively throughout the prolific period of the first three Leipzig cantata *Jahrgänge.*

Turning now to an examination of the musical notation itself, it is apparent, first of all, from the fact that each movement of the work follows directly after—that is, to the right of, or immediately below—the conclusion of the preceding movement (or at the top of a new page when the preceding movement effectively filled the preceding page of the score) that Bach composed the movements in the order in which they were to be performed. This—not at all self-evident—procedure, in fact, is typical of the Bach cantata autographs and indicates that, in this genre, Bach composed the individual movements "linearly"—with the notation of the first measures of the first movement—and proceeded, in principle, to compose the movements in sequence to the final measures of the concluding chorale.

But it is the corrections, revisions, sketches, and even certain notational peculiarities contained in the manuscript that shed the most illuminating light on Bach's evolving conception of the musical particulars of the work. There is a hint, for example, that the composer may not have completely decided upon, or at least have been reluctant to indicate, the precise instrumentation of much of the cantata until the entire manuscript had been completed. Not only are there no instrumental indications in the two recitatives (where they are hardly necessary) or in the final chorale (where they can barely be reconstructed with certainty) but the indications *Corno. è Hautb. 1 all unisoni* and *Hautb. 2. all unison,* entered in the first system of the opening movement above the first two staves, respectively, as well as the words *col Corno in unison* added after the heading *Aria* for the fifth movement, are written in a darker shade of ink than the rest of the headings. These designations, therefore, may well have been added later, perhaps only when Bach was certain that two oboes and a "Corno" would be available for the performance. In Movement 5 the semi-independent "Corno" part is not even notated on its own stave; rather, the part was literally "extracted" from the first violin part (f. 7ᵛ: Plate 26). (It should be observed in this connection that the high range of the part—to d‴—its nontransposing notation, and, above all, its melodic style calling for numerous chromatic pitches and awkward leaps, make it quite unlikely that Bach intended it for a natural horn: it is more probably intended for a *Corno da tirarsi.* Since Bach called explicitly for the *Corno da tirarsi* for the first time in his works in the cantata he wrote for the following week: *Schauet doch und sehet,* BWV 46, first performed on 1 August 1723, it is even conceivable that the instrument only became available to him during the later stages in the composition of our cantata, hence Bach's subsequent addition of these instrumental indications in the autograph. Unfortunately, the original *Corno [da tirarsi?]* part for BWV 105, like all the other original performing parts, is lost, and therefore this, along with other questions bearing on the intended instrumentation—such as the precise role of the "Corno," and, in particular, that of the two oboes, in the final chorale movement (doubling the soprano or one or both of the violin parts?)—cannot be resolved with complete certainty.

PLATE 26.   Autograph score, P 99, f. 7ᵛ: BWV 105/5, mm. 1–4

In Movement 3, as well, the remarkable soprano aria, "Wie zittern und wanken," several notational anomalies in the opening system apparently bear on its scoring [The autograph of this movement is the subject of an independent essay. See Chapter 8.]

With regard to the instrumentation of the work, the autograph reveals, finally, that the idea of treating the continuo part in the accompanied bass recitative, "Wohl aber dem" (Movement 4) as an unbroken stream of pizzicato octave leaps in eighth-notes—surely as a representation of the "Schlagen der Sterbestunde"—was an afterthought. The quarter-rests still visible underneath the final reading reveal that Bach at first had written down the continuo part for mm. 1–7 in the rhythm [♩↟♩↟]. It was only after he had completely entered the continuo part in this form in these measures that Bach returned to the beginning and entered the final reading, perhaps at this time also adding the word *pizzicat[o]* under the first measure (f. 6ᵛ: Plate 27). (This, incidentally, is the first appearance of the term in a surviving Bach autograph. In the autograph score of the Weimar cantata *Nun komm, der Heiden Heiland,* BWV 61 (P 45/6), for example, Bach wrote not *pizzicato* but rather *senza l'arco* in the string parts of a similar movement, the accompanied bass recitative "Siehe, ich stehe vor der Tür und klopfe an.")

The fact that the autograph contains few corrections affecting the main thematic material of the cantata is, of course, itself significant. The relatively clean appearance of the opening measures reveals that the composer had a clear idea of the means he would use to convey the primary affects and images of the text. It is evident, however, that Bach revised the fugue subject at m. 48 of the first movement. As in other works, the first notated form of this fugal theme made more use of repeated notes than the final version (Ex. 7.1).

Example 7.1.   Movement 1, mm. 47–50: Original reading (f. 2ᵛ–3ʳ)

While retaining the same declamatory rhythm of this first conception Bach changed but a single pitch, the fifth note, of the theme—from d' to g'. The resulting tonic–dominant alternation not only creates a sharper melodic profile, but also heightens the theme's quality of decisiveness and lends effective emphasis to the text word *kein* (Ex. 7.2). (In the preceding measure, at the change of tempo to *allegro,* the continuo

[Example 7.2.   Movement 1, mm. 47–50: Final reading]

PLATE 27.   P 99, f. 6ᵛ: BWV 105/4, mm. 1–3a

part has been changed from a half-note to the present sixteenth-note figure—a figure which, in m. 57 and elsewhere, returns, under the new time signature [¢], notated in eighth-notes. The addition of this connecting figure in m. 47 helps establish the precise tempo relation between the two sections as ¢ ♩ = ¢ ♩. There are, of course, two changes of tempo here: in m. 47, third beat, the change is marked by the word *allego*; in m. 48, first beat, in the change of time signature. Although there is no tempo indication in the autograph for the opening section of the movement, two surviving eighteenth-century sources which were prepared from the lost original parts—P 48/4 copied by S. Hering, an occasional copyist of C. P. E. Bach, and P Amalienbibliothek 37, copied by Johann Friedrich Agricola—contain the surely authentic designation *adagio*.)

On f. 3ᵛ, on a blank stave underneath mm. 77–93 of Movement 1, Bach jotted down a thematic idea (Ex. 7.3) easily recognizable as

Example 7.3.   Movement 5: Sketch for ritornello theme (f. 3ᵛ)

a tentative formulation of the opening motif of the tenor aria, "Kann ich nur Jesum mir zum Freunde machen" (Movement 5). The sketch reveals Bach's interest in formulating a ritornello theme that would later bear the first line of the text. A neutral melodic and rhythmic impulse (repeated f', repeated eighth-notes) was to function as a springboard for an *exclamatio* emphasizing the word *Jesum*, after which the rhythmic and melodic tension would be released. This germinal idea was retained in the final version of the theme (Ex. 7.4) but refined in accordance

[Example 7.4.   Movement 5, mm. 1–3: Violino I and Corno, final version]

with purely musical considerations. By removing the fourth beat from the first measure of the original conception Bach avoided the double skip of a sixth plus a fourth and rendered the melody both more concise (one beat shorter) and, by virtue of the minor seventh f' to e"-flat, tonally more focused. It is worth noting that the ritornello melody of the soprano aria also begins with a rhetorical leap of a minor seventh—but this time from the tonic e'-flat to the unexpected pitch d"-flat: a chromatic alteration that serves not to secure the principal tonality, as in the tenor aria, but rather to obscure it—to introduce a degree of ambiguity ("wanken") concerning the tonal orientation of the movement. (See Chapter 8).

The emphatic leap of a minor seventh appearing in the main theme of the two solo arias of the cantata serves as a unifying element: introducing a significant thematic connection between, and thus binding, separate movements of the work into a larger whole. A similar function is fulfilled, even more obviously, by the recurrent appearance (much in the manner of a Leitmotiv) of the "trembling" repeated-note accompaniment in Movements 1 and 3 and again in the final chorale. (The relentless eighth-note pizzicato bass in Movement 4—which, as described above, was added as an afterthought—is clearly closely related to the repeated-note figure.) The autograph score suggests in fact that Bach only gradually became fully aware of the programmatic and unifying potential of this figure during the course of composition. For, in addition to the accompanied recitative, the final chorale movement, too, contains a particularly pertinent and far-reaching change involving the figure, in this case affecting not only pictorial representation but indeed the formal design of the movement as well. The manuscript reveals that Bach had not conceived the idea of having instrumental interludes between the phrases of the chorale strophe until after he had written the outer voices of the two *Stollen* (but not yet the melody of the *Abgesang*). To accommodate the interludes Bach now had to re-bar the two *Stollen,* adding half-measure rests between the phrases of the chorale melody (f. 9v: Plate 28). It is significant, too, that Bach decided to disturb the exact melodic identity of the two chorale *Stollen.* He altered the fourth note of the melody from b'-flat to b'-natural in order to concord with the descending chromatic bass line that effects the transition from the B-flat-major conclusion of the preceding aria to the G-minor tonality of the chorale. (There was originally a natural sign before the corresponding note of the second *Stollen* [m. 7, note 2] as well, but it was later smudged out.) The ascending scalar motion of the bass at the beginning of the second *Stollen* constitutes an obvious antithesis to the motion of the first phrase. (Both span a seventh before momentarily changing direction.) In the second *Stollen* the function of the bass line, however, is not modulatory; on the contrary, it affirms the newly established tonality of G minor. Furthermore, the tone-painting chromaticism of the first phrase of the chorale (Text: *Nun, ich weiß, du wirst mir stillen/Mein Gewissen, das mich plagt*) is replaced by diatonic motion and primary I, IV, and V harmonies of the Aeolian mode (Text of the second *Stollen: Es wird deine Treu erfüllen,/ Was du selber hast gesagt*). The dotted rhythm of the melody in m. 7 seems also to be the result of a correction which, by removing the four equal quarter-notes of the original reading, also eliminates the rhythmic correspondence with the melody of the first *Stollen.* (The corrected version treats the b'-flat as a nonharmonic passing tone which takes up and continues the rising eighth-note motion of the lower voices in mm. 6 and 7.)

The final movement of BWV 105 is the only chorale among the fifty-six *Barform* chorales preserved in autograph scores in which Bach

PLATE 28.   P 99, f. 9ᵛ: BWV 105/6, mm. 1–14

made a correction to disturb the perfect melodic identity of the two *Stollen*. In most *Barform* chorale settings, in fact, not only the melodies but the harmonizations of the two *Stollen*, too, are identical. Bach, therefore, generally notated only one *Stollen* and indicated the second with a repeat sign. [See the related correction in the autograph of Cantata No. 33, described in Chapter 5.]

The subsequent interpolation of instrumental interludes between vocal phrases that originally followed directly upon one another, such as just described in the chorale movement, can be observed elsewhere in the cantata autograph as well. In the opening chorus, at m. 29 (f. 2ʳ: Plate 29), it is clear that Bach at first had begun a new set of imitative choral entries directly after the cadence on the downbeat of the measure. The first few notes in the soprano (♩♪ e″♮ a′) and alto parts (𝄾 𝄾 ♩ a′) were then smudged out, and the present two-measure orchestral interlude was inserted. The following choral entry (mm. 31b–33) apparently caused Bach considerable difficulty and led to the only completely crossed-out passage in the autograph. Since the draft of the two upper instrumental staves cannot be reconciled harmonically with the vocal parts and the continuo, what we have here, evidently, are two unrelated drafts which were tried out one after the other but entered (no doubt only in order to save space) into the same system at the same spot. Bach, at first, had apparently intended at this point, as he had done in the first instrumental interlude (m. 15ff.), to reintroduce the opening motif of the movement, this time—after the previous entries in the tonic (m. 1ff.) and the dominant (m. 15ff.)—in the key of F major (functioning as the dominant of B-flat) while subtly transforming the motivic material of mm. 29–31 into that of the opening ritornello theme itself. Accordingly, the first sketch of mm. 31–32 in the upper instrumental staves reads as shown in Ex. 7.5

Example 7.5.   Movement 1, mm. 31–32: First reading (f. 2ʳ)

Bach then hit upon the idea of introducing a *Choreinbau* into a repetition of the opening measures of the ritornello (mm. 34ff) but only after a renewed statement of the canonic choral theme—first heard in G minor (m. 9), then in D minor (m. 23)—now in the key of B-flat major: the third member of the arpeggiated G-minor triad that constitutes the harmonic groundplan of the adagio. In executing this plan in mm. 31b–33 Bach first set down the order of vocal entries as

PLATE 29.   P 99, f. 2ʳ: BWV 105/1, mm. 27–33

tenor-bass-alto-soprano, but then rejected it, perhaps not only because it may have seemed redundant—too similar to the succession tenor-alto-bass-soprano of m. 9—but in order to underline the entrance of this last of three choral invocations, with its dramatic modulation to the major mode, by means of a more climactic, and brighter, order of imitation: one beginning with the soprano (followed by alto, bass, and tenor).

In the soprano aria there are two interpolated instrumental interludes. Both serve not only to "punctuate" the text but also, like the other interlude interpolations discussed above, to extend the dimensions—to effect a formal expansion—of the movement. In mm. 21b–22 (f. 5ᵛ) the words *indem sie sich* were at first entered beneath the soprano stave but were immediately smudged out. (This correction, of course, can be understood not only as the introduction of an interlude but as the formation of a vocal "motto," a common formal element in concertante arias of this period.) In mm. 74ff. (f. 6ᵛ) the decision to add an interlude between the last line of the A section and the beginning of the B section was not made quite so immediately (just after having written down the text) but only after the notation of the corresponding theme—precisely the same theme with which the soprano enters in m. 78 of the final version.

Bach, as Philipp Spitta (1892) knew, was a remarkably "clean" worker. As he remarked in his essay *Beethoveniana*:

> Despite the great complexity of [Bach's] music, we know of few cases where the layout of a piece was rejected once it had been worked out. Nor did he often falter while working out the details. Sometimes he made changes when he took up a work again at a later date; but for an understanding of the way it was formed in the beginning, the evidence provided by such changes tells us nothing. (p. 181)

Many of the corrections Bach made in the composing score of *Herr, gehe nicht ins Gericht* are clearly concerned with more than "details." They reveal the composer deciding larger issues of scoring, thematic invention, and even aspects of formal design. They would seem, then, to provide one of those rare occasions that enables us to attain, at the least, a modest understanding of the way a work was formed "in the beginning."

8

THE GENESIS OF AN
ARIA RITORNELLO

Observations on the Autograph Score of
"Wie zittern und wanken," BWV 105/3

In his address to the International Musicological Society in 1961, Arthur Mendel offered at one point a paraphrase of a suggestion by Benedetto Croce in these terms: "Do you wish to understand the true history of the *Missa Pange lingua?* Try, if you can, to become Josquin Desprez composing the *Missa Pange lingua."* He went on to caution against the perils of such a project and wondered aloud "to what extent, then, can we imaginatively 'become Josquin Desprez composing the Mass' and to what extent is it necessary that we should? Can we do so by analysis of the work?"[1]

The following is an attempt to "become" Johann Sebastian Bach "composing" the aria—more specifically, the ritornello of the aria—"Wie zittern und wanken" from the cantata *Herr, gehe nicht ins Gericht,* BWV 105. Guidance will be provided by the composer in the form of the earliest notation of the ritornello preserved on f. 5ʳ of the autograph composing score of the complete cantata: P 99. For it seems clear that if we are to try to "become" Bach, or any other composer, "composing" a work, we should first try to witness him in the act of composition; and the evidence for this should be preserved, if at all, in the original autograph score of the work.

The specific wording of the Croce-Mendel exhortation deserves close attention. The aim of the attempt is to "understand" the "true" history of the composition. This suggests that our aim, or "wish," is not particularly to narrate the chronicle of what may be called its "external" history, for example, the order in which its constituent sections or lines were entered, or even to establish, say, what aspects of the work proved more difficult to compose than others, or whether the composer made extensive or minimal use of preliminary sketches and drafts, or whether he tended to elaborate or simplify his initial ideas. For such information is ultimately biographical in nature—concerned with the composer and how he went about putting the particular work together. "Understanding the true history" of the work rather implies empathetically re-creating its "internal" history—reconstructing from moment to moment the compositional motivations that guided and justified the determination of each specific reading. This "internal" history is indeed to some extent recorded in the autograph score, but only when the autograph contains a correction; for only corrections (along perhaps with other anomalies visible in an *Urschrift* but nowhere else) provide evidence of the internal dialogue—the weighing of choices—entailed in the compositional act. For the rest we witness little more than the composer copying—writing out music.

To the extent that we can reconstruct the musical logic that led first to a rejected reading, then uncover the perceived consequences of that reading which led to its rejection, and thereupon do the same with regard to the final reading and its acceptance, we are, it would seem, to the same extent, "imaginatively becoming" the composer composing and hence deriving an "understanding of the true history" of the work. We should therefore be willing to consider every such clue that the composer has left, that is, to discuss and interpret every observable correction and anomaly, no matter how unimportant its significance may appear at first (or may even turn out to be in the end) in terms of its compositional rationale.

In choosing a Bach composition we are perhaps in a relatively favorable position to pursue an experiment of this kind. A similar approach to a composition by Beethoven, for example—the attempt to uncover the compositional meaning of every detail in a Beethoven autograph—would surely prove to be an enterprise of infinite tedium and perhaps ultimate futility. The problems of decipherment posed by a Beethoven autograph or sketch and the sheer number of details demanding individual explication would make the project forbidding if not impossible. Furthermore, the investigator of a Beethoven autograph can rarely be certain that he has assembled all the material, scattered quasi-chaotically over numerous volumes and sheets, that may be related to the work under consideration, or that he has successfully determined the chronological order of this material—a step that must precede any meaningful analytical scrutiny.

The student of Bach's autographs is not so plagued. Since Bach was a "clean" worker, the absolute number of corrections in any particular composition is rarely overwhelming, and legibility is not usually problematic. Moreover, after Bach settled in Leipzig, he apparently always composed (vocal works at least) directly in score and made no use of independent sketchbooks or sheets. The analyst, therefore, can be reasonably certain that the autograph score of P 99, for example, contains all, or almost all,[2] the autograph material that ever existed in connection with the structural origin of Cantata No. 105. Finally, since all compositional corrections were entered into an integral score of the work, questions of chronology are simplified considerably; for one may proceed on the initial assumption that corrections were entered into the score approximately in the order in which they appear.[3] The reduced volume of data, then, the more limited number of known, unknown, and complicating factors, encourage an attempt in Bach's case to "become the composer composing."

This attempt will be limited to the opening ritornello of "Wie zittern und wanken," since a discussion of all the corrections visible in the entire aria autograph—although relatively few in number—would require a full-length study. But the present limitation should not prevent a meaningful conduct and evaluation of the experiment; for it is in the ritornello that the operating forces of the composition are set in motion, and the ritornello, designed to function as both the beginning and end of the aria, is, to some extent, an autonomous, if miniature, composition.

The approach chosen here will often expose a basic article of faith surrounding autograph evidence that should be confessed at once. It is the assumption—or prejudice—throughout that in every instance—unless the contrary is blatantly obvious—the final reading is superior to the rejected reading. On the other hand, it should be emphasized that when, in speculating about the meaning of the autograph corrections of Bach—or of any creative artist, for that matter—we attribute to the artist certain reasons for writing this or changing that, we only seem to be guilty of some form of the "intentional fallacy." It is more than obvious that we can never know what in fact went on in Bach's mind at the moment he wrote down or corrected any symbol. Such phrases as "Bach changed x to y because . . ." or "the a′♭ was rejected for the following reasons . . ." are expressions of convenience which really mean "the observable effects or consequences of this reading or that correction are the following. . . ." The composer may well have been totally unaware in any verbally conscious sense of these "reasons"—as they are perceived by a later observer. The very fact that we can never know what the composer himself really meant should encourage us, not inhibit us, to speculate about the meaning of autograph revisions.[4]

For convenience, the autograph of the aria ritornello is reproduced here in facsimile (Plate 30) and in transcription (Ex. 8.1). As an aid to legibility, the original readings of corrections have been placed on in-

PLATE 30.   P 99, f. 5ʳ: BWV 105/3, "Wie zittern und wanken", mm. 1–21a

Example 8.1.   "Wie zittern," mm. 1–21a: Transcription of autograph. P 99, f. 5ʳ

Example 8.1. (*Continued*)

terlinear staves above the final readings. A number of idiosyncrasies
of the autograph—the duplication of accidentals in key signatures
and within measures, as well as beaming and the placement of autograph slurs—have been retained in the transcription. Any nonautograph entries in the manuscript—occasional slurs (discussed later), the
quarter-rests in the oboe part of m. 17, and the presumably nonautograph entry of the aria text below the score—have been omitted.[5]

The first observable correction in the autograph, the extension of
the score bracket before the first system from four to five staves, seems
to confront us at once with an "external historical" problem of the kind
just described. It also makes us aware of several peculiarities in the
opening score system which do not entail any visible corrections. The

first of these is the designation "Soprano" above the fourth stave—a totally superfluous entry, for the clef on the stave sufficiently identifies the vocal part. The entry is particularly puzzling since there is no (necessary) verbal identification for any of the instrumental parts.[6] A further anomaly is the appearance of the calligraphic form of the C-clefs in this system; the remaining systems of the movement (and of the entire cantata) make exclusive use of the "hook"-form C-clefs which are the norm in Leipzig composing scores. The ornate form is typical of the earliest Bach autographs and is found in fair copies throughout Bach's career, but it rarely appears in composing scores of the post-Mühlhausen period. In the early sources they were sometimes restricted in use—to vocal staves as a means of visually differentiating them from instrumental staves.[7] The presence of the calligraphic form in both the vocal and instrumental staves of the first score system here cannot be explained by the rationale of Bach's pre-Leipzig practice. The following hypothesis, admittedly elaborate and tentative, does manage to account for the constellation of anomalies.

The clean appearance of the opening measures of the aria reveals that the composer had a precise conception from the beginning of the musical means to be employed in creating a vivid "pictorial" representation of the text: broken, "shaking," four-note motives in the melody were to be projected upon a chordal accompaniment of repeated sixteenth-notes "trembling" above ominously thumping eighths, the latter constituting the sole "bass" support in the symbolic absence of a "fundamental" basso continuo. It is evident from the score as well that a five-part texture and—since Bach did not normally enter more than one real part on a single stave—its necessary disposition on a five-stave system had already been determined. In order to economize on space and paper, however, Bach decided at first—here, as elsewhere[8]—to omit the stave of the resting vocal part and drew the initial four-stave bracket. But while so many specifics had been established from the first, there is reason to believe that Bach may not have known, or was perhaps reluctant to indicate, the precise instrumentation for the aria, indeed for much of the cantata, until the entire autograph had been written down.[9] Bach may have intended, for example, to convey the sensation of "groundlessness" not only by dispensing with a continuo but with a lower register (bass and tenor) altogether. It is possible that he planned at first to prevent the "bassetto" from descending below the open g-string of the violin[10] and therefore chose to notate the part in the soprano clef, a practice he occasionally adopted when writing for string parts in this tessitura.[11] In order, now, to call attention to the rather unusual employment of the soprano clef for an instrumental part, Bach introduced the equally unusual calligraphic form of the clef. This recalls the differentiation of vocal and instrumental C-clefs encountered in Weimar autographs but with the specific identifications reversed. Before entering a single note on this stave, however, Bach, according to our hypothesis, realized that in the course of a movement in E-flat major (the key had also been already determined) the bassetto would inevitably descend at least to f—the dominant of the dominant. He therefore added a fifth stave to the system with an alto clef—again in the calligraphic form. This time the calligraphic form was a cautionary signal indicating that the stave with an alto clef below the soprano stave was intended not for an alto voice but for an instrumental part. Finally, Bach extended the score bracket to five staves and added the word "Soprano" over the fourth stave, perhaps as a reminder to himself not to enter the bassetto on that line as he had originally planned.

With the possible exception, then, of the specific scoring,[12] the absence of any visible correction in the first two measures of the autograph discloses that every musical detail related to the rhetorical conception of the aria—the portrayal, with the means described above, of the *zittern und wanken* (trembling and shaking) afflicting the tormented thoughts of sinners—was clear in Bach's mind before he set these measures to paper.[13]

The structural conception of the opening measures was also, despite the presence of corrections as early as m. 3, evidently secure from the first. This was the presentation, after an introductory measure, of a symmetrical four-measure phrase constructed upon the primary harmonies: I–IV, V–I of the tonal cadence, here elaborated to I^{5}_{3}–$^{\flat7}$–IV, V^7–I and grouped into two two-measure pairs of antecedent–consequent subphrases. The melody to be borne by this basic cadential pattern, however, was not to be so straightforward, but rather, in illustration of the tortured conscience, would skip about the constituent tones of the supporting harmonies, suppressing, or, with the aid of sudden shifts to the lower or higher octave, disguising a melodic gesture in essence as basic as the cadential pattern from which it emerges: the direct scalar ascent from the tonic to the mediant, e″ ♭ -f″-g″ (Ex. 8.2).

Example 8.2.   Mm. 1–5: Linear-harmonic plan

The "foreground" of the theme is characterized on the one hand by a direct "rhetorical" leap of a minor seventh[14] to the unexpected pitch d″ ♭, a chromatic alteration that introduces a degree of ambiguity ("wanken") concerning the tonal orientation of the movement—an ambiguity often attending the early introduction of the I♭^{7} sonority. The almost inevitable resolution of the melodic seventh, e′ ♭ -d″ ♭, to the sixth, e′ ♭ -c″, in the context of an A-flat chord hardly reinforces the impression of E-flat as the true tonic, which had of course been assumed on the basis of the atmospheric E-flat triad in the introductory measure. Just as characteristic of the theme as the initial leap is the slow, mordent-like decoration of the downbeats in these opening measures, a device suggestive of the sense of dizziness again conveyed by the word "wanken."

Each of the details of this foreground, which together constitute the realization of a common underlying harmonic and linear ground-plan as a unique, indeed particularly complex, "theme," carries its own implications for continuation. By the third measure of the composition these have become numerous enough to make the specific readings of even the second half of the phrase—in principle only a symmetrical complement of the first half—anything but self-evident.

The change of pitch in the Violin 2 part on the first beat of m. 3 is the first correction of musical substance to appear in the autograph. Although, as will be shown presently, it could not have been the first correction entered, it is advisable to consider it first. The change has more than one effect. The friction of the simultaneous and repeated minor seconds g′–a′ ♭ in the violins may be interpreted as an expressive nuance in the service of the general Affect, perhaps related to (and thus "implied" by) the melodic minor and major seconds in the mordent figures of the theme.[15] But the correction also has structural significance. The four-measure design of the opening phrase with its harmonic plan I(♭7)–IV, V7–I was surely intended as a cogent, yet spacious expression of the basic tonality of the aria. But the "inevitable" resolution of the antecedent (and dissonant) E♭ dominant seventh to the consequent (and consonant) A-flat major triad this early in the movement and at the relatively slow tempo at which the aria should doubtless be performed creates a sense of closure strong enough to jeopardize the larger four-measure phrase. The insertion of g′ into the A-flat triad insures the cohesion of the four-measure unit. There is now, despite the fragmented character of the theme and the 7–6 intervallic succession embodied in the first subphrase, no interruption in the continuity of the phrase until the kinetic series of sevenths, I♭7–IV7–V7, is resolved with the arrival of the E-flat major triad in the middle of m. 5.

The layout of the autograph makes clear that throughout the ritornello the oboe part was as a rule written down first in any measure. (After the barlines were then drawn to accommodate this part, the inner parts—Violins 1 and 2—were entered, which with their greater number of notes were necessarily crowded into the space thus marked off and often extended over the barline.) It is almost certain therefore, that the upbeat to m. 4 was entered, and, as the readings make clear, corrected (more than once) before the inner parts were entered at all. Here, too, as with the later change of the Violin 2 part on the first beat of m. 3, considerations of continuity seem to have motivated the corrections.

The first reading of the upbeat seems to have been f'. Assuming that the e"♭ downbeat of m. 4 was entered together with this reading, then the f'–e"♭ leap would disclose an early intention to relate the second antecedent–consequent pair of subphrases to the first by repeating in transposition the opening melodic interval. This parallelism may have been sensed as overarticulating the subdivision of the four-measure phrase and, accordingly, was smudged away. Another rejected reading for the upbeat is probably covered by the heavy penstrokes before the final reading. They may cover a ♭-sign applying to the a'. An a'♮–e"♭ configuration here would testify to an intermediate attempt by Bach to retain more than a suggestion of a caesura at midphrase but one with less interruptive force. The diminished fifth, as a controlling interval of the dominant seventh harmony, could, like the minor seventh, form the core of an antecedent subphrase. In the present context, moreover, it would not create a parallelism with the first pair nor would it merely contrast with it, but would rather issue from the first pair; for the tritone would be heard as part of a series of contracting intervallic leaps: minor seventh, major sixth, and now the tritone, within the succession of upbeat patterns. The inappropriateness, however, of the particular tritone, a'♮–e"♭ (or for that matter, but to a lesser extent, the minor seventh f'–e"♭), with its suggestion of the applied dominant of the dominant, is evident.[16] The necessity of some form of B-flat resolution for the interval would either have provoked an expansion of the second half of the phrase, thereby destroying its 2×2-measure symmetry, or it would have disturbed the regular one-measure harmonic rhythm underlying the phrase. In either event the fine balance with the first half would have been sacrificed, and, more critical, the momentary tonicizing of the dominant would have anticipated the cadence on B-flat undoubtedly already planned for m. 9 at the midpoint of the ritornello. In the final reading the perfect fifth, a'♭–e"♭ retains the idea of a progression of contracting upbeat intervals discovered with the a'♮ experiment, while the need for an unstable "antecedent" sonority is fulfilled by treating the e"♭ downbeat as a dissonant appoggiatura to d". In this particular context, then, the perfect melodic fifth, a'♭–c"♭, is less stable, that is, more dissonant, than the tritone a'♭–d" to which it "resolves." The formulation: "dissonant appoggiatura resolving to a weaker dissonance" is in addition a harmonic intensification—hence in yet another respect an organic outgrowth—of the dissonance–consonance pattern of the first subphrase.

The new reading, finally, calls attention to and at the same time reinterprets the motivic role of the descending half-step in the melody. The melodic minor second was first introduced within the expressive mordent d"♭–c"–d"♭ on the downbeat of m. 2, the c" functioning as a decorative lower neighbor to the d"♭. In the following measure, the d"♭, now regarded as the upper member of a minor seventh, is resolved, by half-step motion, to the same c". The half-step has thereupon been elevated from decorative to structural significance. In m. 4, the half-step progression, now associated as "appoggiatura-plus-resolution," takes place from one beat to the next rather than from measure to measure; and this rhythmic acceleration impresses the melodic half-step as a thematic motive while providing a "drive" to the cadence. In the cadential measure itself Bach apparently was tempted to suggest a further acceleration of the half-step by anticipating the resolution tone, g', of the appoggiatura resolution pattern, a'♭-g', on the second eighth-note of the measure. But this would have released the accumulated tension of the entire four-measure construction anticlimactically on the weakest metrical position of the measure: the second half of the downbeat. The final reading, f', removes this infelicity, and, by repeating the double appoggiatura pattern introduced in m. 4, creates a further source of unity within the second subphrase contrasting with the simple mordent figure of the first subphrase. The changing significance of the half-step in the opening phrase can be summarized with an analytical diagram (Ex. 8.3).

Example 8.3.   Mm. 1–5: Structural and thematic representation of half-step motif

Multilevel consequences attending seemingly modest corrections of detail are not only present in the opening phrase, where crucial interrelationships and governing patterns are normally first established, but are encountered throughout the ritornello. The correction of the viola in m. 6—at the beginning of the second phrase—from e'♭ to e'♮ replaces a redundant repetition of the E♭ dominant seventh chord which occupies the same position in the first phrase with a coloristic chromatic alteration. The resulting sonority, though, the VII^7 of F, reveals at once the formal significance of the second phrase to be the gradual but inevitable motion away from the tonic and hints as well at the specific goal: a full cadence on the dominant, B-flat. In the Violin 2 part of m. 7 Bach changed the original reading (repeated f' on beat 1 followed by repeated e'♭ on beat 2) by crossing out the second group and inserting a group of four b'♭s on the barline between m. 6 and 7. The substitution of b'♭ for f' on the first beat results in a complete triad; the rationale for the correction of the second beat is not found in local considerations. The F-dominant seventh chord created by the presence of e'♭ on the second beat (and presumably to have been maintained through the third beat as well) would either have forced a premature arrival of the B-flat cadence in m. 8 or have obliged the composer to invent some kind of time-marking and tension-dissipating filler material for the remainder of that measure. As it happened, the problem posed by m. 8 was to cost the composer further pains.

As in m. 4, the challenge here was to generate an accumulation of tension before its release at the cadence while insuring that the means employed would be perceived as a logical, organic consequence of preceding events. In contrast to its treatment throughout the first phrase as a static pedal unaffected by the harmonic motion of the other parts, the bassetto is activated in the second phrase (an event also signaled by the correction in m. 6), and, through mm. 6, 7, and the beginning of m. 8, ascends one step per measure. The sense of the original reading, f′, in the viola on the second beat of m. 8 seems to have been to take up the ♩♩ harmonic rhythm introduced in the upper strings in the preceding measure and to extend it to all the voices of the accompaniment. But before completing this initial conception, Bach evidently felt the need for an accompaniment that would provide more active rhythmic reinforcement for the melodic climax on b″♭ and for the release of rhythmic motion issuing from it. The new reading of the viola part, e′♮, introduces together with the motion of the upper accompanimental parts a quarter-note harmonic rhythm that forms the climax of a paced accelerando in harmonic rhythm that, one realizes in retrospect, was initiated in m. 6:

m.   6   7   8   (9)

| ♩. | ♩ ♩ | ♩ ♩ ♩ | (♩.) |

The e′♮, in addition, is the bass of the same E-diminished seventh chord added as an afterthought in m. 6; and here again it proceeds to an F-major triad. The last two beats of m. 8 accordingly recapitulate in diminution the harmonic content of mm. 6 and 7, this time including (as a passing tone in the oboe) the seventh, e″♭, which had been removed from the harmony of m. 7. In moving on—this time at the proper formal moment—to the B-flat cadence, the new formulation brings to fulfillment the harmonic scheme which at the beginning of the phrase could only be suggested.[17]

There is also a correction in the oboe part in the same measure: a descending hook added to the accidental before the second a″ reveals that it has been changed from ♭ to ♮. From the beginning of the second phrase in m. 6, the presence of d♭ has created doubt about the modal character of the imminent B-flat cadence. The harmonic context of these measures, in fact, is hardly ambiguous at all but quite definitely belongs to B-flat minor.[18] Within such a context the melodic line would normally descend from the b″♭ through the lowered seventh, a″♭;

and this is what Bach wrote down at first. The a″♭ was then rejected for the following reasons. An a″♭ in the melody on the second beat of the measure would have created a cross-relation with the a′♮ of the F-dominant seventh harmony on the third beat and would have weakened the effect of the more dramatic cross-relation impending between the d″♭ in the oboe melody at the end of the measure and the now not-quite-unexpected but still stunning appearance of d′♮ in the long-awaited B-flat major cadence in m. 9.[19] In addition, the appearance of a″♭ here would have been undesirable with respect to the larger structural design of the ritornello. As indicated in the accompanying diagram, the basic linear motion of the complete ritornello describes an almost perfectly symmetrical arc which in the first half rises by step from e″♭ to b″♭ and in the second half returns, again by step, to e″♭ (Ex. 8.4).

Example 8.4.   Opening ritornello: Linear-harmonic plan

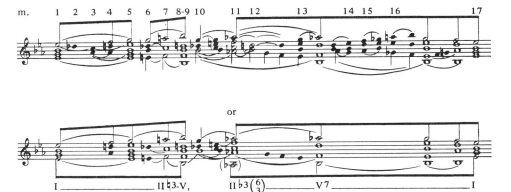

It is part of the tonal logic of this scheme that the approach to b″♭ be reinforced harmonically with an applied dominant sonority and melodically with its leading tone, a″♮, and that the return from b″♭ to e″♭ be underlined by the cancellation of that a″♮, or, what is the same thing, by the definitive reinstatement of a″♭, now as part of the "natural" dominant seventh, B♭[7]. In short, the essential tonal drama of this design centers on the changing inflection of the fourth degree in ascent and descent within the basic arc.[20] It will therefore be the first substantial piece of business of the second half of the ritornello to introduce the a″♭ in the appropriate harmonic context (this occurs in m. 11). An a″♭ in m. 8 would have been, in the truest sense of the word, "profoundly" premature.

The corrections encountered in the opening nine measures of the aria, then, are few in number; but each of them has turned out to be of crucial importance in establishing the structural framework, the stylistic

idiom, and the expressive means for the entire aria. With the resolution
of these fundamental concerns the composition of the second half of
the ritornello was, as the autograph confirms, relatively unproblematic.
There are fewer corrections, and they belong to a lower order of significance. No further correction in fact is clearly visible until the pitch
change in m. 12 (Violin 2).[21] It is possible, however, that the first beat
of the oboe in m. 11 at first read ♩♩♩, f"–g"–a"♭, and was later changed
to ♫♩ f"–g"–a"♭–a"♭.[22] The present reading can be understood, in any
event, as a motivic derivation from, and thus a justification in the large
for the dactylic ♫♫ rhythm which was introduced in m. 8, along with
the syncopation on the first beat, as a necessary but local effect providing the climactic concentration and release of tension at the approach
to the medial cadence.

The introduction of the dactylic rhythm in m. 11 (whether as an
afterthought or not) thus creates a perceptible link between the end
of the first half of the ritornello and the beginning of the second. It
also prepares for the intensified treatment of this rhythm throughout
the second half, that will culminate in its ultimate dissolution at the
final cadence of m. 16–17. In this regard it is worth noting as well that
there is a parallelism between the two interior phrases of the ritornello
which serves both to unify its two halves further and to underline the
crucial transformation of the fourth degree that takes place within these
phrases. The initial oboe motif in both phrases is identical (Ex. 8.5), and

Example 8.5.   Mm. 5–6, 9–10: Upbeat figure

part of the accompanimental sonority (the d"♭ and b'♭ in the inner
voices supporting the mordent figure, mm. 6 and 10) has been retained.
In the following measure of phrase 2 (m. 7), the oboe motif ends on
the critical a'♮—a pitch emphasized at first by skip (the first skip to
appear in this position within the four-note motivic cell) and later, as
the original parts reveal, by a trill.[23] The corresponding measure of the
third phrase (m. 11) reinstates a"♭ which, too, is emphasized by special
means, this time, by the ♫♫ rhythm. The treatment of a'♮ in m. 7 as part
of the pivotal F-major applied dominant harmony is balanced here by
the incorporation of a"♭ within an F-minor triad in ⁶₃ position. This
harmony is experienced as the supertonic of E-flat, owing to the linear
conduct of the bassetto following an authentic B-flat major cadence,
that is, with the return of a'♭ just after the b'♭ and precipitating the
stepwise progression in m. 12 (a'♭, g', f') to e'♭ in m. 13.

Disregarding the questionable existence of a change in the oboe
part of m. 11, the first unambiguous correction in the second half of

the ritornello appears on the second beat of the Violin 2 part in m. 12. The original reading of the measure—repeated f', g', a'♭—would have been the first obviously melodic gesture to appear in an inner part and would have formed a contrary motion relationship between the Violin 2 and the viola. It would thus in two ways have articulated the strategic moment of the scalar descent of the bassetto from the by-now famous a'♭ in m. 11 to the original e'♭ tonic.[24] This basically contrapuntal conception, however, created an incomplete and awkwardly spaced sonority on the second beat (Oboe: b"♭, Violin 1: b'♭, Violin 2, Viola: g') and was modified by adding the root, e'♭, in the Violin 2 part while retaining the original viola reading. Precisely Bach's concern for the linear integrity of the bassetto, incidentally, reveals that the viola part throughout this passage is conceived—and indeed perceived—as the true bass, even though the e'♭ in the new reading of the Violin 2 crosses below the viola. (The same is evident in mm. 8–9 where the f'— b♭ progression in the viola, presented in the differentiated portamento eighth-note rhythm reserved for this part, functions as the harmonic bass of an authentic V⁷—I cadence, although the second violin here, too, crosses below the viola.[25]

The concentration of corrections in the approach to the final cadence is restricted to the inner parts, particularly to the Violin 2 in mm. 15–16. These particular corrections pose an insoluble problem of transcription. It is not certain, first of all, whether m. 15, first quarter, originally read 4 × c", 4 × b'♭, or 2 × c" plus 2 × b'♭. Furthermore, it is not clear whether the corrections on the first and third beats of m. 15 and on the first and second beats of m. 16 were made in one gesture, and accordingly the original readings of these four beats together with the second beat of m. 15 were conceived as one integral version (see Ex. 8.6) or whether each of the beats was drafted and corrected independently of the others (as suggested by the broken interlinear stave in Ex. 8.1), or, finally, whether some of the original readings were rejected in one gesture and the others in one—or more—further gestures.

Example 8.6.   Mm. 15–16: Violino II, ante correcturam

The most satisfactory reconstruction seems to be the following. After having initially harmonized the first beat of m. 15 as a sequential repetition of the same beat in the preceding measure, Bach changed the harmonic color from that of the dominant triad to the more kinetic dominant seventh sonority that had been associated with the dominant pedal point since its inception in m. 13.[26] This change also inspired the idea of leading the first and second violins in parallel motion to the cadence, and accordingly suggested the reading c″ for the third beat of the measure. But this reading resulted, once again, in the omission of the seventh, a′♭, from the dominant sonority. The reintroduction of a′♭ at this point proved particularly fortunate. It allowed for an unobtrusive shift from parallel fourths between the violin parts to the more sonorous and usable sixths, and not only maintained the conjunct motion of the second violin part, but insinuated into this part yet another exposition of the scalar descent from the fourth degree to the tonic (Violin 2: m. 15, third beat, through m. 16, second beat). The same a′♭ also results in a cross-relation with the a″♮ of the oboe in the following measure which dovetails with the g′♭ -g″♮ clash taking place between the Violin 2 and oboe on the first and second beats of m. 16—the latter cross-relation recalling in transposition and transformation the powerful d♭ -d♮ succession of the medial cadence (mm. 8–9).

The absence of a correction in the Violin 1 part on the first beat of m. 16 suggests that the correction in the Violin 2 part on this beat can be dismissed as a slip of the pen; for there is reason to believe that Bach composed the inner parts within a homophonic texture from "the top down."[27] The unchanged reading in the Violin 1 part therefore reveals that the accelerated rate of pitch change in the inner parts from the quarter to the eighth at the approach to the final cadence was determined from the first. The correction in the Violin 2 part on the second beat, however, is not trivial. It was probably related to—and entered after—the correction of the Violin 1 part on beat 3.

The original conception—partially carried out—evidently was to lead the Violin 1 to the cadence in the smoothest manner with the Violin 2 following in its train (Ex. 8.7).[28]

Example 8.7.   Mm. 16–17: Violino I–II, original conception

Ex. 8.7:

This reading would not have been altogether satisfactory, though, since the mediant was not represented on the second half of beat 2,[29] the fifth, f′, was missing from the first part of beat 3, and, finally, the pattern of pitch change in the accompaniment every half-beat which had just been established on the first beat of m. 16 was already abandoned on the second beat.

But it is altogether possible that this last observable correction in the ritornello was not primarily concerned with local details of chord-tone disposition and voice leading but rather with matters of larger design. The new disposition of the cadential V^7–I harmonies projects just those pitches, f″ and e″♭, necessary—and expected—for the completion of the structural arc illustrated in Ex. 8.4 into the highest voice of the texture, and exposes them in the same register in which the earlier tones of the arc appeared. Bach may well have been consciously aware of the artistic necessity of this[30] and understood that only by thus redistributing the accompanying harmonies would the oboe part be freed to fulfill a further imperative residing in the symmetrical design of the ritornello. For the climactic, but seemingly rhapsodic, cadenza is in fact a retrospective review of the entire compass gradually spanned by the ritornello melody in its first nine measures, now compressed into a single measure and returning the melody from the high b″♭ at midpoint to its point of origin, e′♭.

Would it be hubris to assert that in the course of this discussion we have—to some extent—imaginatively become Johann Sebastian Bach composing the ritornello of "Wie zittern und wanken"? Perhaps; but by consulting—or confronting—the composer's own record of its genesis we have surely adopted the approach most likely to have any degree of success. Moreover, the exercise has led to some understanding of the work, particularly in regard to the logical relationship between immediate detail and larger design, that is perhaps not so readily discovered in an analytical study devoted exclusively to the finished, frozen, product. And the discovery of this logic has perhaps given us some idea at least of what it must have felt like to be Bach composing. The definition of "internal history" offered at the beginning of this essay suggests the notion of an active, "guiding" intelligence "determining" and "justifying" every detail of the work. The composer may not have experienced the creative act quite that way. He may rather have felt aware of an inherent and perhaps inexorable logic governing the evolution of the work "from within." And, in attempting to recreate the "internal history" of the work here, we seem indeed, upon reflection, to have been tracing the composer's responses to the ramifications of his own ideas, as these ramifications became ever clearer to him in the course of composition. For once the "operating forces" are set in motion, the creative process is not so much the active exercise of arbitrary jovian will as it is a process of discovery and response. This brings to mind a remark that Albert Einstein is said to have made to an assistant apropos his search for the basic laws at work in the universe:

"What really interests me is whether God had any choice in the creation of the world."[31]

9

ON THE ORIGIN OF
THE *MAGNIFICAT*
A Lutheran Composer's Challenge

How do we cope with masterpieces? There is probably a branch of psychology that deals with this—if not, there should be. For our encounter with a great work of art is undeniably a powerful experience, indeed, an unsettling one: an experience that—for the moment, at least—leaves us emotionally and intellectually transformed. Moreover, our responses to the momentary "trauma" of great art are not only strong but quite complex. As with other traumatic experiences, we seem, after our "exposure" to the great work, to pass through a series of stages in our more-or-less conscious, more-or-less "rational" efforts to come to terms with what we have read or seen or heard or performed.

Our initial reaction is surely mostly an emotional one. It is an amalgam of strongly felt "affects," consisting most immediately of those feelings directly (and, we may assume, deliberately) generated by the content of the particular work and broadly describable as "happy" or "sad." But this, as it were, "directed" response is accompanied by an "uplifting" feeling, best described, perhaps, as one of elation—often approaching euphoria. From the creator's point of view, this is of course a most desirable and flattering result, but one which he could hardly have counted on. But there is also the admixture of yet another affect in this initial, emotional, response: it is the not altogether comfortable feeling of awe—that is, boundless admiration subtly blended with a touch of envy!

161

It is clear that most of us never have the opportunity—or the inclination—to pass beyond this multilayered, and ultimately ambivalent, emotional stage in our experience of the great work. This calls to mind the following remark by Albert Einstein: "This is what I have to say about Bach's life work: listen, play, love, revere—and keep your mouth shut." Very well. Perhaps that is good, eminently wise advice. But there is a further stage, one of which Einstein himself was quite well aware in other realms of experience: a stage of reflection. In art, the existence of this stage is a testimony of course to the fact that the masterpiece challenges our minds as much as it excites our feelings. We are moved to try to understand it and not just respond to it: to try to discover the sources of its remarkable power by subjecting it to rational examination: that is, to an analysis aimed at uncovering the principles of its construction, at identifying the elements of its style, and at recognizing the terms of its expressive vocabulary. We also hope to understand the work by considering it historically—setting it against larger cultural contexts of time, place, genre, and tradition. This "analytical" stage, this attempt to grasp the work with our intellect surely represents an attempt to master its power over us, and testifies to our need to assert some kind of control over great works of art—crudely put: to cut them down to manageable size.

Inevitably, though, we continue, even after such intellectual efforts, to remain spellbound and bewildered in the presence of great works; and we may, accordingly, find ourselves progressing to yet a further stage of confrontation: a stage that may be described as an attempt at demystification. In this last stage we seek to gain control, to master the masterpiece, and its hold over us, by remembering that it is, after all, not some natural phenomenon, the work of a supernatural God, but the artifact of someone not altogether unlike ourselves—some flesh-and-blood mortal. Therefore, we now address our questions to the maker of the masterpiece—the artist—rather than to the work itself and begin to learn as much as we can about him in order, finally, to obtain some sort of answer to a new question: how he did it. This question may be irreverent—even, in some sense, an indiscrete invasion of privacy. (It may in fact be such a consideration that moved Einstein to offer his sobering advice.) But the issue of origins—of genesis—is one of the eternal questions we ask of all mysteries, and so it is almost invariably raised with respect to great works of art as well; for answering this question seems to hold out the prospect of illuminating the masterpiece from an altogether different and promising direction: from within.

What this pursuit implies is nothing less than the attempt to enter into the mind of the creator: in the case of music, to try, with a leap of the imagination, to "become the composer composing"—to reconstruct, as far as possible, what he must have perceived as the options and choices available to him in matters large and small, as he was absorbed in the act of creation; in other words, we try to re-create the inner dialogue of the compositional process.[1]

The following, admittedly, is such a self-indulgent exercise in de-mystification, if that indeed is the correct word—or perhaps even, as Einstein implied, an inexcusable act of hubris. It will have as its object one of the greatest masterpieces of church music: Johann Sebastian Bach's *Magnificat.*

In attempting a reconstruction of the "inner dialogue of the com-positional process," it is crucial to realize that much, if not in fact most, of the creative act is actually done internally: in the mind, and not on paper.[2] The written notation at any moment may represent a rather advanced stage in the weighing of alternatives—any number of which may have been already generated, evaluated, and rejected in the com-poser's mind before he set down what he thought, at least for the moment, was the solution he was seeking. He might then reconsider his choice once again—and make a visible correction on the page. What might appear to us, then, when we examine a composer's working score or sketch, to be his first and last (i.e., his second) thoughts, may in reality be the penultimate and final choices in a considerably longer succession of options that never had to be written down. In fact, it turns out to be the case with the *Magnificat* that the most important decisions were made before the composer ever put pen to paper. To gain insight into these decisions it is necessary to record other kinds of evidence—and also to engage in speculation of the kind that, de-pending on one's intellectual disposition, can be described either as "unfounded" or "imaginative."

In contrast to the vast majority of his vocal music, which was writ-ten within a three-year period at the breathtaking rate of approximately one composition per week, Bach had considerably more time at his dis-posal for the composition of the *Magnificat.* For it was to be performed on Christmas day, 1723; and, in Leipzig, Bach was not obliged to com-pose and perform cantatas during the preceding Advent season. Specif-ically, from November 29, the day following the performance of his can-tata for the First Sunday of Advent, and the *Magnificat* performance on December 25, Bach was freed of the obligation of performing regular Sunday cantatas. Actually, Bach's last *new* composition before the *Mag-nificat* was composed earlier still: during the week preceding Sunday, November 14; for both his Advent cantata (Cantata No. 61, performed on November 28), and his cantata for the Twenty-sixth Sunday after Trinity (Cantata No. 70, performed a week earlier, on November 21) had been composed years before—in Weimar.[3]

In short, Bach had the "luxury" of almost six *weeks* (from November 15 to December 24), rather than the usual six (or even three) *days* for the composition of the *Magnificat.*[4] And he obviously was intent to take advantage of the extra time. The *Magnificat* was by far Bach's most ambitious vocal composition since his assumption six months earlier of the position of Thomaskantor and Director of Church Music for the city of Leipzig. With its twelve movements (sixteen, counting four interpolations about which there will be more to say), the *Magnificat* is easily twice as long as the normal six-movement cantata.

Moreover, the *Magnificat* contains no "easy" movements: secco recitatives or plain four-part chorale harmonizations—forms which, after all, pose far fewer compositional problems on the whole than do elaborate arias and choruses. Indeed, in the *Magnificat* there is not just one full-scale choral movement, as in the usual Sunday cantata, but no fewer than five. It is also necessary to recall that for the same day—Christmas day, 1723—for which Bach composed the *Magnificat,* he also composed a second new work, a *Sanctus* setting for chorus and orchestra (BWV 238). Finally, he revised for performance yet a third work—the quite extensive cantata, *Christen ätzet diesen Tag,* BWV 63, a work *composed,* though, ten years earlier, in Weimar.[5] All things considered, then, six weeks' time could not have been that much of a luxury, after all, for the composition of the *Magnificat.*

But composing at breakneck speed was simply a fact of life for a composer in the early eighteenth century. And it was this fact that dictated how composers of the time approached the act of composition in the first place and molded their attitude toward the question of Originality. Originality, as a conscious concern, could hardly have existed for Bach and his contemporaries. Quite the contrary: they were far more interested in drawing on the accumulated experience and the techniques developed by their predecessors and contemporaries, for doing so obviously facilitated their task. Therefore, in setting out to compose a sacred work like the *Magnificat,* Bach had at his disposal, and was willing to adopt virtually without reservation, a broad array of time-tested (that is, "conventional") formal and stylistic procedures that governed the typical arias and choruses of the late baroque era and that included rhythmic and melodic figures, harmonic groundplans, and fairly standardized formal patterns of repetition.[6]

As is well known, the *Magnificat* is preserved in two distinct versions. The first, in the key of E-flat (BWV 243a), was the one written for Christmas day, 1723—Bach's first Christmas in Leipzig as Thomaskantor. The far more familiar second version in D major (BWV 243) is now known to have been prepared sometime between 1732 and 1735, very likely just about ten years after the first, for a performance on 2 July 1733: the feast of the Visitation of Mary, and, most significantly, the day decreed to mark the official end of the five-month period of national mourning that followed upon the death of the Saxon Elector Friedrich August I the previous February.[7] For both versions, the only surviving original sources are the autograph scores, documents that serve as perfect examples of the two extremes found among Bach's musical manuscripts: the working or "composing score," on the one hand, and the "fair copy," on the other. (Both scores are housed in the Deutsche Staatsbibliothek, East Berlin: P 38, E-flat version, and P 39, D-major version, respectively.)[8]

It is not surprising that the autograph of the D-major version is by far the more handsome of the two, whereas that of the E-flat version is vastly more informative as to the formation of the work. But it, too, represents a relatively advanced stage in the composition's genesis. Accordingly, it will be necessary not so much to examine the autograph evidence—the marginal sketches and the fairly numerous corrections of relatively minor details (an issue treated elsewhere)[9]—as to attempt to trace the process of composition back to an even more embryonic stage: its *prehistory*, the stage at which the planning of the work had not yet reached the point where Bach was prepared to take up a sheet of manuscript paper and rule lines on it, the stage at which the piece was still being formulated in general terms—in the composer's mind. To a stage, as it were, "before genesis."

It is clear that before the first musical notations could be set down they had to be preceded by what may be called "precompositional" planning. During this stage Bach considered his "given" material, the text, in order, first, to uncover its various implications for the musical setting and then, once uncovered, essentially to implement them directly. For example, the general design and structure of the text were allowed to dictate the general design and structure of the music; that is, the number of text verses largely determined the number of movements, while the accentual patterns of the text, its prosody, obviously influenced the choice of meter as well as specific decisions regarding the rhythm of thematic ideas and even the choice of pitches.

But there were considerations even more "preliminary" and fundamental than these. Bach had to take into account local conditions and traditions and also the particular purpose of the pending performance of the *Magnificat*. Like countless settings of the work extending back to the early Middle Ages, Bach's *Magnificat* was to be performed as part of a Vespers service; but it was to be part, specifically, of a Lutheran Vespers service—in eighteenth-century Leipzig, and for Christmas day. According to the liturgical usage in Leipzig at the time, the *Magnificat* was to be sung on high feasts of the church year not, as was the case on regular Sundays, in German and in a simple unaccompanied motet or a cappella style, or as an even simpler harmonized congregational hymn; rather, it was to be performed as a full-scale concert piece for voices and instruments, and in Latin. Furthermore, for the specific high feast of Christmas, a longstanding Leipzig custom called for the inclusion, within the performance of the *Magnificat* proper, of a series of hymn texts (both in German and in Latin) that were completely independent of the *Magnificat* text. They provided something like a miniature summary of the Christmas story. But, as we shall see, they also presented a German Lutheran composer of the early eighteenth century with a unique compositional challenge.[10]

Bach's 1723 version of the *Magnificat* contained four such hymns—or *Laudes,* as they were called at the time. They are designated in the Bach literature as Movements A through D. The first is a setting of Martin Luther's chorale "Vom Himmel hoch"; the second is a setting of an anonymous text, "Freut euch und jubiliert"; the third, Movement C, is based on the first lines of the greater doxology, "Gloria in excelsis Deo"; Movement D, finally, is a strophe from a Christmas hymn dating back to the late sixteenth century: "Virga Jesse floruit."

In addition to Bach's setting there is a manuscript, of Leipzig provenance, containing exactly the same four hymns—in exactly the same order. They were presumably composed by Johann Kuhnau; the only source, however, is an anonymous set of parts.[11] The existence of this setting underlines the fact that Bach, in planning his *Magnificat* composition, found his artistic freedom circumscribed not only by the requirements of the Leipzig liturgy but also by the precedents established by his musical predecessors.

Indeed, Bach's *Laudes* are particularly fascinating in that they seem to survey in almost systematic fashion the various historical styles of vocal music. "Von Himmel hoch" is an a cappella chorale *cantus-firmus* motet in the strict *stile antico.* "Freut euch und jubiliert" is still basically polyphonic but considerably lighter in texture and with an independent basso continuo; its copius voice-pairings in parallel motion are obviously indebted to early baroque practice. (The movement has been shown in fact to bear a strong similarity to a setting of the same text by Sethus Calvisius, himself a Thomaskantor in Leipzig in the early seventeenth century. It was published in 1603, along with Calvisius's settings of other Christmas *Laudes*—including "Vom Himmel hoch" and "Gloria in excelsis Deo.")[12] "Gloria in excelsis Deo" is characterized by more fundamentally chordal, more declamatory, writing, reminiscent perhaps of the later seventeenth-century Venetian tradition as cultivated in Germany by the Thomaskantors Johann Schelle, Johann Kuhnau, and others. The "Virga Jesse" movement, finally, is set in the very latest operatic style as a modern duet for soprano, bass, and continuo.

The musical influences to which Bach was subjected, however, were not limited to those connected with strictly local customs such as the Leipzig Christmas hymns but inevitably extended to the vast repertory of earlier settings of the venerable *Magnificat* text itself. Bach was not only familiar with many *Magnificat* settings: he copied out several himself and performed them in Leipzig. In fact, a number of remarkable formal details in his setting were apparently gleaned from earlier models. The universal Christian musical heritage, then, along with the particular musical and liturgical traditions of Lutheran Leipzig necessarily shaped the direction of Bach's thinking as he turned his attention to the traditional twelve-verse text of the *Magnificat,* consisting of the ten verses of the Gospel according to St. Luke, 1:46–55, augmented by the two additional verses of the lesser doxology "Gloria Patri et Filio."

In formulating his general plan Bach was obliged to observe the contemporary musical conventions that dictated that each of the twelve verses of the *Magnificat* was to be set as a separate movement—with effective contrast insured by the juxtaposition and alternation of solo and choral numbers. The work would begin and end with choral movements, which thus provided an exterior frame. There were perhaps one or more further internal choruses as well that served to punctuate a series of solo numbers: arias and possibly duets and other vocal combinations.

There was also an extramusical constraint impinging on the composer's artistic autonomy: one that critically affected the temporal dimensions of the work. For there were time limitations imposed by the overall duration and full schedule of the Leipzig Vespers service as a whole. The *Magnificat* setting, after all, was to be only one item on a long agenda.[13] These limitations of time, together with the stylistic convention that fairly dictated that just about every verse of the *Magnificat* text was to be set as a separate movement, conspired to assure that the individual movements of Bach's setting were kept short. In fact, no single movement of Bach's *Magnificat* is more than one hundred measures long, and the entire twelve-movement work (i.e., not counting the extra hymns) fills less than six hundred measures. This is most untypical for an obviously ambitious composition from the pen of Johann Sebastian Bach.

Bach may have made some jottings as to the succession and alternation of movement types on a separate piece of paper. But it is just as possible that he worked this out entirely in his head. In any event, the overall design of the work, as well as the tonal relationships for the whole work—that is, the order of keys for the individual movements—was evidently firmly decided upon well before Bach began to write down any musical notation in the surviving composing score: the autograph simply contains no corrections that bear on these fundamental matters. Therefore, we may conclude that Bach decided before he began what may be called the stage of "formal composition"—the writing down—that the work would have the design depicted in Table 9.1.[14]

The outline calls for five choral and seven solo movements, the choruses appearing as structural pillars after every two (or three) solo numbers, with the final choral pillar reinforced and doubly anchored, as it were. There is, in addition, a progressive increase in the number of

TABLE 9.1   The Order of Movements and Keys

Movement	Type	Key
1. Magnificat	Chorus	I
2. Et exultavit	Solo	(I
3. Quia respexit	• Solo	vi
4. Omnes generationes	Chorus	iii
5. Quia fecit mihi magna	Solo	V
6. Et misericordia	• Duet	ii
7. Fecit potentiam	Chorus	IV-I
8. Deposuit	Solo	iii
9. Esurientes	Solo	II#
10. Suscepit Israel	• Trio	vi
11. Sicut locutus est	Chorus	(I
12. Gloria Patri—Sicut erat in principio	Chorus	V-I

vocal soloists in the movements just *preceding* each successive chorus: Movement 3 ("Quia respexit") is a solo aria (for soprano); Movement 6 ("Et misericordia"), a duet (for alto and tenor); Movement 10 ("Suscepit Israel"), a trio (for two sopranos and alto). (Incidentally, assuming this interpretation of the rationale of Bach's scheme is correct—that it systematically observes such a principle of successive increase in the number of soloists—then it would settle a troubling question of performance practice related to this work by indicating that the "Suscepit Israel" movement was conceived and, accordingly, should be performed not as a chorus but as a trio.)

The tonal plan of the work is largely symmetrical as well (Ex. 9.1)[15]

Example 9.1.   The Tonal Plan

The tonic is doubly presented at both the beginning and end (Movements 1–2, 11–12); these tonic pillars enclose at each end movements in the key of the relative minor (Movements 3 and 10). The next two movements in the first half of the composition (Movements 4 and 5)

are on the third and fifth degrees, respectively; that is, together with the two opening movements in the home key, they outline the tonic chord. The keys of the movements in the second half of the work do not arpeggiate a triad but rather descend by step from the dominant back to the tonic, with the fifth and fourth degrees in effect "shadowed" by *their* own dominants, that is, the second and tonic degrees of the home key. In the case of the chorus "Fecit potentiam," the centerpiece of the composition (Movement 7), this "shadow" relationship is expressed within the movement itself. It begins in the subdominant and ends a fifth higher on the tonic. In this way Bach has managed to reintroduce the home key of the *Magnificat* most strategically at the midpoint of the work. [This gesture in turn has its counterpart in the final movement (or double movement): the lesser doxology, whose first part, the "Gloria Patri," just as strategically reintroduces the dominant—from a Schenkerian point of view, the decisive dominant—as the penultimate tonal moment of the work. The inevitable and definitive resolution of this harmony is ushered in at the words "sicut erat in principio."

From a slightly different point of view the tonal design can be represented as the traversal—within framing tonic pillars at beginning and end—of the descending diatonic scale from vi to I, each scale degree trailed by its dominant (see Ex. 9.2). Only the seventh degree, owing to the impurity of its diminished triad, has been omitted:

I; vi–iii, V–ii, IV–I, iii (–vii), II–vi, I–V–I]

Example 9.2.   The Tonal Plan, Alternative Representation

To repeat the main point: Bach's composing score contains no corrections testifying to any changes of mind bearing on these fundamental matters of movement type and tonal design. These issues were decided before Bach wrote down a single note.

The autograph also reveals—again by virtue of the absence of any pertinent changes—that Bach had reached his basic decisions concerning style, scoring, and form with respect to the individual movements during the precompositional stage. This applies not only to such matters as tempo, meter, thematic character, and compositional technique but also to the most striking formal refinements of Bach's setting: the decision to detach the words "omnes generationes" from the third verse of the *Magnificat* text (the "Quia respexit") and to set them as an independent chorus; the decision to conclude the central "Fecit potentiam" chorus with a sudden tempo shift to *adagio* and a change from polyphonic to chordal texture at the final words of the verse, "mente cordis sui"; and, finally, to repeat the music of the first movement at the words "sicut erat in principio" at the end of the final chorus.

Of course, none of these formal effects was original to Bach. They can all be found in *Magnificat* settings by Bach's forerunners and contemporaries. For example, as Terry was apparently the first to observe, a *Magnificat* attributed to Albinoni manifests the same treatment of the "omnes generationes" and the "mente cordis sui" passages as found in Bach.[16] And Monteverdi, as early as 1610, brought back the opening material of the first chorus at the words "sicut erat in principio." But all this is only further evidence that Bach took the occasion of the planning stage of the compositional process not only to ponder the musical implications of the particular liturgical constraints attached to the task but also to survey—and indeed to exploit—the rich artistic tradition which he had inherited and to which of course he himself belonged.

We have yet to address the basic issue bearing on the origin and conception of the *Magnificat* raised by the fact that the work exists in two versions (and two manuscripts). It is clear from the autograph score of the E-flat version that Bach entered and, accordingly, composed, the movements in the normal order. As the score is laid out, Movement 2 follows Movement 1, Movement 3 follows Movement 2, and so on up to the end of the work. This is typical of Bach's practice. There is, in fact, only one unambiguous exception to the rule that Bach normally composed the movements of a vocal work in the sequence in which they were to be performed. And that exception, paradoxically enough, is the score of the same E-flat version of the *Magnificat.* The autograph reveals that the four supplementary movements were not composed (i.e., written down) until the entire standard Latin text had been set. Verbal directions in the score indicate at what points in the work the *Laudes* are to be performed.

It is difficult to know exactly what to make of the fact that the Christmas interpolations appear at the very end of the composing score. It may mean that Bach was not yet aware, or informed—or it had simply slipped his mind for the moment—when he began to set down the *Magnificat* that the local Leipzig Christmas tradition called for these interpolations. If this was the case (and it may have been), then we would have a true, but trivial, instance in which Bach indeed composed the movements of a work out of their expected sounding order—trivial, because it would have been the consequence of mere ignorance, not choice. But it is also possible that Bach well knew about the four interpolations when he began writing but intended at first to make use of some preexistent setting, such as Kuhnau's,[17] and that in any case he preferred to approach the Latin *Magnificat* as an integral work that should maintain its formal integrity and self-sufficiency—that it should be readily performable without the supplemental items. There would also have been a practical advantage to that approach, for Bach would surely have been interested in insuring that his composition was usable on those high feasts other than Christmas when the elaborate *Magnificat* settings were performed in Leipzig—but without the Christmas movements.[18] And, again, Bach did in fact remove them when he prepared the score for the D-major version around ten years later.

It would seem, then, that the four interpolated movements were not—and were not intended to be—an integral part of Bach's conception of the work. And we have seen the logical plan that underlies the organization of the 12 movements of the Latin composition (Table 9.1, Ex. 9.1 and 9.2). The four additional movements, then, must have constituted a considerable problem for Bach: namely, how to insert these foreign bodies into the carefully designed order in a way that not only caused minimal disruption but, if possible, managed to produce a logical—even compelling—formal organization of its own. This, I submit, was this Lutheran composer's particular challenge.

It will come as no surprise to learn that Bach solved the problem both effectively and economically. He indicated that the four hymns were to follow after Movements 2, 5, 7, and 9. This particular placement was not preordained. It differs, for example from that found in a recently recovered, anonymous *Magnificat,* of Leipzig provenance, into which Kuhnau's *Laudes* were evidently inserted.[19] The result of Bach's disposition is that the sixteen movements of the E-flat version are so ordered that the work falls into two large parts or sections (Table 9.2).

It is now a bipartite work in a way that it was not (and is not) when the hymns are absent. The first Part consists of Movements 1 through 7, along with Movements A and B: nine movements in all. The second Part consists of Movements 8 through 12, along with Movements C and D: seven in all. The nine movements of the first Part present a strict alternation of choruses and solo numbers that culminate in the tutti chorus "Fecit potentiam."

The second Part is based not on the alternation of choral and solo movements but rather on a different principle of organization, one consisting of choruses only at the beginning and end. Moreover, both the opening and final movements of Part II—Movements C and 12—are set to "Gloria" texts: the greater and lesser doxologies, "Gloria in excelsis" and "Gloria Patri," respectively. These framing choruses enclose a succession of five movements that observe a principle of increasing textural density: Movement 8, "Deposuit," is a solo aria (for tenor) and unison strings; Movement 9, "Esurientes," is again a solo aria (for alto) but this time with two obbligato instrumental parts (two

TABLE 9.2   The Christmas *Magnificat* (BWV 243a): Order of
            Movements and Keys

Movement	Type	Key
1. Magnificat	Chorus	I
2. Et exultavit	Solo	I
Ⓐ Vom Himmel hoch	Chorus	I
3. Quia respexit	Solo	vi
4. Omnes generationes	Chorus	iii
5. Quia fecit mihi magna	Solo	V
Ⓑ Freut euch und jubiliert	Chorus	V
6. Et misericordia	Duet	ii
7. Fecit potentiam	Chorus	IV-I
Ⓒ Gloria in excelsis Deo	Chorus	I
8. Deposuit	Solo	iii
9. Esurientes	Solo	II♭
Ⓓ Virga Jesse floruit	Duet	II♮
10. Suscepit Israel	Trio	vi
11. Sicut locutus est	Chorus	I
12. Gloria Patri	Chorus	V-I

recorders); Movement D, "Virga Jesse floruit," calls for a vocal duet;
Movement 10, "Suscepit Israel," is a vocal trio; and Movement 11, "Sicut
locutus est," finally, is a five-part, a cappella chorus with basso continuo.
Bach also insured that the four interpolated movements did not disturb
the careful tonal design simply by having each of them duplicate and
reinforce the key of the preceding number.[20]

There can be little doubt, however, that Bach regarded this solution, as resourceful and even as elegant as it is, as less than ideal from
the aesthetic and perhaps even from a theological or Christian point of
view. For the E-flat *Magnificat* is, after all, in the final analysis, a hybrid
both musically and textually and even constitutes a questionable vio-
lation of a sacred, biblical, text. (This is probably also the reason that
the Leipzig town council had attempted to ban the singing of *Laudes* as
early as 1702.)[21] One suspects, therefore, that Bach must have been eager for the opportunity to recast it—and did so, as we now know, some
ten years later, around 1733: that is, at about the same time that he be-

gan to compose the Mass in B minor and in general began to display
increased interest in the composition of Latin sacred texts.[22]

What has this attempt to imagine how Johann Sebastian Bach
approached the composition of his *Magnificat* accomplished? It has
demonstrated that Bach must have arrived at just about all of the
fundamental decisions bearing on the design and the dimensions of
one of his most majestic works before he had written a single note on
paper. I return again to Philipp Spitta's provocative characterization of
Bach's creative process cited earlier:

> In general the creative act [for Bach] was an internal one. . . . Despite
> the great complexity of his music we know of few cases where the
> layout of a piece was rejected once it had been worked out. Nor did he
> often falter while working out the details. Sometimes he made changes
> when he took up a work again at a later date; but for an understanding
> of the way it was formed in the beginning, the evidence provided by
> such changes tells us nothing.[23]

It is easy to imagine that Spitta was thinking of the *Magnificat* when
he wrote these words. The composing score certainly does contain a
great number of corrections of detail, and Bach certainly made changes
when he took up the work again and penned the D-major version. But,
as Spitta said, they tell us virtually nothing of the way the work was
formed "in the beginning." In order to come closer to that mystery it
turned out to be necessary to get behind the written record and, in
effect, to stand the usual method for investigating the compositional
process on its head. Instead of analyzing sketches and autograph corrections, it proved more fruitful to ascertain what aspects of the work
underwent no visible changes and to assess the implications of such
negative evidence. The results necessarily are conjectural: they amount
virtually to an attempt to read Bach's mind. But since the conclusions
do after all derive from objective observations of "hard" manuscript evidence, buttressed with historically verifiable information bearing on
the religious and musical traditions to which the work belongs, there
is reason to think that they are not just idle guesses but to some (unfortunately unknowable) extent—resemble what really must have been
Bach's earliest reflections and decisions as he embarked on the creation
of one of the grandest masterpieces in the history of sacred music.

10

THE MASS IN B MINOR
The Autograph Scores and
the Compositional Process

For virtually every work of Bach's for which an autograph score survives we can usually tell at a glance whether the manuscript is a composing score or a fair copy. With the B-minor Mass this is not always so. As in so many others, in this respect, too, Bach's Mass in B minor is extraordinary.[1] Nonetheless, the available sources do enable us to observe Bach confronting and resolving compositional issues of greater and lesser magnitude posed by this monumental composition as it assumed its ultimate shape in his mind and under his pen. Some of the more enlightening of these are the object of this chapter.

To a great extent the curious nature of the sources is a consequence of the curious history and chronology of the Mass.[2] Unlike most of Bach's vocal music the work was not written within a week or even a month but rather in several discrete stages years apart. The earliest part was the *Sanctus:* composed in Leipzig in late 1724 for performance during the regular liturgical service on Christmas day, 25 December. The *Kyrie* and *Gloria* sections—that is, the *Missa,* as it was called in contemporary Lutheran terminology (and as it is designated by Bach on the surviving title pages of the score and the original set of parts)—was next: composed, as far as is known with any certainty, during the first half of 1733, not for Leipzig at all but for the Catholic court at Dresden.[3] Finally, toward the end of his life, Bach added the missing sections necessary to form a complete, traditional Mass Ordinary: the *Credo* (or, in Bach's words, the *Symbolum Nicenum*), as well as the concluding portions: "Osanna," "Benedictus," "Agnus Dei" and "Dona nobis pacem."

175

According to Friedrich Smend, the editor of the Mass for the *Neue Bach-Ausgabe* (NBA II/1), the autograph of the complete Mass, (SPK) P 180, represents the composing score, or *Urschrift*, for virtually the entire work.[4] The only exception, in his view, was the *Sanctus*, for which a separate manuscript, clearly a composing score—P 13/1—happens to survive.[5] Smend in fact criticized Philipp Spitta for taking P 180 to be a fair copy.[6]

MISSA: KYRIE AND GLORIA

As far as the three movements of the *Kyrie* section of the Mass are concerned, it was Spitta who was essentially right. The script is unarguably calligraphic: the written symbols are carefully aligned, the stems of the individual notes straight and upright. The musical content of the manuscript provides further corroboration. For the most part, Bach's corrections are concerned with rectifying copying errors or slips of the pen. No obviously substantial, "formative," corrections are readily discernible. Many corrections seem to be concerned with transposition errors.[7] The manuscript certainly does not contain any sketches or drafts. Finally, even the ruling of the staves was carefully planned: there are only as many staves on a page as the music requires. This is typical of a Bach fair copy and indicates that the composer had a clear conception of the layout and dimensions of the music he was about to set down. In short, it is clearly impossible to reconstruct the earliest stages in the conception of the *Kyrie* from this source.

On the other hand, the autograph reveals that a number of decisions were reached relatively late in the composition of the work. The inclusion of transverse flutes, for example, was evidently an afterthought; for unlike the other parts, the flutes are not notated on their own staves but share those of the oboes. Moreover, the designations "Traversi et," found at the beginning of the top two staves of the score (i.e., the oboe staves), were a later addition (see Plate 31).

But the first page of the autograph score also contains a fairly large number of corrections in the first four measures of "Kyrie I"—large especially in comparison with the following fugue. The corrections are concentrated in the voice-leading of the inner parts (Viola, Soprano 2, Tenor) and are mostly concerned with voice-leading; but they suffice to reveal that the manuscript here is a composing score. And this fact reveals in turn that even seemingly minor corrections of detail, despite initial appearances, at times can document a substantive change of considerable significance. They indicate here that Bach had decided very late in the conception of the movement—literally "at the last moment" before embarking on the writing down of the autograph score—to begin the work with a massive four-measure adagio introduction and there-

PLATE 31.   Autograph score, SPK P 180, f. 1ʳ: BWV 232/1, mm. 1–10

upon proceeded to compose the introduction directly into the otherwise fair-copy manuscript.

It may well be that on one level Bach was influenced in his decision to add the introduction by a precedent he had found in a Mass in G minor by the Palatine court composer Johann Hugo Wilderer (1670–1724).[8] But there can be little doubt that the decision was ultimately dictated and justified to the composer by his own artistic intuition. The late addition of the adagio introduction—that is, of a completely new and separate, if brief, formal element—would seem to testify to Bach's growing awareness of the aesthetic consequences flowing from the grandiose design of the work: not only of the *Kyrie* section but of the entire *Missa*, if not, indeed (and, if at all, then necessarily only on an unconscious level), of the still-unwritten and, as far as we can know, still-uncontemplated setting of the complete Mass Ordinary. It had presumably become clear to Bach that the *Missa*, given its enormous dimensions, could not begin effectively with the conventional orchestral ritornello but had to be, as it were, much more firmly "anchored" and proclaimed. He therefore decided to preface the ritornello with those majestic block chords serving as powerful supporting pillars. (Perhaps it is not completely far-fetched to perceive a similarity in function here to the long E-flat sonority that both launches and "grounds" Wagner's *Rheingold*—and indeed the entire *Ring des Nibelungen*—that is, another work conceived on the grandest possible scale.)

With respect to the *Gloria* section it is once again not quite accurate to describe the autograph score, as Smend does, as an *Urschrift*. It has long been known that two movements of the *Gloria*—the "Gratias agimus tibi" and the "Qui tollis peccata mundi"—are not original compositions at all but rather revised versions of movements originally written to different texts. That is, they are "parody" compositions.[9] The "Gratias" is based on the music of the opening chorus, "Wir danken dir, Gott, wir danken dir," of Cantata No. 29, the "Qui tollis" on the first part of the opening chorus, "Schauet doch und sehet," of Cantata No. 46. In addition, Smend has demonstrated that the "Gloria in excelsis Deo" movement is most likely an arrangement of the final movement of a lost Köthen instrumental concerto.[10] Smend is certainly correct when he describes P 180 as the *Urschrift* of these three movements in the sense that Bach adjusted the preexistent music to the new Mass text as he wrote out this manuscript. But it is clear that the compositional origins of these movements are not to be found in this source. In each instance the formative stages took place while writing the composing scores of the original compositions—the parody "models." Nonetheless, the Mass version of these movements contains a number of instructive variants, so that a comparison of the model with the later version affords additional insight into the rationale behind Bach's changes.

In the model of the "Qui tollis," for example—the chorus "Schauet

doch"—the first eight measures of the instrumental bass part consisted
only of single quarter-notes followed by rests (Ex. 10.1).

Example 10.1.   BWV 46/1, "Schauet Doch," mm. 1ff: Continuo rhythm

The idea of adding to this isolated downbeat stroke a further rhythmic
level in the cello to provide the underlying quarter-note pulse (Ex. 10.2)
was an afterthought.[11]

Example 10.2.   BWV 232/9, "Qui tollis," mm. 1ff: Cello and Continuo rhythmic
patterns

Violoncello: ... etc.

Continuo:

As a consequence, each of the several instrumental parts is now associated with one of the four rhythmic planes represented in the movement: the continuo with the downbeat, the cello with the quarter-note
pulse, the viola with the eighth-note level, and the flutes, finally, with
the sixteenth-note embellishments. That is, Bach had not decided until
he embarked on the parody version to introduce this abstract rhythmic schema. Corrections of this kind, having as their goal the creation
of "sounding hierarchies" of note values, can be found in other Bach
manuscripts as well.[12]

   It is particularly instructive to consider the differences between the
two versions of the theme itself (Ex. 10.3).

Example 10.3.

In both versions the theme is clearly divided into three segments
(A, B, C), as suggested by the syntactical structure of the text. But
the formal relationships between the segments have been redefined
by seemingly minor changes of detail. Specifically, in "Schauet doch"

the third segment, owing to the return of both the $|\text{♩}\,\text{♩}\,\text{♩}\,|\text{♩}|$ rhythm and of the opening falling third f'–d', serves to round off the theme. That is, in principle the theme is in ABA' form. In the "Qui tollis," on the other hand, the addition of a few passing tones in the penultimate measure is enough to alter the functional meaning of the third segment. It no longer represents a varied return of the opening A motif but is perceived rather as an outgrowth of the B motif. It now seems to be derived from the second—to develop it by means of sequential repetition and rhythmic acceleration. In other words, a symmetrical formal conception—ABA'—has been transformed into an "organic" developmental one: ABB'. Bach was no doubt able to accomplish this transformation so economically because the final thematic segment happened to combine salient characteristics of the two preceding ones. Like Motif A it begins after a rest, on a weak beat; like Motif B it spans the characteristic falling interval of the diminished fourth.

Finally, the rhythmic structure of the theme has been transformed, as well. By replacing the repeated quarter-notes in m. 3 with a dotted half-note (suspended into the following measure), by introducing the eighth-note acceleration in the penultimate measure, and by sharpening the upbeat rhythm at the beginning, the smooth, rather serene rhythmic profile of "Schauet doch" (proceeding as it does exclusively in quarters and half-notes), has been rendered more intense, more sharply profiled, and more dramatic in the "Qui tollis" setting.

In sum, a subtle but fundamental transformation has taken place here: the essentially closed, symmetrical patterning of form and rhythm evident in the cantata version has, in the "Qui tollis," yielded to an emphatically dynamic, organic conception of these same elements.

To return to the autograph: The main impression conveyed by the autograph score of the *Missa*, especially in those movements not known to be parodies, is not that of a composing score. This is especially true of the arias and the duets. In the "Christe," "Laudamus," "Domine Deus," "Qui sedes," and "Quoniam" movements, the autograph score, especially in the instrumental lines, is not only largely free of corrections but is also quite copiously marked with slurs, articulation marks, ornaments, and dynamic indications. Moreover, those corrections and changes that do appear are concentrated in the vocal parts. All this feeds the suspicion that most, if not indeed all, the solo movements of the *Missa*—like, demonstrably, three of the four choral movements of the *Gloria*—are not new compositions but rather parodies of lost originals.

SYMBOLUM NICENUM: CREDO

The second half of the autograph score of the Mass in B minor was not written down until the 1740s. According to Kobayashi, the *Symbolum*

Nicenum, in fact, was penned toward the very end of Bach's life—in late 1748 or even 1749.[13] Moreover, since it is likely that the *Art of Fugue* was largely completed by the early 1740s,[14] the *Credo* of the Mass would seem to be Bach's last significant composition, perhaps indeed his very last. In contrast to the autograph of the *Missa,* written some fifteen years earlier, an investigation of the *Credo* manuscript leaves no doubt that Smend this time was right: the score is an *Urschrift.* Again, though, as in the case of the *Missa,* the term has to be used in a restricted sense: some of the movements of the *Credo* are known to be parodies. The opening chorus of the Leipzig cantata, *Gott wie dein Name, so ist auch dein Ruhm,* BWV 171, served as the model of the "Patrem omnipotentem";[15] the "Crucifixus" is based on the first section of the opening chorus of Cantata No. 12, *Weinen, Klagen, Sorgen, Zagen,* composed in Weimar in 1714; and the *Et expecto* is a heavily revised arrangement of the principal section of the chorus "Jauchzet, ihr erfreuten Stimmen" from Cantata No. 120, a work presumably composed in 1728. In addition, Smend has demonstrated that the "Et resurrexit" chorus—like the "Gloria in excelsis"—is most likely based on a movement from a lost instrumental concerto (in the case of the "Et resurrexit," a first movement).[16] The manuscript contains numerous traces of the composer at work on the new version of these movements. Finally, the clean appearance of the manuscript in the "Et in unum Dominum" and the "Et in Spiritum sanctum" movements, together with the relatively large number of performance indications, again raises the suspicion—as in the *Gloria*—that the two solo numbers, like most of the choruses, are based on lost models, as well. Of the choral movements only the "Credo in unum Deum" appears to be a fair copy.

The autograph also contains evidence of a radical change of mind regarding the form and the dimensions of the *Credo.* As is clear from the text of the *NBA* edition (p. 155f.), the words "et incarnatus est de Spiritu sancto ex Maria virgine, et homo factus est" were, at one time, incorporated into the "Et in unum Dominum" duet, as the fourth of four formal segments. Sometime afterward Bach decided to set the "Et incarnatus est" as a separate movement—a chorus. That is, the total number of movements in the *Credo*—and with it, the formal design underlying this section of the Mass—was altered. Belated decisions operating on this level of magnitude are rarely observable in the Bach manuscripts.[17] Bach almost always knew "at once" how many movements a work would contain, and what type they would be—recitative, aria, chorus, chorale. After all, the text of a cantata, for example, practically dictated that to him. Such matters, therefore, were usually decided before "formal" composition—that is, the putting of notes on paper—had begun. But external circumstances, too, such as the availability (and ability) of particular singers and instrumentalists, normally played a large role in Bach's preliminary but basic deliberations, notably as to the scoring of the several movements.

The text of the Mass Ordinary—at least in the two lengthy sections, the *Gloria* and the *Credo*—does not unambiguously suggest any
particular subdivision or formal ordering. The design is therefore up to
the composer. The autograph of the B-minor Mass reveals that Bach at
first had conceived of the *Symbolum* as a symmetrical arrangement of
eight movements, as follows:

1, 2: Two connected choruses ("Credo" and "Patrem") in direct
   succession, both in D major (more precisely: D mixolydian—D
   major)

3: A solo movement (the duet "Et in unum Dominum") in G major

4, 5: Two choruses in succession ("Crucifixus" and "Et resurrexit"),
   in E minor and D major, respectively

6: A solo movement ("Et in Spiritum sanctum") in A major

7, 8: Two connected choruses ("Confiteor" and "Et expecto") in
   direct succession, in F-sharp minor and D major, respectively

As Smend observes, the modulation plan underlying this sequence
of movements was as follows: The tonic, D major, prevails at the
beginning ("Credo" and "Patrem"), in the middle ("Et resurrexit"), and
at the end ("Et expecto").

> We hear the two "dominants,"—the lower (sub)dominant and the
> upper dominant—in the solo movements: "Et in unum Dominum" (G
> major) and "Et in Spiritum sanctum" (A major). The relative minors of
> the two dominants appear as well: in the "Crucifixus" (E minor), and in
> the "Confiteor unum baptisma" (F-sharp minor). So much, then, for the
> original disposition of the movements. Note that it lacked the relative
> minor of the tonic degree itself. Bach therefore inserted a chorus in B
> minor [the "Et incarnatus"]. But doing so substantially enhances the
> effect of the E-minor tonality of the following "Crucifixus." In the first
> version it was preceded by the C-major conclusion of the duet. But
> when the E-minor chorus follows a movement a fifth higher than itself,
> then the plunge into the depths, into the night of the cross, becomes
> immeasurably more expressive." (pp. 155–56)

In short, the often-mentioned Trinitarian attributes of Bach's *Credo*
setting—a total of nine movements with a central core consisting of
three choruses which together constitute the central core of Christian
faith: Incarnation, Crucifixion, Resurrection[18]—that conceit, which one
would have assumed was the point of departure, the initial inspiration, for Bach's formal conception of the *Symbolum*, was in fact an afterthought! It is not clear whether Bach executed this change soon after the first draft (i.e., as a later stage during the course of the main
period of work on the score) or whether it was truly a later revi-

sion: that is, whether the eight-movement form ever actually existed as an independent, complete entity. There is no doubt, though, that the nine-movement version is the final version.

It is not surprising that this fundamental revision brought a series of further changes in its wake, changes that are visible in the autograph, as well. As mentioned earlier, it was necessary to revise the text setting of the "Et in unum Dominum" duet in order to remove from it the words "et incarnatus est," and so forth. For this purpose Bach wrote out the two vocal parts on an extra leaf inserted into the autograph at the end of the *Symbolum Nicenum* (pp. 151–52 of the manuscript). This version has been reproduced in the *NBA* edition (p. 216) as a variant, since Smend was of the opinion that Bach, as part of a later stage in the history of the work—years later, according to Smend's chronology—had reinstated the earlier version of the duet, despite its redundant presentation of the "et incarnatus" text, because the word–tone relationship in that version, as Smend convincingly demonstrates, was far superior to the later one.[19]

As for the duet, it must be mentioned that despite its remarkably apt text setting—especially in the first version—it was not originally composed to this text at all. It is a parody. The first four measures of the Violin I part appear—in C major and crossed out—in the autograph score of the secular cantata *Lasst uns sorgen, lasst uns wachen*, BWV 213 (Ex. 10.4).

Example 10.4.   BWV 213/11: Rejected thematic sketch

The theme was evidently intended for the duet "Ich bin deine, du bist meine," whose text so happily fits the opening measures of the "Et in unum Dominum." In the end Bach composed different music for the secular text. But the sketch reveals clearly that the music which was ultimately used for the "Et in unum Dominum" had already existed even before the composition of Cantata No. 213. The sketch does not represent the formulation of a new melodic idea. If it had, Bach would surely have composed the two canonic parts simultaneously and would not have written out one part through to the cadence, leaving the imitation to be worked into the rests and held notes of the *dux*. On the other hand, when Bach copied from a source, he first wrote in the top part for a whole line—as he did here—before writing the other parts.

Bach's decision to set the "Et incarnatus" as an independent chorus had consequences not only for the preceding movement, but for the following one, the "Crucifixus," as well. The autograph reveals that the

"Crucifixus" originally began—as does its model, the chorus "Weinen, Klagen, Sorgen, Zagen"—directly with the choral entrance, that is, with what is now the fifth measure. The instrumental introduction, accordingly, was an afterthought. It is not difficult to imagine what motivated the change. The movement that had originally preceded the "Crucifixus" (the "Et in Dominum" duet) contains an instrumental epilogue, but the "Et incarnatus" chorus does not. Bach evidently wished to avoid the direct juxtaposition of two radically contrasting choral statements, unmediated by any kind of instrumental interlude. More precisely: he surely wished to reserve this unusually daring and powerfully dramatic formal gesture for the transition from the "Crucifixus" to the "Et Resurrexit"—and certainly not dilute its effect by anticipating the device here between the "Et incarnatus" and the "Crucifixus." He therefore appended a four-measure instrumental introduction to the "Crucifixus." Owing to lack of space in the autograph he had to insert it at the conclusion of the Duet, on p. 110 of the score—before the inserted leaf containing the "Et incarnatus" (pp. 111–12).[20]

Additional changes from the model to the parody affect the instrumental accompaniment. The rhythm of the continuo in the cantata movement consists of simple half-notes (Ex. 10.5) in contrast to the subdivided, pulsating rhythm in the Mass movement (Ex. 10.6).

Example 10.5.   BWV12/2, "Weinen, Klagen," mm. 1ff: Continuo rhythm

Example 10.6.   BWV 232/16, "Crucifixus," mm. 1ff: Continuo rhythm

The rhythmic texture of the upper instrumental parts has also been enriched. In the cantata the accompaniment consists exclusively of strings, which play the pattern shown in Ex. 10.7.

Example 10.7.   BWV 12/2, "Weinen, Klagen," mm. 1ff: Strings, rhythmic pattern

In the Mass Bach has introduced a complementary rhythm in the flutes (Ex. 10.8).

Example 10.8.   BWV 232/16, "Crucifixus," mm. 1ff: Strings and Traversi, rhyth-
                   mic pattern

There is one further correction in the autograph which reveals
how much value Bach set on the symbolic interconnections among
the individual movements of this central section of the Mass. The half-
cadence on the dominant at the end of the "Credo" chorus originally
sufficed to bind the two opening choruses together. Bach then decided
to add an even more palpable link. In the following movement, the
"Patrem" chorus, all the voices began at first by declaiming "Patrem
omnipotentem" together. These words had been entered in all voices
through m. 3. It then occurred to Bach to have the bass alone introduce
the new text while the opening incipit of the *Symbolum Nicenum*, the
words "Credo in unum Deum," continued to resound in the upper
parts—Soprano I and II, Alto, and Tenor—as an emblematic motto. The
"Patrem" text would eventually suffuse all the parts as they entered
one by one with the fugue subject. All this was an afterthought.

The conscious—even self-conscious—preoccupation with issues of
large-scale formal design that is manifested in the changes and corrections of the *Credo* autograph is unique for Bach. Such fundamental
changes affecting the number, genre, succession, and interconnection
of movements are hardly ever encountered in earlier manuscripts of
the composer—certainly not in such concentration. They bear witness
to the aging Bach's intensified interest in the problems of cyclical unity
in multimovement compositions. These, of course, are the same problems that he had already pursued to their ultimate consequences in
such late works as the "Goldberg" Variations, the *Musical Offering,* and
the *Art of Fugue.*[21]

SANCTUS TO "DONA NOBIS PACEM"

In contrast to all the other parts of the Mass, the *Sanctus* section
survives not only in the autograph of the complete work but also in
a separate autograph score. This score can be dated with certainty to
the end of 1724, the *Sanctus* having been composed for a performance
on Christmas day of that year.[22] The 1724 autograph of the Sanctus, P
13/1, is clearly the composing score for the movement: hastily written
and heavily corrected (with numerous formative changes), and also

containing several sketches and preliminary drafts. For an attempt to reconstruct Bach's compositional process, then, the situation with regard to the *Sanctus* and *Pleni* sections is as favorable as it ever is. We possess two autograph scores: the fair copy, as a constituent part of the complete Mass, and also the composing score.

Bach's sketches, as we have seen in Chapter 6, are not to be compared with those of a composer like Beethoven. For the most part they are brief marginal notations that served primarily as memory aids when work was temporarily interrupted (as for example at the bottom of a page, before a turn, while the ink was drying). But they did on occasion record the composer's first written formulation of a thematic idea.

Both sketch types are represented in the *Sanctus* manuscript. On the bottom of the first page of P 13/1, under the first six measures of the *Sanctus* section, Bach entered a sketch for the theme of the *Pleni* section. It is reproduced and discussed in Chapter 6 (Ex. 6.2). As we have seen, the sketch can best be understood as Bach's first attempt to render the declamation and the imagery of the text in musical terms. A second sketch, however, entered on p. 8 (f. 4ᵛ) of the manuscript—under the score system containing mm. 41–46a of the *Sanctus* (the final measures of the section)—is in effect both a thematic and a continuation sketch. In it Bach was concerned with purely musical issues (Ex. 10.9).

Example 10.9.   BWV 232/21, "Sanctus," mm. 46b–53: Second sketch. P 13/1, f. 4ᵛ

Not only is the text missing in this entry, it was apparently neglected entirely: the beaming of the eighth-note passage in the third measure of the theme overlooks the syllabic requirements of the text. The opening interval has been sharpened from an octave to a sixth—probably not only to increase the "kinetic energy" of the melody (a sixth is far less stable than an octave), but for tonal reasons as well. The new tone, f'♯, serves a pivotal function in the transition from the end of the *Sanctus* section in F-sharp minor to the D-major beginning of the *Pleni*. The first two melodic and harmonic intervals formed by the two principal voices

	a		f'♯
		and	
	F♯		D

were to negotiate between the two tonalities via the ambiguous pitch combination a-F♯, while the entire configuration (a, f♯, d) formed a D-major chord. (It should be noted, however, that in the final instrumentation the orchestra provides the c♯ of the F-sharp minor chord that concludes the *Sanctus* section.) Bach's concern for a subtle transition between the two tonalities, along with his interest in introducing a counterfigure to the fugue subject, no doubt explains why the continuo part was entered in this draft—a rare occurrence in the thematic sketches.

The final version, found on the following page of the manuscript (f. 5ʳ) can be understood as a synthesis of the two tentative sketches, combining the opening motif of the second sketch (the ascending sixth) with the continuation of the first version (Ex. 10.10).

Example 10.10.   BWV 232/21, "Sanctus," mm. 46–54: Final version. P 13/1, f. 5ʳ

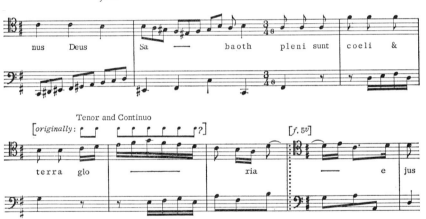

After writing down the third measure (or perhaps the fourth) of the *Pleni,* Bach changed the meter from ¾ to ⅜, probably to clarify the tempo relation between the two sections.[23]

The second sketch of the *Pleni* theme (Ex. 10.9) is instructive in another respect as well. It begins not with the *Pleni* itself but rather with last two measures of the *Sanctus* section, specifically with the continuo part for those measures. It is thus one of those instances where Bach drafted the harmonic progression of a passage as represented by the continuo before the melodic line. (See Chapter 6, p. 122.) One could argue, however, that the continuo (and bass) line in fact constitutes the "melody" in this particular case, developing as it does the pervasive triplet motif that dominates the movement. But its primary function is clearly to spin out via this motif the harmonic sequence of fifths initiated in m. 41 in B minor to the final F-sharp minor cadence. In the fully-scored form the violins move largely in parallel with the continuo, while the upper voices of the chorus (and the doubling instrumental parts) provide what is in effect a chordal thoroughbass realization—"rhythmicized" to accommodate the syllables of the text.

The concluding portions of the Mass—from the "Osanna" through the "Dona nobis pacem"—are contained in the autograph of the entire Mass. Although we are dealing, once again, with a fair copy and not a composing score, the autograph does allow us a final observation—one bearing on the final movement of the work, the "Dona nobis pacem." As mentioned earlier, Bach penned the autograph score of the Mass with extreme care. His clear intent was to produce a particularly fine fair copy. For this reason he set out to rule exactly as many staves on each page of the score as the music required—and managed to do so with but three exceptions. Two of them relate to his subsequent decision, discussed above, to set the "Et incarnatus est" as an independent chorus (entered on pp. 111–12 of the score, with seven unused staves on p. 112) and the consequent need to revise the text of the "Et in unum Dominum" (appended at the end of the *Symbolum Nicenum,* on pp. 151–52 of the score, after the conclusion of the "Et expecto" chorus, with two unused staves on the bottom of p. 152, and followed by a completely ruled but unused—and unpaginated—page with fourteen staves).[24]

The third instance concerns the "Dona nobis pacem" movement. Here Bach could rule the staves for a fair copy—since the movement is a parody of the "Gratias agimus," its layout was clear. But in doing so he seemingly miscalculated the number of staves required. The score for the movement is notated on a fourteen-stave system; yet the pages on which the chorus appears (pp. 183–88) are consistently ruled with eighteen staves. The most obvious explanation for this would be that Bach had originally planned to write out separately each of the eight voice parts of the double chorus employed in this movement—as he had done in the "Osanna"—and had therefore chosen an eighteen-stave layout for the score. Thereupon—presumably as soon as he recalled that, in contrast to the "Osanna," the second chorus in this movement was not independently led—he decided simply to indicate at the beginning of the movement that each voice part was to be doubled as "Soprano 1 + 2," Alto 1 et 2," and so on.

There is a more fascinating explanation, however, for Bach's "miscalculation"—one that was once suggested to the author by Arthur Mendel—namely, that Bach may originally have intended some completely different music for the "Dona nobis pacem" before he hit upon the splendid idea of returning to the music of the "Gratias agimus tibi" for the conclusion of the Mass. One would love to believe that this is the true explanation of the evidence, for it would bear witness to considerably more than the composer's momentary forgetfulness about the number of voices in a particular chorus—to testify, as it were, to his mortality. It would declare rather that Johann Sebastian Bach, in a final flash of inspiration close to the end of his life, had found a decisive way of assuring that posterity would understand that his last and greatest church composition, despite its protracted and sporadic gestation extending over a full quarter-century (virtually the entirety of his career in Leipzig), was indeed an emphatically unified whole: a single, profoundly monumental, yet integral masterpiece.

III

Questions of Authenticity and Chronology

11

THE AUTOGRAPH FAIR
COPIES OF THE *FANTASIA*
PER IL CEMBALO, BWV 906

Among the small number of musical autographs of Johann Sebastian Bach located in American collections,[1] none is more handsome—or more puzzling—than the fair-copy holograph of the Harpsichord Fantasia in C minor, BWV 906. The manuscript, presently housed in the library of Lehigh University, belongs to the Bach Choir of Bethlehem, Pennsylvania (Plates 32 and 33).

The autograph consists of a single leaf measuring approximately 34.5 × 20.5 cm. and apparently was trimmed on the bottom and both sides.[2] With the exception of the word "autograph" added in the upper left-hand corner of the first page in red ink, there are no notations in the manuscript by anyone but the composer. The ink color of the original is a consistent brownish black throughout, which suggests that the score was penned at one sitting; but the heading is written in a browner shade of ink and may have been added at a different time.

The leaf contains a watermark which is visible enough to be identified as that designated [in the *NBA* watermark catalogue as No. 47: a rare variant of the watermark representing the heraldic coat of arms of Zedwitz. This particular watermark has been dated generally to the period 1726-31. Its only other—and only datable—appearance in the Bach manuscripts is in an alto part for the motet *Der Geist hilft unsrer Schwachheit auf,* BWV 226, a work originally performed on 20 October 1729.[3] Another, more common variant of the same watermark (No. 48 in the *NBA* catalogue) is found in a number of Bach manuscripts, all

PLATE 32.   Autograph score, Bach Choir, Bethlehem, Pa., f. 1ʳ: BWV 906, mm.
1–16

PLATE 33.   Bach Choir, f. 1ᵛ: BWV 906, mm. 17–40

PLATE 34a. Autograph score, Dresden, Sachsische Landesbibliothek, *Mus. 2405-T-52*, p. 1 (=f. 1ᵛ): BWV 906, mm. 1–18a

PLATE 34b.   Dresden, p. 3 (=f. 2ᵛ): BWV 906/1 (*Fantasia*), mm. 32b–end; BWV
906/2 (*Fuga*), mm. 1–12

197

evidently dating from about 1738 on.] Included in this group is a second autograph of BWV 906—again a fair copy (Plate 34)—which is now preserved in the Sächsische Landesbibliothek, Dresden, with the shelf number *Mus. 2405-T-52*.[4] The two sets of dates associated with the watermarks of the two autographs of BWV 906–ca. 1726–31 for the Bethlehem autograph and ca. [1738]–40 for the Dresden autograph—while separated by about a decade, are both quite plausible and suggestive. Their implications will be explored presently.

The condition of the paper of the Bethlehem autograph can be described as good, although there are one or two instances of paper damage. The manuscript has darkened with time to a brownish-buff color. It is clear that it was folded at some time (into three vertical and six horizontal sections), presumably to fit into a pocket or an envelope.

The existence of the Bethlehem autograph seems to have been [virtually] unknown until it was brought to public notice in 1945 by Otto E. Albrecht in an article surveying musical autographs in American collections.[5] The manuscript had been brought to the United States in the late 1930s by the son and widow of the famous German musicologist, Max Friedländer (1852–1934). After passing through the hands of several dealers, it was purchased in April 1958 by the Bach Choir of Bethlehem. The whereabouts of the Bethlehem autograph before it was acquired by Max Friedländer cannot be traced at the present time [with any certainty.][5a]

The obscure early history of the Bethlehem autograph is shared to a great extent by the Dresden autograph, which was not known until its [presence in] the music collection of King Albrecht of Saxony was announced in 1876 by Moritz Fürstenau.[6] But even more puzzling than their [largely] unexplained and evidently unusual destinies during the eighteenth and most of the nineteenth centuries is the very existence in Bach's own hand of two fair copies of the same work. This is a most exceptional circumstance among the Bach sources, and it seems to call for some attempt, even if quite tentative, at an explanation.

Although the musical text of the Fantasia is virtually identical in the two autograph sources, there are fundamental differences between them that can be summarized in tabular form as follows:

Bethlehem	*Dresden*
1. has an autograph heading	1. has no heading
2. notates the right hand in treble clef	2. notates the right hand in soprano clef
3. contains first and second endings for the first part (m. 16)[7]	3. has the "second" ending only
4. has no fugue	4. contains a 48-measure-fragment of a fugue in C minor (BWV 906/2)

An examination of the readings of the two manuscripts reveals the curious circumstance that, despite the fact that the Bethlehem autograph is a veritably perfect fair copy containing practically no corrections of any musical significance, it seems to be earlier than the Dresden autograph.[8] Indeed, the latter may have been copied directly from the former; for there is an erasure in m. 9 of the Dresden autograph which reveals that Bach had been copying from a source in which the right-hand part was written in the treble clef.[9] An earlier date for the Bethlehem autograph, moreover, accords better with the evidence of the watermarks presented above.

While neither the internal evidence (the correction in m. 9 of the Dresden autograph) nor the external evidence (the watermarks), taken alone, is decisive, the cumulative impression conveyed when both are considered together makes the case for a dating of the Bethlehem autograph between ca. 1726–31 and for the Dresden autograph about a decade later, that is, ca. 1738–40, more plausible than the converse.[10] Moreover, such an assumption, when considered in the context of Bach's known activities during the late 1720s and again in the late 1730s suggests a possible explanation for many of the discrepancies between the two autographs.

It was precisely during the period 1726–31 that Bach turned his attention away from the composition of a "regulated church music" for the Leipzig service and began to take up again the production of keyboard music.[11] This redirection of his artistic efforts is marked most notably by the serial publication of the six partitas of the *Clavier-Übung,* Part I (BWV 825–30) between 1726 and 1730 which culminated in the appearance of the collected edition in 1731.[12] Now, as is well known, the opening movement of each partita bears a different designation and is cast in a different form. Notably absent from the series, however, is the form of the binary sonata; and it does not seem unreasonable to suspect that Bach may have in fact planned to have the binary sonata form represented in the *Clavier-Übung,* Part I, at some time. Indeed, it is conceivable that he intended specifically to include our Fantasia (in actuality a sonata or sinfonia), which is not only cast in binary form but contains a regular, if abbreviated, recapitulation (mm. 34ff.) as the opening movement of the Partita No. 2 in C minor, BWV 826—a movement which carries the heading *Sinfonia*—and that he prepared a fair copy [either the Bethlehem autograph itself or one substantially identical to it] to serve perhaps as the printer's copy for the edition. [This might explain the use of treble clef for the right-hand staff in the Bethlehem autograph, which would accord with the notation of the *Clavier-Übung.*][13] The exploitation of handcrossing that is such a prominent feature of the keyboard idiom of BWV 906 would have carried over to the opening movement of the second partita the device that Bach had introduced so effectively in the concluding movement, the "Giga," of the first partita.[14] Bach may ultimately have concluded, however, that it was not advisable to cast the introductory movement of the C minor partita in the same basic binary form that underlay all the remaining dance movements and therefore (or for some other reason) decided against including BWV 906 in the partita.

We can entertain similar speculations in connection with the Dresden autograph. When the Dresden autograph of BWV 906 was penned during the second half of the 1730s, Bach was again deeply involved with keyboard music. He had resumed publication of the *Clavier-Übung* and had begun to assemble the *Well-Tempered Clavier II*.[15]

Like the Fantasia, BWV 906, ten preludes in the *Well-Tempered Clavier II* are bipartite in form, and elements of the sonata form, especially a clearly recognizable recapitulation, appear in three of them.[16] Philipp Spitta had even asserted that the rather extensive cultivation of the bipartite form in the preludes of the *Well-Tempered Clavier II* had been anticipated in the Fantasia, BWV 906.[17] It seems justifiable, in view of the formal and chronological proximity, to go one step further and raise the possibility that Bach may have in fact considered incorporating the Fantasia, BWV 906, itself into the *Well-Tempered Clavier II* as the representative of C minor and had therefore written out the Dresden autograph in the late 1730s, notating the right-hand part—as is the case in all but two of the preludes and fugues in the London "Autograph"— in the soprano clef and appending the following fugue.[18] Why Bach would then have removed BWV 906 in favor of the present prelude and fugue in C minor is not clear, but the reasons may be the same as those that prompted him to abandon the Dresden autograph altogether before he had finished copying the highly chromatic C-minor fugue.[19] At all events, even speculation and conjecture have their limits, and it is likely that the questions raised by the appearance and the existence of the two fair copies of the C-minor Fantasia will continue to provoke, even—indeed, especially—if they are never completely answered.

12

THE COMPOSITIONS FOR SOLO FLUTE

A Reconsideration of Their Authenticity and Chronology*

Since the publication of the "New Chronology" of Bach's vocal music by Alfred Dürr and Georg von Dadelsen more than twenty years ago,[1] there have been almost no important advances in Bach chronology. Although we have now reached the point in Bach research where, in effect, the last scribe and the last watermark have been traced, catalogued, and assimilated, we are left with countless unanswered questions regarding the fundamentals: chronology and even authenticity. We still know next to nothing, for example, except in the very broadest terms, about when most of Bach's instrumental compositions were written.[2]

The reasons for this impasse are not hard to find. Whereas for the vocal works large numbers of composing-score autographs and original performing materials have survived, there are virtually no primary sources for the instrumental compositions.[2a] Most frequently we have scribal copies of greater or lesser authority, occasionally a later fair copy in Bach's hand. This means that there is almost no unambiguous, hard, external evidence that would permit us to date these compositions with

*This study was originally delivered as a paper at the Midwest Chapter meeting of the American Musicological Society in November 1977; at Brandeis University; and at the Bachfest of the Neue Bachgesellschaft, Marburg, 1978. The present revised and expanded version has greatly benefited from comments made during the discussions following those presentations. I should like in particular to express my gratitude to Joshua Rifkin, Hans-Joachim Schulze and Alfred Dürr for having called my attention to a number of items that had escaped my notice.

certainty, or, in some cases, even to be sure that a work is indeed by J. S. Bach.

Because Bach's compositions for solo flute are so few in number and so typical in their source transmission, they can be taken as a paradigm of the problems of authenticity and chronology posed by his instrumental music in general. They offer also a convenient arena for a discussion of the conventional means and for the testing of alternative means of dealing with these problems.

The basic questions about the flute sonatas have still not been satisfactorily answered. For example, how many compositions for solo flute did Bach write, or more precisely, how many of the flute pieces that have been attributed to him can be considered authentic? When were they written? For whom? Were they originally conceived as flute sonatas or are they arrangements of works first written for another medium?

It is still widely believed that Bach wrote eight works for the solo flute. But the view that has prevailed among Bach specialists for the past fifteen years is that the rather similar Sonatas for flute and harpsichord obbligato in G minor (BWV 1020) and E Flat major (BWV 1031) were probably composed by someone else—most likely Carl Philipp Emanuel Bach—and that the Sonata in C major for flute and continuo (BWV 1033) was written by one—or two—of Bach's students (one of them, again, might have been Emanuel Bach), presumably in part under the composer's active supervision and intervention. All three works were excluded from the *Neue Bach-Ausgabe* (NBA);[3] but they have recently appeared in the Bärenreiter series, "Flötenmusik," in an edition prepared by Alfred Dürr. The composer of the pieces is identified only as "Bach," with the tag "überliefert als Werke Johann Sebastian Bachs."[4] The NBA has left us, then, with literally a handful of authentic works for solo flute: the Unaccompanied Partita in A minor (BWV 1013); the Sonatas in E minor and E major for flute and continuo (BWV 1034 and 1035); and the Sonatas in B minor and A major for flute and harpsichord obbligato (BWV 1030 and 1032).

It is no small irony that the Sonatas in G minor, E Flat major and C major were eliminated from the NBA—the veritable symbol today of text-critical objectivity and responsibility—on the basis of unstated stylistic criteria. The only reference to the omitted compositions in the critical report appears under the list of abbreviations and reads in its entirety as follows:

> Because of the strong doubts concerning their authenticity, the three-voice Sonatas in G Minor (BWV 1020), E Flat (BWV 1031) and in G Major (BWV 1038), as well as the two-voice Sonata in C Major (BWV 1033), have not been included in this volume; which of them will appear in Volume 4 of this series [i.e., Chamber Works of Dubious Authenticity] has yet to be determined.[5]

We learn from Hans Eppstein that at least the C-major Sonata—and by implication all of them—was excluded because Friedrich Blume declared it, in passing and without any explanation, to be "sicher nicht von Bach."[6] In the meantime, Eppstein, in his *Bach-Jahrbuch* article and in an important monograph,[7] has presented a strong case against the authenticity of the three compositions on the basis of a careful, specific, and altogether admirable stylistic analysis. There is no need here to review his arguments except to say that he successfully demonstrates that the compositions, at the least, are not typical of J. S. Bach.

The source transmission of these three sonatas, as reported by Eppstein and by Dürr in his new edition, is summarized in Table 12.1.[8]

TABLE 12.1   The Principal Sources for the Challenged Flute Sonatas

Call No.	Copyist	Date	Title
Sonata in C Major for Flute and Basso Continuo, BWV 1033			
St 460	C. P. E. Bach	c. 1731	SONATA / a / Traversa / e / Continuo / di / Joh. Seb. Bach
Sonata in E Flat Major for Flute and Harpsichord Obbligato, BWV 1031			
a. P 649	"Anonymous 4" Title: C. P. E. Bach	mid-18th century	Es d[ur] / Trio / Furs obligate Clavier u. die Flöte / Von / J. S. Bach.
b. P 1056	C. F. Penzel (in part)	c. 1755	Sonata / a / Flauto Travers. / ed / Cembalo obligato / di / I. S. Bach. / Poss. Penzel.
Sonata in G Minor for "Flute" and Harpischord Obbligato, BWV 1020			
a. P 1059	Unknown (Owner: Schicht)	2nd half of 18th century	SONATA. / del Signore Bach. [lower right:] Schicht.
b. Vienna XI 36271	Michel (Owner: Brahms)	2nd half of 18th century	G. moll / SONATA. / Cembalo obligato. / con / Violino / Del Signore / C. P. E. Bach
c. P 471	A. Werner	c. 1840	Sonata in G^mol / per il / Clavicembalo e Violino obligato comp: da / G. Seb. Bach.
d. Breitkopf Catalogue of Music in Manuscript		1763	Sonata del Sigr. C. P. E. Bach, a Cl. ob. c. V. [with incipit]

This table is based on information in Dürr 1975 (see n. 4). Unless otherwise stated the MSS are in SPK. The letters St (*Stimmen*) and P (*Partitur*) are abbreviations for Mus.ms.Bach St. and Mus.ms.Bach P. respectively.

The principal source for the C-major Sonata was written by C. P. E. Bach around 1731, that is, when he was about seventeen years old and still living in his father's house. The manuscript ascribes the work to "Joh. Seb. Bach." As Dürr observes, few works attributed to J. S. Bach have such clear and impeccable credentials.[9] The main source for the E-flat Sonata dates from the mid-eighteenth century and was written out by an anonymous copyist who worked for both Sebastian and Emanuel.

The title page of the sonata, however, is in Emanuel's mature (that is, not late) hand and identifies "J. S. Bach" as the composer, as does the heading of the manuscript, which is in the hand of the scribe. There is another mid-century copy of the E-flat Sonata which was once in the possession of Christian Friedrich Penzel (1737–1801). Penzel is one of the most important and reliable[9a] transmitters and copyists of Sebastian Bach's music.[10] This copy, partly in Penzel's handwriting, also names Sebastian as the composer. For neither the C-major nor the E-flat Sonata is there any conflicting attribution in any source.

The situation is different for the G-minor Sonata. There are three known sources for this work. The first, from the second half of the eighteenth century, has the noncommittal title "Sonata del Signore Bach." The title of a set of parts prepared by Emanuel's Hamburg copyist Michel and now in the Vienna Gesellschaft der Musikfreunde (from Johannes Brahms's estate) attributes the work to "Signore C. P. E. Bach";[11] but a mid-nineteenth-century copy ascribes it to "G. Seb. Bach." The work is listed also in Breitkopf's catalogue of 1763 as a composition of Emanuel's.[12]

I will take these cases in order. Eppstein points, among other things, to the uneven quality of the C-major Sonata. He considers the first two movements to be quite mediocre and the last two rather fine, observing that the first minuet resembles the first minuet of the Partita in B Flat from the *Clavier-Übung,* Part I. He concludes that the sonata was likely written by two pupils of J. S. Bach, the second one superior to the first and enjoying, moreover, Bach's active supervision and assistance.[13] Dürr is tempted to identify C. P. E. Bach as the composer of the entire work.[14] Both Dürr and Eppstein suggest that Emanuel ascribed the work to Sebastian in recognition of his helping, if limited, role in the composition.

Now it seems implausible that the young and, like most young artists, surely proud C. P. E. Bach would have attributed a work basically of his own composition to his father, especially while he lived at home. This surely stretches credibility. On the other hand, the composition is strangely primitive, especially in the first two movements with their rudimentary bass part. It is particularly hard to believe that J. S. Bach could have been responsible for that bass part. We may indeed be dealing here with a hybrid composition, but not one in which a student (say, C. P. E. Bach) did the lion's share and the master lent a helping hand only in the last two movements. The fact alone that the first minuet has an obbligato right-hand harpsichord part, while the rest of the sonata is for basso continuo, is sufficient indication of the hybrid nature of the piece.

Almost all the problems of this composition disappear, it seems, as soon as one entertains the possibility that the piece may in fact have been written by J. S. Bach, but as a composition for unaccompanied flute. The basso continuo in the first two movements clearly detracts from rather than adds anything to them (see Ex. 12.1 and 12.2).[14a] The flute line of the original version of the first minuet would have been what is transmitted to us as the right-hand line of the harpsichord part, with occasional borrowings from the other lines. The flute part of the extant version is obviously a derivation of this right-hand line (see Ex. 12.3). The right-hand part never descends below middle d'—the lowest note on the eighteenth-century flute—even though the piece is in the key of C. It is even more significant that the C-major Sonata, like BWV 1013, and in contrast to the compositions for accompanied flute, contains practically no rests for the flute. With the exception of a few quarter-rests in the first part of Movement II the flute plays constantly.[15]

The resemblance of the minuet to that of the B-flat Partita may even suggest a possible date of composition—or, more likely, compilation—for the sonata. The partita was first printed singly in September 1726

Example 12.1.   BWV 1033/1

a. mm. 1–5

b. mm. 10–15

Example 12.2.   BWV 1033/2, mm. 1–6

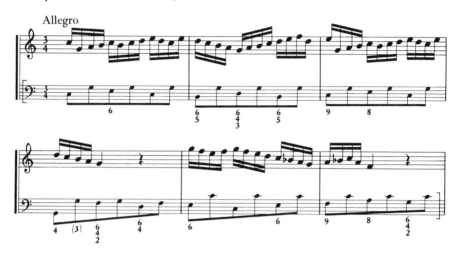

Example 12.3.   BWV 1033/4: Suggested original version for flute alone

(a) mm. 1–4

(b) mm. 9–10

with a dedication to the newborn son of Prince Leopold of Köthen. It was reprinted as part of the *Clavier-Übung* in 1731—the time of Emanuel's copy of the C-major flute sonata. It seems altogether possible that J. S. Bach had assigned C. P. E. Bach the exercise of fitting the sonata with a bass, or arranging it for flute and continuo or harpsichord at that time. Hence the character of the surviving version of the piece. The original—unaccompanied—sonata itself may have been composed around the same time as the Unaccompanied Partita in A minor, and conceived perhaps as a counterpart to it.

It is known, incidentally, that at about this time C. P. E. Bach made arrangements of other instrumental compositions of his father's, namely, of the lost Violin Concerto in D minor and of the Sonata in G major for violin and continuo, BWV 1021. Emanuel's harpsichord version of the violin concerto is different from that known as BWV 1052. Werner Breig suggests in passing that the transcription (BWV 1052a) may well have been prepared at the request of Sebastian Bach.[16] Breig's conjecture and mine concerning the Flute Sonata in C major would seem to support one another, and to shed light, moreover, on J. S. Bach's method of teaching composition. Even more telling is the case of the Trio Sonata in G major for flute, violin, and continuo, BWV 1038. Ulrich Siegele has convincingly argued that this composition, which uses basically the same continuo part as that of J. S. Bach's Sonata in G major for violin and continuo, BWV 1021, is actually a work by C. P. E. Bach. In two respects this case represents the converse of that of the Flute Sonata in C. In the trio sonata, J. S. Bach evidently had Emanuel invent new upper parts to a given bass; in the flute sonata, as we have seen, his assignment was the opposite. Second, whereas the C-major sonata is apparently a work essentially of J. S. Bach's composition surviving in the hand of C. P. E. Bach, the trio sonata is preserved in a manuscript penned by J. S. Bach.[17]

For the E-flat Sonata, the most popular and indeed the most attractive of the three questionable sonatas, the argument against its authenticity has been based first on its "un-Bachian" features (as Dürr puts it: the thumping basses; the triadic, *galant*-sounding melodies; the short-breathed phrases) and second on the fact that it has clear similarities with the G-minor Sonata.[18] The latter, as we have seen, is frequently ascribed to C. P. E. Bach in the early sources. Dürr's conclusion is that both the E-flat and the G-minor sonatas may have been compositions of Emanuel's, that the E-flat was still written under his father's supervision, and that the G-minor, while directly modeled on the E-flat, was a sufficiently independent effort on C. P. E. Bach's part for him to justify his identifying himself this time as the composer. But again, on the face of it, it seems unlikely that C. P. E. Bach would wish to attribute a work of his own entirely to his father, even if he enjoyed the latter's guidance, without at least providing an explanation for such a peculiar action.[19]

Now the E-flat Sonata is ascribed to J. S. Bach not only by Emanuel but also by Penzel, whose connections with the Bach sources seem to derive primarily from Wilhelm Friedemann, not Emanuel Bach.[20] In any case, Penzel's copy is demonstrably independent of Emanuel's.[21] Therefore, it seems likely that the two attributions to Sebastian are likewise independent. This, in fact, is the crux of the external argument for BWV 1031; for both Penzel and C. P. E. Bach have attributed to J. S. Bach elsewhere compositions whose authenticity is highly questionable, if not altogether without credibility: in Penzel's case the Christmas cantata, *Uns ist ein Kind geboren,* BWV 142; in the case of Emanuel the Suite in A Major for violin and harpsichord obbligato, BWV 1025. Since the existence of the latter attribution, in particular, has been adduced to buttress the challenge to the credentials of the E-flat Sonata (and the C-major, too, for that matter),[22] it is important to emphasize that the attributions of the cantata and the suite, unlike that of BWV 1031, are uncorroborated.[23]

The obviously *galant* style of the E-flat Sonata should perhaps be considered as a clue to its dating rather than a judgment of its authenticity. As I have attempted to develop elsewhere, Bach seems to have been increasingly influenced by the *galant* style during the 1730s and early 1740s, when he was interested in strengthening his connections with the musical establishment in Dresden.[24] That the E-flat Sonata could have been written by J. S. Bach in the early 1730s and that it could have served as a model for C. P. E. Bach when he composed the G-minor Sonata—for violin[25]—at around the same time (that is, before Emanuel left Leipzig in 1734), is not only plausible but seems to be the explanation that accords best with the external evidence. In brief, the greater part of valor would seem to dictate that both the C-major—as an unaccompanied sonata, perhaps—and the E-flat Sonata, as it has come down to us, should be restored to the Bach canon. They should, at the least, be included in the NBA among the *opera dubia;* but even that would be perhaps more of a stigma than the evidence warrants.[26]

The discussion so far has been rather agreeable; for the weapons employed have been the conventional ones—external source evidence—used in the widely accepted manner: namely, according to a "strict constructionist" view of the objective data. In turning now to the five authenticated compositions I shall be standing, quite a bit less comfortably, on the other side of the fence. The following remarks will be, frankly, quite speculative. The point of departure, however (and this needs to be emphasized), will again be the sources.

The five flute compositions have reached us singly. It does not seem that they were ever gathered together into a set in any eighteenth-century source. Table 12.2 offers a brief description of the principal sources.[27] We have a manuscript for BWV 1013 dating from the late

TABLE 12.2   The Principal Sources for the Authenticated Flute Sonatas

Call No.	Copyist	Date	Title
Partita in A minor for Unaccompanied Flute, BWV 1013			
P 968	1) "Anonymous 5"	ca. 1722–23	Solo pour la Flute traversiere par
			J. S. Bach
	2) Anonymous		
Sonata in E minor for Flute and Basso Continuo, BWV 1034			
P 804/23	J. P. Kellner	ca. [1726–27]	Sonata per la Flaute / Traversière e
			Basso di / J. S. Bach / J. P. Kellner.
Sonata in E Major for Flute and Basso Continuo, BWV 1035			
P 622	Unknown	early 19th	SONATA / per / Traverso Solo e
		century	Continuo / del S^{gre} / Giov: Seb:
			Bach.
			[Notation in the hand of Count Voss-Buch:] Auf dem Exemplare, von welchem diese Abschrift genommen worden ist, steht die Bemerkung: "nach dem Autographo des Verfassers welches o. 17 da er in Potsdam war, für den Geh. Kämmerir Fredersdorf von ihm angefertigt worden."
Sonata in B minor for Flute and Harpsichord Obbligato, BWV 1030			
P 975	J. S. Bach	ca. 1736	Sonata a Cembalo obligato e
			Travers. solo di J.S. Bach
The G-minor Version of BWV 1030			
P 1008	"Anonymous 300"	2nd half	G. moll / Sonata / al / Cembalo
	(C. P. E. Bach's	of 18th	obligato / e / Flauto traverso /
	copyist)	century	composta / da / Giov. Seb. Bach
	Title: Voss-Buch		
Sonata in A Major for Flute and Harpsichord Obbligato, BWV 1032			
P 612	J. S. Bach	ca. 1736	Sonata a 1 Traversa è Cembalo
			obligato di J. S. Bach

The information in this table is based on NBA. VI/3 (see n. 3). The MSS are in the SPK, except for P 975 and P 612, which are in the Deutsche Staatsbibliothek, Berlin, German Democratic Republic. For the abbreviation P and St see the notes to Table 12.1.

Köthen period, about 1722–23; a manuscript for BWV 1034 probably dating from 1725 or 1726; autograph score copies for BWV 1030 and 1032, both dating from around 1736; and a nineteenth-century manuscript for BWV 1035 associating the piece with a visit by Bach to Potsdam, and thus dating it presumably 1741 or 1747. That is, of the five compositions for solo flute accepted by the NBA as genuine, only one, the A-minor partita, BWV 1013, survives in a source evidently dating from the Köthen period. Let us reflect on this.

It used to be thought that Bach's instrumental music (with the exception of the organ works) was concentrated into a brief period, the six years 1717–23, when Bach served as Kapellmeister in Köthen, and that his church music was written gradually over the course of his life. Can it be that just the opposite might be the case? It is now known that Bach wrote the great majority of his church cantatas during the concentrated period 1723–27, his first four years as Thomaskantor in Leipzig. Perhaps, conversely, his instrumental music was written at various times throughout his career. The manuscript evidence in the case of the flute sonatas does not preclude that possibility. And we know that the preparation and publication of the four parts of the *Clavier-Übung* and the composition of the *Well-Tempered Clavier II* as well extended from at least the mid-1720s to the early 1740s.[28]

Even the dating of instrumental works apparently most securely associated with the Köthen period cannot always be accepted without qualification. In a reference to the sonatas for violin and obbligato harpsichord, BWV 1014–19, Johann Nikolaus Forkel remarked in Chapter 9 of his biography that they were composed at Köthen.[29] It must be noted, however, not only that the earliest surviving manuscript of the final version of the set (in the hand of Johann Christoph Altnikol) presumably dates from the last years of Bach's life (when Altnikol was a pupil of Bach's),[30] but that a copy of what is apparently the earliest of the three known versions of the sonatas would seem also to have been prepared during the Leipzig period. For the principal copyist of the keyboard part is Bach's "Hauptkopist C,"[30a] an important scribe who is represented in the manuscripts of Bach's vocal works from April 1724 to February 1727.[31]

This issue cannot be pursued here. Suffice it to say that it is of course conceivable that Bach had drafted the first version of the sonatas in Köthen and wished to make a copy of them after settling in Leipzig where he eventually (sometime between the date of St 162, that is, ca. 1724–25, and that of P 229, ca. 1747–49?) composed the intermediate and final versions. It is hardly plausible—at least it would be most uncharacteristic of Bach—that the composer would have recopied in Leipzig the earliest version of a work that had already been brought to a more advanced form in Köthen. That is, the sonatas for violin and obbligato harpsichord, in their familiar, final form, are almost certainly a product not of Köthen, but Leipzig.[32]

In brief, the assumption that Bach wrote all or almost all of his instrumental chamber and ensemble music in Köthen is, in fact, nothing *but* an assumption. The notion may have started with Spitta, who apparently expanded on the report in the obituary prepared by Emanuel Bach and Johann Friedrich Agricola, and repeated by Forkel, that Bach composed most of his organ music in Weimar.[33] Spitta elaborated this into the admittedly very elegant conceit that Bach's artistic career followed a rational plan: the bulk of the organ music composed in Weimar, the keyboard and chamber works in Köthen, the church music in

Leipzig. I suspect that we may be laboring under the burden of an unchallenged, comfortable myth that might have been keeping generations of Bach scholars from noticing rather obvious clues in the sources themselves.[33a]

To return to the flute music. There is no autograph for the A-minor partita. The composition survives in a single manuscript that was written out by two copyists, one of whom, known in the literature as Anonymous 5, was associated with Bach in both Köthen and Leipzig. The manuscript represents the earlier, Köthen stage, in his script, and dates from 1722-23.[34]

In contrast to all of Bach's other flute music, the partita is considered unidiomatic by many flautists—especially the first movement, where there are practically no natural places to take a breath, and the second, where some extended arpeggio patterns are quite awkward. Moreover, it is Bach's only flute composition to call for the high a′′′—the highest note on the baroque flute.[35] For these reasons it is assumed by some (including Schmitz) that the composition must have been written originally for some other instrument.[36] But the work obviously can be played on the flute; and it could have been conceived originally for the instrument—if Bach had reason to believe that there was a virtuoso able to play it.

Now the modest technical demands of the surviving flute parts in Bach's Köthen cantatas, the birthday cantata, *Durchlauchtster Leopold,* BWV 173a, and the (New York's?) cantata, BWV 184a (the text for which is lost)[37] suggest that Bach's regular flautists in Köthen, the Chamber Musicians Johann Heinrich Freytag and Johann Gottlieb Würdig, had rather limited abilities on the instrument.[38] (Even the flute part of the Fifth Brandenburg Concerto, assuming for the moment that it was intended for a performance by Bach's Köthen ensemble, is not particularly difficult.[39] We may possess a clue, however, as to the identity of the flautist Bach may have had in mind for the partita.

The heading of the A-minor Partita, in the hand of the original copyist, is in French. It reads: "Solo pour la flute traversiere par J. S. Bach." This could be significant.[40] The greatest flute virtuoso in Germany during Bach's lifetime was the Frenchman Pierre Gabriel Buffardin (1689-1768). Buffardin was the principal flautist in Dresden from 1715 to 1749.[41] (Another flautist resident in Dresden during much of that time, incidentally, was Buffardin's pupil, Johann Joachim Quantz.)[42]

We have it on the testimony of C. P. E. Bach that J. S. Bach knew Buffardin personally. In 1774 Carl Philipp Emanuel sent along a copy of the genealogy of the Bach family, a document prepared by his father, to Johann Nikolaus Forkel, together with his own emendations. Entry no. 23 referred to Johann Sebastian Bach's well-traveled elder brother Johann Jacob Bach, for whom J. S. Bach had composed the "Capriccio on the Absence of the Most Beloved Brother" (BWV 992), around 1704. Emanuel added the following gloss to his father's account:

> From [the Turkish town of] Bender [Johann Jacob] journeyed to Constantinople, and there had instruction on the flute from the famous flutist Buffardin, who had traveled to Constantinople with a French ambassador. This information was furnished by Buffardin himself when he once visited J. S. Bach in Leipzig.[43]

It does not seem unreasonable to suppose that Bach had already met Buffardin before he settled in Leipzig. The most likely occasion for their first encounter would surely have been Bach's first documented visit to Dresden in the fall of 1717 for his celebrated and well-publicized recital—the remnant of the notorious, aborted contest with Louis Marchand. This visit took place shortly before Bach was to assume his new duties as court Kapellmeister to Prince Leopold of Anhalt-Köthen in December 1717.[44] Since the contest with Marchand was arranged by the Konzertmeister of the Dresden Court Chapel, Jean Baptiste Volumier (1670-1728), it is evident that Bach's reputation had already reached the musicians of the Saxon capital.[45] Indeed, we know that Bach had connections with Dresden musicians even earlier. He is known to have met the brilliant German violinst, and Volumier's successor as Konzertmeister, Johann Georg Pisendel (1687-1755), as early as March 1709, when the latter passed through Weimar and took the trouble of introducing himself to Bach.[46] It is easy to imagine that it was Pisendel, a member of the Dresden Court Chapel since 1712, who brought Bach to the attention of Volumier.

In 1717 Pisendel (or Volumier—it does not matter) could not have failed to introduce Bach in his moment of triumph to his other Dresden colleagues, Buffardin among them. During the course of this sojourn we can assume also that Bach had an opportunity to hear the French flute virtuoso and to form, very likely for the first time, an impression of the character and capabilities of the transverse flute in the hands of a first-rate player. For, as far as is known, Bach had never, up to that time, composed anything at all for the instrument. There are no transverse flutes in any of the Mühlhausen or Weimar cantatas. The instrument makes its first appearance no earlier than the year 1720 in one or the other of the two Köthen cantatas mentioned above.[47]

While we are speculating about Bach's experiences in Dresden in the fall of 1717, we can assume further that Pisendel spoke with him about his own recent personal experiences with one of the musicians Bach most admired: Antonio Vivaldi. For not long before Bach's visit to Dresden Pisendel himself had just returned there—in September—after a year's study with Vivaldi in Venice.[48] Pisendel may have shown Bach on this occasion some of the most recent Vivaldi concertos he is known to have brought back to Dresden with him from Venice.[49] One or another may indeed have provided a direct impetus to the composition of several of Bach's concertos. Pisendel may also have shown Bach one of his own compositions, considered to be a product of his Venetian sojourn: a sonata, in A minor, for unaccompanied violin.[50] This work, it has been claimed (quite plausibly), could have served as the direct model for Bach's sonatas and partitas for unaccompanied violin.[51] (It does not seem ever to have been stressed that, with the exception of Heinrich Biber's "passagaglia" [sic] from the "Rosary Sonatas" (ca. 1674), all known precursors of Bach's unaccompanied works are associated in one way or another with Dresden: Pisendel's sonata; a suite published in 1682 by the Dresden composer Johann Paul Westhoff; and Francesco Geminiani's Sonata in B Flat *a violino solo senza basso*, which survives only in a Dresden manuscript.)[52]

It is tempting to think then, that it was Buffardin who stimulated Bach's interest in the transverse flute, that the unaccompanied partita was Bach's first composition for the instrument, that it was written shortly after he had met the French virtuoso, and that it was inspired by his having seen or heard, on the same occasion, Pisendel's unaccompanied sonata for violin in the same key.[52a] The unidiomatic character of the partita, in that event, could be attributed to the composer's inexperience in writing for the flute.[53]

After the unaccompanied partita, the earliesst source for any of Bach's flute compositions is a manuscript of the Sonata in E minor, BWV 1034. It was copied out, most likely in [1726 or 1727], by Johann Peter Kellner (1705–72) and entered into his large collection of Bach manuscripts.[54] Now it is not clear whether the E-minor Sonata was composed in Leipzig or Köthen. The consensus of opinion has automatically assumed a Köthen origin.[55] But the fact that the earliest manuscript of the work dates from around [1726/27] may not be altogether coincidental. There is evidence that Bach had become intensely interested in the flute shortly before then, specifically in the summer and autumn of 1724. William H. Scheide was the first to observe that Bach wrote more than a dozen church cantatas between the months of July and November 1724 that contain especially elaborate and often difficult solos for the transverse flute.[56] (See Table 12.3.)

Would these obbligato parts have been intended for Bach's regular flute player in Leipzig? First of all, it does not seem that there was a regular, competent player of the flute available to Bach in Leipzig before this time at all.[57] Bach began the weekly composition of church cantatas on 30 May 1723, the First Sunday after Trinity, with *Die Elenden sollen essen*, BWV 75. The transverse flute makes its first appearance almost eleven months (and around fifty cantatas) later, on 16 April 1724, with a modest ripieno part in Cantata No. 67: *Halt im Gedächtnis Jesum*

TABLE 12.3   The Series of Cantatas from July to November 1724
with Extended Parts for Solo or Obbligato Flute(s)

Date	Occasion	BWV/ movement	Description
23 July	7 p. Trin.	107/6	Aria, D major: flutes 1 and 2 *all'unisono*, tenor, continuo
(30 July	8 p. Trin.	178	No flute parts)
6 August	9 p. Trin.	94/1	Chorus, D major: flute obbligato
		94/4	Aria, E minor: flute, alto, continuo
13 August	10 p. Trin.	101/2	Aria, G minor: flute (replaced by violin before the first performance), tenor, continuo
		101/6	Duet, D minor: flute, oboe da caccia, soprano, alto, continuo
20 August	11 p. Trin.	113/5	Aria, D major: flute, tenor, continuo
(27 August	12 p. Trin.	?)	
(28 August	Inauguration	?)	
(3 September	13 p. Trin.	33	No flute parts)
10 September	14 p. Trin.	78/4	Aria, G minor: flute, tenor, continuo
17 September	15 p. Trin.	99/3	Aria, E minor: flute, tenor, continuo
		99/5	Duet, B minor: flute, oboe d'amore, soprano, alto, continuo
24 September	16 p. Trin.	8/1	Chorus, E major (later D): flauto piccolo (replaced by flute before the first performance)
		8/4	Aria, A major (later G): flute, strings, bass, continuo
29 September	St. Michael	130/5	Aria, G major: flute, tenor, continuo
1 October	17 p. Trin.	114/2	Aria, D minor: flute, tenor, continuo
8 October	18 p. Trin.	96/3	Aria, C major: flute, tenor, continuo
(15 October	19 p. Trin	5	No flute parts)
22 October	20 p. Trin.	180/2	Aria, C major: flute, tenor, continuo
(29 October	21 p. Trin.	38	No flute parts)
(31 October	Reformation	80? 76?	No flute parts)
5 November	22 p. Trin.	115/4	Aria, B minor: flute, violoncello piccolo, soprano, continuo
(12 November	23 p. Trin.	139	No flute parts)
19 November	24 p. Trin.	26/2	Aria, C major: violin solo, flute (partially in unison with violin), tenor, continuo

Christ.[58] Bach did not call for the instrument again until he prepared the cantatas for Pentecost Monday and Tuesday, 29 and 30 May 1724. The compositions performed on those occasions were, respectively, *Erhöhtes Fleisch und Blut,* BWV 173, and *Erwünschtes Freudenlicht,* BWV 184.[59] These are parodies of the two secular Köthen cantatas, BWV 173a and 184a, mentioned earlier. Like the originals, both of the Pentecost cantatas employ a pair of flutes. The parts, as stated before, are quite simple.[60]

On 11 June 1724, the First Sunday after Trinity, Bach began the so-called Second Leipzig *Jahrgang* with the famous cycle of chorale cantatas. There are no flute parts in any of them until the four-month series of flute solos under discussion was initiated with Cantata No. 107 on 23 July.[61] After the conclusion of that series with Cantata No. 26 on 19 November, the flute disappears once again until Epiphany, that is, 25 January 1725 (BWV 123), and only turns up sporadically thereafter.

The sudden appearance and disappearance of such extensive flute writing, much of it quite difficult, suggests that it was inspired by the temporary and irregular presence in Leipzig of an unusually fine visiting flautist. We can, however, identify one of Bach's regular flautists in Leipzig. On 18 May 1727, Bach wrote a testimonial for Friedrich Gottlieb Wild, a law student, and remarked:

> Mons. Wild, during the four years [i.e., from the beginning of Bach's Cantorate] that he has lived here at the University . . . not only . . . helped adorn the church music with his well-learned accomplishments on the *Flaute traversière* and *Clavecin*, but has also taken special instruction from me in the Clavier, Thorough Bass and the fundamental rules of composition.[62]

It is not difficult to imagine that Wild was entrusted with routine parts on the flute or even, in time, with more challenging ones; but if he was really a virtuoso of the first rank as early as the summer of 1724, capable of executing the rapid and ornate parts in Cantata Nos. 94, 113, 99 or 114, then one is baffled by the chronological concentration and isolation of these parts within a single four-month period. But the possibility that these parts were indeed written for Wild or some other regular member of Bach's Leipzig ensemble can by no means be eliminated.

The name of the player of the obbligato flute parts is unimportant.[63] What is significant here is Bach's unusual, concentrated interest in the transverse flute during the second half of the year 1724—shortly before the presumed date of origin of the earliest surviving copy of the E-minor Sonata. At the least, it is altogether conceivable that the sonata was composed at about the same time as the series of obbligato flute parts in the cantatas.

It is worth observing, too, that in a significant respect the texture of the E-minor Sonata, scored as it is for basso continuo, is more closely related to the "impure" texture of the continuo-accompanied arias with obbligato flute than to the "pure," "clean" texture of Bach's mature "duo" sonatas from the Köthen period: the sonatas for melody instrument and obbligato keyboard.[64]

The probable (approximate) date of the earliest manuscript, then, along with a constellation of biographical and stylistic data (the concentrated series of flute solos in the cantatas, as well as the "reversion" in the sonata to the texture of the continuo-accompanied solo sonata), suggests that the Sonata in E minor was composed in Leipzig sometime in the late summer or fall of 1724.[64a]

The B-minor Sonata, BWV 1030, survives also in a G-minor version. (At least the harpsichord part does.)[65] While the G-minor version is definitely earlier than the B-minor,[66] it survives only in a posthumous copy (P 1008), so that it is impossible to determine its date. But the vocally inspired opening theme of the sonata bears an uncanny resemblance to the beginning of the opening chorus of Cantata No. 117, *Sei Lob und Ehr' dem höchsten Gut,* a movement in G major, composed some time between 1728 and 1731 and scored with flutes.[67] More striking is the remarkable correspondence between the idiomatic right-hand accompanimental figure in the sonata and the equally characteristic, but highly unusual, obbligato cello accompaniment in the cantata movement (see Ex. 12.4 and 12.5). Since it was in 1729 that Bach took up the directorship of the Collegium Musicum and turned his attention to the performance—and composition—of instrumental music, it does not seem too audacious to entertain the possibility that the G-minor version of the sonata, BWV 1030, may have been prepared between 1729 and 1731, that is, within the chronological limits established by Dürr and von Dadelsen for Cantata No. 117.[68] When Bach prepared the fair copy of BWV 1030 (P 975) around 1736, he decided on the new key, B minor—a key, among other things, much better suited to the flute than G minor.[69]

Example 12.4.   BWV 1030/1, mm. 1–2

The B-minor Sonata is exceptionally demanding. The presto fugue with the breakneck gigue conclusion, in particular, is a *tour de force* of technical virtuosity. The inordinate difficulty of this movement, along with the fact (touched upon earlier) that Bach's connections with Dresden had increased considerably during the 1730s and indeed culminated in November 1736 with his receiving the title of Composer to the Royal Court Chapel, suggest that Bach prepared the final version of his

Example 12.5.   BWV 117/1, mm. 1–4

greatest and most difficult flute composition, too, for the master flautist Buffardin. As in the whirlwind *badinerie* that concludes the B-minor Suite for Flute and Strings, BWV 1067, Bach seems to have had Buffardin in mind in this treacherous gigue. Buffardin's greatest strength, after all, was, according to Quantz, playing rapid pieces (*geshwinde Sachen*).[70]

The A-major Sonata, BWV 1032, also survives in an autograph, a fair or revision copy dating from around 1736.[71] The piece, then, was definitely composed earlier. Indeed, the retention of the same tonic for all three movements of the sonata (A major–A minor–A major) is totally unknown otherwise in Bach's compositions in this genre and lends support to Eppstein's suggestion that the outer movements were originally in C major. Eppstein, however, has argued in addition that the work must have existed in one or more earlier versions—possibly as a trio sonata for flute, violin, and continuo (and/or as a flute concerto)—that were substantially different from the surviving version. Moreover, he seems to be asserting that all of these versions must have originated in Köthen.[72]

Actually, Eppstein is quite vague—even ambivalent—about the chronology of this sonata. Since the autograph was not available to him, he was obviously greatly handicapped in dealing with the problem.

On the one hand he argues, among other things on the basis of the restricted compass of the harpsichord part (from C♯ to b″), that even the surviving version (but not of course the autograph itself) must have been one of Bach's first chamber compositions—or transcriptions—with obbligato harpsichord (p. 169). It was written, he thinks, along with the B-minor Sonata and the sonatas for viola da gamba and harpsichord, BWV 1027-29, before the violin sonatas, BWV 1014-19. These, in his view, as we have seen, were not only composed but given their final form during the Köthen period (p. 159). Since Eppstein dates the violin sonatas during the "later Köthen period," that is, 1720-23, he concludes that the flute sonatas, BWV 1030 and 1032, must have been written by 1720 (p. 160).

Eppstein is extremely critical of the musical quality of the A-major Sonata, specifically the first movement, in its present and only known form. He points to the lack of "polyphonic intensity," the thin texture, the "careless compositional technique" (especially the redundant E-major cadences in mm. 33 and 35), and the "stylistic unevenness" (pp. 100-02). Indeed, one suspects that Eppstein would have been pleased to strike BWV 1032 from the canon of authentic works, were it not for the known existence of the autograph.[73] His solution is to conjecture—again without having been able to see the autograph—that the version preserved in it was probably not really the final, that is, "finished," version of the sonata. He accepts Spitta's dating of ca. 1736—a dating now known to be correct—but he argues that it may have been some kind of sketch or draft which in some sections was still so unsatisfactory that Bach himself perhaps cut out the missing leaves of the manuscript.[74] That is, while Eppstein seems to argue explicitly that BWV 1032 was written early in the Köthen period, he is also hinting at the same time that the present state of the sonata is really a product of the 1730s and not quite finished even then.

It turns out that the autograph for the first two movements is a neatly penned fair copy, showing absolutely no traces of the substantial rewriting of parts from a preexistent model that Eppstein has argued must have taken place in the process of transcription and transposition and which he has attempted in part to reconstruct (pp. 193-97).[75] The third movement, however, can best be described as a revision copy. There are corrections of detail in all parts (especially the bass), although none, again, is of major structural importance. More pertinent to our discussion is the presence of a few corrections which indicate that Bach may have been copying from a C-major source.[76] The condition of the manuscript, then, reveals only that the sonata had achieved its present compositional state some time before it was copied. The corrections of a third suggest that, as in the case of BWV 1030, Bach may have decided on a new key for the sonata at the time he penned the manuscript and transposed the outer movements (or, to be more cautious, at least the final movement) on the spot from C to A. Moreover, the calligraphy indicates that Bach apparently intended this to be the finished version of the work.

Whether in fact the composition, with the likely exception of the slow movement,[77] ever existed in a substantially different "gestalt" is not at all clear, and certainly not evident from the autograph. The very fact that Eppstein is ultimately unable to decide whether the original form of the first movement was a concerto or a trio sonata or both (pp. 98, 100) raises the suspicion that there may have been no earlier form—that Bach had conceived this movement, and by extension perhaps the final movement as well, from the beginning as a sonata for flute and obbligato harpsichord.[78]

As for the suggestion (p. 162) that the character of the opening theme of BWV 1032—in Heinrich Besseler's terminology a *Laufthema* (Ex. 12.6)—argues for a quite early dating,[79] it should be mentioned

Example 12.6.   BWV 1032/1, mm. 1–3

that the theme also bears a strong resemblance to the opening of the aria, "Halleluia, Stärk' und Macht," from Cantata No. 29, *Wir danken dir, Gott,* a work composed for 28 August 1731, that is, at just about the date suggested above for the challenged Sonata in E Flat major, BWV 1031 (Ex. 12.7).[80]

Example 12.7.   BWV 29/3, mm. 20–23

It is not necessary to entertain here (aloud) any naive speculations as to whether this thematic similarity has any bearing on the dating of the pre-autograph version of the A-major sonata. But considered in the light of the severity of Eppstein's criticism of the work's artistic value, and, moreover, the similarity of his arguments on that point to those adduced in his challenge to the authenticity of BWV 1031, one is inclined to whisper one's suspicion that the A-major Sonata, too, may have been composed—as a work indeed in C major, but in its present scoring for flute and obbligato harpsichord—in the early 1730s, at about the same time that Bach composed the E-flat Sonata. Both works, along with the Sonata in B minor, were presumably written in conjunction with Bach's activities with the Collegium Musicum;[81] the A-major and E-flat sonatas being slightly later than the B-minor and reflecting, moreover, Bach's flirtation at the time with a lighter, simpler style.

With the fifth of the "authentic" flute pieces, the Sonata in E major for flute and continuo, BWV 1035, we would seem, at first glance, to be on firmer ground again. An old archival notice on the title page of a nineteenth-century copy declares that Bach prepared the score of the work "when he was in Potsdam in 17 [sic] for the royal valet Fredersdorf."[82] Bach is known to have gone to Berlin in 1741 and 1747. It is, nonetheless, rather curious that the identity of the composer of the E-major Sonata has apparently never been called into question. The sources for the sonata are not only all posthumous, but they all date from the nineteenth century. Furthermore, the sonata (one is inclined to add, "as usual") is not at all "typical" of J. S. Bach. As Eppstein observes, the composition, first of all, dispenses with imitative polyphony almost entirely; in addition, it is Bach's only ensemble sonata to adopt the form of the sonata da camera.[83]

The biographical circumstances alleged by the nineteenth-century annotators to have surrounded the work seem to have been sufficient, however, to forestall any doubts about its authenticity. The lighter texture and the freer form of the sonata lead Eppstein, for example, to conjecture that Bach not only delivered the sonata in Potsdam in the 1740s but that he may well have composed it at that time with a view to pleasing the *galant* taste that prevailed in Frederick's court.[84] It is certainly not my intention to challenge the authenticity of the E-major sonata here. On the contrary, in light of Bach's progressive tendencies in the 1730s and early 1740s and the increasingly archaic and contrapuntal nature of his music after about 1745, I am inclined to accept Eppstein's suggestion that the sonata was composed specifically for Bach's first known visit to the Prussian capital in 1741.[85]

But it must be reported that almost nothing is known about Bach's 1741 visit to Berlin except that it took place some time between late July and mid-August, and that it began before 5 August and concluded after 9 August—those being the dates of two letters sent to the composer in Berlin by his cousin, Johann Elias (who was living with the Bach household in Leipzig at the time).[86] There is no evidence that Bach went to Potsdam during this sojourn. Elias makes no allusion or response to any important or exciting business such as an appearance at court that might have been mentioned in J. S. Bach's letters. In fact, he apologizes in his letter of 5 August for disturbing the composer's "present peace and contentment"—a formulation that suggests that the Berlin visit was private—even recreational—in nature.

Moreover, it seems that Frederick was away from Berlin on a military campaign in connection with the First Silesian War for much of 1741.[87] And it would be odd that there should be absolutely no documentation of any contact between Bach and Potsdam in 1741, whereas the famous visit of 1747 not only found its way into the eighteenth-century anecdotal literature and, of course, into Forkel's biography, but was even covered at the time by the Berlin newspapers.[88] Finally, as Wolff has demonstrated, Bach was able, even within the stylistic framework of the *Musical Offering*, to make a gesture toward the musical taste of Potsdam.[89] In short, Bach could conceivably have composed BWV 1035 some time shortly before his celebrated journey to Potsdam in May 1747 as an homage to be presented to the king on that occasion. Eppstein's objection to this notion[90] on the ground that such a gesture would have been unnecessary in view of the fact that Bach had been invited to appear before the court is not compelling. Even invited guests, after all, sometimes bring gifts. On the other hand, if Bach had "prepared" the E-major Sonata in connection with the royal invitation of 1747, then he surely would have prepared the score not for Fredersdorf but for the king himself. In any case the work would surely have been mentioned somewhere in the contemporary commentaries on the famous visit.

The case for 1741, then, can not be discounted by any means. Again, the musical evidence of the E-major Sonata itself favors this date. In addition, it was just about this time, shortly after his accession to the throne on 31 May 1740, that Frederick began the elaborate expansion of his musical establishment. Within two months the king sent Carl Heinrich Graun to Italy to recruit singers for the new opera house whose construction he had just ordered. In the same year, 1740, C. P. E. Bach was called to Potsdam to serve as principal cembalist.[91] It is easy to imagine that J. S. Bach would have sought to establish an early contact of his own with the new, musically ambitious monarch by offering (through the agency of Philipp Emanuel, perhaps) a composition—BWV 1035—to the king's flute partner, Fredersdorf. And it is most plausible to think that such an approach specifically to Fredersdorf would have been made before, rather than after, the arrival in Potsdam in December 1741 of a new, most highly favored, flute partner for Frederick: Johann Joachim Quantz.[92] But the sonata, of course, could have been prepared for Fredersdorf even after Quantz's arrival—indeed at almost any time, in connection with some journey by Bach to Potsdam of which we have no specific information at all.[93] Prudence dictates, however, that speculation be confined to Bach's two documented visits to Berlin (or Potsdam), and, on balance, the case for a 1741 origin of the Sonata in E major is rather more persuasive.

It is difficult at this point to suppress the suspicion that the problems of style, idiom, and authenticity (not to mention the questions of chronology) posed variously by the flute sonatas in C, E-flat, A, and E and by the A-minor Partita derive not so much from the shortcomings or idiosyncrasies perceived in them as from our own still underdeveloped knowledge of the stages of Bach's stylistic development and also, perhaps, from our underestimation of the breadth of his style—perhaps even our refusal to acknowledge the extraordinary extent of its range. Just as the traditional notion of the general outlines of Bach's artistic career is apparently an oversimplification resting on largely unsubstantiated preconceptions, it seems that our notions of the Bach style itself have been unjustifiably restricted and marked by our inability to imagine that the greatest master of the arts of counterpoint, the "fifth evangelist," could, at certain times and on certain appropriate occasions, also deliberately cultivate a lighter, more popular idiom.

A proper understanding of the music has also been hindered by one further assumption: that Bach's music is in some particularly profound way abstract, "pure" music—*musica mundana*. Bach, in this view, was, in the most literal sense, "profoundly" unconcerned about the actual sounding, acoustical realization of his creations, unconcerned about their technical difficulties or their idiomatic effectiveness, and "sublimely" unaware of the abilities of the musicians actually available to him.[94] But perhaps Bach was quite concerned about all these things. As noted above, the flute parts in the works known to have been written for Köthen are quite simple; and in the permutation fugue Bach developed a choral form that was relatively easy for young, nonprofessional singers to learn; finally, the opening choruses of the chorale cantatas make use characteristically of a simple soprano *cantus firmus* that obviously takes cognizance of the limitations of young children. Conversely, the trumpet parts of the Leipzig cantatas surely testify to the specific, perhaps unique, abilities of the brilliant virtuoso, Gottfried Reiche, Bach's regular trumpeter. And there is, in the last analysis, no reason not to assume that Bach—who was presumably able to play all of his own keyboard music—had personal knowledge of, say, a violinist who would have been able to play the unaccompanied sonatas and partitas (Pisendel? whose own sonata for unaccompanied violin is in some ways technically more difficult than Bach's), or a flute player—who shall remain nameless—who would have been able to play the opening Allemande of the A-minor Partita or the concluding gigue of the B-minor Sonata.

And there is every objective indication that it may in fact have mattered more to Bach than to most of his contemporaries whether, say, an ensemble sonata was played by a particular solo instrument. None of the original sources, definitely none of the surviving autographs, suggest that any sonata for melody instrument and keyboard could be played, for example, alternatively on "violino o flauto traverso." Could it be that Bach had a quite definite conception of the proper style of music for the flute that was clearly different from music for solo violin, that music for the one instrument should not necessarily be played (or even playable) or be effective on the other, that is, that he was "profoundly" concerned about the "instrumental, sounding, and other performance-related realities" (Eppstein, p. 32)?

When Bach made the acquaintance of the transverse flute it was preeminently a French instrument nourished by a French repertoire—a musical tradition characterized by light textures, clearly articulated phrases, and dance-inspired rhythms and forms. Should it be unimaginable or even particularly surprising that in his own chamber music for the instrument Bach would frequently wish to draw on this fresh style and not invariably impress upon it all the compositional rigor and sophistication at his command?

To summarize briefly: A review of the sources, in conjunction with a consideration of some neglected biographical information and a number of stylistic observations, has suggested the outlines of a chronology of Bach's music for solo flute.

1. The first of Bach's flute compositions seems to have been the unaccompanied partita, BWV 1013, a work presumably composed around 1718 for Pierre Gabriel Buffardin, whom Bach would have met in Dresden in the fall of 1717.

2. The C-major Sonata, BWV 1033, too, may have been composed originally as an unaccompanied work at around the same time—or even slightly earlier.

3. The earliest, lost, versions—if such indeed existed—of the two sonatas for flute and harpsichord obbligato, BWV 1030 and 1032, may have been composed, in different instrumentations, in Köthen.[94a]

4. The E-minor Sonata, BWV 1034, may have been composed in the [mid–1720s] in Leipzig (that is, shortly before the probable date of the earliest surviving manuscript) at a time when Bach was writing an elaborate series of obbligato flute parts in his church cantatas—in themselves an indication that he then enjoyed the services of a virtuoso of the first rank.

5. The G-minor version of BWV 1030, now scored for flute and harpsichord obbligato, may have been prepared (or composed) around

1729, perhaps in connection with Bach's having assumed the directorship of the Collegium Musicum.

6. Sometime in the early 1730s, and before 1734, Bach probably composed the E-flat Sonata for flute and harpsichord obbligato (BWV 1031). The composition then evidently served as a model for Philipp Emanuel Bach's Sonata in G minor for violin and harpsichord (BWV 1020).

7. At about the same time, perhaps in the year 1731, Bach may have prepared (or composed) the C-major version of BWV 1032.

8. Fair copies of both BWV 1030 and 1032, the former transposed on this occasion to B minor, the latter to A major, were prepared about 1736, perhaps, again, with a view towards a performance with the Collegium Musicum in Leipzig—or, conceivably by Buffardin in Dresden.

9. BWV 1035 was probably composed at the time of Bach's first known visit to Potsdam, in 1741, for Frederick the Great's flute partner, Fredersdorf.

Bach's involvement with the flute as a solo chamber instrument, then, apparently was not restricted to his five-and-a-half year sojourn in Köthen but rather spanned close to a quarter-century of his maturity, extending from around 1718 to around 1741.

Since the second world war Bach research has been dominated, appropriately, by textual criticism.[95] But the text-critical techniques that have achieved such sensational results in investigations of Bach's vocal music seem to have reached—or are rapidly approaching—their limits in dealing with his instrumental music, since (as mentioned at the outset) virtually no primary sources for these compositions survive, and it is not very likely that many new ones will turn up. Faced with such a situation we can obviously either abandon the effort to solve the remaining problems, or we can attempt to approach them anew. We should, at the least, attempt to augment the meager, fragmentary, inadequate or contradictory source evidence we might have with whatever potentially enlightening information we are able to obtain from other domains.

Two important areas of Bach research that have stood in the shadow of textual criticism over the past few decades—biographical studies and stylistic analysis—have in fact registered substantial achievements during that time as well.[96] But until now these three disciplines have largely been pursued independently of one another, indeed by different specialists in each case. I suspect that in the future the most important advances in Bach scholarship are likely to be achieved only by uniting these disciplines.

Of course, it is possible, indeed probable, that even if we make this effort, we shall never be able to obtain the quality of proof and verifiability we have become accustomed to. But do we really have much choice?

Postscript

Hans Eppstein's "Zur Problematik von Johann Sebastian Bachs Flötensonaten" (Eppstein 1981) is a direct rejoinder to the preceding essay. In it the author reaffirms his earlier assertions against the authenticity of the E-flat and C-major sonatas. There is little point in extending the debate for another round here; for Eppstein presents no fresh evidence in support of his position. As in his previous discussion of this issue (Eppstein 1972), the new argument is based entirely on stylistic criteria. Again he succeeds admirably in demonstrating that the compositions, as I put it in my essay, "are not typical of J. S. Bach." That is, they do not conform to the traditional, romantic (and romanticized) understanding of Bach inherited from the nineteenth century. The critical stance, once again, reflects, in my opinion, "an underestimation of . . . and a refusal to acknowledge" the breadth, the range, and the variety of Bach's style.

Why should Johann Sebastian Bach, any more than Mozart or Beethoven, have been "incapable" of composing, on occasion, in a lighter, less rigorous vein? Or, for that matter, less capable of producing anything other than masterpieces of the first order? The eminent Mozart scholar Wolfgang Plath once observed, "What we really need to know is not how well but how 'poorly' Mozart was able to compose,"[1] and pointed out that a number of works once considered, on stylistic grounds, to be spurious later turned out in fact to be by Mozart.[2]

In the postscript to "Bach the Progressive" (Chapter 2) I have already had to return to these issues in connection with Frederick Neumann's attempt to deny Bach's authorship of the theme of the "Goldberg" Variations. I referred to the undeniably authentic "Peasant" and "Coffee" Cantatas. It is surely inconceivable that these slight and silly works would ever have been accepted as authentic works by J. S. Bach under the earlier dispensation, if they did not happen to survive in autograph composing scores. And yet Bach did compose them—and rather late in his life at that. The moral should be clear.

IV

*Aspects of
Performance
Practice*

13

"AUTHENTIC" PERFORMANCE
Musical Text, Performing Forces, Performance Style (a Review Essay)*

What can a Bach scholar say about a plan to record the complete cantatas, under the direction of two of the most enlightened musicians on the current scene, and with as much fidelity to Bach's own intentions as we can possibly hope to achieve? He can begin by mentioning the obvious. The project is auspicious—one, incidentally, that had been proposed (as wishful thinking, perhaps) in the pages of this journal twenty years ago[1] but has only become possible—and then all but inevitable—in recent years. (At this moment, in fact, there are two projects under way with the aim of making all the surviving Bach cantatas available on records. In addition to Telefunken's intention to record all the numbered cantatas in order from BWV 1 through, presumably, BWV 216, the Claudius-Verlag of Munich has begun to release recordings under the direction of Helmuth Rilling mainly of those cantatas not currently on the market; this series will be distributed domestically by The Musical Heritage Society.)[1a] He must go on to acknowledge not only that Nikolaus Harnoncourt's Bach interpretations are quite well known—through his earlier recordings of the Brandenburg Concertos, Orchestral Suites, St. John and St. Matthew Passions, and the B-minor Mass—but that they are extremely controversial. The opposing arguments, which have been forcefully presented by eminent proponents of both sides—in part and very recently in the editorial pages of *The Musical Quarterly*[2]—are equally familiar to all interested readers and listeners. And since the basic critical positions have long since hardened, the chances of changing minds on the matter at this time are surely remote. But that will not be the purpose of this review.

Anyone considering these performances and the controversy surrounding them soon realizes that the conflicting assessments are not reflections of personal taste alone. The dispute centers to a great extent on the claim to "authenticity" asserted by the artists and producers of the Telefunken Bach recordings in their attempt to reconstruct the original scoring, instruments, performance techniques and styles. Accordingly, the initiation of the Telefunken series provides a fitting occasion to take stock of the present state of our knowledge—and ignorance—of baroque performance practice in general and of Bach's in particular and to consider the significance of several recent developments and directions in Bach research for our present understanding of "authenticity" in Bach.[2a]

THE MUSICAL TEXT

How authentic, first of all, is the musical text—the edition—used for the Telefunken project? Since the cantatas are being produced in the standard order of the old Bach-Gesellschaft edition (miniature scores reproduced from the BG are in fact included in each album) the implication is that the BG edition is authentic enough, at least for the purposes of these recordings. Is it? In his program notes for the St. Matthew Passion and B-minor Mass recordings Harnoncourt emphasized that he personally consulted the original scores and parts for the works. He thus suggested that the BG edition (and in the case of the Mass even the *Neue Bach-Ausgabe*) is not necessarily a trustworthy guide to the authentic text and that the truly responsible performer must turn to the sources himself. Indeed, the quality of both the BG and NBA is mixed. Occasionally, the BG edition has turned out to be more authentic—better—than that of the NBA.[3] And it may be that in the case of the only cantata among the eight under discussion here which [had] already appeared in the NBA [at the time the recordings were made]—BWV 6—Harnoncourt was well advised (or fortunate) to ignore the new edition and to base his performance on the BG or, conceivably, on his own redaction of the sources.[4] For even though Moritz Hauptmann, the editor of the first volume of the BG, did not prepare Cantata No. 6 from the original sources (although they would have been available to him) but on the nineteenth-century copies of them, the readings in a number of particulars seem to me—after a definitely casual comparison—to be preferable to those printed in the NBA.[5] The reason may be that the NBA edition of Cantata No. 6, like that of the BG, appears in an early volume of the edition. Here, however, limited experience did not lead to a casual attitude toward the original sources, but on the contrary to one of uncompromising and, occasionally, pedantic *Quellentreue*. In the case of BWV 6 this resulted in a number of unconvincing inconsistencies such as the treatment of slurs, trills, and so on, in corresponding sections or simultaneous lines of movements.[5a]

In general, though, the NBA offers the better text. And while the differences between the old and new editions for any given composition as a rule are relatively few and concerned with relatively minor details, there have been instances already where the NBA has been able to offer dramatically superior readings. In Volume I/12, for example, an obbligato part for the tenor aria, "Ich will an den Himmel denken," from Cantata No. 166, omitted in the BG edition, is reconstructed almost entirely; and fourteen measures of the tenor aria, "Mein Jesus soll mein Alles sein," BWV 75/3, have been restored in NBA I/15.

In regard to textual authenticity, then, the Telefunken project is assuming some risk whenever it records any work—such as Cantata Nos. 1–5, 7–8—that has not yet been published in the NBA. Shortcomings similar to those in the BG editions of BWV 75 and 166 conceivably exist in one or another of these seven cantatas. But the likelihood that many more failings on that order in the BG have still not been discovered seems to me too remote to justify a recommendation that future recordings in the series be synchronized with the progress of the NBA and thus be prolonged over twenty years or more.[6] On the other hand, it would clearly be absurd to ignore the NBA when it is there: the Rilling recording of BWV 75 omits the fourteen measures in the tenor aria.[7]

THE PERFORMING FORCES

The truly authentic performance of a composition has always been expected to be faithful to all the known hard historical facts pertaining to performance practice at the time the work was written. But we are now wise enough to realize that not all the known facts may be relevant; and many of them may even contradict each other. This touches the heart of the authenticity dispute, which is primarily a matter not of facts but of discretion. The attributes of authenticity can readily be agreed upon, but they can be so variously evaluated in relation to one another that unanimity on even the "objective" criteria for judging a conscientious, that is, historically minded, performance of older music will never readily be attained. In addition, the question of authenticity involves a crucial dimension of historical focus raised by Professor Lang in his critique of Harnoncourt's Bach performances[8] which I should like to formulate as follows: Even if we could determine precisely what *all* the facts are and then go on to reconstruct the original historical situation in every detail, we still would not be justified to claim authenticity unless we had established that the particular factual constellation was intentional and not accidental. In his famous memorandum of 1730, Bach, after all, documented the qualitative and quantitative inadequacies of his singers and players.

Harnoncourt is quite aware of all this, though; and, as he puts it in the program notes to the B-minor Mass, his aim has been to reconstruct not the actual sound of J. S. Bach's performances but the type of sound Bach would have considered "optimal." His success in this, too, however, has been disputed. For Dr. Lang's point is not just that the immediate playing conditions in Bach's churches were poor but that they were untypical. Moreover, the local aesthetics that underlay and were perhaps responsible for the local conditions contradicted the aesthetic that prevailed in the larger musical world at the time—and was shared (according to Lang) by J. S. Bach. What really has to be determined, then, is whether the style and structure—the "spirit," if you will—of the music itself was more definitively shaped by the larger or smaller historical context.

Walter Kolneder has shown[9] that the unique texture of Bach's concerto style, with its intricately motivic and contrapuntal interplay between solo and tutti, presupposes the small, indeed miniature, ensemble at Bach's disposal in Köthen; just as, on the other hand, there is a direct correlation between the simpler textures and the coloristic emphasis on stark tutti–solo contrasts in the concertos of the Italians Corelli, Torelli, Vivaldi, and the larger, sometimes enormous, string ensembles available in Rome, Bologna, and Venice. Now, it is possible to demonstrate that the conditions under which Bach composed his church cantatas just as profoundly influenced his treatment of this genre as they did his approach to the concerto. The typical intoning of the unadorned chorale *cantus firmus* by the sopranos in the opening choruses of most of the chorale cantatas—often reinforced by some wind instrument—while the lower voices engage in a relatively complex contrapuntal commentary reflects the fact that the soprano part had to be simple enough to be quickly learned and adequately sung by young boys. The obvious technical and musical limitations of boy sopranos also help explain why the soprano appears only once as a soloist in these eight cantatas in what can be considered a vocally elaborate aria: BWV 1/3.[10] In the chorale aria "Ach bleib bei uns," BWV 6/3, the soprano sings a bare chorale *cantus firmus* in long notes. The neutral quality of the boy's voice here is altogether appropriate for the abstract, organ-like character of this part in a way that a mature woman's voice would not be.

Bach's extensive cultivation of the "permutation fugue" in cantata choruses before he turned to the chorale-cantata genre had a similar rationale. The technique obliged each member of the chorus to learn only four or five phrases: the four or five mutually invertible contrapuntal elements. These were then kaleidoscopically combined and recombined from one end of the fugue to the other,[11] "automatically" generating a highly unified yet varied composition that never overtaxed the technical capacities or the musicianship of the choir boys of the Thomasschule.

These examples are offered in illustration of the fact that during the late baroque the composer in a particular milieu inherited a local performance practice together with a performance ideal. Both not only left the deepest imprint on the externals of his personal style but helped inspire his musical imagination. The examples are offered also—turning to the performances under review—in support and approval of the Telefunken decision to use boy sopranos and, by extension, an all-male chorus.

The approval cannot be extended unconditionally to the employment of original or reconstructed eighteenth-century instruments in these recordings. The use of old instruments inevitably creates difficult problems relating to pitch, tuning, and intonation; and it is not clear that Harnoncourt and Leonhardt have always been successful in resolving them. It is hard not to be skeptical, for example, about the authenticity of Harnoncourt's adoption of a very low tuning (based, as he indicates in a private communication that has come to my attention, on $a' = 421$), in view of the evidence brought together by Arthur Mendel in support of his contention that the basic *Kammerton* pitch in Bach's day was no lower than it is now.[12] Harnoncourt may have persuasive, even historical, justification for this decision. If he does, it ought to be set forth somewhere.

Harnoncourt does present his views in reference to intonation,[13] maintaining that the construction of early-eighteenth-century instruments accounted for the numerous coloristic and tonal inflections that arose when playing in different keys and that these to a large extent determined the affective character associated at the time with each key. This seems at first quite plausible; and the prospect that the modern listener after some exposure to old instruments would eventually acquire the same sensitivity to their subtle shadings that the eighteenth-century listener allegedly had is attractive indeed. But this view has to be reconciled with the fact that such mechanical limitations differed radically from one type of instrument to the other. And since the various instruments were called upon to play together in the same pieces—often in unison—one of the primary responsibilities of eighteenth-century players necessarily had to be to minimize as much as possible the discrepancies between the unlimited tonal flexibility of string instruments on the one hand, and the relatively or severely reduced control over intonation available on woodwinds and brasses. Therefore, it is not at all clear that the "colorful and continuous changes of nuances"[14] encountered—by modern players, in any event—in the use of cross fingerings on the one-key flute and the two-key oboe were in fact appreciated or even tolerated at the time. They may well have been considered (like the clicking of the keys audible rather frequently on these records) imperfections that the expert player would attempt, with a large degree of success, to eliminate.[15]

It is questionable, too, whether Harnoncourt and Leonhardt have managed to overcome all the difficulties entailed in reconstructing a thoroughly authentic instrumentarium. While there is no reason to doubt the authenticity—and, in my opinion, the general artistic success—of the standard orchestral instruments (violins, oboes, trumpets, recorders, traversi, etc.), there is a question as to whether some of the more exceptional instruments have been accurately recreated. I suspect that the solo instrument used in BWV 6/3, for example, is not Bach's own "violoncello piccolo,"[16] but rather a normal (baroque) cello. And the enclosed literature reveals that the wind instrument used to reinforce the chorale *cantus firmus* in the first and last movements of BWV 5, designated *Tromba da tirarsi* in the original parts, is an alto trombone (or *Zugtrompete*) in E-flat. But Bach may have had in mind the instrument illustrated in Filippo Bonanni's *Gabinetto Armonico* of 1723 as the *Altra Tromba Spezzata,* where the player slid the entire instrument back and forth on the neck of the mouthpiece.[17] While granting that there may well be little appreciable difference between the timbre of the violoncello piccolo vis-à-vis the standard (baroque) cello, Bach, who reputedly invented the former, must have thought there was enough. And we are not justified in dismissing without good reason what seems to have been a careful differentiation by Bach between *Trombone, Cornetto, Corno, Corno da tirarsi, Tromba,* and *Tromba da tirarsi.*[17a]

Of considerable consequence, in any event, were artistic decisions affecting the scoring of the continuo. Beyond the facts that Bach used the organ almost exclusively for the continuo realization in his church music[17b]—a practice observed in the Telefunken performances—and that the continuo line was normally reinforced by two additional "foundation" instruments, we know little about his specific practice. What rationale, for example, governed the octave doubling of the continuo line? The opening of Cantata No. 2, *Ach Gott vom Himmel sieh' darein,* to take a particular instance, is a chorale motet for four-part chorus with colla parte instruments and an independent continuo line. Throughout the movement the continuo line frequently crosses above the vocal bass line, while the figures in such passages indicate that the continuo was considered by Bach to represent the true harmonic bass. This was perhaps understood by Harnoncourt to imply, perhaps demand, con-

trabass doubling by a violone. Harnoncourt may well be right; but the
decision could be disputed. Not only does the continuo often cross
above the bass; it is also led in unison with it (mm. 161-166), and quite
often it explicitly doubles the vocal bass an octave lower (mm. 36-44,
86-94, 114-115). In mm. 119-135 all three relationships—unison, crossing, and octave doubling—appear in rapid succession and alternation.
The effect of this is weakened when the continuo is doubled at the
lower octave throughout. Therefore, one could maintain that where
Bach desired contrabass doubling he explicitly notated it or prescribed
it by specifically designating one of the continuo parts *Violone* or *Bassono gross*.[18] Indeed, in arias for bass voice with reduced instrumental
forces (such as the continuo aria "Empfind ich Höllenangst und Pein,"
BWV 3/3) where contrabass doubling is most unlikely, and indeed not
supplied in the Harnoncourt performance,[19] Bach still allows the continuo and vocal bass lines to cross. There seems, then, to be reason for
believing that Bach, and perhaps the late baroque in general, conceived
of obbligato bass and continuo lines as belonging to two distinct strata
within a composition which were to a large degree "heard" separately.
The instrumental continuo was to be perceived at all times as the true
harmonic bass even when some other part incidentally crossed below
it. There is clearly a need for a study of Bach's continuo scoring based
on analysis of the music, a consultation of the theoretical sources, and a
more extensive examination of the autographs and original performing
materials than has been undertaken heretofore.[20] But practical experience resulting from the kind of experimentation surely being conducted
in the course of the Telefunken recording sessions, if it were ultimately
reported, would obviously have unique musicological value.[21]

The wisdom, finally, of adhering to the absolute size and the proportions of Bach's preferred ensemble, as these are set forth in the 1730
memorandum, has been questioned. The bright sound of the smaller ensemble undoubtedly comes at first as something of a shock. But the employment of the small ensemble seems to me to be artistically sound as
well as historically correct.[21a] On the one hand, not only is the texture
of relatively elaborate contrapuntal movements such as choral fugues
rendered more "transparent," but, in losing much of their accustomed
weight, these choruses also cast off the weighty sluggishness which has
so regularly attended Bach performances by large ensembles that we
have come to assume it to be a quality inherent in the style, perhaps
regarding it as an attribute of profundity. In homophonic movements,
too—arias or duets (e.g., BWV 3/5, 4/4, 6/5)—in which florid melodic
lines are to be performed in unison, the reduced forces permit a degree of rhythmic flexibility approaching that of the soloist with whom
the unison players are often engaged in contrapuntal dialogue. In such
musical situations we become aware of the existence of a fusion of

performance medium and performance style as compelling for the interpreter as the mutual interdependence of performing conditions and ideals (described above) represents for the composer.

THE PERFORMANCE STYLE

The artists participating in the Telefunken series demonstrate to a remarkable degree not only their knowledge of the conventions associated with Bach performance but in addition their empathetic grasp of the spirit informing these conventions. In observing, for example, the eighteenth-century practice of sustaining continuo notes in recitatives for only a fraction of their written value, the notes are not shortened uniformly but are held for a longer or shorter time as seems appropriate for the affective content of the text.[22] The same musicality and intelligence is evident in the discrete vocal or instrumental embellishments added in the da-capo sections of some arias (e.g., BWV 3/3, 5/5), or in the rendition of end-line fermatas in chorale settings. Similarly, tempos, while considerably faster in most cases than those one is accustomed to, rarely seem hurried or nervous.[23]

This instinct for capturing the essence of a convention is on one occasion so acute that the performers permit themselves to disregard what Bach allegedly wrote down himself (assuming they were aware of it) in order to play a variant that he would surely have approved. For the bass aria "'Empfind' ich Höllenangst und Pein," BWV 3/3, a continuo realization for the first fifteen measures survives in what has been taken to be Bach's hand.[24] According to this source (whose actual provenance has [now been] established) the right hand was to supply a modest three-part chordal accompaniment that rather mechanically marks the quarter-note pulse in each phrase (Ex. 13.1a).

Example 13.1a.   BWV 3/3: Rhythm of continuo realization in the hand of Christian Friedrich Penzel

While retaining a similar rudimentary harmonization, Harnoncourt's organist quite effectively and validly alters the rhythm of the right hand to provide a more structurally meaningful if even simpler pattern (Ex. 13.1b).

Example 13.1b.   BWV 3/3: Rhythm of continuo realization in Harnoncourt performance

With respect to ornamentation, it is no small irony that just as performers have begun to discover, appreciate, and apply old musicological lessons on the proper execution of trills, ornaments, and other nuances in the music of Bach, these same prescriptions have been thrown into question by further musicological research itself. In particular, several articles published by Frederick Neumann during the 1960s[25] potentially offer almost as profound a challenge to the prevailing musicological wisdom in regard to Bach performance as the chronology established by Alfred Dürr and Georg von Dadelsen during the 1950s represented for the traditional understanding of Bach's biography and artistic development. In many respects, Neumann's proposals seem on first reading to contradict directly and radically the interpretation of baroque performance conventions first propounded over fifty years ago by Arnold Dolmetsch and elaborated upon since by many intelligent scholars and musicians. For Neumann contends that the French system of *notes inégales* does not apply to Bach's music; that the doctrine of overdotting in the overture style is a myth; finally, that—as dictated by good taste—trills may just as well begin on the principal note as on the upper auxiliary and, along with grace notes of all kinds, may begin before or "straddling" the beat as well as on it. The theoretical and practical documentation that Neumann has already presented and continues to amass in support of his views is impressive.

My suspicion is that Neumann's ideas were unknown to Leonhardt and Harnoncourt at the time they recorded these eight cantatas, and perhaps are unknown to them still. But this suspicion cannot be unambiguously confirmed or discounted on the evidence of the recordings alone. Paradoxically, the (presumed) ignorance of these new theories on baroque performance practice does not here—and perhaps rarely will—make much real difference in the audible gestalt of any competent historical performance of baroque music. For although, like many first discoverers of precedent shattering truths, Neumann has been tempted from time to time to be overly doctrinaire in advancing his findings, these discoveries are not a total repudiation of our accustomed understanding of the baroque conventions but only of their inflexible, rigid application. The general principles, for the most part, remain valid: trills should, after all, normally, if not always, begin on the upper auxiliary and on the beat. And since the start of each individual trill or grace note lasts only an instant, the audible difference between a performance in which all the ornaments are rigorously executed according to the rules and one in which they are usually but not exclusively so performed would—all other things being equal—surely be negligible. (In fact, however, a performance characterized by a relentlessly uniform rendition of the ornaments would almost surely betray a mechanical rigidity in other musical respects as well.) At all events, the execution of the embellishments in these recordings is musicologically orthodox but not fussy. Here, too, the performers have evidently assimilated the essence of the conventions and can apply them un-self-consciously.

This, unfortunately, is not always the case in regard to the liberties they take with agogics and dynamics. Many of these liberties are unobtrusive and convincing—perhaps falling within the framework of "agogic articulation" approved of by Neumann as "one of the many freedoms inherent in a flexible performance."[26] Others constitute an inappropriate or exaggerated application of "the rules." The consistent rendering of the figure Ex. 13.2a from the ritornello of BWV 1/5 (mm. 5–6 and analogous measures) as it is shown in Ex. 13.2b is a disturbing—and invalid—use of the French *inégales*.

Example 13.2a.   BWV 1/5, mm. 5–6: Violino I, II concertante

Example 13.2b.   BWV 1/5, mm. 5–6: Harnoncourt rendition

Other agogic, and particularly, dynamic mannerisms introduced in the declared service of a motive-oriented, rhetorical conception of phrasing[27] result all too frequently in a short-winded articulation of phrases and motives that is rather affected than affective. Such exaggerations as the rendition of staccatos and legatos in the opening ritornello of the St. Matthew Passion criticized by Lang[28] and the widely fluctuating *messa di voce* (particularly in the strings) as in the themes in Ex. 13.3a and 13.3b must surely be a caricature of what was in fact eighteenth-century practice.[28a] Moreover, this overly "expressive" string playing contradicts the "neutral" sound and expression implied by the use of boy's voices. And this incongruity or tension, like that existing between the flexible intonation of the strings and the limited

Example 13.3a.   BWV 1/1, m. 1: Violino II concertante, Harnoncourt rendition

Example 13.3b.   BWV 2/5, mm. 1–3a: Violino I, Harnoncourt rendition

tonal control of the winds mentioned above, prevents these performances from achieving a completely convincing stylistic unity.

It would be unfair to conclude on such a disapproving note; for this essay is intended as a strongly favorable review of the Telefunken project. The astounding accomplishments of both the Concentus Musicus and the Leonhardt Consort in the light of formidable difficulties have been so highly praised so often, however, that it would have been rather patronizing and pointless to issue further mere compliments here. Moreover, I feel compelled rather to append a somewhat embarrassing confession: for pure enjoyment I would prefer to listen to the Bach performances of, say, Karl Richter or Helmuth Rilling, with their straightforward phrasing and articulation, their impeccable intonation and familiar timbres, and their admittedly loose approximation to authenticity.[29] But I must add at once that my delight in the Telefunken performances has grown with each hearing. Like so many new and unfamiliar experiences, they obviously demand a lot of getting used to. There can be little doubt that beauty, its recognition, and its delectation are direct functions of familiarity and that we must be on our guard not to judge the aesthetic validity—much less the historical authenticity—of any rendition of an artwork by our first (or even ultimate) response to it. The notion that "Beauty is truth, truth beauty" may be a poet's profound wisdom, but it is a seductive, if splendid, fallacy for the historian.

14

"EDITORE TRADITORE"
Suspicious Performance Indications in the Bach Sources

Anyone who has had occasion to examine the original sources of the works of Johann Sebastian Bach knows that they often contain a multitude of variants, internal contradictions, ambiguous readings, and a not inconsiderable number of plain mistakes. This state of affairs inevitably confronts an editor of Bach's music with an array of uncommonly difficult, if not indeed simply insoluble problems: problems that appear in particular concentration and in a particularly intractable form with respect to articulation, or, more specifically, with respect to slurring—what Georg von Dadelsen has described as "Die Crux der Nebensache" (The Crux of the Trivial) in an article of that name.[1] Needless to say, these problems, and their resolution (successful or not), are ultimately passed on to the performer.

As von Dadelsen remarks, the most elusive editorial problems usually result from the ambiguous placement of Bach's own slurring indications—markings that the composer evidently added, at least in the case of the original performing parts of his vocal works, in great haste and at "the last moment," or, in his composing scores, as an afterthought or private cue. To quote von Dadelsen:

> When Bach was in a hurry, slurs placed over the notes are usually too high above them, or they are shifted to one side, or they are written so small that it is impossible to know at first glance whether they are

241

meant to apply to the entire group or just a portion of it. If one were to take them at their face, the results would be thoroughly irrational and arbitrary. Slurs below the notes are as a rule not symmetrically curved but rather begin with a fine line at the left, then thicken substantially before being extended towards the right. Often enough they begin too far to the right. . . . Therefore, it is easy to read them as applying just to the second-to-fourth notes [of a four-note group, for example] rather than to all four or perhaps just to the first three notes of the group.[2]

As von Dadelsen attempts to show throughout his article, it is often possible to resolve these ambiguities by carefully considering both the immediate context and the treatment of corresponding, or parallel sections (repeated passages and the like) and also by developing a familiarity with Bach's script and writing habits. Of course, even then one can rarely achieve more than a rendering that is consistent and plausible and that just may reflect Bach's intention. But that can almost never be proven. What one quite frankly settles for in most cases, then, is a fairly reasonable fiction.

In light of this situation one's initial response on those rare occasions where the slurring in a Bach manuscript was evidently entered with particular precision is one of pleasant surprise approaching elation. A moment's reflection, however, often suggests that the circumstance is too good to be true. Such slurs are especially striking—and suspicious—when they appear not in the original parts but in an original score. The autograph score of the cantata *Herr, deine Augen sehen nach dem Glauben*, BWV 102, P 97, is clearly a composing score throughout. In Movements 1, 3, and 4, however, it contains a number of slurs—in Movement 4 staccato dots as well—that were entered with a fine pen point and blackish ink. It is not possible, though, on the basis of appearance alone, to determine with any certainty, whether or not these slurs and dots are autograph (see Plate 35). Their ink color clearly differs from the other slurs found in the score which, like the score itself, are entered in a dark brown ink.[3] Among the figures bearing one of these blackish slurs is the principal motif of the cantata, which is articulated as shown in Ex. 14.1.[4]

Example 14.1.   BWV 102/1, mm. 1–2: Oboe I. P 97, f. 1ʳ

This pattern was adopted by Wilhelm Rust in his edition of the cantata in Volume 23 of the *Bach-Gesellschaft* edition (BG).

It would be quite untypical in any case for Bach to have so carefully entered the articulation of a motif in a composing score—and to have

PLATE 35.   Autograph score, P 97, f. 1ʳ (top): BWV 102/1, mm. 1–11a

done so, indeed, not just at its first appearance but at many recurrences as well. In the present instance we can be certain that the slurs—at least in Movement 1-are *not* Bach's. For it so happens that a quite reliable control of their authenticity exists. It is a score—SPK P 98—that was prepared around 1800 by the Hamburg musician Christian Gottlieb Schwencke (1767-1822), a Kirnberger pupil who early on served as an accompanist for C. P. E. Bach and ultimately was to be C. P. E. Bach's successor as director of church music for the city of Hamburg.

Schwencke had had access to Johann Sebastian Bach's music as early as 1779. A comparison of the slurring reveals that the questionable slurs in the autograph are all absent from Schwencke's score, whereas those slurs that were doubtless entered by *Bach* in the autograph—in brown ink—are all present in Schwencke's score—at least those in the instrumental parts. We have, in addition, two further sources—a score and a set of parts—that derive from the largely lost, original performing parts of the cantata. These sources preserve the original version of the cantata as it read before it was significantly revised by C. P. E. Bach (see below). Of these two manuscripts, the score was written out entirely, the set of parts to a large extent, by one S. Hering, a musician about whom little is known except that he served as a copyist for C. P. E. Bach in Berlin in the 1760s. (The pertinent sources for Cantata No. 102 are summarized in Table 14.1).

TABLE 14.1   The Sources for Cantata No. 102: Original Version

Source	Location and Shelf Number
A. Autograph Composing Score	P 97
B. Two Original Performing Parts	
1. *Soprano*	St 41
2. *Continuo*	bound with P 97
C. Set of Thirteen Parts,	West Berlin: Hochschule der
ca. 1760 (S. Hering et al.)	Künste: 6138/5
D. Score Copy,	SPK P 48/3
ca. 1760 (S. Hering)	
E. Score Copy, Movement 1,	
ca. 1800 (C. G. Schwencke)	SPK P 98

It can be demonstrated (1) that the Hering parts were copied directly from the (largely lost) original parts and (2) that Hering apparently copied his score from his own newly copied set of parts but occasionally in addition consulted the original parts directly—especially with regard to the placement slurs.[5] In Hering's score, SPK P 48, the slurs of the principal motif in the opening ritornello read unambiguously, as in Ex. 14.2.

Example 14.2.   BWV 102/1, mm. 1–2: Oboe I. (SPK) P 48/3

This pattern was also the *original* slurring in the Hering parts and was presumably also the slurring found in the lost, original, parts.[6] In the Hering parts, however, this pattern was changed, by a second hand, to the slurring found in the autograph (see Plate 36). In fact, the Hering parts contain a large number of slurs that were added in a grayish-black ink (and with a fine penpoint). They can be readily distinguished in most cases from the original Hering slurs that were penned in brown ink. Most of these grayish-black slurs are completely new, that is, they were added at points where there were previously no slurs at all in the manuscript. Frequently, however, the original slurs entered by Hering were in effect canceled and altered by the new ones, in that the new slurs were written directly over the old ones and are obviously intended as changes. There are a considerable number of additional slurs in the most important instrumental parts: in the oboe and violin parts of the opening chorus; in the solo oboe part of the alto aria "Weh der Seele" (Movement 3); in the strings and principal continuo part of the

PLATE 36.   Anonymous copyist ("Anonymous 307") of Carl Philipp Emanuel
Bach's circle, with later altered or added articulation markings,
Hochschule für Musik, Berlin-Charlottenburg, 6138[5], p. 1 (= f.
2[v]): BWV 102/1, mm. 1–23a: *Hautbois Primo*

bass aria "Verachtest du den Reichtum seiner Gnade" (Movement 4);
and in the obbligato flute part for the tenor aria "Erschrecke doch"
(Movement 5). The newly added slurs are particularly extensive in the
obbligato wind parts of Movements 3 and 5. Moreover, these new slurs
are highly differentiated, musically intelligent, and convincing; and they
are executed with the care and precision that a modern editor longs for
but really never finds in the original Bach sources (see Plates 37 and
38). All of these slurs, too, were incorporated by Wilhelm Rust in his
edition of the cantata.

What is the origin of these slurs? Who was responsible for them—
both those in the autograph score and those in the Hering parts? It is
clear, first of all, that the new slurs in the autograph could not have
been introduced before ca. 1800—the time when the Schwencke score
(which does not contain them) was copied. Second, it is striking that
the new articulation marks found in the autograph correspond with
those in the Hering parts—to the far more limited extent that they are
present.[7]

In addition to the sources for *Herr, deine Augen* just discussed, there
are others as well. All of them, however, record an entirely discrete,
and posthumous, version of the work—one issuing from the pen of
Carl Philipp Emanuel Bach.[8] Sometime after J. S. Bach's death, Philipp
Emanuel subjected the cantata to a quite extensive revision. Part of
the process of his revision is reflected in a series of corrections and

PLATE 37.   Hochschule für Musik, p. 3 (= f. 1ᵛ): BWV 102/3, mm. 1–10a: *Hautbois Primo*

PLATE 38.   Anonymous copyist ("Anonymous 300") of Carl Philipp Emanuel Bach's circle, with later altered or added articulation markings, Hochschule für Musik, p. 1: BWV 102/5, mm. 1–19: *Traversière*

cross-outs penned (in brown ink) in the two surviving original parts (see Plate 39). The resulting version, like the original, consists of seven movements, but there are some major differences, as outlined in Table 14.2.

All the movements in C. P. E. Bach's version, with the exception of the final chorale, contain changes of greater or lesser magnitude vis-à-vis J. S. Bach's original, ranging from minor details of harmony in the opening chorus, to substantial rewriting of the vocal lines in the two recitatives (associated in the secco recitative—Movement 2—with a completely new text), to the addition of a string section to the recitativo accompagnato (Movement 6). The most striking difference between the two versions, however, is the deletion of the alto aria, "Weh der Seele."[9]

PLATE 39. Original Continuo Part of BWV 102, P 97/3, with C. P. E. Bach's alterations.
a) F. 1ᵛ: End of Movement 2 with deletion of Movement 3
b) F. 2ᵛ: Indication for the insertion of a chorale between Movements 4 and 5

That is, one of the movements for which the Hering parts displayed an especially large number of added and altered slurs (Plate 37) is completely absent from C. P. E. Bach's arrangement of the cantata.

The fact that all surviving nineteenth-century sources of Cantata No. 102—including a published edition—transmit the work in C. P. E. Bach's version[10] is one of considerable historical importance. It reveals, first of all, that from about 1830 at the latest until the appearance of the BG edition in 1876 the work was known mainly—perhaps exclusively—in C. P. E. Bach's revision. Furthermore, this version was apparently considered to be the original—J. S. Bach's own. None of the later nineteenth-century sources contain any comment to the effect that they transmitted a posthumous arrangement of the work. All of this has obvious implications for the study of Bach "reception" in the nineteenth century. For our immediate purposes, however, the fact that the copyists (and editor) of these scores completely ignored the sources of the original version allows the conclusion that they were completely

TABLE 14.2   The C. P. E. Bach Version of Cantata No. 102

Movement	BWV/movement: Description
1	= BWV 102/1: Chorus
2	= BWV 102/2: Secco recitative (with new text)
3	= BWV 102/4: Basso arioso
4	= BWV 102/7: Chorale (with Strophe 2 of "So wahr ich leb")
5	= BWV 102/5: Tenor aria (partially retexted; with obbligato for Violins 1 and 2 in unison)
6	= BWV 102/6: Accompanied recitative (with added string choir; partially retexted)
7	= BWV 102/7: Four-part chorale

unaware of them. It follows that they could hardly have made entries into them.[11]

So far as is known, only one individual ever consulted these sources during the nineteenth century: the editor of the first edition of the original version of the cantata, Wilhelm Rust. Rust's foreword to Volume 23 of the BG is dated May/June 1876. It is, accordingly, one of the last volumes that Rust prepared for the Bach-Gesellschaft. He lists the following sources for his edition: the autograph score, the two surviving original parts, the two Hering manuscripts, C. P. E. Bach's organ part and score for the arrangement of Movement 6, the Masses in G minor and F major, BWV 235 and 233.[12] As mentioned earlier, Rust's edition contains all the additional articulation marks found in the Hering parts.

There is in fact good reason to think that they and not the autograph score served as Rust's principal source. The Hering parts include an old title page which contains, in addition to the original heading written by Hering, a number of notations entered onto it by Rust himself: his own signature and also the words "Stim[m]en von Hering." He also wrote down (in ink) the name "Rudorff"—a reference to Ernst Rudorff (1840–1916), the owner of the manuscript at the time. Ernst Rudorff was also a professor of violin at the Berlin Conservatory of Music and the owner of other Bach manuscripts as well.[13] Preserved along with the original title page, however, is a new one. This page bears a heading, written by Rudorff, which includes a reference to the BG edition and, most important, the following remark, written in pencil and most likely in Rudorff's hand as well: "Muster für die Redaktion gewesen" ("was the source for the edition").

The facts, then, (1) that Rust not only consulted the Hering parts but used them as the *Muster* for his edition, (2) that he felt free to make notations on the original title page of the source, and (3) that the source contains far-reaching, carefully drawn, and musically subtle slurrings that were clearly later additions and are found nowhere else but in the BG edition—all these considerations suggest that it was Rust himself who actually entered the new articulation in the Hering parts. This in turn leads to the suspicion—which one mentions with considerably more hesitation—that it may have been Rust again who added the (far less numerous) supplemental slurs and staccato dots in the autograph score. The evidence for this assertion is (1) their agreement with those in the Hering parts and (2) the fact that they almost certainly were added not only after 1800 (the time of the Schwencke copy) but indeed after 1841, the year in which the autograph was acquired by the Prussian State Library from its previous owner, the autograph collector Georg Poelchau, and became—for the first time, really—generally accessible. Other considerations leading to this suspicion are the absence of any other person known to, or even likely to, have examined both the autograph score and the Hering parts in the nineteenth century and, finally, an admittedly subjective impression that the handwriting of the slurs in both sources is not dissimilar (see the plates). But, once again, it is a difficult matter indeed to identify with certainty the hand that drew a slur.[14]

It must be emphasized that the previous discussion falls far short of conclusive proof that it was Wilhelm Rust and no one else who entered and altered articulation marks not only in an important secondary copy but even in an autograph manuscript of Bach himself. The evidence at this point is quite circumstantial. Such an intimation, moreover, must not be made lightly. It is a charge tantamount to falsification of documents and would be an accusation of the gravest sort.

The fact is, however, that Wilhelm Rust's reputation as a reliable and conscientious editor has been seriously tarnished before—but not with reference to his still monumental achievements as an editor of the works of J. S. Bach. It is known that Rust was the perpetrator of one of the boldest hoaxes in the history of musicology. In 1912 Ernst Neufeldt, in his article "Der Fall Rust" (The Rust Case), was the first to discover that Wilhelm Rust's editions of piano and violin sonatas composed by his grandfather Friedrich Wilhelm Rust (1739-96; a pupil, incidentally, of both C. P. E. and W. F. Bach), were thoroughly rewritten—without any indication to that effect—by Wilhelm Rust. Rust's object was to endow them with the stylistic features of a later epoch: instrumental recitatives, thematic reminiscences, rich keyboard doublings and textures, harmonies and formal procedures characteristic of, and traditionally claimed as the historical achievements of, Beethoven, Schumann, Chopin, even Wagner—in order to support the claim that his grandfather was not only a major composer and innovator but indeed a genius of the first magnitude and (in the words of Vincent d'Indy) "the connecting link between Haydn and Mozart on the one hand and Beethoven on the other." The revelation was a cause célèbre and need not be pursued further here except to provide an example of Rust's editorial method with regard to his grandfather's music (see Ex. 14.3).[15]

Example 14.3.   *"F. W. Rust:" Violin Sonata (after Calvocoressi 1914)*

Its relevance for the present inquiry should be abundantly obvious.

Neufeldt himself was quite aware of the larger implications of his discovery. He wrote:

> Will we not be obliged at this point to entertain justified doubts about Rust's other scholarly work? At least until a precise control has been established to evaluate it? For more than ten years [actually more than a quarter century] Rust was the sole editor of the great Bach edition—work that until now has been duly acknowledged as a lofty achievement. And one that should continue to be so acknowledged— as soon as it has been seriously tested. That, in the light of our recent experience, is surely necessary, indeed.[16]

Another scholar, Erich Prieger, who had been among the most deceived by the Rust editions and had written a pamphlet called *Friedrich Wilhelm Rust, ein Vorläufer Beethovens,* asked:

> In light of such editorial practice one question insists on being addressed: If Wilhelm Rust took such liberties with the compositions of his grandfather, how did he behave with regard to the works of Johann Sebastian Bach? It is impossible to resent anyone's posing the question who has now become suspicious.[17]

Wilhelm Rust's editions of his grandfather's music appeared between 1885 and 1892:[18] that is, after the appearance (in 1881) of Volume 28 of the BG Edition, the last of the twenty-six volumes he had edited, from 1855 on, for the Bach-Gesellschaft. As Hermann Kretzschmar related in his summary report on the Bach-Gesellschaft, published in the final volume of the BG edition, the last years of Rust's activity as principal editor of the BG were problematic.

> In Rust's case, too, the time came when he began to lose pleasure in his work. From Volume 16 on it is possible to discern a change in his attitude—sometimes quite noticeable, sometimes less so. The editorial board at the time, owing to Rust's failure to submit his material on time, was forced to publish volumes years late; his forewords failed to include thorough discussions where they would be expected; rather, they became more careless and suffused with mystical, pietistic meditations. Arbitrary additions began to appear in the body of the edition itself: citations of bible passages and identifications of chorale texts were appended to Bach's music—with or without parentheses. Essential titles and headings, on the other hand, were omitted or banished to the foreword. Complaints from the subscribers arrived at the office of the Board of Directors. Among these angry voices was that of the Bach biographer Philipp Spitta.[19]

Georg von Dadelsen, too, in his encyclopedia article on Rust, remarks:

Fully aware of his authority, Rust increasingly inclined to editorial idiosyncrasies and was no longer willing to take the Bach research of Philipp Spitta seriously into account. The reasons for his ceasing his editorial work for the BG Edition in 1882 and, in 1888, resigning from the editorial committee altogether, can be found in this posture.[20]

In light of these reports and the famous "Fall Rust" itself, the possibility raised here—that Rust may have deliberately made entries in Bach manuscripts, becomes, sorry to say, less unthinkable. Again, however, there is still no conclusive proof of this. It is still quite possible that Rust was acting in the best faith in his edition of Cantata No. 102: that he had found—to his delight—some unusually explicit and plausible articulation markings in the principal sources, which he was overly eager to adopt. His only misdeed in that case was an honest failure to notice that the markings were hardly authentic.[21] In short, it would be premature at this time to find Wilhelm Rust guilty beyond a doubt of deliberate falsification.

In the case of Cantata No. 102 the existence of a control (the Schwencke score) and above all the state of the Hering parts, where the actual process of revision can be observed, makes it possible to recognize the questionable articulation marks in the autograph score as posthumous additions and, accordingly, to eliminate them from the New Bach Edition, the NBA. Unfortunately, such favorable circumstances do not always obtain. Editorial work on Volume I/19 of the NBA, undertaken by the present writer, uncovered other instances of uncharacteristically precise slurring in the original Bach sources.[22] The most problematic case concerns several of the original instrumental parts of Cantata No. 94, *Was frag ich nach der Welt.*[23] The Oboe I and Oboe II parts in Movement 3 and the principal (untransposed) continuo part in Movement 7 all contain a series of slurs written with a fine penpoint that awaken strong suspicions as to their authenticity by virtue of their precise placement: the beginnings and endings of slurs often actually touch the noteheads they apply to (see Plate 40). The suspicions are increased by the fact that the slurs in the continuo part for Movement 7, in contrast to the vast majority of autograph additions contained in it, were not copied into the surviving duplicate continuo part.[24] But such duplicate parts belonging to the original part sets of Bach are notoriously unreliable and incomplete: especially with respect to articulation marks. In the case of Cantata No. 94, moreover, we possess no later source which was copied directly from the original parts and could therefore serve as a control as to its original state—such as we have in the Schwencke score with respect to the autograph score of Cantata No. 102. That is, it is not possible to say with any certainty in the case of Cantata No. 94 whether the clearly later slurs in the original parts

PLATE 40.   Original Continuo Part in the hand of Johann Andreas Kuhnau, with articulation markings of doubtful origin, Thomasschule, Leipzig, f. 4ʳ (bottom): BWV 94/7, mm. 1–17

were in fact entered either by Bach himself or on his authority. It is easy to imagine, judging both by their differentiated musical character and their handwriting features, that they were added by the same hand that was at work in the autograph score of Cantata No. 102, the hand that, for its part, could well have been the same that revised the slurring in the Hering parts for that work—the hand (it seems) of Wilhelm Rust. But, to repeat, in the case of Cantata No. 94 there is no reliable control to confirm this suspicion—or to refute it, for that matter. Therefore, it would be more arbitrary to condemn the slurs—which, after all, are present in an original Bach source—as spurious and, on the (ultimately subjective) basis of their questionable appearance, to eliminate them from a source-critical edition, than to include them. The appearance of even an authentic slur, after all, can vary according to the condition of the quill, the composition of the ink, the amount of time at the composer's disposal for the task. These slurs, in short, appear in the NBA and, owing to the editorial principles of the edition, appear without any typographical differentiation. There is an explicit statement of caution in the foreword of the music volume, and there will be a more extensive discussion in the Critical Report making clear the editor's reservations and doubts. But it seems certain that the mere presence, in normal type, of some precisely indicated slurs on the authoritative pages of the NBA—an always welcome, because rare, circumstance—will assure that they are observed in practically every performance of the work. The poignant result will be that the editor will have been compelled by the inherent authority of an original source to perpetuate a rendition of the work that he does not himself believe was what the composer had in mind.

At issue in all of this is more than the familiar matter of the imperfect reliability of the Bach manuscripts. The contraditions and ambiguities and other manifestations of haste and carelessness in their production, after all, are quite well known. Rather it is the possibility, never before raised, apparently, that in some cases the very integrity and legitimacy—the authenticity, in a word—of even the most important sources of Bach's music, including autograph scores and original performing materials, may be suspect: that they may have been subjected to posthumous tampering even as late as the nineteenth century, tampering that went beyond overt and well-meaning clarification and emendation (such as we know was exercised by C. P. E. Bach and even Zelter) but may have constituted deliberate alteration, if not deception. At the least, it would be good to know whether the editor of the New Edition of Cantata Nos. 94 and 102 (the writer of these lines) has been the butt of mischief perpetrated perhaps by the editor of the Old Bach Edition, or whether both of us have been compelled by still unclarified events in the history of the Bach sources to play the role—to a still unclarified degree—of what may be called "editore traditore."

Postscript

Conclusive identification of the hand—or hands—involved in the articulation markings discussed here may yet be forthcoming. Since the original publication of this essay, sophisticated techniques of ink analysis have been successfully applied to Bach sources: most notably the "proton milliprobe" analysis of the hand-penned annotations in Bach's personal copy of the Calov Bible, carried out in 1982 by the Crocker Nuclear Laboratory of the University of California at Davis but first reported in 1985 (see Cox 1985). Even more recently, in West Berlin, Rainer Kaiser, a musicologist, and Dieter M. Kolb, a physicist, making use of the facilities of the Max Planck Society, have collaborated in conducting an ink analysis of a number of performance indications in several Bach manuscripts long thought to be, and now confirmed to be, in the hand of Carl Friedrich Zelter. These findings have not yet been "formally" published in the musicological literature but have been briefly reported in the March 1987 newsletter of the Max Planck Society as well as in the German press (see the 17 July 1987 issue of *Die Zeit*, p. 20). We may presume that it is only a matter of time until the mystery tale related here will be definitively solved.

15

TEMPO AND DYNAMICS
The Original Terminology

Unlike many of the leading musicians of his time, Johann Sebastian
Bach took no active part in that most characteristic enterprise of the
Age of the Enlightenment: the literally encyclopedic effort to organize
the inherited corpus of musical knowledge and experience in a systematic and rational fashion. We possess no lengthy theoretical treatises,
no musical dictionaries, *Versuche*, or *Anleitungen* from his pen. Perhaps
Bach remained aloof from such activity because he was skeptical about
such a self-conscious process of verbal conceptualization about music,
with its underlying assumption that by describing, defining, classify-
ing musical phenomena in words (or mathematical formulas) one could
capture their essence. But it may be that he was simply too busy. As
C. P. E. Bach related to Johann Nicolaus Forkel, "Bey seinen vielen
Beschäftigungen hatte er kaum zu der nöthigsten Correspondenz Zeit"
("With his many activities [Sebastian] hardly had time for the most
necessary correspondence").[a] Indeed, the definitive edition of the surviving documents from his hand, which includes the texts not only of
letters and formal reports but also of every bill and every receipt (be it
ever so brief or trivial) and even the title-pages of a number of musical compositions, nonetheless contains fewer than two hundred items
and would surely run to fewer than a hundred pages if one could strip
away the elaborate critical apparatus.

Bach, then, was clearly not disposed to write extensively about
music; but he could by no means altogether escape the necessity of
using words to deal with it. First of all, part of the written form of

any musical composition necessarily had to be set down in words. There was (and is) simply no other way for a composer to communicate his intentions regarding tempo, dynamics, instrumentation, and other aspects of the physical realization of his work (e.g., directions like *arco* or *pizzicato, con* or *senza sordino, tutti* or *solo,* etc.). Second, Bach was not only a composer and performer but also a teacher. It was in this capacity that he prepared the explanatory material about the rudiments of musical notation and the proper rendition of ornaments that introduces the *Clavier-Büchlein vor Wilhelm Friedemann Bach;*[1] and it was surely during the course of music lessons that he dictated the elementary rules of thoroughbass that survive in Anna Magdalena Bach's *Clavier-Büchlein.*[2] Moreover, the title-pages and prefaces of the Two- and Three-part Inventions, the *Orgel-Büchlein, Well-Tempered Clavier, Musical Offering,* and *Art of Fugue* all provide explicit testimony as to the didactic function of these monumental works. In fact, it would not be difficult to argue that Bach was the most self-consciously pedagogical of the great composers.

Third, owing to his reputation as an expert on organs, Bach was often called upon not only to try out newly built or renovated instruments but also to submit written evaluations of them or to draft proposals for the construction or repair of others. Finally, Johann Sebastian Bach was a civil servant whose official duties—or sense of responsibility and equity—frequently obliged him to write letters of recommendation, status reports, or even petitions and formal complaints bearing on this or that aspect of the current musical situation. The sum of these various activities and responsibilities, then, repeatedly presented Bach with opportunities to express himself in words about music or to use words simply as a necessary and unavoidable part of the process of composition. Fairly inevitably, then, he evolved a personal musical vocabulary whose range and character—as well as the manner of its expansion and revision over time—would seem destined, if seriously investigated, to provide valuable insight into his traditional and intellectual roots, his aesthetic attitudes, and his development as a teacher, performer, and composer. Such a study could even uncover welcome information of a quite practical kind.

With such reflections in mind, I have begun a compilation of the musical terms preserved in the Bach sources. So far I have managed to survey approximately six hundred sources drawn from the following "pools":

The original documents published in the first volume of *Bach-Dokumente,* that is, those letters, testimonials, reports, receipts, dedications, etc., written by, or at least signed and thus authenticated by, Bach himself.

The available autograph scores of the instrumental music.

The surviving autograph scores of the vocal compositions spanning

> the period from the earliest Mühlhausen cantatas of ca. 1707–08
> to the end of the first Leipzig cantata *Jahrgang* (May 1724).

A selection of autograph scores from the later Leipzig period chosen
to represent the principal vocal genres: cantata, motet, oratorio,
passion, mass.

The original editions of Bach's music published or prepared for
publication during his lifetime.

It has not yet been possible for me to examine more than cur-
sorily either the extensive body of original performing parts that are
preserved for numerous vocal works (and for some of the instrumental ensemble compositions) or the early sources for those instrumental
and vocal compositions which, in the absence of autographs and other
original materials (e.g., copies prepared directly under the composer's
supervision), may be regarded as relatively authentic.

Bach's musical vocabulary encompasses Italian, French, Latin, and
German terms. The "functional" terminology in the musical manuscripts
themselves is overwhelmingly Italian, although Bach clearly prefers
Hautbois (*Hautb.*) over *Oboe* (*Ob., Obui,* also *Obboe*) and favors French
terminology in general for the dance genres. On the other hand, the
musical terms found in the text documents, as well as those in the
title-pages, dedications, and prefaces to both manuscript and printed
musical collections, are mostly German.

At this point the compilation contains over a thousand entries—an
impressive figure, indeed, especially when one considers that even Johann Gottfried Walther's comprehensive *Musicalisches Lexicon* contains
only about three thousand musical terms.[3] It seems prudent, incidentally, to avoid citing a more precise figure—not only because the compilation is still incomplete but also because the material inherently defies
strict quantifiction, for we encounter not only equivalent terms in different languages but also numerous variant spellings and grammatical
inflections (along with the uninhibited use of a variety of abbreviations) for what is presumably one and the same term in a single language. Finally, there are alternative phonetic forms (as distinct from
variant spellings or grammatical forms) of the same term in the same
language. (I have generally considered the latter, unlike orthographi-
cal variants and abbreviations, to be separate items.) The difficulty can
best be illustrated by reproducing the five separate entries I have so
far for Bach's various designations for the transverse flute. They consist of no fewer than fourteen forms: *Flaute traverso* (*Flaut: Travers:*); *Flute
Traversa* (*Flute Travers.*); *Flute Traversiere; Traverso* (*Trav., Travers., Traversa,
Traversi*); *Traversiere* (*Traversier., Traversiera, Traversieri*)—to which could be
added *Flöte(n)-Traversier,* but not *Fleute-Travers,* since for Bach the latter
refers only to an organ stop.

The following discussion, owing to space constraints, will be limited in its scope to a portion of the Bach terminology dealing with performance: specifically, dynamic and tempo indications. It is intended to be regarded as a sample illustrating the potential value, and perhaps also the inherent limitations, of a systematic study of the musical terminology contained in the Bach sources.

DYNAMICS

The entire corpus of Bach's dynamic markings, as revealed (so far) by the sources, consists—even if one reckons single letters separately from other abbreviations and fully written-out terms—of only seventeen items (see Table 15.1).[4] The meanings of most of these terms are neither problematic nor surprising. Walther (1732, pp. 257, 479) defines *forte* as "stark, hefftig, jedoch auf eine natürliche Art, ohne die Stimme, oder das Instrument gar zu sehr zu zwingen' ("strong, intense, but in a natural manner, without forcing the voice or instrument too much") and *piano* as "so viel als leise; dass man nemlich die Stärcke der Stimme oder des Instruments dermassen lieblich machen, oder mindern soll, dass es wie ein Echo lasse" ("in effect, soft; one should adjust or reduce the strength of the voice or instrument so that it may have the effect of an echo"). But one must nonetheless proceed with caution. The letters *pp*, for example,

TABLE 15.1   Dynamic Indications in the Bach Sources

| | Earliest Observed Appearance | |
Term	Year	BWV
1 *f* [*forte*]	1707	131
2 *forte* (*for:, fort.*)	1713	208; 596
3 *m. f.* [*mezzo forte*]	1736	244
4 *mezo forte* [*sic*]	1736	244
5 *p* [*piano*]	1707	131
6 *p.* [*pianissimo*]	1721	1046
7 *p: pian* [*più piano*]	1723	95
8 *pi p* [*più piano*]	1715	132
9 *pianissimo* (*pianiβimo, pianiss.*)	ca. 1707	106
10 *piano* (*pi, pia, pian.*)	1707	131
11 *piano piano*	1715	165
12 *piu piano* (*piu p:, piu pian*)	1707	131
13 *poco forte*	1713?	63
14 (*un*) *poco piano*	1733	232
15 *pp.* [*più piano*]	1707	131
16 *p. s.* [*pianissimo sempre*]	1721	1046
17 *sempre piano* (*piano sempre*)	1713?	63

contrary to the expectations of the modern musician, are reported by Walther to stand not for *pianissimo* but for *più piano*;[5] and the sources reveal that Bach observed this usage.[6] For example, in the autograph score of the Mühlhausen cantata *Aus der Tiefen*, BWV 131, dating from ca. 1707, three of the upper instrumental parts at one point (m. 298) read *pp* while the continuo at the same time has *piu p.*[7] Similarly, we find basically the same combination in the autograph score[8] of the Weimar cantata *Bereitet die Wege*, BWV 132 (composed December 1715), at m. 87 of the first movement: *pp* in two upper parts (Violino II and Viola) and, simultaneously, *pi p* in another (Violino I). (This reveals, incidentally, that *pi p* is to be deciphered as *più piano*, and not, say, *piano piano*.)

Decisive confirmation of Bach's distinction between *pp* (*più piano*) and *pianissimo* is provided by a passage from the final chorus of the St. Matthew Passion as preserved in the 1736 version of the work. In several of the performing parts (violin, viola, traverso, continuo), Bach marked the final measures of the B section of the movement preceding the *da capo* (mm. 76–79) with the following sequence of dynamics: *piano—pp—pianissimo.*[9] At the same time this passage constitutes the earliest unambiguous indication of graduated dynamics—the succession clearly amounts to a *de facto* decrescendo—that I have encountered so far in the Bach sources. (The same sequence appears in another autograph source[10] dating from about the same time: the score of the Harpsichord Concerto in D Major, BWV 1054, ca. 1735–45, in the viola part of the first movement, at mm. 17–19 and again mm. 35–37.)

The dynamic markings discussed so far—*f*, *p*, *piano*, *piu p*, *pp*, *pianissimo*—were all used by Bach from the beginning of his career. They all appear as early as 1707 in his first Mühlhausen cantatas: *pianissimo* in the (posthumous) manuscript of Cantata No. 106, *Gottes Zeit ist die allerbeste Zeit*, the others in the autograph score of Cantata No. 131.[11] The preponderance of the softer dynamic markings here is striking; moreover, on the basis of the evidence so far assembled, it remains a hallmark of Bach's practice henceforth. More precisely, Bach not only continues to exploit the soft extreme of the dynamic range beyond *piano* to *più piano* and *pianissimo*, but will also eventually fill in the gap between *piano* and *forte* by introducing such designations as *poco piano*, *mezo forte* [sic], *poco forte*. But evidently he will never prescribe a dynamic level above a simple *forte*. Bach's entire dynamic spectrum, in other words, remains fundamentally "skewed" toward the soft end; and this asymmetry would seem to reflect a basic attitude toward the performance of musical dynamics. Bach could and frequently did, of course, augment the volume level of a passage or a composition by adding more and louder instruments—a *forte* in a work scored with trumpets and drums, after all, is considerably louder than one scored for strings alone—or perhaps simply by increasing the number of polyphonic parts. (A celebrated example occurs in mm. 20–22 of the B Flat minor Prelude, BWV 867 of the *Well-Tempered Clavier I,* which one may or may not regard as ultimately rising above *forte.*)[12] But the remarkable fact remains that Bach chose, apparently, to call for more volume (power, brilliance) only by such compositional or orchestrational means rather than by the introduction of dynamic markings (*più forte, ff, fortissimo*), something he was quite willing to do in the case of the softer dynamic levels. The practical consequences of this for anyone concerned about "historically authentic" Bach performance seem fairly clear.

We shall shortly turn to a consideration of the later additions to Bach's palette of dynamic markings. It is first necessary, however, to make some observations about the general patterns apparently governing Bach's use or nonuse of dynamic indications at all. For example, it must be mentioned that the original sources for Bach's solo keyboard and organ works—whether autographs, copies, or prints—contain (as every player familiar with *Urtext* editions has long since surmised) virtually no dynamic indications. There are of course exceptions, such as the indication of registral differentiation between leading and accompanimental parts by the simultaneous employment of *piano* and *forte* markings throughout the original 1735 edition of the *Italian Concerto* or the equally special instance of relatively rapid, echo-like *forte-piano* alternations.[13] By and large, however, it is clear that Bach considered the prescription of dynamics to be necessary only in ensemble compositions; in solo works the choice almost invariably could be left entirely to the discretion of the autonomous performer.[14]

With respect to ensemble works, Bach's normal practice—at least in the case of movements in ritornello form (arias, choruses, concerto movements)—was, as is well known, to have the tutti ensemble play *forte* during the ritornellos and *piano* during the solo sections. The principal instrumental performing parts were marked, almost always by Bach himself, according to this principle.[15] The opening ritornellos, however, typically bear no dynamic marking at all, *forte* being implied until the first (explicit) *piano* marking makes its appearance in the accompanying parts together with the (unmarked but clearly *forte*) entrance of the instrumental or vocal soloist (or chorus). It is important to recognize that the dynamic markings here are obviously fulfilling a formal rather than an expressive function: a *forte* in the accompanying parts in the later course of the movement signals the return of the ritornello or of an instrumental interlude for the ripieno ensemble, while *piano,* conversely, signals the beginning of a solo episode. The unambiguous, if tacit, assumption of a *forte* dynamic at the opening of such movements is particularly significant, for it strongly suggests that Bach regarded the simple *forte* as the normal dynamic level prevailing in a composition in the absence of any indication to the contrary.

As early as 1713 Bach began to modify this schematic loud–soft alternation. In the Weimar Christmas cantata *Christen ätzet diesen Tag,* BWV

63, the duet "Gott du hast es wohl gefüget" calls for soprano, bass, obbligato oboe, and continuo. During the course of the first vocal section (specifically, at mm. 10, 15, 18), the oboe part is sporadically marked *poco forte*, in alternation with *piano*.[16] The reason for this refinement is clearly to call attention to the introduction of a thematic quotation from the ritornello in these bars and to instruct the oboist to emphasize them accordingly, despite the continued activity of the vocal soloists. The same dynamic marking, in a similar context and serving the same purpose of eliciting a "discreet emphasis" from an instrumental accompaniment, is found throughout the aria "Mein Erlöser und Erhalter" from the early Leipzig cantata *Lobe den Herrn, meine Seele*, BWV 69a (August 1723).[17] The function of *poco forte*, then, as it is used by Bach, is still primarily formal, and this would seem to be the case as well with regard to Bach's use of *m.f.* and *mezo forte*. Both designations appear for the first (and so far only) time in the 1736 sources of the St. Matthew Passion, where they are found in the instrumental parts of the opening chorus at most of the vocal entrances.[18] Bach's similar use of *poco forte*, on the one hand, and *mezo forte*, on the other—both as accompanimental dynamics—would seem to argue that he considered the two terms essentially synonymous. It is worth noting, however, that in the example cited above, *poco forte* follows, and thus contrasts with, a *piano*, whereas in the St. Matthew chorus *m.f.* largely alternates with, and apparently modifies, a *forte* marking. This suggests that *poco forte* implied for Bach a more forceful rendering than *m.f.*, and that it therefore probably represented a dynamic level between *m.f.* and *f.*

The indication *un poco piano* in the string parts of the opening ritornello of the *aria a doi chori* "So ist mein Jesus nun gefangen" (again preserved in the 1736 layer of performing parts) serves once again—like the *m.f.* markings in the opening chorus—to refine the contrast between melody and accompaniment by insuring, in this instance, that the relatively active, but secondary, strings are subordinated in volume to the thematically dominant woodwinds. That is, *poco piano* here seems actually to be quite close in meaning to the comparative *più piano*—this time "softer" with reference to the (presumably *forte*) volume of the flute and oboes—in our terms, then, *meno forte*.[19]

The introduction in the St. Matthew Passion of such subtle, more shaded dynamics—as well as the graduated dynamics in the final chorus mentioned earlier—seems to be symptomatic of a general tendency on Bach's part during the decade of the 1730s toward greater differentiation in his performance indications. The *Missa* of the B-minor Mass, composed before July 1733, provides a different manifestation of the same tendency. The opening ritornello of the first *Kyrie* commences in the instruments only after the dramatic four-measure choral invocation at the outset of the movement. Attached to some of the upper string parts at the change of tempo at this point (m. 5) from *Adagio* to *Largo* is once again the dynamic marking *poco piano*.[20] This time the marking serves not only the familiar formal function of clarifying the design of the movement (by introducing a dynamic contrast between vocal and instrumental sections) but also and primarily an expressive function (by contributing to the evocation of the appropriate *Affekt* of the movement—call it "meditative" or "somber"). That is, perhaps for the first time (at least through written prescription), Bach here is exploiting the purely expressive potential of musical dynamics.

The term *piano piano* has so far turned up only once. Like *poco piano* it is used to an expressive end—not in order to help evoke the general *Affekt*, however, but rather in the age-old service of text-illustration. The term appears in the string parts, to the accompaniment of the line "wenn alle Kraft vergehen," in the last measure of the recitative "Ich habe ja, mein Seelenbräutigam" from the Weimar cantata *O heil'ges Geist-und Wasserbad*, BWV 165. Now although it is clear that *piano piano* is meant to be distinctly softer than simple *piano*, it is not clear whether Bach regarded it as synonymous with *piu piano*, with *pianissimo*, or perhaps with neither.[21] (It may, admittedly, be pedantic even to raise this question. Walther, at all events, was not inclined to split hairs as fine as this. Although he goes so far as to accord *piano piano* its own entry in his *Lexicon*, he is content to define it as "wie *piu piano* oder *pianissimo*.") At the beginning of 'Ich habe ja," incidentally, the string parts are marked *piano sempre*. This term (along with *sempre piano*) frequently appears in the string parts of accompanied recitatives, the first such use occurring in the recitative "O sel'ger Tag" from Cantata No. 63 (1713). *Piano sempre* also appears on occasion in the accompanying parts of concerto slow movements: for example, in the First Brandenburg Concerto and in the D-Major Harpsichord Concerto, BWV 1054.

As has been mentioned earlier with reference to the Italian Concerto, Bach at times took the trouble to prescribe different, but simultaneously executed, dynamic levels. Since such notation was, in effect, a way of indicating manual registration, it is encountered mostly in the sources of organ compositions. The autograph score of the D-minor Concerto after Vivaldi (BWV 596), penned ca. 1713–14,[22] provides the earliest instance. In the fourth movement, a *Largo* in 12/8 meter, the upper staff is marked *forte*, the lower *piano*. Similarly, in the chorale prelude *Liebster Jesu wir sind hier*, BWV 634, a setting entered into the *Orgel-Büchlein* ca. 1715,[23] the canonic parts on the top staff are *forte*, the accompaniment on the bottom staff *piano*. The most striking example of simultaneous differentiated dynamics, however, occurs in an ensemble work, the opening movement of the [Second] Brandenburg Concerto. In the meticulously prepared fair-copy score Bach has carefully marked the momentarily leading parts *f* in mm. 45, 51–54 and elsewhere, while the surrounding subordinate parts have *p*.[24]

TEMPO AND *AFFEKT* INDICATIONS

According to the sources consulted so far, there would seem to be forty-five discrete terms that fall into this category.[25] They are listed in alphabetical order—and according to Bach's usual orthography and capitalization—in Table 15.2. It is apparent at once, from Bach's use of such double (and from our point of view contradictory) formulations as *Vivace è allegro* or *Allegro e presto,* that he could not have regarded the terms belonging to this category entirely in the modern sense as objective indications of tempo (i.e., velocity) alone but must still have understood them in their earlier sense as characterizations, at least in part, of *Affekt.* Moreover, since such "tempo" designations had their origins in (and owed their very existence to) the breakdown of the absolute temporal values of the mensural system, they could hardly have been expected in any case to serve as precise indicators of the absolute, metronomic tempo of any compositions. Quite the contrary: the very wealth, variety, and even fussiness (or ambivalence) of a surprisingly large number of Bach's tempo markings—the *assais, un pocos,* and *ma nons*—strongly suggest that they eluded exact quantification and were for Bach ultimately as subjective as the moods and *Affekte* from which they derived their names. Accordingly, it seems proper to group together such terms as *adagio, allegro, largo* and *presto,* which today unambiguously define tempo, along with more evocative ones such as *grave, affettuoso, gay, spirituoso,* and even *cantabile* and *dolce.* Bach, in fact, not only used all of these terms himself basically in the same way—almost invariably placing them at the beginning of a movement or formal section of a movement—but even had many of them serve, at least in his earliest cantatas, as, in effect, movement headings in the absence of form or genre designations *per se,* such as *Aria* or *Recitativo* (terms that were not to appear in his vocal compositions for another few years).[26]

The domination of Italian terminology in this category is overwhelming. Not only is the mere handful of French terms here limited to compositions in the French style—suite movements and overtures—but they are all *unica,* at least so far: *lentement* appears only in the "Polonoise" of the orchestral Suite in B minor, BWV 1067; *gay* only at the beginning of the fast section of the opening chorus of Cantata No. 61, *Nun komm, der Heiden Heiland; vistement* in the prelude of the English Suite in F major, BWV 809; *tres viste* at the ³⁄₈ section of the prelude of the Lute Suite in G minor, BWV 995, and *fort gai* in the prelude of the Keyboard Suite in A minor, BWV 818a.[27] This enumeration, admittedly, could be augmented by considering *grave* and *lente* to be French words. But Bach evidently did not, since *grave* and *lente,* unlike the clearly French terms, are not restricted to compositions in

TABLE 15.2   Tempo and *Affekt* Designations in the Bach Sources

Term	Earliest Observed Appearance		Number of appearances		
	Year	BWV	1	2–5	25+
1 *Adagio*	1704	992			x
2 *adagio assai*	ca. 1707	106		x	
3 *Adagio mà non tanto*	1721	1051			
4 *Adagio o vero Largo*	Köthen?	1061	x		
5 *adagißimo*	ca. 1704?	565		x	
6 *adagiosissimo*	1704	992		x	
7 *Affettuoso*	1708	71 (libretto)		x	
8 *Allabreve*	1733	232		x	
9 *Allegro*	1705?	535a			x
10 *Allegro assai*	1720	1005			
11 *Allegro e presto*	Weimar?	916	x		
12 *allegro ma non presto*	ca. 1726	1039	x		
13 *Allegro ma non tanto*	ca. 1735	1027		x	
14 *Allegro moderato*	ca. 1735	1027		x	
15 *Allegro poco*	1704	992	x		
16 *Andante*	1707	131			x
17 *Andante un poco*	ca. 1725	1015	x		
18 *Animose*	1708	71 (libretto)	x		
19 *cantabile*	1721	1050		x	
20 *con discretione*	ca. 1710	912	x		
21 *dolce*	ca. 1727–30	527		x	
22 *Fort gai*	ca. 1725	818a	x		
23 *gay*	1714	61	x		
24 *Grave*	ca. 1713–14	596			
25 *Larghetto*	1708	71		x	
26 *Largo*	1707	131			x
27 *Largo ma non tanto*	Köthen?	1043	x		
28 *Lente*	1707	131		x	
29 *Lentement*	ca. 1738	1067	x		
30 *Lento*	ca. 1707	106	x		
31 *moderato*	1736	244	x		
32 *molt'adagio*	ca. 1704?	565		x	
33 *molt'allegro*	1731	36	x		
34 *più presto*	1713	208	x		
35 *prestissimo*	ca. 1704?	565		x	
36 *Presto*	ca. 1706–10?	911			x
37 *Spirituoso*	1714	21	x		
38 *Tardò*	1707	524	x		
39 *Tempo di (Borea, Gavotta, Giga, Minuetta)*	Köthen	173a			
40 *tres viste*	ca. 1730	995	x		
41 *un poc'allegro*	1707	131			
42 *un poco Adagio*	Köthen	1019a	x		
43 *vistement*	ca. 1725	809	x		
44 *Vivace*	1707	131			x
45 *Vivace è allegro*	1723	24		x	

264

French style. Moreover, Walther identifies *grave* as Italian (in contrast to *gravement*) and, while omitting *lente,* offers *lento* as Italian and *lent* as French.[28] The whole thrust of Bach's usage, in any case, indicates that in general, and certainly in this connection, he viewed Italian as the standard currency of musical terminology and drew on French only when he wished to emphasize the French character of a style or genre.

It will be helpful to begin our consideration of this material with something of a statistical survey, noting, for example, that of the forty-five tempo markings no fewer than twenty appear quite early on in Bach's career, before ca. 1710. They are (here only retaining Bach's spelling and capitalization): *Adagio, Adagio assai, adagissimo, adagiosissimo, Affettuoso, allegro, allegro poco, andante, animose, con discretione, Larghetto, Largo, Lente, lento, molto adagio, prestissimo, presto, Tardò, un poc'allegro,* and *vivace.* The earliest works, in fact—the Mühlhausen cantatas BWV 131, 106, 71; the *Quodlibet,* BWV 524; the organ Prelude and Fugue in G minor, BWV 535a; the Toccata and Fugue in D minor, BWV 565; and the *Capriccio on the Absence of His Most Beloved Brother,* BWV 992—are particularly rich in such terms, especially the more extreme as well as some of the most uncommon indications. Twelve of these early terms, indeed, appear no more than five times in all in the Bach sources: *adagissimo, adagiosissimo, adagio assai, affettuoso, allegro poco, animose, con discretione, larghetto, lento, molto adagio, prestissimo, tardò.* But the fact is that almost three-quarters of all the tempo designations contained in the Bach sources reviewed so far (thirty-three of the forty-five, to be precise) are "uncommon" in that they occur only five or fewer times. (In addition to the twelve just listed, the remaining twenty-one are *adagio o vero largo, allabreve, allegro e presto, allegro ma non presto, allegro ma non tanto, allegro moderato, andante un poco, cantabile, dolce, fort gai, gay, largo ma non tanto, lentement, moderato, molt'allegro, più presto, spirituoso, tres viste, un poco adagio, vistement, vivace e allegro.*) And of these, twenty—or more than forty percent of the total—are *unica* (*Adagio o vero largo, allegro e presto, allegro ma non presto, allegro poco, andante un poco, animose, con discretione, fort gai, gay, largo ma non tanto, lentement, lento, moderato, molt'allegro, più presto, spirituoso, tardò, tres viste, un poco adagio, vistement*).

Considered from the other end, there are only six tempo indications that occur twenty-five or more times: *adagio, allegro, andante, largo, presto, vivace.* These six would seem, then, to constitute the "fixed points" for Bach in the scale of tempo markings, a scale which, in its essential outlines, was established early in his career and maintained thereafter. Of these six terms there is reason to believe that Bach regarded *allegro* as representing the normal tempo—the *tempo ordinario*—just as he evidently took *forte* to be the basic dynamic level. As with *forte,* there is a notable absence in the Bach sources of a simple *allegro* marking in certain strategic positions. In the cantatas, for example, *allegro* almost never appears at the beginning of a movement but only after a section in a different—typically, slow—tempo such as *adagio* or *grave*.[29] Similarly, the opening movements of the vast majority of instrumental works,[30] whether for keyboard, organ, or ensemble, carry no tempo indication—unless it is something other than a simple *allegro*. On the other hand, the second (i.e., fast) movements of instrumental compositions in *sonata da chiesa* form (e.g., BWV 1001, 1014, 1016–1018, 1028, 1034–1035) are usually marked *allegro,* as are the final movements of three-movement concertos. In both situations, of course, *allegro* invariably follows (i.e., cancels) a different (slow) indication—that of the preceding movement—and thereby serves to restore the *tempo ordinario.* The suspicion, finally, that an *allegro* tempo constituted Bach's norm receives virtually explicit corroboration from the *Necrology:* "und im Zeitmasse, welches or gemeiniglich sehr lebhaft nahm [war er] überaus sicher" ("of the tempo, which [Bach] generally took very lively, he was uncommonly sure").[30a]

Having ascertained the "center," as it were, of Bach's scale of tempo designations, it is necessary to establish the extremes. The manner in which Bach linguistically manipulates the terms at the outer ends of the tempo continuum proves to be most enlightening in this connection. Whereas he exaggerates *adagio* (altering it to *adagissimo, adagiosissimo, adagio assai, molto adagio*), he moderates *largo* (changing it to *larghetto* or *largo ma non tanto*). At the other extreme Bach accelerates *presto* to *prestissimo* and avoids too rapid a tempo with the formulation *allegro ma non presto.* There are no corresponding qualifications or modifications of *vivace*—say, to *molto vivace* or *vivacissimo.* All this allows the conclusion that for Bach the slow end of the tempo continuum was generally represented by *adagio,* not *largo,* and the fast end (less surprisingly) by *presto,* not *vivace.*

It is now a simple matter to arrange Bach's six principal tempo designations into what was almost certainly for him their proper sequential order of increasing velocity, namely, *adagio—largo—andante—allegro—vivace—presto.* This accords only in part with the ranking implied by Walther's *Lexicon* which, in its operative phrases, defines these terms as follows:[31]

> *Adagio:* "gemächlich, langsam" ("leisurely, slow")
>
> *Largo:* "sehr langsam, den Tact gleichsam erweiternd" ("very slow, as if expanding the measure")
>
> *Andante:* "alle Noten fein gleich . . . executirt . . . und etwas geschwinder als *adagio*" ("all the notes executed nice and evenly . . . and somewhat quicker than *adagio*")
>
> *Allegro:* "frölich, lustig, wohl belebt oder erweckt; sehr offt auch: geschwinde und flüchtig: manchmal aber auch, einen

gemässigten, obschon frölichen und belebten Tact" ("happy, merry, quite lively or awake; very often also quick or fleeting; but sometimes also a moderate but happy, lively measure")

Vivace: "lebhafft. *Vivacissimo.* sehr lebhafft" ("lively; *Vivacissimo,* very lively")

Presto: "geschwind" ("quick": Walther does not list *Prestissimo*)

Walther, then, seems to be suggesting the order *largo—adagio—andante—allegro—presto—vivace.*

From the instances where different tempo designations appear simultaneously (and presumably unintentionally) in different lines or parts of the same work, we can safely infer that Bach regarded the terms involved as synonymous. In the autograph score of Cantata No. 131, for example, the opening measures of the work are marked *Lente* over the continuo staff of the score and, simultaneously, *adagio* over the top staff (oboe);[31a] and the "Qui tollis" movement from the Mass in B minor is marked *Adagio* in the autograph Violin I part but *Lente* in the equally autograph alto, cello, and continuo parts.[32] Similarly, in the autograph score of the early *Quodlibet,* BWV 524, the continuo part at m. 15 is marked *Tardò* while the tenor has *Adagio.*[33]

A related situation is presented by the work-pair consisting of the G-Major Trio Sonata for Flute, Violin, and Continuo, BWV 1039, and its later reworking, the Sonata for Viola da Gamba and Obbligato Harpsichord, BWV 1027. The sources for both compositions date from the Leipzig period: the anonymous copyists' parts for BWV 1039 (St 431) from ca. 1726, the autograph score of BWV 1027 (P 226) from ca. 1735.[34] In the trio version the tempo for the second movement is given as *allegro ma non presto;* in the gamba version it is *allegro ma non tanto.* It seems justified to conclude from this that Bach considered the two designations to be virtually identical in meaning. On the other hand, the fourth movement of the trio is marked *presto* while that of the gamba sonata reads *allegro moderato.* Here it would surely be difficult to maintain that the two different tempo markings are to be understood as synonymous. Quite the contrary; it would seem clear in this instance that Bach intended the gamba version to be taken at a distinctly slower tempo than the trio, and changed the tempo marking accordingly.

I have already indicated that the most extreme tempo markings in the Bach repertory are concentrated in the early works. Conversely, most of the more subtle shadings do not appear before the 1720s or even the 1730s, although there are some exceptions. *Allegro poco, larghetto,* and *un poc'allegro* all make their first appearance in the sources of pre-Weimar compositions. To these we should perhaps add *con discretione,* a term which Bach apparently prescribes only once, in a passage from the Keyboard Toccata in D Major, BWV 912 (presumably composed ca.

1710). The musical context in which the term appears—a passage of decorated chords marked with fermatas occurring during the course of a section marked *adagio* (mm. 111-18)—strongly suggests that *con discretione* must have meant to Bach something like *ad libitum*, that is, in free rhythm. Indeed, this impression is emphatically confirmed by Mattheson in his discussion of the fantasy style in *Der vollkommene Capellmeister* (Part 1, Chapter 10): "Man pfleget sonst bey dergleichen Sachen wol die Worte zu schreiben: *ceci se joue à discretion,* oder im Italienischen: *con discrezione,* um zu bemercken, dass man sich an den Tact gar nicht binden dürffe; sondern nach Belieben bald langsam bald geschwinde spielen möge" ("One is probably also in the habit, with such pieces, of writing the words *ceci se joue à discretion,* or in Italian *con discrezione,* in order to indicate that one need not be confined to the beat at all, but according to one's pleasure might play sometimes slow, sometimes fast").[35] On the other hand, it must be reported that Walther defines *con discretione* as "bescheidentlich, mit Masse, nemlich nicht zu geschwinde noch zu langsam" ("discreet, restrained, neither too fast nor too slow"). The expression, then, could well have signified, at least to Bach's contemporaries, a tempo much like *moderato*.[36]

As for *moderato* itself, it appears (like its counterpart among the dynamic markings, *mezzo forte*) for the first and so far only time in the St. Matthew Passion, at the end of the accompanied recitative "Und da sie den Lobgesang gesprochen haben" at Jesus's words "Wenn ich aber auferstehe." Here *moderato* follows, and in effect cancels, a *vivace* marking over a passage set to the words "Ich werde den Hirten schlagen."

Since in vocal music the character and meaning of the text normally suffice to define the *Affekt* and thereby suggest the appropriate tempo, it is not surprising to discover that the "uncommon" as well as the more extreme and the more differentiated tempo markings encountered in the Bach sources are concentrated in his instrumental compositions. The extreme tempos, whether fast or slow, are largely confined to the early keyboard and organ works of the pre- and early Weimar periods: that is, to compositions for a solo instrument that were intended typically as strongly individualistic, if not unabashedly virtuoso vehicles. The more moderate, more meticulously qualified tempo markings, on the other hand, are found mainly in the later ensemble compositions: the concertos and chamber works composed during the Köthen or even the Leipzig years. Among the latter group of designations should be included the terms *dolce* and *cantabile.* They too appear only in Bach's instrumental music: *dolce* invariably in works in 6/8 time and usually in conjunction with a *largo* or *adagio* indication (thus forming part of the movement heading),[37] *cantabile* either as a movement heading[38] or as an expression mark functioning virtually as a dynamic indication. In each of the two instances of the latter type uncovered so far, the *cantabile* indication reinforces a striking formal nuance. In the third movement of the Fifth Brandenburg Concerto at m. 148, the term calls attention to the radical transformation of the principal theme in the ripieno strings; in the final movement of the Gamba Sonata in G minor, BWV 1029, at mm. 19 and 24, it emphasizes the arrival and the contrasting lyric character of the secondary theme as well as the establishment of the new key of the relative major. *Affettuoso* and *grave*—like *dolce* and *cantabile* primarily character designations, although carrying obvious implications for the tempo—turn up in both vocal and instrumental works. *Affettuoso* appears for the first time in the surviving printed libretto of the Mühlhausen cantata *Gott ist mein König*, BWV 71 (as part of the movement heading, *Affettuoso e Larghetto*, of the chorus "Du wollest dem Feinde"),[39] and thereafter only in the headings of instrumental compositions; the third movement of the C-minor Sonata for Violin and Continuo, BWV 1024 (a work of doubtful authenticity),[40] and—its most familiar occurrence—the second movement of the Fifth Brandenburg Concerto.[41] The term *grave*, too, except for its isolated appearance in the Weimar cantata *Ich hatte viel Bekümmernis*, BWV 21 (at the block-chord choral introduction to the final movement), is found only in instrumental compositions, in works belonging to virtually every medium: keyboard, organ, solo violin, ensemble.[42]

It is tempting to conclude this survey by presenting a grand tabulation in which all of Bach's tempo indications would be placed in their proper positions along the terminological continuum. Such a representation would of course take cognizance of the existence of synonyms: those that have been made explicit in the sources themselves through simultaneous usage, as well as those that can be plausibly inferred from linguistic equivalence (e.g., *adagio:lente, allegro:gay, presto:tres viste*, and so on). But depending on whether one adopts a "strict" or "free" approach to the identification of synonyms, that is, to the separating or coupling of terms, there could be as many as twenty-two discrete points on the scale or as few as fourteen. For example: Should *largo ma non tanto* be treated as a synonym of *larghtetto*, or should it be placed between *largo* and *larghetto*? Does *allegro moderato* belong between *moderato* and *un poc'allegro* or coupled with the latter? The heading *Adagio o vero Largo* (from the second movement of the C-major Concerto for Two Harpsichords, BWV 1061) would seem to mean something like "between *adagio* and *largo*." If that is so, then does it follow that the expression is synonymous with *adagio ma non tanto*, or does it mean something else? And, if it means something else, then does it signify a tempo faster or slower than *adagio ma non tanto*? In view of these and other uncertainties, it seems the better part of valor to refrain at this juncture from an all-too-ambitious peroration. We may hope and expect, though, that many of these uncertainties will be satisfactorily resolved in time as Bach's music is more closely examined and more extensively correlated with the terminological evidence than could be attempted here.

16

ORGAN OR "KLAVIER"?

Instrumental Prescriptions in the Sources of the Keyboard Works

As everyone knows, during the baroque era the various keyboard instruments, including the organ, largely shared a common repertoire. Most standard discussions of early keyboard music in fact begin with a statement to that effect. For example, we read at the start of Willi Apel's *The History of Keyboard Music to 1700*:

> The word *keyboard* in the title of this book . . . suits our purpose not only because of its brevity but also because it eliminates the need to differentiate between the organ and other keyboard instruments—a decision that is simply not feasible for most types of early keyboard music. . . .[1]

With respect to the music of Johann Sebastian Bach, however, musicians and scholars have never been comfortable with this information and have suspected that the practical reality in Bach's case could not have been so casual. Since at least the beginning of the nineteenth century until quite recently, all serious editions of Bach's keyboard music—publications that include both the Bach-Gesellschaft edition and the *Neue Bach-Ausgabe*—have proceeded on the assumption (usually unstated) that it is not only possible but altogether appropriate to separate this repertoire rather strictly into two discrete parts: one consisting of "organ" music, the other of music for the string keyboard

instruments. The scholarly literature, too, has approached the repertoire in largely the same way, that is, with separate discussions of each
corpus of works.

Nor has it been difficult to devise simple rules to help decide in
which category a given work belonged. Compositions with an independent pedal part (especially one with an obbligato character) or that
make use of liturgical material (i.e., a chorale melody) are normally clas-
sified as organ works. Conversely, keyboard compositions apparently
lacking a pedal part or chorale-derived material are assumed to have
been conceived for the harpsichord or the clavichord. This division has
the double virtue of being not only easy to implement but also eminently useful in that it has satisfied the very practical needs of the
most-interested constituencies—organists and other keyboard players.

These criteria, in fact, are already implicit in the Obituary of 1754,[2]
where the pertinent "unpublished works of the late Bach" are grouped
as follows:

> 5) Many free preludes, fugues, and similar pieces for organ, with
> obbligato pedal
> 6) Six trios for organ with obbligato pedal
> 7) Many preludes on chorales for the organ
> 8) A book of short preludes on most of the hymns of the church
> for the organ
> 9) Twice twenty-four preludes and fugues, in all keys, for the
> clavier
> 10) Six toccatas for the clavier
> 11) Six suites for the same
> 12) Six more of the same, somewhat shorter

And Forkel, in his biography, not only devoted separate chapters to
"Bach the Clavier Player" (Chapter III) and "Bach the Organist" (Chapter
IV), but, in his own list of works, expanded upon the separation of
the two repertoires already found in the Obituary. Moreover, in his
introduction to the organ pieces, he emphasized the indispensability of
the pedals, literally regarding them as the "essential part of the organ."[3]

The formal and official codification of the subdivision of Bach's keyboard repertoire is found in the pages of the *Bach-Werke Verzeichnis*, the
BWV, where the "Works for Organ" occupy numbers 525 through 771,
the "Works for Klavier," numbers 772 to 994. (Throughout this study,
too, the modern German term *Klavier* is used to denote the string keyboard instruments only, as opposed to the eighteenth-century *clavier*,
which, like the English, *keyboard*, embraces all keyboard instruments,
including the organ.)

A brief scanning of these sections of the BWV will show that a
discrete and systematic classification was not without its difficulties.
Indeed, for the very first entry among the organ works, the six sonatas,

BWV 525-30, the setting has been qualified as "Orgel. In erster Linie für Pedalclavichord oder Pedalcembalo geschrieben." The Fantasia and Fugue in A minor, BWV 561 (now considered to be a spurious work, perhaps by J. C. Kittel), although listed in the BWV among the organ works, carries the indication "Pedalcembalo (Orgel)." Similarly indecisive designations are offered for the Fugue in C minor, BWV 575: "Pedalcembalo (Orgel)"; the (presumably) spurious fugues in G major, BWV 576 and BWV 577: "Orgel (Pedalcembalo?)"; the Passacaglia in C minor, BWV 582: "Orgel oder Cembalo"; the Pastorale in F major, BWV 590: "Orgel (Pedalcembalo)"; and even the chorale partitas on *Christ, der du bist der helle Tag,* BWV 766: "Pedalflügel (Orgel)"; *O Gott, du frommer Gott,* BWV 767: "Orgel (Pedalflügel?)"; and *Ach, was soll ich Sünder machen,* BWV 770: "Orgel (Pedalflügel)."

The "Works for Klavier" evidently presented fewer ambiguities of this kind. Nonetheless, the four duets from *Clavier-Übung* III, BWV 802-05, are designated in the BWV for "Klavier (Orgel?)"; the Fugue in C major, BWV 946, for "Klavier (Pedalcembalo)"; the Fugue in A major, BWV 949, for "Klavier (Pedalflügel)"; and, finally, the Capriccio in E major, "In honorem Joh. Christoph Bachii," BWV 993, for "Klavier (Pedalcembalo)".

The main reason for Schmieder's occasional uncertainty is not difficult to find. As his curiously varying formulations in these questionable instances remind us, string keyboard instruments—especially clavichords but also harpsichords—as well as organs could be equipped with pedals. But what could have prompted Schmieder to weigh this possibility seriously enough to suggest it in no fewer than nineteen instances, when he is willing to entertain the opposite alternative—the performance on the organ of a "Klavier" work requiring only manual(s)—only once: in the special case of the four duets, BWV 802-05? This tendency is particularly strange since the option of writing an organ work without an obbligato pedal part was readily available for any baroque composer. Indeed, the notion that performance on the organ of a number of Bach's compositions calling for manual(s) alone was not only tolerated but actually preferred—that such compositions were perhaps conceived in the first instance as organ works—has not received much serious consideration.

In view of the common repertoire tradition as well as the baroque era's uninhibited practice of transcribing virtually any work from one medium to another, it is difficult to imagine that Bach would have objected to organ renditions of most of his keyboard compositions. But this proposition cannot be proven. Moreover, there is reason to believe that he was more sensitive than many of his contemporaries to the matter of scoring. It is striking, for example, that in his chamber music he consistently avoided such typical formulations of the period as "Violino ò traverso." If it could be demonstrated that some of Bach's compositions for manuals alone were probably conceived as organ works, that fact should be of considerable interest not only to scholars but even more so to organists and keyboard players.

Heinz Lohmann is apparently the first to take advantage of the practical implications of the common repertoire tradition as it affects Johann Sebastian Bach.[4] In the Short Afterword to his edition of the complete organ works for Breitkopf und Härtel, dated "Summer, 1979" (and reproduced identically in vols. 1–3, i.e., the volumes devoted to the preludes, fantasias, toccatas, fugues, and single pieces), Lohmann remarks:

> [T]he attempt to recover many *manualiter* works for the organ—and also for the Positive—has substantially expanded [the] range [of this edition] in comparison with other organ editions of the past and present. That this recovery could only be achieved for a selection of works is self-evident.

Lohmann has in fact carried out his selection with few restraints evidently guided by little more than personal taste and inclination. His edition includes about 50 compositions hitherto regarded as belonging to the province of "Klaviermusik." The "new" works are drawn chiefly from the larger and smaller preludes, toccatas, fantasies, and fugues. (Almost all the compositions in vol. 3 are new to editions of Bach's organ works.) But the edition also includes several of the concerto arrangements for manuals alone and, more surprisingly, such compositions as the Ouverture in F major, BWV 820; the *Aria variata alla maniera italiana*, BWV 989; and even the *Capriccio sopra la lontananza del suo fratello dilettissimo*, BWV 992.

In adopting this extremely "loose" approach, it seems that Lohmann has refrained only from recruiting compositions whose identification as works for string keyboard instrument is by now apparently unshakable: the *Well-Tempered Clavier*; the Two- and Three-part Inventions; the French and English Suites; and Parts I, II, and IV of the *Clavier-Übung*.[5] Lohmann's approach to Bach's repertoire is not only bold but clearly justified by early-eighteenth-century practice, although it is not entirely satisfying in its reliance on personal taste and preference. One wonders whether there may not be more objective criteria on which to base the inclusion or exclusion of particular compositions from a conscientious edition of Bach's organ works.

ORIGINAL INSTRUMENTAL DESIGNATIONS

Perhaps the most reliable source of Bach's intentions with regard to instrumentation are in the headings or on the title pages of the primary sources: the autographs and the original editions prepared under the composer's supervision. Contrary to the impression often conveyed by the secondary literature, there are in fact a respectable number of keyboard compositions by Bach preserved in such sources (see Tables 16.1 and 16.2).

TABLE 16.1   Work Headings in the Primary Sources of Bach's Organ Compositions*

BWV	Heading	Source	Date	Comment
525–30	Sonata 1[–6] à 2 Clav. et Pedal	P 271	ca. 1730	Autograph
535	Preludio con Fuga per il Organo	Lpz *III.8.7*	ca. 1740–50	Apograph with autograph additions
535a	Praeludium cum Fuga— ex. Gb. Pedaliter	SPK *Mus. ms. 10614*	ca. 1707	Autograph fragment
541	Praeludium pro Organo con Pedal: obligat:	SPK *N. Mus. ms. 378*	ca. 1733–42	Autograph
544	Praeludium pro Organo cum pedale obligato (Title page)	Private collection	ca. 1727–31	Autograph
	Praeludium in Organo pleno, pedal: (Heading)	Private collection	ca. 1727–31	Autograph
545	Praeludium pro Organo cum Pedale obligato (Title page)	Lost	?	Autograph
	Praeludium in Organo pleno pedaliter (Heading)	Lost	?	Autograph
548	Praeludium pedaliter pro Organo	SPK P 274	ca. 1727–31	Partial autograph (to m.21 of Fugue; thereafter: Kellner)
550	Praeludium pedaliter	SPK P 1210	?	Apograph with autograph additions
552/1	Praeludium pro Organo pleno	*Clavier Übung* III	1739	Original edition
552/2	Fuga à 5. con pedale. pro Organo pleno	*Clavier-Übung* III	1739	Original edition
562/1	Fantasia pro Organo. a. 5 Vocum, cum pedali obligato	SPK P 490	ca. 1720–30	Autograph

Table 16.1   (Continued)

BWV	Heading	Source	Date	Comment
562/2	Fuga. a 5	SPK P 490	ca. 1745?	Autograph fragment
573	Fantasia pro Organo	P 224	ca. 1722–23	Autograph
596	Concerto a 2 Clav: & Pedale	SPK P 330	ca. 1713	Autograph
599–644	Orgel-Büchlein Worinne einem anfahenden Organisten Anleitung gegeben wird . . . sich im *Pedal studio* zu *habilitiren,* indem . . . das Pedal gantz *obligat tractiret* wird.	P 283	1713 ff.	Autograph title added during Köthen period
645–50	Sechs Chorale von verschiedener Art auf einer Orgel mit 2 Clavieren und Pedal. . . .	Print	ca. 1748	Original edition
651–65	[From the "Seventeen Great Chorales"]	P 271	1740–48?	Autograph
651	Fantasia . . . in organo pleno			
652	alio modo a 2 Clav. et Ped			
653	a 2 Clav. e Pedal			
654	a 2 Clav. e Pedal			
655	Trio a 2 Clav. e Pedal			
656	Versus. manualiter [3rd verse:] Pedal			
657	a 2 Clav. et Ped.			
658	[over Staff:] Ped.			
659	a 2 Clav. et Ped.			
660	a due Bassi è canto fermo			
661	in organo pleno. Canto fermo in Pedal			
662	a 2 Clav. et Ped.			
663	a 2 Clav. et Ped.			
664	Trio . . . a 2 Clav. et Ped			
665	sub communione . . . pedaliter			*pedaliter* possibly added later
669–89, etc.	Dritter Theil der Clavier-Übung bestehend in verschiedenen Vorspielen über die Catechismus- und andere Gesaenge, vor die Orgel	*Clavier-Übung* III	1739	Original edition

Table 16.1   (Continued)

BWV	Heading	Source	Date	Comment
669	à 2 Clav. et Ped			
670	à 2 Clav. et Ped			
671	a 5 Canto fermo in Bassi cum Organo Pleno			
672	alio modo manualiter			
675	Canto fermo in alto			
676	à 2 Clav. et Pedal			
677	. . . manualiter			
678	à 2 Clav. et Ped.			
679	. . . manualiter			
680	In Organo pleno con Pedali			
681	. . . manualiter			
682	à 2 Clav. et Pedal			
683	alio modo manualiter			
684	à 2 Clav. è Canto fermo in Pedal			
685	alio modo manualiter			
686	à 6 in Organo pleno con Pedale doppio			
687	à 4 alio modo manualiter			
688	à 2 Clav. e Canto fermo in Pedal			
689	a 4 manualiter			
691	Wer nur den lieben Gott läßt walten	Yale: (Clavier-Büchlein WFB)	ca. 1720	Autograph
728	Jesus mein Zuversicht	P 224	ca. 1722-23	Autograph
739	Wie schön leuchtet . . . a 2 Clav. Ped.	SPK P 488	ca. 1705?	Autograph
753	Jesu meine Freude	Yale: (Clavier-Büchlein	ca. 1720	Autograph
764	[No heading]	P 488	ca. 1705?	Autograph
769	Einige canonische Veraenderungen . . . vor die Orgel mit 2. Clavieren und dem Pedal	Print	ca. 1747?	Original edition
769a	Vom Himmel hoch . . . [Var. 1, 2, 4:] a 2 Clav. et Pedal	P 271	ca. 1748?	Autograph

*See the source descriptions in the pertinent *Kritische Berichte* of the NBA and *Bach-Dokumente* I; also George Stauffer, *The Organ Preludes of Johann Sebastian Bach* (Ann Arbor, 1980). Appendix I: and Peter Williams, *The Organ Music of J. S. Bach* (Cambridge, 1980-1984), vols. 1 and 2.

TABLE 16.2   Work Headings in the Primary Sources of Bach's
             "Klavier" Compositions*

BWV	Heading	Source	Date	Comment
772–801	[No general title]	Yale *Clavier-Büchlein*	ca. 1722–23	Autograph
772–86	Praeambulum 1 [-15] (Headings)			Partial autograph
787–801	Fantasia 1[-15] (Headings)			Autograph
772–801	Auffrichtige Anleitung, Wormit denen Liebhabern des *Clavires* . . . eine deütliche Art gezeiget wird . . . eine *cantable* Art im Spielen zu erlangen	P 610	1723	Autograph
772–87	Inventio 1[-15] (Headings)	P 610	1723	Autograph
788–801	Sinfonia 1[-15] (Headings)	P 610	1723	Autograph
802–805	Duetto I[-IV]	*Clavier-Übung* III	1739	Original edition
814	Suite pour le Clavessin	P 224	1722	Autograph
815	Suite ex Dis pour le Clavessin	P 224	1722	Autograph
816	Suite pour le Clavessin ex G♮	P 224	1722	Autograph
825–30	Clavier Ubung bestehend in Praeludien, Allemanden, Couranten, Sarabanden, Giquen, Menuetten, und andern Galanterien [Individual compositions: Partita I[-VI]	*Clavier-Übung* I	1731 (1726–30)	Original edition
827	[No heading]	SPK P 225	1725	Autograph
830	[No heading]	SPK P 225	1725	Autograph
831a	Ouverture pour le Clavesin	SPK P 226	ca. 1730	Apograph with autograph heading
971, 831	Zweyter Theil der Clavier Ubung . . . vor ein Clavicymbel mit zweyen Manualen	*Clavier Übung* II	1735	Original edition
846–69	Das Wohl*temperirte Clavier*, oder *Praeludia*, und Fugen durch alle *Tone* und *Semitonia* . . .	P 415	1722– ca. 1740	Autograph

Table 16.2   *(Continued)*

BWV	Heading	Source	Date	Comment
870–93	[*Well-Tempered Clavier* II: No title page]	London British Library *Add. 35021*	ca. 1738–41	Partially autograph
886	Fuga ex Gis dur	SPK P 274	1730s?	Autograph
906/1	Fantasia per il Cembalo	Bethlehem Bach Choir	1726–31	Autograph
906/1–2	[No heading]	Dresden Sächsische Landes-bibliothek 2405-T-52	ca. 1735–40	Autograph fragment
924	Praeambulum I	Yale *Clavier-Büchlein*	1720	Autograph
930	Praeambulum	Yale *Clavier-Büchlein*	1720–22	Autograph
953	Fuga à 3	Yale *Clavier-Büchlein*	ca. 1724	Autograph
988	Clavier Ubung be-stehend in einer ARIA mit verschiedenen Veraenderungen vors Clavicimbal mit 2 Manualen . . .	*Clavier-Übung* [IV]	ca. 1742	Original edition
991	Air	P 224	1722	Autograph
994	Applicatio	Yale *Clavier-Büchlein*	1720	Autograph

*See the source descriptions in the pertinent *Kritische Berichte* of the NBA and *Bach-Dokumente* I, as well as in the various published facsimile editions.

It is significant that Bach has usually troubled to provide some kind of instrumental designation along with the title or the genre indication of a composition. But it is admittedly disappointing that many of these designations, at least at first glance, are ambiguous. They usually do not contain explicit prescriptions, such as "pro organo" or "per il cembalo," but are as likely to read "a 2 Clav. et Pedal," "pedaliter," "manualiter," or, simply, "Clavier." These formulations, however, may be more informative than would at first appear. But it is advisable to proceed cautiously, even if that at times entails belaboring the obvious.

Organo; Cembalo; Clavessin

The almost invariable inclusion of a reference to the pedals in any original heading explicitly mentioning "Orgel" or "Organo," as in the phrases "Organo con/cum Pedal(e)" or "Organo pedaliter," certainly suggests (as Forkel argued) that Bach must have regarded the pedals as an "essential" part of the organ. But it also suggests that organists of the time expected to be informed (or forewarned) whether an organ composition contained an obbligato pedal part. Otherwise such phrases would be tautological. At all events, it is safer to assume that Bach had reason to add such written qualifications. (The only instances in which he apparently failed to mention the pedals in connection with an "Organo" heading are the autograph of the *Fantasia pro Organo* in C major, BWV 573, preserved in the 1722 *Clavier-Büchlein* for Anna Magdalena Bach; and the *Praeludium pro Organo pleno*, BWV 552/1, printed at the beginning of *Clavier-Übung* III. However, the indications "Ped." and "Pedal," respectively, are present in the first measures of these works.) As for the harpsichord, it is not surprising, but worth noting, that no Bach autograph or original print specifying "Clavessin/Clavecin," "Cembalo," or "Clavicymbel/Clavicimbal" contains an independent pedal part.[6] And, from the titles of *Clavier-Übung* II and IV, it seems safe to conclude that Bach normally had to reckon with a single-manual harpsichord.

Pedal Clavichord; Pedal Harpsichord

The consistent presence of pedal indications in the primary sources of Bach's keyboard compositions explicitly for organ and, conversely, their consistent absence in the primary sources of works explicitly for harpsichord would seem to support a number of corollaries: for example, that compositions with pedal indications but no instrumental designation per se—for example, the isolated *pedaliter* indication in BWV 535a or, far more common, the prescription "a 2 Clav. e(t) Ped(al)" alone—were in fact intended for the organ and only the organ. There is absolutely no evidence that they were intended for the pedal harpsichord or pedal clavichord. These instruments are not mentioned in the original sources for any Bach compositions or in any authentic Bach document.[7] Much has been made of a statement in a document dated November 11, 1750, shortly after the death of J. S. Bach, to the effect that he had once given his son Johann Christian "3. Clavire nebst Pedal" (translated in *The Bach Reader* as "3 claviers with a set of pedals").[8] To assume automatically that the formulation must have been synonymous with "3 Pedalcembali"[9] is dangerous, since it seems most unlikely that Bach would have possessed three complete pedal harpsichords and given them all to the same son. It is far more likely that he had once owned, in addition to the various clavecins mentioned in Chapter 6 of the Estate Catalogue of July 28, 1750,[10] three *claviers*, that is, manuals (perhaps the otherwise unmentioned clavichords; see below), along with a set of pedals that could be played together with one (or more?) of the manuals in the manner described by Jakob Adlung in his *Musica mechanica Organoedi.* [11]

In any case, it seems that pedal harpsichords and clavichords served primarily as practice instruments,[12] on which a keyboard player not only practiced pedal technique but also prepared compositions that were ultimately to be performed on a full-sized pedal organ, no doubt in a church. As for Bach's use of the contraption, Forkel reports in Chapter 3 of his biography that the composer used it for such private purposes as sight reading ensemble pieces at the keyboard(s) and improvising upon them.[13]

2 Clav. et Pedal; Pedaliter

There is ample evidence that Bach regarded the designation "2 Clav. e(t) Ped(al)" as a synonym for the (full-sized) organ. The title page of the Schübler Chorales mentions an "Orgel mit 2 Clavieren und Pedal," as do numerous headings of the individual chorale settings in *Clavier-Übung* III, the title page of which specifies "vor die Orgel." Also, the surviving autograph scores for the early chorale prelude *Wie schön leuchtet uns der Morgenstern,* BWV 739, whose heading reads "a 2 Clav. Ped.," and the "Concerto a 2 Clav: & Pedale," BWV 596, both contain the organ registration indications "BR" and "Brustpos." (i.e., *Brustwerk, Brustpositiv*), "O" and "ObW" (i.e., *Oberwerk*), and, in the case of BWV 596, "R" (i.e., Rückpositiv). It should be recalled, too, that even the Trio Sonatas, BWV 525-30, "a 2 Clav. et Pedal"—the works that have been suggested as candidates for the pedal harpsichord most frequently and most seriously (as, for example, in the BWV citation)—were catalogued as early as 1754, in the Obituary, as organ compositions.[14]

The use of the term *pedaliter* alone—that is, unattached to an organ prescription—is found in a Bach autograph only once: in the pre-1707 version of the Prelude and Fugue in G minor, BWV 535a, preserved in the *Möllersche Handschrift,* (SPK) *Mus. ms. 40644*. Confirmation for the view that here again Bach could have had only the organ in mind (not that there was ever much doubt), is provided by a manuscript containing the revised form of the work, BWV 535 (Leipzig, Musikbibliothek der Stadt Leipzig III.8.7). The presence of autograph entries in the manuscript also lends the authority of a primary source to the title page, which reads, "Preludio con Fuga per il Organo."[15] *Pedaliter*, in any case, was a very common designation in the late seventeenth and early eighteenth century for North German organ works requiring obbligato pedals; for example, in the compositions of Scheidemann, Tunder, and Buxtehude.[16] In fact, of the presumed organ works in the *Möllersche Handschrift* with any instrumental designations at all, five carry the *pedaliter* designation. (In addition to BWV 535a, they are the Prelude and Fugue in C major, BWV 531; the Prelude and Fugue in D minor BWV 549a; and Nikolaus Bruhns, Preludes in G major, and E minor. One also finds "con Pedale" for a Prelude and Fugue in A major by Buxtehude, and "2 Clav. con Ped." for BWV 739.) None make specific reference to "organo."[17] In sum, the proposition entertained, if not quite advocated, in the pages of the BWV that any composition of Johann Sebastian Bach's could have been seriously intended for—as distinct from merely tolerated on—a pedal harpsichord or clavichord is surely nothing but a red herring.

When we attempt to determine the instrument(s) Bach had in mind for his keyboard compositions lacking obbligato pedal parts the difficulties multiply. We have only been able to establish so far that there are no pedal parts in any of Bach's compositions explicitly for harpsichord (i.e., "cembalo" or "clavecin"). Can anything more useful be learned beyond this not very surprising fact?

Clavichord

The clavichord is never mentioned in any original or early sources of Bach's keyboard music, nor—despite Forkel's well-known claim in Chapter 3 of his biography that Bach "liked best to play upon the clavichord"—is the instrument mentioned in the catalogue of his estate.[18] Forkel does go on to say in the same context, though, that Bach "considered the clavichord as the best instrument for *study* and, in general, for *private* musical entertainment [emphasis added]."[19] The tacit implication of this remark is, at the least, that Bach did not regard the clavichord as the "best instrument" for his more ambitious keyboard compositions. Indeed, Johann Gottfried Walther, in the entry "clavicordo" in his *Musikalisches Lexikon* (p. 169) notes that the instrument "is, so to speak, for all players the first grammar," that is, a "primer"[20]—in effect, a practice instrument, perhaps not substantially different in function from the domestic pedal board instruments. (This usage may be the reason that the pedal clavichord was more common than the pedal harpsichord at the time.[21] It also lends strength to the suspicion, already expressed above, that the "3. Clavire nebst Pedal" Bach gave to Johann Christian were, in all likelihood, so many clavichords, along with a pedal board.)

Manualiter

There can be little doubt that Bach had the organ in mind for the eight chorale settings in *Clavier-Übung* III that both lack pedals and are specifically marked *manualiter.* Not only does the title page of the collection specify the organ in connection with the "various preludes on the Catechism and other hymns" but its internal ordering—along with the occasional addition of an "alio modo" indication (in *Kyrie, Gott Vater in Ewigkreit,* BWV 672; *Vater unser im Himmelreich,* BWV 683; *Christ, unser Herr, zum Jordan kam,* BWV 685; and *Aus tiefer Not schrei' ich zu dir,* BWV 687)— makes clear that the pieces were offered as alternatives to the setting(s) of the same chorales "a 2 Clav. et Pedal." Furthermore, since in Bach's usage, keyboard works specifically intended for harpsichord have no pedal parts (almost by definition, we might say), the only meaning the *manualiter* indication could have had (beyond mere redundancy) would be in connection with organ rendition.[21a] That is, under normal circumstances the term must have been the *de facto* equivalent of an organ indication. If so—unfortunately, Walther does not include entries for *manualiter* or *pedaliter* in his dictionary—then the presence of the term in reliable Bach sources could be taken as *prima facie* evidence that the compositions were conceived in the first instance as organ works.

THE TOCCATAS, BWV 910–16

Apart from *Clavier-Übung* III, the *manualiter* indication appears in the heading of only one other primary Bach source: the autograph of the three-strophe chorale setting *O Lamm Gottes unschuldig,* BWV 656, from the "Great Eighteen Collection." (The third strophe, or verse, calls for "Pedal.") But the term does appear in a few early, if nonautograph, Bach sources. Many of them—such as the *Andreas-Bach-Buch,* Johann Peter Kellner's voluminous miscellany (SPK, P 804), and a Preller manuscript (SPK P 1082)—originated either within or reassuringly close to Bach's own circle.[22] Most significantly, the compositions involved are virtually all confined to a single genre, the toccata, and indeed include all the surviving "Klavier" toccatas, BWV 910–16 (see Table 16.3).[23] The clear implication is that the "Klavier" toccatas must have been intended by Bach for the organ. And there is evidence, apart from the presence of the *manualiter* indications, to support this assertion. Table 16.4 shows the ranges of the principal instruments at Bach's disposal throughout his career.[24]

   In his study of the compass of Bach's "Klavier" works, Alfred Dürr points out that in the Toccata in D minor, BWV 913 (at m. 89), and the

TABLE 16.3   Representative Early Sources of Bach's Keyboard Toccatas
(by Key)

Key	BWV	Heading	Source	Comment
C major	564	Toccata ex C♮. pedaliter	P 286	Copyist[s]: Kellner [and anonymous][24a] range: to d″
C minor	911	Toccata C♭. Manualiter	ABB*	Copyist: Hauptschreiber
D major	912a	Toccata ex D fis	*Mus. ms. 40644*	Copyist: Hauptschreiber
D major	912	Toccata. Manualiter del . . . Bach. Organista	P 289	Anonymous copyist: 2d half of 18th century
D minor	565	Toccata Con Fuga: pedaliter. ex d♯ [*sic*]	P 595	Copyist: Ringk
D minor	538	Toccata con Fuga D♭.	P 803	Copyist: Walther
D minor	913	Toccata Prima. ex Clave D♭ manualiter	P 281	Copyist: Joh. Christoph Georg Bach?
E minor	914	Toccata ex E♭. manualiter	Private collection, Germany	Copyist: H. N. Gerber
F major	540	Toccata col pedale obligato	P 803	Copyists: J. T. Krebs, 540/1; J. L. Krebs, 540/2
F♯ minor	910	Toccata ex Fis. Manualiter	ABB	Copyist: Hauptschreiber
G major	916	Toccata. Manualiter	ABB	Copyist: Hauptschreiber (and Nebenschreiber)
G minor	915	Toccata manualiter in G mol	P 1082	Copyist: Preller

Andreas-Bach-Buch

Toccata in G minor, BWV 915 (at m. 186). B♭$_1$ has been conspicuously avoided; as has d‴ in the Toccata in G, BWV 916, (at m. 134; i.e., Movement 3, m. 54).[25] That is, at these points in the compositions the logical continuation of a sequential pattern has been broken, evidently because the composer was constrained by the compass limitations of his instrument. Apart from such adjustments, the keyboard ranges found in the Toccatas, BWV 910–16, are as shown in Table 16.5.

It is important to realize that although such range limitations do prevail in Bach's "Klavier" works up to the mid-1720s (more precisely, until 1726—with the publication of the first of the partitas belonging

TABLE 16.4   The Compass of the "Bach" Organs

Arnstadt (Neue Kirche)	manuals: CDE–d'''
	pedals: CDE–d'
Mühlhausen (Divi Blasii)	manuals: CD–d'''
	pedals: CD–d'
Weimar (Schlosskirche)	manuals: C–c'''
	pedals: C–e'(?)
Köthen (Schlosskapelle)	manuals: C–e'''
	pedals: C–e'
Köthen (St. Agnus-kirche)	manuals: C–d'''(?)
	pedals: CD–d'e'f'
Leipzig*	manuals: CD–c'''
	pedals: CD–d'

*The range observed in the organ works presumably composed during the Leipzig period.

to *Clavier-Übung* I), they are not universal—not even in his early compositions. Most significant for our concerns is the appearance of A_1 in the *Aria variata*, BWV 989. Like three of the toccatas under consideration here, it is transmitted in the *Andreas-Bach-Buch.*[26]

Several other features related to keyboard range in the "Klavier" toccatas are worth noting. Bach calls for the complete chromatic range only in the Toccata in F♯ minor, BWV 910, which is an emphatically chromatic work in every respect, a "chromatic fantasy" of sorts. None of the others contain the low C♯, not even the Toccatas in G minor, BWV 915, and G major, BWV 916, where the pitch could have been employed effectively as the leading tone of the dominant. Bach did find ample opportunity in the Toccata in F♯ minor, after all, to prescribe the low C several times—notated as B♯$_1$ and serving just this function (mm. 13, 104, and 134).

It is tempting to try to connect the individual toccatas, on the basis of their ranges, with the various "Bach" organs—associating the

TABLE 16.5   The Ranges of the "Klavier" Toccatas

BWV	Key	Range
910	F♯ minor	C(B♯$_1$)–b''
911	C minor	CD–c'''
912/912a	D major	CDE–c'''
913	D minor	CDE–c'''
914	E minor	CD–c'''
915	G minor	CD–c'''
916	G major	CDE–c'''

toccatas that omit both C♯ and D♯ (the Toccatas in D major, D minor, and G major) with Arnstadt, linking those omitting only the C♯ (the Toccatas in C minor, E minor, and G minor) with Mühlhausen, and ascribing the fully chromatic Toccata in F♯ minor to Weimar. (The latter's inclusion in the *Andreas-Bach-Buch* precludes a later origin.[27]) But this chronological placement is too bold. There was nothing to prevent Bach from composing the Toccatas in D major, D minor, or G major despite their lack of C♯ and D♯ , after the Arnstadt period, or the Toccatas in C minor, E minor, or G minor, despite their lack of C♯, after the Mühlhausen period.

On the other hand, the appearance of the Toccata in D major, BWV 912a, in the *Möllersche Handschrift* (in close proximity to the autograph entry of the Prelude and Fugue in G minor, BWV 535a), along with its undeniably primitive stylistic features—conventional thematic material, stereotyped sequential patterns[28]—argues strongly for an early date of composition (before 1707, i.e., Arnstadt?). And if one assumes that Bach normally composed keyboard works for the instruments regularly at his disposal, then it follows that he would have written the Toccata in F♯ minor at Weimar, since the work, with its fully chromatic range, could only have been performed on the Weimar organ. Moreover, both the advanced chromatic language and the more-sophisticated organization of the composition[29] argue for such a dating.[29a]

Finally, in the case of the Toccata in G major, BWV 916, there is strong stylistic as well as external evidence supporting not an Arnstadt origin, as entertained above, but one in Weimar. The deliberate avoidance of d‴ (noted by Dürr) would have been necessary only on the Weimar organ (the note was available on the Arnstadt and Mühlhausen manuals). The three-movement concerto form of the composition also provides a compelling argument (made by Schulze and others), for Weimar. It points specifically toward the later Weimar period, ca. 1713-14, when Bach seems to have been preoccupied with the Italian concerto form.[30]

The conclusion that the Toccatas, BWV 910-16, were in all likelihood conceived as *manualiter* organ pieces inevitably demands that they be considered in connection with the *pedaliter* Toccatas in D minor ("Dorian," BWV 538), F Major (BWV 540), C Major (BWV 564), and D minor (BWV 565). If one "collates" the two groups, their keys seem to complement each other (see Table 16.3 above). The C-major *Toccata ex C♮. pedaliter*, BWV 564,[31] corresponds, as it were, to the *Toccata C♭. Manualiter*, BWV 911; the D-major *manualiter* Toccata, BWV 912/912a, to one or the other of the D-minor *pedaliter* Toccatas, BWV 538 or 565. (But then there is also the D-minor *manualiter* Toccata, BWV 913.) The obvious tonal and even stylistic counterpart to the E-minor *manualiter* Toccata, BWV 914, would be the E-major *pedaliter* "Toccata," BWV 566, although it must be reported that the work is called "Praeludium" or "Preludio" in the eighteenth-century sources with unusual unanimity.[32]

It is particularly tempting to try to associate the *Toccata col pedale obligato,* in F, BWV 540 (thus headed in P 803), with the Toccata in F♯ minor, BWV 910. We have seen that both the range and the mature style of the Toccata in F♯ minor argue for a Weimar origin. As for the Toccata in F, its unique pedal range—to f' (and including e' ♭)—makes it virtually certain that the work was written for the organ at Weissenfels.[33] And since the copy of the work entered into the Walther manuscript, P 803 (by Johann Tobias Krebs), seems to be dateable to ca. 1714,[34] one can conclude that Bach composed at least the toccata section of BWV 540 during the Weimar years, almost certainly in connection with his visit to Weissenfels in February 1713, at which time the "Hunting" Cantata, BWV 208, was composed and performed in honor of the birthday of Duke Christian.[35]

Whatever principle of alternation between *manualiter* and *pedaliter* settings may have been operating—intentionally or not—in the surviving corpus of toccatas, it was evidently abandoned by Bach when he composed the Toccatas in G major and G minor, BWV 916 and 915, for manuals alone.

"ALIO MODO" SETTINGS; CONCERTO ARRANGEMENTS

Other keyboard works by Bach seem to be related to one another according to what may be called an "alio modo" principle based on the alternation of *manualiter* vis-à-vis *pedaliter* settings of similar material. For example, the Toccata in D major, BWV 912/912a, not only exists in two alternative *manualiter* settings but shares its striking opening flourishes with the Prelude and Fugue in D major, BWV 532, a work dated by Stauffer to the early Weimar period or perhaps even earlier.[36] The general resemblance between the clavier Fugue in A minor, BWV 944, the the organ Fugue in A minor, BWV 543/543a, has often been noted.[37] (In the *Andreas-Bach-Buch,* the fugue of BWV 944 is preceded by a free prelude in arpeggio style with the heading "Fantasia in A♭ pour le Clavessin."[38] It is not clear whether the harpsichord prescription is meant to apply to the Fugue as well as to the "cembalistic" Fantasia. The Fugue contains rather long sustained notes in the bass and has a range of CD–c'''.)[38a]

Finally, among the keyboard transcriptions of concertos five are *pedaliter,* BWV 592–96,[39] and sixteen are *manualiter,* BWV 972–87—seventeen, if one includes the questionable Concerto in G major, BWV 592a. If the concerto is authentic, then there are two instances of "alio modo" settings in the strict sense (i.e., alternative versions based on the same material) within this repertoire. The first is the pair of arrangements of Duke Johann Ernst's Violin Concerto in G major, consisting of BWV 592 and BWV 592a. The former is preserved in the manuscript (SPK) P 280, where it has the heading "Concerto a 2 Clav. et Ped." The latter apparently survives in a single source, Leipzig, Musikbibliothek der Stadt Leipzig *Poel. mus. MS 29* (a manuscript that has been dated ca. 1780/90), with the heading "Concerto per il Cembalo Solo."[40] The second "alio modo" pair, both members of which are certainly authentic, consists of alternative settings of another work by Johann Ernst, the Violin Concerto in C major. The heading of the *pedaliter* arrangement, BWV 595, in a copy found in the Kellner-circle manuscript, (SPK) P 286, reads "Concerto . . . appropriato all Organo à 2 Clavier: et Pedal." The *manualiter* arrangement, BWV 984, copied into the Kellner miscellany, P 804, by Johannes Ringk,[41] contains no instrumental designation.

With the exception of the arrangement of Vivaldi's Concerto in D minor, Op. 3, No. 11, "a 2 Clav: & Pedale," BWV 596, discussed earlier, none of the concerto transcriptions survive in autograph. The concertos, BWV 972-82, along with BWV 592, are contained in the copy prepared by Bach's cousin, [the Eisenach town organist Johann Bernhard Bach]. (The manuscript, in P 280, carries the inscription "J. E. Bach. Lipsiens. 1739.") The title page, [unlike the rest of the manuscript, is in the hand of Bach's godson, Johann Ernst, and] reads *XII. CONCERTO di Vivaldi [sic] elabor: di J. S. Bach.*[42] Neither the title page nor the headings of the individual concertos contain any instrumental indication except for the "a 2 Clav. et Ped." indication for BWV 592 (see above). Nor are there any instrumental designations in the principal source for BWV 983-87, the Kellner manuscript, P 804.[43] In contrast to the *manualiter* arrangements, the five *pedaliter* settings, BWV 592-96, are scattered over a number of manuscripts, each concerto having its own source constellation.[44] Like the headings of the principal sources for BWV 592 and 596 cited earlier, the copy of BWV 594 in P 286 mentions "2. Clavier et Pedal." (As we have seen, the heading for BWV 595, which is also contained in P 286, specifically mentions the organ.) The late-eighteenth-century source for BWV 593 originally read only "Concerto." (A later hand added "pro organo."[45])

The prevailing assumption—one apparently never really challenged until Lohmann included the *manualiter* concerto transcriptions BWV 973, 974, 978, 984, and 986 in vol. 5 of his edition—has been that only the five concertos "a 2. Clav. et Pedal" were meant for the organ, the other sixteen (or seventeen) for the harpsichord. Once again, there can be no doubt that Bach would have condoned harpsichord performances of these pieces. But whether he actually intended them for the harpsichord in the first place is not at all clear. There is, after all, no explicit indication for the harpsichord in the best sources for BWV 972-87 (P 280 for BWV 972-82, P 804 for BWV 983-87). And, as Hans-Joachim Schulze has convincingly demonstrated, Bach's arrangements must have been prepared, on commission for Johann Ernst, during the period from July

1713 to July 1714, that is, on the Duke's return to Weimar from a tour
of the Netherlands. During the journey the duke acquired numerous
concertos and became familiar at first hand with the Dutch practice
of performing transcriptions of Italian concertos in church—on the
organ—as part of a tradition of nonliturgical concert entertainments.[46]
In 1713, and until March 1714, Bach's official position in Weimar was
as court organist at the Himmelsburg Chapel. In the spring of 1713,
the Weimar court was eagerly awaiting not only the return of the
duke from his travels abroad (with his cache of Italian and French
instrumental music) but also the completion of the renovation of the
organ in the Himmelsburg Chapel.[47] Johann Gottfried Walther, the
duke's instructor in music and the Weimar town organist, as well as
Bach produced a number of concerto transcriptions for the organ, some
of them *manualiter*.[48]

Finally, as Alfred Dürr notes, the keyboard range of BWV 592a and
972–87 largely stays within the four octaves C–c'''. The only exceptions
are the B_1 in BWV 979, a single Bb_1 in BWV 982, and an isolated d''' in
BWV 975-a pitch otherwise regularly avoided in the work. Dürr points
out that the only source for BWV 975 is Johann [Bernhard] Bach's
copy, and that it is possible that here (and in the other instances as
well?) the source "does not reflect the original reading of the Weimar
arrangement in every respect."[49] All this suggests that not only the
concerto transcriptions "a 2 clav. et pedal" but the *manualiter* settings
as well may have originally been intended for the organ.

THE DUETS FROM *CLAVIER-ÜBUNG* III

Whatever one ultimately concludes about the toccatas and the concerto transcriptions, there can hardly be any doubt that Bach must have
reckoned with organ performance of the four duets, BWV 802–05, published in *Clavier-Übung* III. A *manualiter* designation, however, is notably
absent from the headings of these pieces in the print: they are simply called *Duetto* [I–IV]. Nonetheless, since only the organ is specifically
mentioned on the title page, the burden of proof is surely on anyone
who would maintain that the duets were written for some other instrument. One could point out, of course, that the title page refers only to
the chorale settings as "vor die Orgel." But the monumentally organ-
istic Prelude and Fugue in Eb, BWV 552, is not mentioned on the title
page either. Neither that omission, then, nor the remark by Johann Elias
Bach (in a letter of January 1739) that *Clavier-Übung* III was only *"princi-
pally* for those who play organ"[50] seems sufficient to challenge the *prima
facie* case favoring the organ as the instrument of choice for the entire
collection. Indeed, the range of all four duets keeps within the lim-

ited organ compass of CDE-c'''. As the other parts of the *Clavier-Übung* abundantly testify, Bach was rather keen at this time on extending the range of his harpsichord works well beyond this compass (from G_1A_1 to d'''). It would thus seem that Bach was concerned that the duets be playable on almost any organ.

CLAVIER

There was surely more involved in Bach's self-imposed restraint. A keyboard composition that was restricted to a single manual and to a C-c''' compass could have been played on virtually any keyboard instrument of the time, especially if it also largely avoided the low chromatic pitches C♯ and/or D♯. In other words, the absence of the pedal and the restriction of the range to C-c''' were the two—and the only two—"universal characteristics" common to both the organ and the string keyboard instruments, that is, to the *clavier*. During the baroque era *clavier* was the general designation for all keyboard instruments; and Bach confirmed that usage when, following the precedent of Johann Kuhnau, he chose *Clavier-Übung* as the title for his ambitious series of keyboard publications.

But in his practical realization of this project, Bach provided explicit instrumental designations: in Parts II and IV for a Clavicymbel/Clavicimbal with two manuals, in Part III for an organ. Needless to say, he felt free—though not obliged—to take advantage of the specific capacities of each; but he could not ignore their limitations. Thus, Part III of the *Clavier-Übung,* "vor die Orgel," keeps within the four-octave range throughout, even though it does not always prescribe the pedal; and the harpsichord works of the remaining parts necessarily dispense with a pedal part even though they do not necessarily exploit the complete G_1A_1-d''' range.[51] Part I contains no instrumental designation, but both the genre to which the collection is devoted (the suite, with its strong identification with the harpsichord) and the expansive compass of the pieces make it clear that only the harpsichord was intended. Furthermore, since these suites can all be played on a single manual, there was no need for any additional prescription, as was the case in Parts II and IV. (The presence of the designation "pour le Clavessin" in the headings of the French Suites, BWV 814–16, in the 1722 *Clavier-Büchlein* for Anna Magdalena Bach provides explicit confirmation—if any were needed—that Bach associated the suite genre with the harpsichord. The formulation "Suite . . . pour le Clavessin" itself was obviously borrowed from French publications of the time.)

The term *clavier* also appears in the titles of the *Clavier-Büchlein* volumes for Anna Magdalena and Wilhelm Friedemann Bach. Since these books are eminently personal documents, which reflect the particular needs, tastes, and instrumental resources of their recipients and owners, it would be rash to generalize too much from them. But they do reveal, as Dürr notes, that until ca. 1730 Anna Magdalena must have had at her disposal a *clavier* with a range of C–c''', and thereafter an instrument that extended at least from Bb_1 to d'''. Similarly, the presence of B_1 in both original sources of the Two- and Three-part Inventions and Sinfonias—that is, in both the *Clavier-Büchlein vor Wilhelm Friedemann Bach* and the fair copy, Berlin, P 610—suggests that Bach must have assumed that these avowedly preparatory compositions would be studied at home, no doubt on one of the domestic keyboard instruments. The most likely candidate was surely the traditional "practice" instrument, the clavichord, whose low strings, of course, could also be retuned from one piece to another.[52]

Bach's most enigmatic use of the term *clavier* perhaps is in the title *Das Wohltemperirte Clavier*. The *Well-Tempered Clavier*, of course, cannot properly be compared either to the *Clavier-Büchlein* volumes or to the Two- and Three-part Inventions, even in their fair-copy version with its elaborate title page. Unlike the former, the *Well-Tempered Clavier* is clearly addressed to a general audience; unlike the latter it is not limited to relative beginners but also intended for more advanced students ("also for those who are already skilled in this study," in the words of the title page). Despite the technical difficulties of many of the compositions, it is remarkable that Bach rigorously observes the four-octave compass C–c''', even though in the more than twenty years, beginning in 1722, during which he repeatedly refined the fair copy of the *Well-Tempered Clavier* (P 415),[53] he gradually expanded the compass of his other keyboard works. This process, by the way, is not only observable in the partitas in *Clavier-Übung* I but also in the French and English Suites.[54]

As in the case of the duets, BWV 802–05, the range restriction in the *Well-Tempered Clavier*, taken together with the absence of an obbligato pedal part throughout the work, must mean that the composer was determined to keep the work "universally" accessible to all keyboard players, including organists, and that is confirmed by Bach's choice of the "generic" term *clavier* in the title. (Whether the long pedal points in some of the compositions should be taken as a hint that performance on an organ was more than merely "acceptable" is a question best left unasked. They do suggest that such pieces, for example, the Prelude and Fugue in A minor, BWV 865, may have originally been conceived as organ pieces before their incorporation in the *Well-Tempered Clavier*.)

Dürr notes that the few instances in WTC II in which the four-octave range is exceeded seem to be "exceptional cases, while the compass, on the whole, is retained here as well."[55] However, one should add that, whereas we have Bach's explicit description of WTC I, no autograph title for WTC II, much less an elaborate title page stating its precise purpose, has come down to us.

Let us return now to Heinz Lohmann's edition of the Bach organ works and attempt to assess the validity of his selection in the light of Bach's own instrumental prescriptions and the principles we have been able to derive from them. It would seem that Lohmann was justified in including in his edition not only the toccatas and the concerto arrangements for manuals alone but also the various keyboard preludes and fugues that respect the normal C–c''' compass (so long, of course, as the authenticity of the works is otherwise secure). It is at the least questionable, however, whether it was appropriate to include in an edition of organ works compositions for which the earliest sources carry an explicit prescription for harpsichord, as is the case with the Fantasia in A minor, BWV 904.[56] And there was little or no justification to include compositions that belong to the clearly secular genres, such as the *Fantasie sur un Rondeau*, BWV 918; the *Aria variata*, BWV 989; the *Capriccio sopra la lontananza del suo fratello dilettissimo*, BWV 992; or the *Ouverture* in F major, BWV 820—certainly not if (as is the case with BWV 989) the four-octave range is clearly exceeded. Ironically, Lohmann has resisted the boldest stroke of all—one which, as we have seen, there is reason to believe would have been in conformity with Bach's intentions: the inclusion of the preludes and fugues of the *Well-Tempered Clavier* in an edition of Bach's organ works!

The possibility that compositions such as the Toccatas, BWV 910–16, were conceived as organ pieces raises another issue: What occasion would the young Bach have had to perform such virtuosic and manifestly "public" display pieces on a harpsichord? Whether *manualiter* or *pedaliter*, Bach's toccatas seem designed for large audiences and large rooms which at that time would only have been found in a church. The toccatas presumably composed in Weimar (those in F♯ minor, BWV 910; G major, BWV 916; and perhaps C minor, BWV 911[57]), like the concerto arrangements, could conceivably have been performed at court. But given Bach's position in Weimar as court "organist," it seems more reasonable that he would have made his public appearances in that capacity rather than as a "chamber musician" at the harpsichord, either in the ballroom or in some other "chamber." We know about a number of occasions on which Bach "made himself heard" in public at the organ as a solo recitalist—for example, in Hamburg in 1720, Kassel in 1732, and Dresden in 1736—but there is no evidence that he ever did so as a harpsichordist. Rather, whenever he performed for an audience on the harpsichord it seems to have been in the context of ensemble music and under the auspices of an institution like the Leipzig Collegium Musicum, playing the obbligato cembalo parts in his violin, gamba, and flute sonatas, perhaps, or the solos in his harpsichord concerti. Harpsichord "recitals," to the extent that such things existed at all, apparently were private or quite exclusive occasions: for example, the aborted contest with Marchand, which, according to the Obituary, was to take place "in the home of a leading minister of state [identified by Forkel as one Count Flemming], where a large company of persons of high rank and of both sexes was assembled";[58] or the well-known anecdote, related by Forkel, about Count Keyserlingk, Goldberg, and the origin and purpose of the famous variations; or the command performance at the court of Frederick the Great.

We know very little about concert performance during the Bach era. But the functional division of music at the time into the realms of "church, chamber, and theater" as it applied to keyboard music (and keyboard players) suggests that not only chorale settings but also grandiose compositions like the toccatas and similarly large, serious, and technically demanding works among the preludes and fugues, regardless of whether they invariably contained obbligato pedal parts, were written with a view to church performance. The only keyboard compositions clearly intended for the "chamber," that is, the aristocratic salon or ballroom, were dance suites and such secular entertainments as program pieces or variations on popular tunes. The keyboard parts, both continuo and obbligato, in instrumental ensemble works ("chamber music" in our sense), would normally have been performed on the harpsichord. The theater was of marginal significance in the career of J. S. Bach. The keyboard's role here would have been limited to continuo accompaniment on the harpsichord in the orchestra pit. This picture of baroque musical practice is in accord with that drawn by commentators of the era, from Marco Scacchi to Matheson and Heinichen; and it is largely borne out (and certainly nowhere contradicted) by Bach's own instrumental prescriptions in the original and early sources of his keyboard and chamber compositions.

A fourth sphere of musical activity, one that was fundamental to all the others, was instruction in the art of music itself, both its performance and its creation. It was here that the musicians of the time came as close as they ever would to producing music "for its own sake," where it served no purpose other than self-understanding and self-perfection. The only appropriate instrument for such a purpose was a keyboard, because of its contrapuntal and harmonic capacity. The most appropriate keyboard, paradoxically, was no particular instrument at all but rather the *clavier,* with its "universal characteristics": a single manual with a range of C to c''', regardless of whether it was attached to pipes or a set of strings. It was for this ideal yet "universally" available medium that Bach created works that were to serve, as he put it on the title page of the *Well-Tempered Clavier,* "For the Use and Profit of the Musical Youth Desirous of Learning as well as for the Pastime of those Already Skilled in this Study."

2. BACH THE PROGRESSIVE

1. So described by Bach in his memorandum of June 25, 1708, requesting to be relieved of his post of organist of the Blasiuskirche in Mühlhausen. The original text is transcribed in *Bach-Dokumente I*, No. 1 (pp. 19-21). A translation appears in BR, pp. 60-61.

2. For the "new" chronology, now almost twenty years old, see Dürr 1957/76, Dadelsen 1958, and the English-language summary in Herz 1972, pp. 3-50. On the dating of the St. Matthew Passion, see Rifkin 1975. The historical circumstances and stylistic conventions forming the matrix for Bach's working pace and habits are briefly considered in Marshall 1972, vol. 1, pp. 234-41.

3. See *Kalendarium*, especially pp. 34-35.

4. In any event, early versions of the third and sixth partitas, published, respectively, in 1727 and (almost certainly) 1730, were composed early enough to be entered into the *Clavier-Büchlein* for Anna Magdalena Bach of 1725 by Bach himself as fair or revision copies. See NBA V/4, KB, pp. 73-80.

5. See *Kalendarium*, p. 34, and NBA I/40, KB, pp. 26-40, especially pp. 38-39.

6. *Cantaten / Auf die Sonn- / und / Fest-Tage, durch / das gantze Jahr . . . Leipzig, 1728.* See Spitta 1880, vol. 2, pp. 172 and 174-75, and Dürr 1957/76, p. 18. Considering the biographical context being outlined here, it is quite conceivable that Picander's foreword was a deliberately public appeal to urge the disaffected composer to relent in what may have been his widely known decision to withdraw from active participation in the musical life of the Leipzig churches.

7. One further setting, *Ich bin vergnügt*, BWV 84, was performed on February 9, 1727, that is, before publication of Picander's volume, with a text that differs substantially from the published version. See Dürr 1957/76, pp. 19 and 95, and Trautmann 1969. The only other cantata for this group which is definitely datable is *Ich liebe den Höchsten*, BWV 174, whose manuscript bears the date 1729, and, accordingly, was prepared for the second day of Pentecost, June 6, 1729. See Dürr 1957/76, p. 98, and NBA I/14, KB, pp. 116-17. External evidence—copyists' handwriting and manuscript

watermarks—supports an approximate dating of 1728-29 for the remaining eight cantatas: BWV 197a, *Ehre sei Gott* (ca. 1728); BWV 149, *Man singet mit Freuden* (ca. 1728); BWV 188, *Ich habe meine Zuversicht* (ca. 1728); BWV 171, *Gott, wie dein Name* (January 1, 1729?); BWV 156, *Ich steh mit einem Fuss im Grabe* (January 27, 1729?); BWV 159, *Sehet, wir gehn hinauf* (February 27, 1729?); BWV—, *Ich bin ein Pilgrim* (April 18, 1729?); and BWV 145, *Ich lebe, mein Herze* (April 19, 1729?). See Dürr 1957/76, pp. 18 and 97-99, and *Kalendarium*, pp. 35-36.

8. *Bach-Dokumente I*, No. 20 (pp. 57-58), and BR, pp. 115-16. A close reading of Bach's letter to Wecker, incidentally, provided one of the principal clues that led Rifkin to his redating of the St. Matthew Passion. See Rifkin 1975.

9. See Brainard 1969 and Rifkin 1975.

10. See *Bach-Dokumente II*, No. 260 (p. 191); and W. Neumann 1969, pp. 165-68.

11. Deutsch 1955, p. 243. This seems, incidentally, to be the only reference to an illness at any time during Bach's life with the exception of the events surrounding his blindness and death. In the light of the biographical circumstances of 1729-30, such a reference becomes suggestive indeed.

12. *Bach-Dokumente II*, No. 281 (p. 206); BR, pp. 119-20. Since the establishment of the "new chronology" several differing explanations have been advanced for the crisis Bach experienced after completing the cantata cycles in the mid-1720s. See Herz 1971, especially pp. 11-16; Siegele 1975, pp. 162-68; also Rifkin 1975, pp. 384-87.

13. The entire document is printed in *Bach-Dokumente I*, No. 22 (pp. 60-66); BR, pp. 120-24. See also the facsimile edition: *Kurtzer Entwurff*.

14. On the Leipzig opera, see Spitta 1880, vol. 2, p. 27, and Schering 1926, pp. 469-71; also Schering 1941, p. 271.

15. See Fürstenau 1861, vol. 2, pp. 159-66.

16. On the contest with Marchand, see *Bach-Dokumente I*, No. 6 (pp. 26-27); on the organ recital in the Sophienkirche, see *Bach-Dokumente II*, No. 193 (p. 150). The anecdote about the "lovely ditties" derives from Forkel 1802. See the facsimile edition, p. 48, and BR, p. 335. Bach's alleged comment, as Walter Emery correctly cautioned, was not necessarily meant disparagingly. See Walter Emery, "Bach, Johann Sebastian," *Encyclopaedia Britannica*, fourteenth edition [Emery 1970.] In the course of this article, incidentally, Emery characterizes Bach as a "moderate progressive." This sensible judgment was dropped by the present writer in his revision of the Bach article in the fifteenth edition of the *Britannica* [see Chapter 1, this volume] in order to describe the composer as "basically conservative and traditional"—a judgment no less, but also no more, valid. The present essay is, in some respects, the writer's attempt to make amends to the late Walter Emery.

17. *Bach-Dokumente I*, No. 23 (pp. 67-70); BR, pp. 125-26. [See also the facsimile edition: *Brief 1730*.] It does not seem prudent to attach much significance, as does Siegele 1975, p. 166, to the fact that the prevailing musical taste in Danzig was conservative. It seems reasonable to assume that Bach, like anyone else seeking a new position, must have written letters of inquiry to numerous acquaintances at this time and that it is only coincidence that none have survived except for the letter to Erdmann.

18. Bach's musical activities during the first half of 1730 are unknown, except that he composed three cantatas (BWV 190a, 120b, and Anh. 4a) for the bicentennial celebration of the Augsburg Confession, June 25–27, and earlier (May 1) placed an advertisement for the fifth partita of the *Clavier-Übung* in the Leipzig newspapers. It is perhaps also worth mentioning that for the Passion music in that year Bach performed the St. Luke Passion, BWV 246, a work certainly not of his own composition. See *Kalendarium*, p. 37.

19. BWV Anh. 3: *Gott, gib dein Gerichte dem Könige.* See *Bach-Dokumente II,* No. 264 (p. 194). The text is published in W. Neumann 1956, pp. 375–76. [See also the facsimile in W. Neumann 1974, p. 332.]

20. Dürr 1971, vol. 2, p. 445, notes the Italian character of this scoring.

21. The autograph, P 104, can best be described as a "revision copy" for the first movement and, as the presence of sketches and formative compositional corrections in the remaining movements makes clear, as a "calligraphic composing score" for the rest. See Marshall 1972, vol. 1, pp. 19 and 162–63.

22. Dürr 1957/76, p. 101.

23. Dürr 1971, vol. 2, p. 445. It is also worth observing that the heading on the first page of the score has no indication of the occasion—exceptional in the Bach autographs.

24. Dürr 1971, vol. 2, p. 446, remarks, incidentally, that the infiltration of virtuoso elements is a hallmark of Bach's later cantatas.

25. See Fürstenau 1861, vol. 2, pp. 166 and 168.

26. Dürr 1957/76, p. 101.

27. *Bach-Dokumente II,* No. 294 (p. 214).

28. Johann Mattheson employed female singers in a Hamburg church as early as 1715. See Turnow 1960, col. 1800, and Mattheson 1739, p. 482. (In the very next paragraph Mattheson warns of the deficiencies of boy sopranos.) But women were not permitted to sing in Leipzig services until the nineteenth century. See the literature mentioned in note 30.

29. The surviving original performing parts, SPK St 49, provide little help here. They were evidently retained by Bach in Leipzig, since they ultimately were inherited, along with the autograph score and many other Leipzig materials, by C. P. E. Bach. (See Dürr 1957/76, p. 18.) Therefore, one tends to assume that the presumed performance of September 17, 1730, perhaps with Bindi as the soloist, took place in one of the Leipzig churches. But the possibility of a Dresden performance cannot be dismissed. The presence of a transposed continuo part in St 49, intended for an organ tuned in *Chorton,* excludes a performance in the Sophienkirche with its *Kammerton* organ, but not the Frauenkirche, whose organ, according to a testimonial by Gottfried Silbermann, was still tuned in *Chorton* in October 1734. See Flade 1953, p. 131, also pp. 177–78. I wish to thank Professor Thomas Harmon, University Organist, The University of California, Los Angeles, for bringing this reference to my attention.

30. On Bach's singers and the tradition of falsetto practice in Leipzig at this time, see Spitta 1880, vol. 2, pp. 140–41, and Schering 1936, pp. 39–41, 46, 48. Schering suggested C. P. E. Bach in the introduction of the Eulenburg

edition of the cantata. Philipp Emanuel was over sixteen years old in 1730; there is no record of his having been either a particularly accomplished boy soprano or falsettist.

[30a. Over the years I have become considerably less enamored of the Bindi hypothesis. There is clearly validity to the objection raised by Frederick Neumann (F. Neumann 1985, p. 285) and others that it is unlikely—"inconceivable" (Neumann's word) is perhaps too strong—that an Italian opera star would have been willing (or even linguistically able, perhaps) to sing a Lutheran cantata in German. But to Neumann's assertion that Bach "*must* have had (emphasis added) a talented youngster or falsettist for the vocal part" I repeat the question: if there had been a singer capable of performing the soprano part of *Jauchzet Gott* regularly available in Leipzig, why did Bach evidently write no further music of this nature for him?]

[30b. The likely publication year for the variations is now thought to be 1741. See NBA V/2, KB, p. 94. The credibility of the famous story of Keyserlingk's commission of the work for "his Goldberg"—an anecdote first promulgated by Forkel—is shaky at best. (See Wolff 1984, pp. 18–19, 31–32.)]

31. *Bach-Dokumente II,* No. 389 (pp. 279–80).

32. *Bach-Dokumente III,* No. 803 (p. 289), and BR, p. 279.

33. Among the pertinent studies, in addition to the three-volume critical edition of the *Bach-Dokumente,* are W. Neumann 1960, Eller 1961, and Wolff 1968.

34. See NBA I/36, KB, pp. 7–10, which document the direct connection between Bach's concentrated production of cantatas in the years 1732–41 for the Saxon royalty and his direction of the Collegium Musicum. It seems plausible that Bach's performances of such works with the Collegium Musicum, which began in earnest in August 1732, triggered his decision to apply for the title of Royal Court Composer in the summer of 1733. For further information on Bach's cantatas for the university and for the Collegium, see NBA I/38, KB; and NBA I/40, KB; passim.

35. See Downes 1961, especially p. 279.

36. See, among others, Ratner 1949, Ratner 1956, and Newman 1963, especially Chapters 2 and 6.

37. The presumed date of this cantata has been continually pushed back from 1749 to 1732 to 1731, and, most recently, to 1729/30, that is, just at the beginning of the period of concern to us here. See NBA I/40, KB, pp. 136–37.

38. See Spitta 1880, vol. 2, pp. 473–79, and Dürr 1971, vol. 2, pp. 712–16.

39. Dürr 1971, vol. 2, p. 718, already discusses this periodicity.

40. Bach seems to have given this interpretation *ex post facto* support when he reused Pan's music for the aria "Dein Wachstum sei feste" in the "Peasant" Cantata, where it is introduced in the preceding recitative with the words: "Ich muss mich also zwingen, / Was Städtisches zu singen." See the discussion of the "Peasant" Cantata [p. 40, this volume].

41. See Dürr 1971, vol. 2, pp. 721–23.

42. See *ibid.,* p. 722, and Martin Bernstein's remarks in Congress 1961, vol. 2, p. 127. On Faustina's range and technique, see Högg 1931, especially pp. 68–72.

43. The work is scheduled to be published in the NBA in I/41: "Kantaten zweifelhafter Echtheit."

44. Dürr 1971, vol. 2, p. 720, calls attention to the use of unison doubling in this cantata.

45. Bach, though, could hardly have known this particular work, for the first known German performance took place—in Dresden—in 1740. See Platen 1961, p. 46.

46. For example, Alfred Dürr, in Dürr 1971, vol. 2, p. 718.

47. See Seiffert 1939.

48. See Dürr 1971, vol. 2, p. 696.

49. A fine stylistic study of the "Peasant" Cantata appears in Dürr 1971, vol. 2, pp. 696–99.

50. See Dadelsen 1958, p. 152.

51. Wolff 1968, pp. 132–34.

52. In this connection, see Gerber 1925, pp. 69–71, and Downes 1958, pp. 48–56.

53. The sonority is structurally analogous to, and in every way as shocking as, the famous repeated chord in the "Danses des Adolescents" episode of Stravinsky's *Le Sacre,* written just about two hundred years later. While the date and occasion of Cantata No. 54 is still usually given as the Seventh Sunday after Trinity, July 15, 1714 (see Dürr 1971, vol. 2, p. 369), it seems altogether possible that the composition was written and performed four months earlier, namely, on Oculi Sunday (the designation appearing on the recently rediscovered libretto), March 4, 1714. (See Noack 1970, pp. 13–14, and the facsimile reproduced in W. Neumann 1974, p. 259.) That would be two days after Bach had been appointed Konzertmeister to the Weimar court. The extremely short time available for the composition and rehearsal of the work would seem to explain both the choice of a short, three-movement, cantata text and a scoring limited to just solo alto and string ensemble (i.e., not even a chorus or concluding chorale). Nonetheless, since Cantata No. 54 was to be the work with which Bach introduced himself in the new position, it would be most understandable that the composition was designed to make a memorable impression; hence its bold opening chords, the remarkable deceptive cadences in the same movement (mm. 45 and 51), and perhaps also the chromatic subject of the final aria. With the B-minor Mass, Bach, again, was interested in introducing himself to a court and in making an impression—of a rather different kind.

54. In his program notes for a performance of the B-minor Mass on May 3, 1949, by the Cantata Singers under his direction.

55. See Herz 1974.

56. Dadelsen 1958, pp. 143–56, suggests 1747–49. Wolff 1968, pp. 149–55, attempts to redate the composition of at least the "Credo" and "Confi-

teor" movements to between 1742–45. [These movements have now been definitively dated to the period between August 1748 and October 1749. See Kobayashi 1988, pp. 61–62.]

57. As translated by Ralph Kirkpatrick in his edition of the "Goldberg" Variations, 1938.

58. For the problems of dating the publication, see Kinsky 1937, p. 53; Emery 1963a, and Emery 1963b. [Also NBA V/2, KB, p. 94.]

[58a. The major portion of the *Art of Fugue* was completed in the early 1740s. See Wolff 1983. The *Art of Fugue*, too, then, stands at the beginning, not the end, of Bach's final creative period.]

[58b. It is odd, to say the least, that Bach should have failed to include a volume of fugues in the *Clavier-Übung* and chose instead a set of variations, a genre he had largely neglected heretofore. Certainly a fugue collection would have made a far more obvious, and fitting, conclusion to the series, given Bach's lifelong cultivation and supreme mastery of the form—a supremacy recognized and appreciated by his contemporaries. Indeed, Bach was occupied in the late 1730s and early '40s with the compilation and composition of both the *Well-Tempered Clavier II* and the *Art of Fugue*, a circumstance that lends considerable weight to the possibility (briefly raised and discounted in Wolff 1984, pp. 8, 22) that Bach originally intended to make one or the other of these collections serve as the capstone of the *Clavier-Übung*. For some reason, however—perhaps, after all, an interruption in the form of a commission from Keyserlingk? (but see the next note)—neither work had reached final form by 1741, and this distinction ultimately fell to the "Goldberg" Variations.]

[58c. The arguments against any such commission, notably the lack of a dedication in the print, are presented in Wolff 1984, pp. 19, 32.]

59. Kinsky 1937, p. 32.

60. See Hoffmann-Erbrecht 1973.

61. See Newman 1963, pp. 68–71 and 80.

62. Bukofzer 1947, pp. 297–98.

63. *Ibid.*, p. 297. See also Keller 1950, p. 217, and Spitta 1880, vol. 2, p. 662. Spitta mentions possible Scarlattian influence in reference to the extensive hand crossing in the Fantasia in C minor, BWV 906, a work probably composed [in the late 1720s]. See my foreword to the facsimile edition of the Fantasia [Chapter 11, this volume].

[63a. The dating of Scarlatti's keyboard works is not clear. At all events, Kirkpatrick's suggestion that most of them were composed at about the same time the surviving copies were made, that is, after 1752 (and after Scarlatti was 67 years old—a notion unlikely on its face), has been seriously questioned. See the summary of the chronological problems in Boyd 1987, pp. 160–63.]

64. Kirkpatrick 1953, p. 125.

65. This seems to be the most reasonable conclusion from the chronology outlined in *ibid.*, pp. 74–75: Domenico Scarlatti's return to Italy in 1724 to visit his father; Hasse's studies "with Alessandro in Naples at the same

time"; and Hasse's later report to Burney that he had heard the Scarlattis play.

66. See *Bach-Dokumente II,* No. 597a (pp. 467–68) and No. 600 (p. 469).

67. See Scarlatti, *Complete Keyboard Works,* edited by Ralph Kirkpatrick 1972, vol. I.

68. Tovey 1944, p. 63.

69. Translated in Kirkpatrick 1953, p. 102.

70. The obvious humor of such numbers as variations 14, 23, and others clearly challenges the assertion of Charles Rosen, which, curiously enough, is partly supported by a reference to the "Goldberg" Variations (specifically, the quodlibet), that music could not be "genuinely," that is, intrinsically, funny "without outside help" in the form of nonmusical allusions, before the development of the classical style. See Rosen 1971, p. 95. Such purely musical humor, of course, can also be interpreted, and will be presently, as evidence of the presence of classical or, at least, pre-classical stylistic and structural procedures in the "Goldberg" Variations.

71. For an extensive analysis, see "The Genesis of an Aria Ritornello." [This volume, Chapter 8.]

72. See also the representation in Schenker 1956, Appendix vol. p. 7. Schenker, however, evidently does not call attention to the remarkable rhythmic telescoping of the "Urlinie." (See the discussion in the text volume, pp. 68–69.)

73. The strict periodicity of variation 10 relates it to the "permutation fugue," a genre or technique Bach had already developed in Weimar. See W. Neumann 1938.

74. Lowinsky 1956, pp. 162–63. The article is reprinted in Lang 1963, pp. 31–55.

75. See Platen 1961 and Dürr 1968a. An edition of this work, "Tilge, Höchster, meine Sünden," prepared by Diethard Hellmann, appeared in 1963 as vol. 151 of the series *Die Kantate.* It was published, then, before the original parts for the work were rediscovered by Dürr and described by him in the article just cited. The stylistic features of Bach's arrangement mentioned in this essay are found exclusively in the original parts.

76. See Dürr, *ibid.,* 92–100.

77. Wolff 1971, pp. 401–03. In addition to the traits mentioned by Wolff, the opening movement of the trio sonata, like many pre-classical sonatas of the 1740s, for example, C. P. E. Bach's "Prussian" Sonatas, combines the characteristics of both the "binary" and "ternary" sonata form—with a second section exactly twice as long as the first (16:32 mm.), and with the last sixteen measures functioning much like a formal recapitulation. See David 1945, pp. 111–15. Bach employs clear recapitulation designs elsewhere as well, most notably in the Fantasia in C minor, BWV 906, mentioned earlier in this essay for its exploitation of "Scarlattian" hand-crossing.

78. It seems possible that Bach's growing involvement with recent stylistic developments received repeated impetus during the 1730s and '40s from the external events of his life: 1730, after seven years of service (in

accordance with a well-documented psychological mechanism), disillusionment with his current position in Leipzig; 1733, his application for the Dresden court title; 1737, the famous criticism of his music by his former pupil Johann Adolph Scheibe and the ensuing controversy; 1742, the publication of Philipp Emanuel's "Prussian" Sonatas; 1747, his visit to Frederick the Great in Potsdam.

79. The composition referred to, *Willkommen! Ihr herrschenden Götter der Erden*, BWV Anh. 13, performed on April 28, 1738, is lost. Mizler's remarks are reprinted in *Dokumente II*, No. 436 (p. 336), and BR, p. 249. It should be remembered in this connection that Bach did in fact receive the Dresden court title. Evidently the fashionable court appreciated Bach's various efforts to please.

80. Besseler 1955a, reprinted in Blankenburg 1970, pp. 196–246.

81. Bach's arrangement of Palestrina's *Missa sine nomine* dates from around 1740. See Wolff 1968, p. 145. But Bach's extensive encounter with sixteenth-century music can be assumed to have begun as soon as he arrived in Leipzig. It can be clearly traced to the year 1729 when he ordered new copies of the *Florilegium portense* (Leipzig, 1618, 1621) of Erhard Bodenschatz for the Thomasschule. This motet collection contained works of Lassus, Handl, Ingegneri, the Gabrielis, etc., and had been in use by the Thomana for over a hundred years. It was surely well known to Bach from the moment he became Thomaskantor. See Schering 1936, pp. 121–24.

82. On Bach's familiarity with Polish music, see Hlawiczka 1961 and Hlawiczka 1966.

83. This is an expanded version of a paper originally delivered in Schoenberg Hall, the University of California, Los Angeles, in February 1975. A revised form of the paper was read at Duke University, Rutgers University, and Carleton College.

I wish to thank Professors Joshua Rifkin, Brandeis University, and Edward E. Lowinsky, The University of Chicago, for their helpful suggestions and for their stimulating criticism of many of the assertions made here.

"Bach the Progressive": Notes to the Postscript

1. One need only recall that Forkel's biography concludes with the words: "And this man, the greatest musical orator that ever existed, and probably ever will exist, was a German. Let his country be proud of him; let it be proud, but, at the same time, worthy of him!" (BR, p. 353) and that the first sentence in Spitta's biography begins: "The family/race from which Johann Sebastian Bach descended, was purely and thoroughly German" (Das Geschlecht, dem Johann Sebastian Bach entstammte, ist ein grunddeutsches . . . Spitta 1880, vol. 1, p. 3).

2. I mention in this connection a fact of which Neumann apparently thinks I am ignorant, namely, that "periodic phrase structure was in existence for a long time in dance music, and it is found elsewhere in Bach's music, particularly but not exclusively, in his dance pieces," [p. 350] and go on to

cite emphatically "Bachian" and un-*galant* examples from a cantata and from the St. Matthew Passion.

3. See NBA V/2, KB, pp. 109–10.

4. See NBA V/4, p. 99, and NBA V/4, KB, p. 91.

5. Since Anna Magdalena was frustratingly casual about these things, it is no surprise that she failed to provide either title or attribution for the "Goldberg" aria when she copied it into her notebook, any more than she did for the vast majority of pieces in the notebook, including pieces by her husband, such as the indisputably authentic C-major Prelude from the *Well-Tempered Clavier I* and a recitative and aria from Cantata No. 82, *Ich habe genug*. Nonetheless, Neumann seizes upon the absence of Anna Magdalena's attribution as further evidence against Bach's authorship of the aria.

3. BACH'S *ORCHESTRE*

1. The original letter is reproduced in *Bach-Dokumente I,* No. 27 (p. 74).

2. BR, p. 129.

3. See the original in *Bach-Dokumente I, No. 22* (pp. 60–66), and the English translation in BR, pp. 120–24.

4. See Rifkin 1982a, Marshall 1983, Rifkin 1983.

5. Walther 1732, p. 452.

6. See Fürstenau 1861, vol. 2, pp. 159–66, and Marshall "Bach the Progressive," [Chapter 2, this volume].

7. Heinichen 1728, pp. 36, 37.

8. Mattheson 1739, pp. 83–84; also English translation in Harriss 1981, pp. 210–11.

9. *Ibid.,* paragraph 78, p. 86; English translation, p. 213.

10. *Ibid.,* p. 234; English translation, p. 467. See, in general, the chapters entitled *Vom Unterschiede zwischen den Sing- und Spiel-Melodien* and *Von den Gattungen der Melodien und ihren besondern Abzeichen,* pp. 203–34; English translation, pp. 419–68.

11. Mattheson 1713, p. 34; cited here after Cannon 1947, pp. 114ff.

12. *Ibid.;* see also the longer citation quoted in Staehelin 1981, especially p. 2.

13. Cannon 1947, p. 115.

14. Fürstenau 1861, vol. 2, p. 13.

15. *Ibid.,* vol. 2, p. 99.

4. ON BACH'S UNIVERSALITY

1. Emery–Marshall 1974, [Chapter 1, this volume].

2. Geiringer 1966.

3. Schweitzer 1911, p. 3.

4. "Bach the Progressive," [Chapter 2, this volume].
5. Barth 1956, p. 12.
6. Casals 1970, p. 17.
7. Postscript to a letter of 17 July 1827 addressed to Karl Friedrich Zelter.
8. BR, p. 85 and p. 75, respectively.
9. *Ibid.*, p. 86.
10. *Ibid.*, p. 37.
11. *Ibid.*, pp. 32–33 [slightly revised].
12. Bukofzer 1947, p. 220.
13. BR, p. 123.
14. These quotations are cited in Blume 1970, p. 28.

5. "COMPOSING SCORES" AND "FAIR COPIES"

1. Dürr 1977, pp. 59, 166–67.
2. Herz 1970.
3. See Stinson 1985a.
4. Herz 1970, p. 274.
5. See Dadelsen 1958, pp. 49 and 72ff.
6. See Marshall 1972, vol. 1, pp. 59–61.
7. See Dürr 1977, pp. 217–20; also Mendel 1955.
8. See also "Tempo and Dynamics," [Chapter 15, this volume].
[9. The sketches are treated at length in "The Sketches," Chapter 6, this volume.]
10. For a discussion of the discrepancies between this sketch and the final reading, see Marshall 1972, vol. 1, p. 230.
11. See NBA I/21, KB, especially pp. 48–50, for a detailed description of Zelter's entries.
12. See Dürr 1957/76, p. 99.
13. See NBA I/4, KB, pp. 104–05.
14. *Ibid.*, pp. 96, 98.
15. *Ibid.*, pp. 105–06.
16. For differing views on this question, see Marshall 1972, vol. 1, pp. 27–28, and Dürr 1957/76 [2nd edition], p. 167.
17. See Herz 1984, pp. 73–74.
18. See *ibid.*, p. 75; also Dürr 1971, vol. 2, p. 363.
19. See the transcriptions in Marshall 1972, vol. 2, Sketch 7.
20. Other rhythmic changes in this and the other recitative movements are discussed in Marshall 1972, vol. 1, pp. 103–05.
21. See Dürr 1957/76, pp. 116, 119.
22. See MacCracken 1984, especially pp. 77–78.

[23. I wish to express my gratitude to Gerhard Herz, distinguished emeritus Professor of Music History, the University of Louisville, for his invaluable assistance and advice, and to Leo F. Balk and Garland Publishing for providing the impetus for this publication.]

6. THE SKETCHES

1. [. . .]A summary of this research appears in Mendel 1960a.

2. Schünemann 1935.

3. A more complete treatment, including transcriptions of all extant Bach sketches and drafts forms a major part of the present writer's study, *The Compositional Process of J. S. Bach* [Marshall 1972].

4. In Cantata No. 117, *Sei Lob und Ehr' dem höchsten Gut*, for example, the rejected draft for the first movement appears upside down on the last page of the autograph. Facsimiles of the first and last pages of the manuscript are printed in Schmieder 1939, pp. 6–7; Plate 22 is reproduced from this anthology. See also the transcription in [Marshall 1972, vol. 2, Sketch 88].

5. For the dating, see Dürr 1957/76, pp. 98–99. The autograph is in the SPK P 36/1; Plate 23 is reproduced from the facsimile edition, edited by Konrad Ameln.

6. SPK P 670. See Dürr 1958. A facsimile of this page of the manuscript appears also in NBA I/33, KB, opposite p. 58 [and in Marshall 1972, vol. 1, p. 33].

7. The handwriting of the cello part is identified in Dadelsen 1957, p. 34. Kast 1958, p. 8, attributes the pencil sketch to an unknown copyist. The pencil, incidentally, was invented long before Bach's time.

8. Professor Werner Neumann of the Bach-Archiv, Leipzig, writes that the psalm was part of the service for the Sunday after New Year in the Leipzig liturgy of the time. Since there are only two extant Bach cantatas for this feast—BWV 58 and 153 (excluding Part 5 of the Christmas Oratorio)—it is particularly tempting to reckon with lost cantatas for this Sunday. It must be pointed out, however, that this liturgy for the Sunday after New Year did not fall in every liturgical year, so that the three extant works may have been adequate for Bach's needs.

   A word about the musical examples. The transcriptions of sketches attempt to reproduce any corrections found in the original manuscript unless the contrary is stated. The original readings appear in normal engraving; corrections in small or shaded notes. Corrections of time signatures are given in larger type. It is hoped that this method draws the reader's attention first to the original reading and thereafter to the correction, thereby encouraging the reader to reconstruct the genesis of the passage. Musical examples devoted to the final readings only, however, are based on the complete editions, unless the heading specifically refers to the original manuscript.

9. The question whether the Bach autographs can contribute to an understanding of his "creative process" was raised and briefly discussed at the

Leipzig Bach festival of 1950 at the inception of the current philological activity, but the problem has apparently not been seriously investigated since. See the discussion following Schmieder 1951, pp. 229-30.

[10. The composing scores of several Leipzig cantatas are described and discussed in Chapter 5, this volume. See also Chapters 7 and 8, this volume, devoted to the composing score of Cantata No. 105, *Herr, gehe nicht ins Gericht.*]

11. The royal visit, for example, for which Bach composed *Preise dein Glücke* (BWV 215) was announced three days in advance. See NBA I/37, KB, p. 66.

12. It is clear that we have to reckon with the loss—presumably with the destruction by Bach himself—of the initial manuscripts of such works as the *Well-Tempered Clavier,* the Brandenburg Concertos, and the sonatas for unaccompanied violin. Since this paper (and the writer) is concerned primarily with the cantata autographs, the manuscripts for instrumental works will for the most part not be considered here. [But see Chapter 11, this volume, on the autograph(s) of the Harpsichord Fantasia in C minor, BWV 906.]

13. Dürr 1951, pp. 52-57 [or Dürr 1977, pp. 63-69].

14. It is tempting to speculate whether Bach's well-known rejection of Rameau's theories cannot perhaps best be explained from this point of view. We know from the obituary written by Philipp Emanuel Bach and J. F. Agricola that ". . . Bach did not engage in deep theoretical reflections about music. . . ." (reprinted in Richter 1920, pp. 25- 26, [also *Bach-Dokumente III,* No. 666, p. 89]), and since there was no German translation of Rameau's theoretical writings during his lifetime, it is improbable that Bach was familiar at first hand with the details of Rameau's doctrines. It is quite conceivable, however, that Bach had heard Rameau's tenet: "it is harmony . . . that is generated first" (translated in Strunk 1950, p. 571), and that he shared Mattheson's opinion that "We consider the Melody as the basis of the entire art of composition, and cannot understand it . . . when for example it is maintained counter to all reason that the melody is derived from the harmony+. . . .+ See *Traité de l'Harmonie* par M. *Rameau,* L. II Ch. 19 p. 139, Ch. 21 p. 147. Most astonishing, it is maintained that the harmony is engendered first. I submit: what is engendered must have parents" (Mattheson 1739, p. 133).

15. See the statement of Bach's pupil Johann Gottfried Ziegler, quoted in Spitta 1880, vol. 1, p. 519.

16. Bach's historical connection with the *Figurenlehre* and the use of rhetorical figures in his music have been investigated primarily by Schmitz 1950.

17. In several manuscripts thematic sketches for the later movements appear on the bottom of the first page of the score, but it would be rash to assume that Bach got the initial idea for the "Pleni" while working on the opening measures of the *Sanctus,* or, in a similar case, that he interrupted his work on the first movement of Cantata No. 57 (P 144, f. 1ʳ-1ᵛ) to jot down the ritornello theme for Movement 7. While these are of course possibilities, it is equally likely, if not more likely, that the completed first page lay uppermost on the composer's desk and within his reach. The only reasonable certainty is that Bach wrote down such sketches—there

are about half a dozen—some time before beginning actual work on the movement concerned.

18. As the transcription shows, Bach began to draft the theme in the alto clef but changed his mind after writing the clef and the first note. See note 8.

19. See the comments in the second paragraph of this essay. The draft is catalogued in *BWV*, p. xiv, as an unidentified sketch, presumably after Schünemann 1935, pp. 25–26.

20. Plate 24 is reprinted from the facsimile edition of the Christmas Oratorio, edited by Alfred Dürr. A facsimile of f. 31ᵛ appears also in NBA II/6, p. x. The most accurate and complete transcription is in [Marshall 1972, vol. 2, Sketch 162].

21. The draft is found upside down in the autograph to Cantata No. 79, *Gott, der Herr, ist Sonn' und Schild* (P 89, f. 10ᵛ). Although the Reformation cantata was probably written for October 31, 1725, and BWV 183 for Exaudi, May 13, 1725, the key, the instrumentation, and the watermark of the paper of the draft are the same as that found in the original sources for the Exaudi cantata (see Dürr 1957/76, pp. 81, 83) so that it is clear—as Spitta 1880 pointed out (vol. 2, pp. 831–33)—that the draft indeed belongs to BWV 183 and not to a third setting of this text (besides BWV 183 and 44). The draft is not mentioned, however, in the critical report to this cantata in NBA I/12, KB, pp. 294–318.

22. The writer is indebted to Dr. Ulrich Siegele, Tübingen, for pointing out this model to him. See also Siegele 1960 for a discussion of a similar contrary motion model underlying the Gigue of the sixth English Suite (BWV 811).

23. The evidence for this is not provided by any extant sketches and therefore will not be presented here; it is discussed in Marshall 1972, vol. 1, pp. 173–74.

24. The sketch illustrates primarily Bach's manner of writing *cantus-firmus* compositions in the style of the *Orgel-Büchlein*. See the discussion below on the order in which the parts were written down.

25. Bach probably ruled the staves for an entire sheet—all four pages—in advance, before beginning to write on it. Therefore, the need to rule staves in the middle of work on a composition occurred only when Bach completed one sheet and took a new one, assuming he had not ruled enough paper beforehand for the whole composition. Presumably, however, he usually had an adequate supply of ruled sheets on hand, for continuation sketches on the last page—verso—of a sheet are exceedingly rare. The second sketch to the "Pleni" theme of the B-minor Mass is such an instance—particularly the sketch of the continuo part for the final measures of the *Sanctus* section. [See the discussion of this sketch, Chapter 10, this volume, p. 186.]

26. The most complete analysis of the compositional designs of Bach's arias is found in Dürr 1951, pp. 104–51 [=Dürr 1977, pp. 118–63]. The choral fugues are analyzed in W. Neumann 1938. [See also Crist 1988.]

27. The placement of the syllable "-fer" at the beginning of m. 59 in the sketch suggests, as the transcription illustrates, that the text was written down before the music in this instance. The beaming here, however, makes the underlaying unambiguous. See the final version of the passage in [NBA I/15, p. 225].

28. Platen 1959, especially pp. 164-204.

29. There are several sketches for the continuo ritornelli of quasi-*basso-ostinato* movements, but here of course the continuo is the principal, indeed only, melodic part of the ritornello. See the sketch for Movement 4 of Cantata No. 62, transcribed in [NBA I/15, KB, p. 80].

30. Bach often sketched the melody for the entire ritornello theme. See the sketches of the (almost) complete ritornello themes of Movement 10 of BWV 198 (P 41/1, f. 1ʳ) transcribed in NBA I/38, KB, p. 100, [also Marshall 1972, vol. 2, Sketch 127], and BWV 44, Movement 6 (P 148, f. 6ᵛ) transcribed in NBA I/12, KB, p. 260, [also Marshall 1972, vol. 2, Sketch 130].

31. See Mendel 1960a, pp. 292-93, for such an analysis of the opening exposition of the fugue subject in the autograph (SPK P 103) to Cantata No. 182, *Himmelskönig, sei willkommen.*

32. This seems to be implied in W. Neumann 1938, pp. 14-52. Neumann does not expressly suggest that Bach initially composed homophonic *Stimm-tausch* blocks of invertible counterpoints as the starting point of his compositional activity, but the reader is likely to have this impression from the style of the argumentation.

33. The drafts are found in the autograph to Cantata No. 81, *Jesus schläft, was soll ich hoffen,* below the concluding chorale, leading one to suppose at first—as Schünemann (1935, p. 22) seems to do—that Bach wrote the draft to the middle section of the Epiphany cantata, BWV 65 (first performed January 6, 1724) after completing the cantata for the Fourth Sunday after Epiphany, BWV 81 (first performed January 30, 1724; see the datings in Dürr 1957/76, pp. 65-66). This would clearly have wide-ranging consequences for our notions of Bach's work rhythm in the first Leipzig years. A closer examination of both manuscripts reveals at once, however, that Movement 1, m. 19 of BWV 65 begins a new sheet in the autograph (P 147, f. 3ʳ). Bach, then, had taken a new sheet, left the upper nine staves free for the instrumental parts and had begun to draft the fugue exposition on staves 10-14. After discarding the draft, he laid the sheet aside until beginning to compose BWV 81. The case is completely analogous to those discussed earlier—see nn. 4 and 21, and p. 116—except that this time Bach did not turn the sheet upside down before reusing it.

34. Schünemann's discussions and transcriptions of this sketch, both in Schünemann 1935, pp. 23-25, and in Schünemann 1936, pp. 15-17 (from which Plate 25 is reproduced), are considerably oversimplified. [See Marshall 1972, vol. 1, pp. 134-38.]

35. See also the analysis of dovetailing in m. 45 in W. Neumann 1938, p. 58.

36. The author is indebted to Professor Arthur Mendel for valuable criticisms and suggestions regarding this paper.

8. The Genesis of an Aria Ritornello

1. Mendel 1961, p. 15.

2. While proofreading the original performing parts (which were normally prepared by apprentice copyists from the autograph score), Bach occasionally

introduced corrections of a structural nature along with dynamics, slurs, continuo figures, and other performance indications.

3. The possibility cannot be eliminated, however, that a particular correction may have been "delayed," that is, introduced after—perhaps in response to—corrections affecting later details of the work.

4. It is my personal conviction—unverifiable, of course—that Bach expended practically no conscious verbal effort at all about why he chose or rejected a reading. The internal verbal dialogue probably consisted rarely of expressions more eloquent than "this is not good" or "this is better."

5. I am indebted to Arthur Mendel and Alfred Dürr for their convincing demonstrations of the probably nonautograph nature of this text entry.

6. That the instrumentation is not self-evident is revealed by an early nineteenth-century copy of the cantata, (SPK) P 838, prepared from the autograph (directly or indirectly) by [Christian Friedrich] Knuth [ca. 1793–1849]. The instrumental indications are given as follows: Stave 1: *Violino 1,* Stave 2: *Violino 2,* Stave 3: *Viola,* Stave 5: *Violon* (changed from *Violone*). Wilhelm Rust, who edited the cantata for the Bach-Gesellschaft, conscientiously reproduced the word *Soprano* in the manner of the autograph and refrained from adding indications for the accompanying instruments. He identified the obbligato instrument, within editorial parentheses, as an oboe. See BG 23, p. 131 and p. xxxvi of the foreword.

7. See Dadelsen 1958, p. 86, n. 56, and the facsimile edition of the autograph score of *Gott ist mein König,* BWV 71. The differentiated use of C-clef forms is observable throughout the autograph score of the Mühlhausen cantata, BWV 131 [see Chapter 5, this volume, p. 85, and Plates 6–8], and sporadically in several later autographs, e.g., the scores for BWV 199 (Royal Danish Library, Copenhagen) and BWV 12 (SPK P 44/7) both written in 1714; fairly consistently in the secular Köthen cantata, BWV 173a (SPK P 42/2); and in several movements of the Leipzig cantata, BWV 24 (SPK P 44/4), composed in 1723.

8. Reduced systems without staves for resting parts are frequently found in the Bach autographs. See Marshall 1972, vol. 1, pp. 47–58, [and Plates 6 and 19, this volume].

[9. See Chapter 7, this volume, pp. 133–135.]

10. The lowest pitch in the aria, f, appears for the first time in m. 37, where it is introduced as a correction. (See the facsimile of P 99, f. 5ᵛ, in BG 44, Bl. 38, the second full measure of the third system [also the facsimile edition of the complete autograph, edited by the present writer].) Friedrich Erhardt Niedt's description of the bassetto (or *Bassetgen*) printed in Niedt 1721 is quoted in J. S. Bach, *The Passion According to St. John,* edited by Arthur Mendel, p. vii.

11. The violin–viola unison parts in BWV 115/1, for example, are notated in this fashion in the autograph score (Fitzwilliam Museum, Cambridge). (See the transcription of the first system in Marshall 1972, vol. 2, Sketch 84, Final Version.) In BG 24 the part is reproduced in the treble clef.

12. Although Bach never entered instrumental indications for this aria into the autograph as he did ultimately for the first and fifth movements, there is still hardly any doubt what the scoring of the movement should be. A mid-eighteenth-century score (SPK P 48/4), in the hand of S. Hering, a

copyist for C. P. E. Bach, which was clearly prepared from the lost original performing parts, identifies the obbligato instrument as an oboe and the supporting parts as *Violino 1, Violino 2,* and *Viola.* The parts will be referred to thus in the course of this discussion. The evidence demonstrating the derivation of P 48 from the lost parts is included in NBA I/19, KB.

13. The symbolism of the aria has been commented upon in similar terms by several generations of interpreters. See, for example, Arnold Schering's foreword to the Eulenburg edition of BWV 105, (No. 1040), p. ii; Smend 1950, Heft 3, p. 25; and the standard biographies of Philipp Spitta and Albert Schweitzer.

14. This "exclamatio" figure is used also at the beginning of the tenor aria, where it was introduced as an afterthought and serves rather to define than to obscure the principal tonality. See [Chapter 7, this volume, pp. 137–38].

15. The clash was evidently too strong for the taste of Adolf Bernard Marx, the first editor of the cantata, who in his editions of the full and vocal scores of the aria published by Simrock (Bonn, 1830) removed the g' from the chord. Günther Raphael, who arranged the vocal score of BWV 105 for the Breitkopf edition, did the same. Both editors may have justified their emendation by noting that there is no similar dissonance in m. 19. Here, however, the continuity of phrase which the addition of g' effects is provided by the canonic dialogue between soprano and oboe.

16. It is important to remember that the inner parts were almost certainly not entered in m. 3 until the final upbeat reading was determined. Therefore there is no need to speculate as to whether the f' and a' ♮ readings were rejected in order to avoid the unthinkable tone clusters e' ♭ -f'-g'-a' ♭, or e' ♭-g'-a' ♭-a' ♮ on the third beat of the measure.

17. One could speculate as well as to whether the configuration g' ♭-e' ♮-f', in the final reading of the viola is an intentional reference, in augmentation and with more structural weight, to the e" ♭-c"-d", and a' ♭-f'-g' appoggiatura figures in the oboe part of mm. 4–5 which play such a conspicuous role in forming the cadence of the first phrase.

18. This mode-obscuring d♭ should perhaps be heard in connection with the d" ♭ which appeared as the second note of the melody (m.2) and served there to cast momentary doubt on the tonality.

19. The veritably brutal force of this modal shift, along with the less spectacular but equally marked change of modal color from the E-flat major in phrase 1 to the B-flat minor context of phrase 2 and then to the B-flat major cadence, paint yet another aural representation of "wanken."

20. The play upon d" ♭ -d" ♮ within the space of a third: e" ♭-d" ♭-c"-d" ♮ -e" ♭ which fills the first phrase of the aria is perhaps (along with whatever other significance may have been attributed to it in these pages) a reflection in miniature, and as it were in reverse, of the larger arc.

21. The slur over the last five notes of the melody in m. 8 has been corrected—but apparently not by Bach—from ♪♫ ♪♫ . The change is barely apparent in the facsimile; but it is clear in the original that the lower "u"-shaped slur that connects the two autograph overhand slurs was added with the same thin quill and blacker ink found again on this folio in the oboe, mm. 15, 18–21a, and in the viola, mm. 11–12, as well as elsewhere in the movement. These nonautograph slurs have not been reproduced in

Ex. 8.1. [The significance of nonautograph slurs in the autograph scores of J. S. Bach is explored in "Editore traditore," Chapter 14, this volume.]

22. There is some visual evidence for this, although it is not unambiguous. First, the leger line through the a″♭ is unusually long and may have been drawn with the emphatic gesture often characteristic of Bach's corrections. (See, for example, the hook of the corrected ♮-sign in m. 8.) Second, the stem of the g″ does not reach the lower beam of the three-note group, an indication, perhaps, that the note was inserted after what was originally the second note was changed—with the addition of the leger line—from g″ to a″♭.

23. See the [NBA] edition. The trill is found in P 48 and therefore was presumably added, by Bach, in the lost oboe part. Since the trill serves more than a merely ornamental function, its later introduction into the parts should be considered a compositional, if delayed, correction. Evidence that Bach did occasionally enter "ornamental" notes in a composing score is provided in this same phrase by the grace note in m. 9. The grace note not only adds a piquant dissonance to the cadence but completes the scalar descent through the octave from b″♭. It also results in the rhythmically subdivided downbeat pattern characteristic of the theme throughout and thus reserves for the final cadence of the ritornello the conclusiveness of a masculine ending. Perhaps as preparation for this truly "wesentliche Manier" Bach added the trill in m. 7, the upper auxiliary of which by nature fills the skip, c″-a′♮, and provides an accented dissonance on the strong half of the beat, analogous to that in m. 9 and, again, serving to emphasize the appearance of a′♮.

24. The pitch is conspicuously represented in three voices and further emphasized by means of a quasi-*Stimmtausch* interplay between the oboe and viola.

25. The continuo figures for the first movement, preserved in P 48, suggest that the instrumental bass was regarded as the harmonic bass even when the vocal bass crossed below it. (See example).

A passage such as mm. 73–93, moreover, in which the continuo sometimes doubles the vocal bass at the unison, sometimes at the lower octave (descending to C), sometimes crosses above it, and sometimes continues into the bassetto register (mm. 109–112 are notated in P 99 in the tenor clef) [raises the question whether] Bach assumed or even desired contrabass doubling when he determined the continuo-vocal bass relationship or when he entered the figures in the continuo part. (F. E. Niedt, in the passage referred to in n. 10, restricts the use of 16' doubling of continuo parts to heavily orchestrated compositions with trumpets and timpani.)

26. Both the dominant pedal and the dominant-seventh sonority pervading the last phrase of the ritornello serve to raise the harmonic tension during the approach to the final cadence to a level above that attained at the medial cadence where the (applied) dominant-seventh chord sounded only momentarily on the last half-beat of m. 8. The dominant pedal point corresponds, of course, to the tonic pedal of the opening measures.

27. See Marshall 1972, vol. 1, p. 138, and the discussion below.

28. The original reading of the first two notes in Violino I is clear; there seems to be visual evidence for the third note as well in the thickening between the two sixteenth-beams at the base of the stem.

29. The g', however, could and may have been introduced into the Violino II part within the context of this first reading and led by skip to d'.

30. We can infer that Bach recognized the structural ramifications of chord-tone disposition from the fact that the cadence in mm. 24–25, while corresponding to and essentially identical with that in mm. 16–17, has a different configuration of the chord-tones, and that this was brought about in an autograph correction. (See the facsimile [edition and] BG 44, Bl. 38.) In mm. 24–25 the necessity was not to complete the structural line but to leave it open. In the final reading of m. 25 the highest pitch of the cadential complex, g', refers back to the g' of the soprano in m. 21 and carries over to the same pitch in mm. 29–30, now transposed into the "structural register" established in the ritornello in preparation for the ensuing tonal development. In the course of the first vocal section of the aria (mm. 25–45) the g" of mm. 29–30 moves on to f" in m. 35 ("prolonged" through mm. 38, 41, 43), and in mm. 43–45 finally descends e"♭-d"(♭)-c"-b'♭.

31. Quoted by Holton 1971.

9. THE ORIGIN OF THE MAGNIFICAT

1. In this connection see the opening and closing discussions of "The Genesis of an Aria Ritornello" [Chapter 8, this volume].

2. This point was emphasized by Hugo Riemann as early as 1909. See Riemann 1909.

3. See Dürr 1957/76, p. 63.

4. That Bach in Leipzig most likely had only three or four days for the actual composition of a regular Sunday cantata is demonstrated in Marshall 1972, vol. 1, p. 235.

5. See Dürr 1957/76, p. 64.
6. The most extensive discussion of Bach's use of the traditional figures in the *Magnificat* appears in Meyer 1973.
7. See Hans-Joachim Schulze's commentary in the facsimile edition of the *Magnificat*, pp. 7-9.
8. For a closer description of the manuscripts see NBA II/3, KB, pp. 10-15, 18-21, and Marshall 1972, vol. 1, pp. 47-53, 54-56.
9. See Marshall, 1972, *passim.*, and, especially, Alfred Dürr's critical report, NBA II/3, KB, pp. 37-51.
10. The most recent and most comprehensive survey of the Leipzig traditions bearing on Bach's setting is presented in Cammarota 1983.
11. Musikbibliothek der Stadt Leipzig, Sammlung Becker III.2.124.
12. See Tunger 1978.
13. See the order of service in Terry 1929, p. 5. A slightly different, and even longer, program appears in Terry 1925, pp. 66-67.
14. Since the same tonal plan underlies both the E-flat and D-major versions, the keys are indicated here by Roman numerals rather than pitch names (capitals = major mode; lowercase = minor mode).
15. Open noteheads represent movements in the major, filled-in noteheads movements in the minor mode. D major, as the key of the more familiar version, has been selected for the diagram.
16. See Terry 1929, pp. 17, 19. The score is published in the Edition Eulenburg, No. 1074, edited by Felix Schröder. According to Talbot 1980, pp. 216-17, the ascription to Albinoni is "of dubious authenticity."
17. Hans-Joachim Schulze raises this possibility, too. See the *Nachwort* to his edition of the D-major version (Edition Peters), p. 76-77.
18. There were at least fourteen such occasions, besides Christmas. See Stiller 1970, pp. 65, 80-81.
19. See Cammarota 1983, pp. 87-89.
20. Schulze, on the contrary, believes that the inclusion of the hymns "had undesirable consequences for the tonal organization of the whole." See the facsimile edition, pp. 6, 12; and Edition Peters, pp. 76, 79.
21. See Geck 1961, especially p. 264.
22. On this point see Schulze's foreword to the facsimile edition, pp. 8-9.
23. Spitta 1892, p. 181.

10. THE MASS IN B MINOR

1. Some of the Mass's remarkable stylistic features are discussed in "Bach the Progressive" [Chapter 2, this volume].
2. See Dadelsen 1958, pp. 143-56, for a comprehensive discussion of the evidence supporting this chronology.
3. See "Bach's *Orchestre*," [Chapter 3, this volume], also Schulze's commentary in the facsimile edition of the original parts.

4. NBA II/1, KB, pp. 98–113, 130–51, 178–87. Two facsimile editions of P 180 have been published—most recently in 1965 with a commentary by Alfred Dürr. See the review of the latter in Marshall 1967.

5. NBA II/1, KB, pp. 166–68. It is important to recognize, too, that Smend's edition—and his understanding of the chronology of the work as presented in the critical report—appeared in print in 1956 and therefore did not have the benefit of the manuscript and chronological research published by Dürr and von Dadelsen in the late 1950s.

6. NBA II/1, KB, p. 98, and *passim.*

7. Rifkin 1982b suggests that "Kyrie I" was originally in C minor.

8. See Wolff 1967.

9. See also the remarks concerning Cantata No. 171 in "Composing Scores" [Chapter 5, this volume].

10. NBA II/1, KB, pp. 108–12.

11. See the facsimile edition, p. 60.

12. See Marshall 1972, vol. 1, pp. 189–92.

13. See Kobayashi 1988, pp. 61–62.

14. See Wolff 1983.

15. See the discussion of the autograph of BWV 171, pp. 97–99.

16. NBA II/1, KB, pp. 145–47.

17. A related case is found in the *Magnificat.* See "The Origin of the Magnificat" [Chapter 9, this volume]. See also Eric Chafe's illuminating study of the St. Matthew Passion (Chafe 1982).

18. See, for example, Wolff 1968, p. 133.

19. NBA II/1, KB, pp. 147–48, 153–54.

20. See the facsimile edition.

21. In this connection see Wolff 1969.

22. See Dürr 1957/76, p. 77.

23. Exactly what this tempo relation is has been a matter of dispute. See the exchange between Bernard Rose and Arthur Mendel in Mendel 1959, Rose 1959, Mendel 1960b, and B. Rose 1960.

24. See the facsimile edition.

THE AUTOGRAPH FAIR COPIES OF THE
FANTASIA PER IL CEMBALO, BWV 906

[1. Only the following autograph scores of J. S. Bach compositions are presently in American possession, public or private: BWV 9, 10, 33, 80 (fragment), 97, 112, 118[1], 131, 171, 188 (fragment), 197a (fragment), 544, 906, 1073, and the *Clavier-Büchlein vor Wilhelm Friedemann Bach.* See Herz 1984, especially the "Epilogue," p. 303. Marshall 1985 is a facsimile edition of the eight complete cantata autographs. Chapter 5 in this volume is a revised version of the introduction to that volume.]

2. The edges of the paper are presently covered by matting, which makes it impossible to be certain whether the manuscript has indeed been trimmed.

[3. See NBA IX/1, *Textband*, pp. 50–51. The watermark itself is reproduced in NBA IX/1, *Abbildungen*, p. 42.]

[4. See NBA IX/1, *Textband*, p. 51; *Abbildungen*, p. 43. See also Schulze's edition, which is a facsimile of the Dresden autograph with commentary.]

5. Albrecht 1945.

[5a. Schulze, [in the foreword to his facsimile edition,] p. 7, suggests that it may have belonged to Friedrich Konrad Griepenkerl (1782–1849), a pupil of Johann Nikolaus Forkel and an early editor of Bach's keyboard works.]

6. Fürstenau 1876. [According to Schulze, *ibid.*, p. 6, the autograph must have been in the possession of the Saxon royalty in Dresden for a considerable time—perhaps going back to Bach's lifetime—before its presence there was announced by Fürstenau.]

7. Owing to lack of space and the desire to enter the entire first part of the Fantasia on one page, Bach entered m. 16–both first and second endings— on two freely drawn staves on the bottom of the first page. As a result of the (presumably) trimmed lower margin, the precise reading of the left-hand part in the prima volta has been lost. It can be reconstructed from other sources. See Georg von Dadelsen's and Klaus Rönnau's edition of the Bach fantasies, preludes, and fugues, pp. 30ff., and the commentary, p. 136.

8. The only observable corrections in the Bethlehem autograph are changes in the notation of the hand-crossing patterns in mm. 27, 28, and 31. In each case (m. 27, third eighth-note; m. 28, note 1 and m. 31, first and third quarter) the eighth-note in the right hand was first written with a separate flag. This was then changed to a beam and connected with the following eighth (m. 27) or triplet sixteenth group. The Dresden autograph in each instance has the detached notation.

9. Bach had initially written the first four groups of sixteenth-notes a third "too low." It is clear that this was merely a copying error involving the transcription from treble to soprano clef; for, if Bach had actually intended a reading a third lower here, however tentatively, the harmonic content of the first half of m. 9—a diminished seventh—would have obliged him to enter a natural sign before the e′, that is, the note on the second line of the staff (assuming Bach was "thinking in" soprano clef), and there is no trace of such an accidental.

10. Dadelsen and Rönnau, p. 136, suggest that the Dresden autograph ante- dates the Bethlehem. While they present no explicit supporting arguments for their assumption, it is presumably based on internal evidence: the clefs, presence of the prima volta, etc.

11. See Herz 1971, especially pp. 14–15, and Rifkin 1975, especially pp. 384–85.

12. See Kinsky 1937, pp. 20–27; [and the facsimile edition of the *Clavier-Übung*, with commentary by Christoph Wolff (Wolff 1984)].

13. [The C-minor Partita was first published in a separate print in 1727. Al- though the only other Bach manuscript known to contain this watermark is datable to 1729 (see above), there is nothing to exclude an earlier date, ca.1726–27, since the watermark itself, as mentioned earlier, has been dated

to this period. At all events, the Fantasia was clearly composed—and set down at least once (in a composing score)—before the Bethelehem copy was penned.] It is worth mentioning also that the fair copies of the A-minor and E-minor partitas, BWV 827 and 830, that appear in Bach's hand at the beginning of the *Clavier-Büchlein* for Anna Magdalena Bach of 1725 were evidently entered into the volume at just that time. This was presumably before the plan of the *Clavier-Übung* was projected, since the two partitas are notated there with the soprano clef in the right-hand staff. See NBA V/4, KB, pp. 40–46, 69, 73, 76.

14. The manner of notating the hand-crossing in the original edition of the *Giga,* incidentally, is similar to that of the Bethlehem autograph: extra-long note stems extending over the two staves help clarify the disposition of the hands. Conversely, Bach's notation of the hand-crossing passages in the autograph of the B-flat prelude from the *Well-Tempered Clavier II,* BWV 890— the so-called "London Autograph," British Museum: *Add. MS. 35021* (see n. 16)—employs the detached stemming found in the contemporaneous Dresden autograph of our Fantasia. I should like to thank William H. Scheide for bringing these notational idiosyncrasies to my attention.

15. The principal watermark of the "London Autograph"—[the hammer and anvil (No. 105 in the NBA catalogue)—is datable between 1738–40]. This manuscript—or group of manuscripts—presently contains only 21 preludes and fugues from the *Well-Tempered Clavier II* and is not entirely holograph: it is partially in the hand of Anna Magdalena Bach. The greater part, however, was entered by the composer. [See the introduction to the facsimile edition by Don Franklin and Stephen Daw.]

16. The preludes in D, F minor, and B-flat. See Keller 1965, pp. 122, 134, 152, 175.

17. Spitta 1880, vol. 2, pp. 662–63, 667.

18. The absence of a heading from the Fantasia in the Dresden autograph might be explainable, too, since it seems that the headings for many of the preludes in the "London Autograph" of the *Well-Tempered Clavier II* were only added after the individual manuscripts that constitute the "London Autograph" were brought together. See Breckoff 1965, pp. 27–28.

19. See Cone 1974. Cone has convincingly demonstrated that the fugue is indeed unfinished.

12. THE COMPOSITIONS FOR SOLO FLUTE

1. See Dadelsen 1958 and Dürr 1957/76. An English language summary of the chronology appears in Herz 1972, pp. 3–50.

2. Among the [more] significant contributions to the chronology of the instrumental compositions the following should be mentioned. (a) In ref-

erence to the organ and keyboard music: Dadelsen 1963a, Emery 1952, Emery 1966, Kilian 1962, this author's introduction to the facsimile edition of the Fantasia, BWV 906 [see Chapter 11, this volume]; Schulze 1978a. (b) Concertos: Besseler 1955b, Geck 1970. (c) Music for solo instruments: Eppstein 1969, Eppstein 1976, Schulze 1966. [Since the appearance of this essay in 1979 there have been a substantial number of important publications taking up the perennial issues of chronology and authenticity both with regard to Bach's instrumental works in general and the flute compositions in particular. Those dealing with the latter will be addressed in the course of this essay and the Postscript following. I shall refrain from attempting to update the bibliographical survey presented here except to mention Christoph Wolff's redating of the *Art of Fugue* to the early 1740s. See Wolff 1983.]

[2a. The situation, at least for the keyboard works, is actually not so bleak. See the tables of sources in "Organ or 'Klavier?'", Chapter 16, this volume.]

3. NBA VI/3, edited by Hans-Peter Schmitz, published in 1963.

4. Dürr 1975.

5. NBA VI/3, KB, p. 6.

6. Eppstein 1972, especially p. 12. See Blume 1949, cols 1013 and 1023.

7. Eppstein 1966. The discussion of BWV 1031 and 1020 appears on pp. 176–81.

8. The table is based on Durr 1975, pp. 39–40; also Eppstein 1966, pp. 20 and 23; and Eppstein 1972, p. 12.

9. "Wur wären froh, hätten wir für andere Werke eine ähnlich sichere Beglaubigung!" (Dürr 1975, p. 2). This point is made even more emphatically in G. Rose 1970.

[9a. The attribute "most reliable" is perhaps not completely apt for Penzel. See n. 23.]

10. See Schulze 1975, especially pp. 48–52, and Dürr 1962, col. 1022. The most comprehensive discussion and assessment of Penzel appears in Kobayashi 1973, pp. 109–12, 174–83.

11. The copyist, known only by his surname, and the approximate date of the manuscript have recently been ascertained in Kobayashi 1978, especially pp. 52–53.

12. Dürr 1975, p. 40, also refers to an additional source for BWV 1020, said to be part of the "Naumburg Church Archive," and attributing the work to J. S. Bach. Dürr was not able to bring the copy to light.

13. Eppstein 1972, pp. 12–13.

14. Dürr 1975, p. 2. Dürr's suggestion that a correction in Philipp Emanuel's copy of the sonata (St 460) indicates that the scribe was the composer is not convincing. The correction, in m. 8 of the Adagio affects the reading of an ornamental turn figure (changed from d″-c″♯-d″-e″ to d″-e″-d″-e″♯) and could just as easily have resulted from momentary inattention

on the part of the copyist as from the considered reflection of the composer. The minor detail, in any case, has to be weighed against C. P. E. Bach's ascription of the work to his father.

[14a. The even more superfluous bass part in the opening movement of the Sonata for Violin and Basso Continuo in E minor, BWV 1023—a single held tonic pedal throughout—raises the same suspicion: that this movement, too, like the C-major flute sonata, was originally for unaccompanied melody instrument, here a violin. The movement (if not the entire composition) may be the remnant and/or reworking of a projected sonata—more likely, in view of the stylistic heterogeneity and tonal uniformity of BWV 1023, a partita—that was to belong to the cycle of compositions for violin alone. If so, then it may have been rejected in favor of the E-major partita, BWV 1006, that now concludes the famous set of six. Both BWV 1023/1 and BWV 1006/1 are fiery *perpetuum mobile* movements; both feature brilliant bariolage display; both, in effect, are "toccatas" for violin.]

15. It is not really surprising that it took a flautist to be sensitive to the lack of rests in the flute part: I am indebted to Mr. Jacob L. Berg, St. Louis, for this observation.

16. See Breig 1976. I am indebted to Joshua Rifkin for communicating his findings corroborating the assumption of Breig and others that C. P. E. Bach was the author, as well as the scribe, of the cembalo arrangement.

17. See Siegele 1975, pp. 31–46. The manuscript of BWV 1038, in the Germanisches Nationalmuseum, Nuremberg, mentions no composer; it is datable, on the basis of its watermark—"MA, large form"—to the period 1732-35. In this connection, finally, there is a remarkable reference in the catalog of Emanuel's musical estate to a "Trio für die Violine, Bratsche und Bass, mit Johann Sebastian Bach gemeinschaftlich verfertigt." See Miesner 1939, p. 86. I have not been able to identify the composition; no work for this combination is included in Wotquenne 1905.

18. See Dürr 1975, pp. 2–3. One wonders whether the phrase structure of the sonata is accurately characterized as "short-breathed." In the first movement, for example, the keyboard introduction, for all its use of "modern" redicta, proceeds for eight rather long measures quite "breathlessly" over basically a single cadential progression. Similarly, the first "solo episode" after a curious six-measure double motto (mm. 9–14) spins out for 12 full measures (mm. 14–26) before there is any strong caesura.

19. Dürr conjectures that Emanuel's faulty memory in old age could have accounted for the "false" attribution of BWV 1031 to Sebastian (Dürr 1975, pp. 2-3). But the attribution to "J. S. B." also appears, in the hand of the copyist Anonymous 4, in the heading of P 649, and not only (in Emanuel's handwriting) on the title page. And, again, this explanation leaves Penzel's independent and contemporaneous ascription to "J. S. Bach" out of consideration.

20. See Schulze 1975, pp. 49–50.

21. See Dürr 1975, p. 39.

22. Dürr 1975, p. 2. Eppstein 1966, pp. 185-87, offers a cogent characterization of the compositional failings of BWV 1025 (as distinguished from the presumed stylistic anomalies he observes in BWV 1033 and 1031).

23. Penzel's manuscript of BWV 142, SPK P 1042, is the earliest known manuscript of the work and, according to Dürr 1977, pp. 57–58, is the source for all further copies. C. P. E. Bach's copy of BWV 1025, SPK St 462, would seem to have served as the source for the two later manuscripts that attribute the work to Sebastian: SPK St 442 and SPK St 443. St 442 is in the hand of Michel; the wording of the heading of St 443, copied c.1800, is identical to that of St 442. (See also Kast 1958, pp. 87–88.) Another manuscript of the violin suite, bound in the miscellany P 226, consists only of a harpsichord part; the heading of the work mentions no composer. The very first system of the manuscript—and only this much—is in the hand of J. S. Bach. The continuation, which disagrees substantially from the version preserved in the C. P. E. Bach sources, is in the hand of an anonymous scribe. In effect, the violin part has been transferred here to the right hand of the harpsichord part and the piece rearranged for solo keyboard. This, presumably, represents yet another exercise by J. S. Bach the teacher of composition. Having started the pupil off by entering the first system, Bach apparently expected the pupil-scribe to prepare a transcription of the duo. It is conceivable that BWV 1025—whoever may have been the actual composer, and for whatever medium the piece was originally intended—was a favorite instruction piece of Sebastian's for assignments of this kind and was mistakenly taken by Emanuel later on to be an original composition of his father's.

24. "Bach the Progressive," [Chapter 2, this volume].

25. No instrument but the violin is mentioned in any source. The widespread conviction that a flute was intended is based on the fact that the lowest note called for in the piece is d'. (See Eppstein 1972, p. 176, n.2, for a summary of the literature.) This would indeed be odd if the sonata were by J. S. Bach and intended for the violin, since Bach normally exploits the entire available range of his solo instruments. But it is not at all certain that the young C. P. E. Bach would have felt constrained to adopt this characteristic practice of his father.

26. This is Rose's conclusion, too. See G. Rose 1970, p. 368. Rose, though, does not attempt to account for the stylistic peculiarities of BWV 1031 and 1033. For the E-flat sonata she seeks rather to deny them, and she avoids the issue altogether in the case of the C-major sonata. As with the violin suite, BWV 1025, she is content here to accept the attribution on the strength of C. P. E. Bach's authority alone.

27. The table is based on information supplied by Schmitz in NBA VI/3, KB, pp. 7–8, 11, 23, 28–30, 32, 43–44.

28. Early versions of the A-minor and E-minor partitas, BWV 827 and 830, appear in Bach's hand, as fair copies, at the beginning of the *Clavier-Büchlein* for Anna Magdalena Bach of 1725. See NBA V/4, KB, pp. 40–46. The four parts of the *Clavier-Übung* were published in 1731, 1735, 1739, and c.1741. Regarding the origins of the *Well-Tempered Clavier II* see Breckoff 1965, especially pp. 3, 8, 17–24. [Also Brokaw 1985.]

29. BR, p. 343.

30. According to Dürr 1970, especially pp. 46–48, SPK P 229 can be dated no more precisely than "not before 1747."

[30a. "Hauptkopist C" has been identified as Johann Heinrich Bach (1707–83), a nephew of J. S. Bach. (See Schulze 1979, p. 61.) The references to this copyist in nn. 31 and 32 should be emended accordingly.]

31. The remainder of the keyboard part is in the hand of Bach himself. See the description of St 162 in NBA VI/1, KB, pp. 139–40, which, however, does not identify the first hand. A facsimile of a page from St 162 in the hand of Hauptkopist C is reproduced as the frontispiece to Volume II of the *Wiener Urtext Edition* of the sonatas. For the dates of this scribe's appearance in the Bach sources see Dürr 1957/76, p. 148. I should like to thank Dr. Dürr for having confirmed, in a private communication, the identification of the copyist and the continued validity of the dates of his known association with Bach. Actually, the dating of St 162 can be fixed more precisely. The third and fifth movements of this version of Sonata No. 6, BWV 1019, are early versions of the Corrente and Tempo di Gavotte of the E-minor partita from the *Clavier-Übung*, BWV 830—indeed earlier than the versions of the same movements in the *Clavier-Büchlein* for Anna Magdalena Bach of 1725. (See n. 28 above, and NBA V/1, KB, p. 53.) Since this portion of the *Clavier-Büchlein* was written in 1725 and Hauptkopist C's association with Bach began in 1724, St 162 was almost certainly copied in 1724 or 1725. This conclusion is unaffected by the fact that these particular movements were entered into St 162 by Bach himself (in their proper position), since it is hardly likely that Bach would have entered an earlier version of them in St 162 after he had revised them for the version in the *Clavier-Büchlein*.

32. The general conviction, however, as articulated even by Eppstein, who has convincingly established the relative chronology of the three versions of the sonatas, is that the final version, too, is a product of Bach's Köthen period. See Eppstein 1964 and Eppstein 1966, p. 164. In neither publication does Eppstein indicate that the principal scribe of St 162 is Hauptkopist C, nor does he discuss the absolute dating of the source except to suggest, on the basis of its relationship to the *Clavier-Büchlein*, that it must be earlier than 1725. See Eppstein 1964, pp. 223–24.

33. English translations of the obituary and of Forkel's biography are printed in BR, pp. 215–24 and 295–356, respectively.

[33a. This line of inquiry has recently been pursued further by Christoph Wolff. See Wolff 1985.]

34. See NBA VI/3, KB, pp. 7–8. [According to the extensive study of the handwriting of "Anonymous 5" undertaken by Marianne Helms, the attribution in Kast 1958 (and thereupon by Schmitz in NBA VI/3) of the first five staves of BWV 1013 in P 968 (i.e., mm. 1–19 of the Allemande) to the early hand of this copyist is incorrect. More significantly for our purposes, Helms confirms that the manuscript is in the hands of "several of Bach's *Köthen* copyists [emphasis added]." See NBA V/7, KB, pp. 183–85, especially p. 193.]

35. Schmitz claims in fact that the partita is the only work for flute from the first half of the eighteenth century that employs the a‴. See NBA VI/3, KB, p. 8, n.10. But the note does appear in the table of fingerings printed in Johann Joachim Quantz's treatise. (See Quantz-Reilly 1966, p. 42.) The

table of ranges published in the appendix of Terry 1932, pp. 202–03, list the a''' as the highest note in two cantatas, BWV 8 and 145. In the latter instance this is a simple mistake: the highest note in the cantata is g'''. The case of Cantata No. 8 is quite complicated. The Bach-Gesellschaft Edition of the cantata contains a version of the fourth movement, the aria, "Doch weichet, ihr tollen vergeblichen Sorgen," in which the obbligato flute part contains several examples of g♯''' and a'''. It suffices to say here that none of the surviving original sources of the cantata, including the two versions of the flute part, one of which is autograph, demand the a'''.

36. NBA VI/3, KB, p. 8.

37. Only the instrumental parts for BWV 184a survive. They were reused in the Leipzig parody version, BWV 184, *Erwünschtes Freudenlicht*. See the critical reports for both cantatas, prepared in each case by Dürr: NBA I/35, KB, pp. 138ff. (BWV 184a), and NBA I/14, KB, pp. 140ff. (BWV 184).

38. Bach's Köthen flautists are identified by name in König 1959, especially pp. 160–61.

39. The dedication of the concertos, of course, is to the Margrave of Brandenburg, whose residence was in Berlin. Hans-Joachim Schulze, in his foreword to a facsimile edition of the autograph performing parts of the Fifth Concerto (St 130), pp. 7–8, offers the plausible argument that the dedication of the Brandenburg Concertos constituted a barely disguised application for a position at the Margrave's court, made at a time when the musical establishment at Köthen was already in the midst of decline.

40. French titles or headings are extremely rare in the original—or early—sources of Bach's instrumental music. Apart from the flute partita I am aware of only the following examples: the autograph score (P Am. B. 78) of the Brandenburg Concertos; the autographs of the lute compositions, BWV 995 and 998 (the first in the Bibliothèque royale de Belgique, Brussels; the second in private possession in Japan); and Anna Magdalena Bach's copy of the Suites for Unaccompanied Violoncello, BWV 1007–1012 (SPK P 269). It is worth observing that both the score of the Brandenburg Concertos and of the Suite for Lute, BWV 995, are dedication copies; the heading of the latter reads: *Pièces pour la Luth / à / Monsieur Schouster / par / J. S. Bach*. (Finally, for the sake of completeness, it should be mentioned that it is not certain that the title page of Anna Magdalena Bach's copy of the violoncello suites is also in her hand.) [A further example is the Organ Fantasy in G Major, BWV 572, which is transmitted in early sources under the title *Pièce d'Orgue*. See Stauffer 1980, pp. 41, 109, 230–31, and Williams 1980, vol. 1, p. 233. As mentioned in "Tempo and Dynamics," (Chapter 15, this volume), Bach normally employed French terminology for works in French style.]

41. See Härtwig 1973.

42. See Quantz-Reilly 1966, pp. xiii–xv.

43. See BR, pp. 207–08.

44. See the obituary account, *ibid.*, p. 218. For evidence that the contest must have taken place in the fall, no sooner than the end of September 1717, see *Bach-Dokumente I*, No. 6 (pp. 26–27).

45. BR, p. 218.

46. See *Bach-Dokumente III*, No. 735 (p. 189), and Jung 1962, col. 1301.

47. The precise dating, and even the relative chronology of BWV 173a and 184a, are not clear. Owing to the strong stylistic similarities between the two works (Dürr refers to them as "Schwesterwerke"), it has always been assumed that they were composed at about the same time: the birthday cantata, BWV 173a, for 10 December and BWV 184a for the following New Year's Day. But the external evidence contradicts this assumption. The watermark in the autograph composing score of BWV 173a (P 42) is not the same as that found in the surviving parts of BWV 184a (St 24). In his foreword to the facsimile edition of the parts for the Fifth Brandenburg Concerto, Schulze mentions in passing (p. 8) that the watermark in the parts of BWV 184a suggests that the cantata was composed for New Year's Day, 1721. (See also Dürr in NBA I/14, KB, p. 145.) But, according to Dadelsen 1958, pp. 82ff., Bach's handwriting in the score of BWV 173a argues that that work was composed in December 1722. See also NBA I/14, KB, pp. 144-45 (re BWV 184a); NBA I/35, KB, pp. 9-10, 132-33 (re BWV 173a) and 138 (re BWV 184a).

48. See Jung 1962, col. 1301.

49. See Heller 1971, pp. 16-18, 26-27, and Eller 1961.

50. The sonata has been assigned tentatively to the year 1716 by Jung 1962, col. 1301.

51. Such a claim is made, for example, by Günter Hausswald in the foreword to his edition of the Pisendel sonata.

52. See Newman 1966, especially pp. 65, 235, and 322.

[52a. This depiction of Bach's experiences in Dresden in the fall of 1717 is, depending on one's predisposition, either an "imaginative reconstruction" of history or idle speculation. The credibility of the scenario, as conjectural as it admittedly is, can be assessed, I think, simply by postulating the opposite of the events represented here: assuming, for example, that Bach in his moment of triumph was *not* introduced to his Dresden colleagues, that Pisendel did *not* speak to Bach about his recent encounters with Vivaldi and did *not* show or mention his newly composed sonata for unaccompanied violin to him, and so on.]

53. To add to our conjecture: If the C-major sonata, as proposed earlier, was originally composed as an unaccompanied work—perhaps as a companion piece, or even forerunner to the partita—then its deficiencies, too, after subtracting those caused by the addition of the bass part, could be ascribed to the composer's inexperience: inexperience perhaps in composing unaccompanied works for melody instruments. [According to Marcello Castellani, the flute writing in BWV 1013 is not unidiomatic but rather representative of the modern French style and should have been playable by any professional flautist of the time. Rejecting my association with Buffardin, then, but accepting my dating of BWV 1034 (see below), he proposes that the partita, too, was composed in Leipzig, in 1724 (the year of the cantatas with flute obbligato). (See Castellani 1985.) In light of the Köthen provenance of P 968, however, a Leipzig origin for BWV 1013 is effectively excluded.]

54. See NBA VI/3, KB, p. 11. The miscellany, P 804, is described at length in NBA V/5, KB, pp. 24–35. Kellner knew Bach personally; but it is not known precisely when they met, nor how Kellner procured the sources from which he prepared the manuscripts brought together (after his death) to form P 804. It is clear, however, that many, but by no means all, of Kellner's copies must have been made directly from autographs in Bach's possession. (See May 1974, especially pp. 268–70.) Three fascicles in P 804—none including the flute sonata—were dated by Kellner: two with the year 1725, one with 1726. The title page and also the final page of [Fascicle 22 (containing the unaccompanied violin works)] carry the date 1726. The miscellany, however, also contains a copy of the A-minor Partita from the *Clavier-Übung* (BWV 827), which not only reproduces the title page, including the date, 1727, of the original print, but also shares its readings—readings, that is, that postdate those contained in the *Clavier-Büchlein* of 1725. (See NBA V/1, KB, p. 35.) This would seem to constitute conclusive evidence that Kellner had access to Bach sources from the early Leipzig period and not only the Weimar and Köthen periods. Since no systematic study of Kellner's script has ever appeared, it is not yet possible to date these manuscripts precisely. As Dietrich Kilian reports in NBA IV/5–6, KB, *Teilband I*, pp. 194–97, Kellner's handwriting seems to have undergone several stages of development. My own examination of Kellner samples from P 804 reveals that the script found in BWV 1034 shares features with both the manuscripts of 1725 and that of 1726 and would seem to have been copied within that two-year span. [In the meantime a comprehensive and systematic study of Kellner has appeared: Stinson 1985a. According to Stinson (p. 127), the fascicle containing BWV 1034 dates from 1726/27—not 1725/26, as proposed here. This slightly later dating will have a slight impact on the argument developed here. See note 64a.]

55. See, for example, Eppstein 1972, p. 17.

56. Scheide is credited for this by Dürr 1971, vol. 1, p. 50, n. 24.

57. But see the discussion below of Bach's pupil, Friedrich Gottlieb Wild.

58. The flute parts in Cantata No. 181 were only added after the first performance of 13 February 1724. See Dürr 1957/76, p. 66.

59. *Ibid.*, pp. 70–71.

60. The cantatas are published in NBA I/14.

61. It is striking that between 6 August and 8 October the flute appears almost every week. (The cantatas for the Twelfth Sunday after Trinity, 27 August, and for the Town Council Inauguration on 28 August are apparently lost. There are no flute parts in the cantata for the Thirteenth Sunday after Trinity, 3 September [BWV 33].) It is just as striking that from 8 October to 19 November the weekly pattern is broken and the flute appears at two-week intervals.

62. BR, pp. 111–12.

63. That of Buffardin, who "once visited J. S. Bach at Leipzig" also suggests itself. [Yet another candidate is the Bach pupil Christoph Gottlob Wecker, who was in Leipzig from 1723 to 1728 and whose "barely matched . . . dexterity and experience on the Flaute Traver." was specifically attested to

by a contemporary. (See Feldmann 1934, p. 93, n. 4.) Bach's own recommendation for Wecker, however, dated March 1729, does not emphasize his abilities as a flautist. (See BR, p. 116.)]

64. See Eppstein 1966, pp. 29–30.

[64a. Given the redating of P 804/23 to 1726/27 and the undeniable fact that Bach's schedule of cantata production in the late summer and fall of 1724 could hardly have left him much time to compose much else, it is more prudent to date the composition of BWV 1034 even more approximately: to the mid-1720s.]

65. See Table 12.2 and NBA VI/3, KB, pp. 32–33. Eppstein has suggested that the sonata may also have existed in one or more preliminary forms in a different scoring, now lost. See Eppstein 1966, pp. 75–90.

66. The fair-copy autograph of the B-minor version, P 975, contains a number of transposition corrections that reveal that it was prepared from a source in G minor. See the facsimile edition of P 975.

67. For the dating of Cantata No. 117 see Dürr 1957/76, p. 106. It is evident from the incipits compiled in McAll 1962, pp. 55–56, that no other theme by Bach even approximately shares this particular rhythmic-melodic configuration.

68. Dürr 1968b also suggests the possibility that one of the versions of BWV 1030 with keyboard obbligato was prepared in connection with Bach's activities with the Collegium Musicum. (See, especially, p. 340.) It is perhaps not entirely irrelevant to mention here that a number of passages in the sonata call to mind, in a general way, certain numbers in the St. Matthew Passion: shared rhythmic or melodic contours; the use of certain syncopation patterns (for example, tied and decorated suspensions and appoggiaturas approached and/or left by leap); florid, ornamental, but strangely unflowing "jerky" melodies punctuated with erratic, start–stop rhythms that feature short–long anapestic patterns; and so on. Compare, for example, the aria "Erbarme dich, mein Gott," and the "second theme" (mm. 20ff.) of BWV 1030/1, or the gigue from BWV 1030/3 and "Mache dich, mein Herze, rein." But it would surely be premature to speculate as to whether the G-minor version of the sonata was composed perhaps at about the time of the second performance of the St. Matthew Passion in 1729.

69. The watermark of the autograph ("NM + Heraldisches Wappen von Zedwitz") can only be dated to the second half of the 1730s. (See Dürr 1957/76, p. 143.) But it appears in the parts prepared for the 1736 performance of the St. Matthew Passion (Dürr 1957/76, p. 115). The title page of P 1008, incidentally, with its description of the G-minor version as a flute composition, seems to have been written by the nineteenth-century owner of the manuscript (see NBA VI/3, p. 32). Accordingly, it is not inconceivable that the G-minor version was intended for some instrument other than the flute. Indeed, the work is often performed in G minor on the oboe. Eppstein, however, argues on the basis of the compass of all three parts (obbligato instrument and each of the two hands of the harpsichord part) that the solo instrument was the flute. (He also posits yet an earlier version for two flutes and continuo, likewise in G minor. Eppstein 1966, pp. 75–78.

70. Quantz's description of his teacher's playing appeared in Quantz 1755, especially p. 209. Martin Bernstein was the first to doubt that the B-minor suite was written at Köthen and to connect it with Dresden and with the 1730s. See his remarks in Congress 1961, p. 127.

71. See the facsimile edition and the text discussion. P 612 is one of the handful of manuscripts, and the only Bach manuscript, from the Prussian State Library that had been missing since the Second World War and was returned in 1977 to the Deutsche Staatsbibliothek. Its recovery has made it possible to examine the watermark and to confirm the dating c.1736, which had been suggested by Philipp Spitta. The autograph is something of a curiosity in that it contains two works entered one above the other. The score of the concerto in C minor for two harpsichords, BWV 1062, is notated on folios 1ʳ–15ᵛ above the score of the A-major sonata, which occupies the bottom three staves of those leaves and then continues on folio 16ʳ. Another peculiarity of P 612 is that from folio 9ʳ to 14ᵛ the staves for the first movement of the sonata, beginning after m. 62, have been completely removed from the score. That is, over forty percent of the movement is irretrievably lost. [Michael Marissen has successfully repudiated this last assertion and has posited a reconstruction that very likely retrieves the missing measures in most, if not all, significant particulars. See Marissen 1985.]

72. See Eppstein 1966, pp. 90–102, 161–69. In the following [text] discussion page references to specific points in Eppstein's argument will be cited in the text in parentheses.

73. It is of interest to compare Eppstein's characterization of the A-major sonata, BWV 1032/1, or at least the first movement, with his arguments against the authenticity of the E-flat sonata, BWV 1031. (a) Re 1032/1: "it completely lacks . . . the intensive three-part texture which otherwise characterizes all the polyphonic movements of the sonatas for melody instrument and harpsichord. If one disregards the passages in parallel motion (flute, mm. 11–12, 18–19, etc.) and the barely melodic filler parts . . . then the movement is basically for two voices" (pp. 99–100). Re 1031: ". . . a looseness of polyphonic writing [Schlaffheit der polyphonen Arbeit] which finds expression for example in the constant parallel motion between the two upper parts (third movement, mm. 2, 4, 6–8, 10, 12)" (p. 179). (b) Re 1032/1: "In mm. 25–37, where the 'tutti' theme of the beginning is repeated by the flute in the dominant, it is curiously divided between the flute and the right hand of the harpsichord in the manner of 'durchbrochene Arbeit.' This technique is hardly a stylistic feature of Bach's epoch" (p. 93). "Bach draws on this technique again . . . mm. 55ff . . . .The reason for it in this movement, a movement so lacking in polyphony . . . is probably again Bach's desire for quasi-polyphonic activity in the two parts" (p. 93, n.). Re 1031: "Just as unusual is the obvious preference for small-scale voice exchange. . . . This phenomenon is related to another: two-voice episodes are often simply repeated with the voices exchanged" (p. 179). (c) Re 1032/1: "The flute ascends to d‴, the highest note in the movement, only once; for the remainder Bach apparently set c‴♯ as the upper limit" (p. 100). "Neither the highest available notes of the flute nor the harpsichord are exploited" (p. 92). Re 1031: "Incidentally, they [BWV 1031 and 1020] differ from all of Bach's authentic

compositions for flute . . . in that they hardly exploit the high range of the flute: neither exceeds d'''' " (p. 180).

74. "One wonders whether this movement in its present fragmentary state can be considered a finished composition at all, or whether it might not be the sketch of a transcription (arrangement). Could it have been Bach himself, dissatisfied with the result, who cut out the missing portion?" (p. 101).

75. This confirms the conjecture expressed in NBA VI/3, KB, p. 44, that the reading crossed out after m. 21 in the first movement of the score resulted from a copying error and was not a rejected compositional sketch. The latter had been suggested in Schünemann 1935, p. 4. The commentary in Marshall 1972, vol. 2, Sketch 169, should be emended accordingly. P 612 does, however, contain a few interesting corrections, such as the addition of the characteristic written-out thirty-second-note mordents in mm. 3 and 4 of the theme—but not thereafter.

76. Flute part, mm. 122–23; bass part, m. 144, first note, m. 194, first note: all originally a third higher. It is also conceivable, but by no means certain, that Bach entered the right-hand stave of the harpsichord part for the entire sonata in the soprano clef in order to facilitate the transposition down a third (in the outer movements) from a treble-clef source in C major. It should also be mentioned that in mm. 34–35 of the second movement, Bach had at first entered the right-hand part a third too low, which suggests that his source here was written, as presumed, in the same key (A minor) as the current version, but, again, in the treble clef.

77. The Largo survives in a source, SPK St 345, dating from the mid-eighteenth century and scored for violin, cello, and "bass," which presumably has no connection with Bach but which seems to be derived from an (earlier?) version of BWV 1032/2 that was not identical with that in P 612. See Eppstein 1966, pp. 24, 91–92, and NBA VI/3, KB, pp. 43ff. and 55ff.; also Dürr 1968b, p. 336.

78. Eppstein is quite convinced that the third movement was originally a trio. But the fact that it could have been does not, of course, mean that it must have been. (Cf. Dürr's expression of caution in Dürr 1968b, p. 335.) It is curious, moreover, that in presenting his argument for the trio origins of the third movement—as opposed to the uncertain (trio or concerto) prehistory of the first movement—Eppstein points out its similarity to the finale of the Harpsichord Concerto in E Major, BWV 1053 (p. 99). [All of this speculation about the original key, scoring, and style of BWV 1032 has effectively been put to rest by Marissen's compelling demonstration that the work was originally a trio sonata in C major for recorder, violin, and continuo, cast as a *Sonate auf Concertenart* (in the terminology of Johann Adolph Scheibe). As mentioned earlier, Marissen is also able to reconstruct the forty-five missing measures and to argue persuasively that they were in all likelihood removed by Bach himself, not because of any dissatisfaction with their substance but rather in order to expedite the copying of parts for a performance of the work. See Marissen 1985 and also Marissen 1988. (Marissen does not venture a date of composition for the trio version.)]

79. One infers from the context in which this observation is made that Eppstein would be tempted to suggest a Weimar origin for the presumed earliest version of BWV 1032, were it not for the fact that Bach did not begin to compose for the flute until he settled in Köthen.

80. See Marshall 1972, vol. 2, Sketch 19.

81. See also Dürr 1968b, p. 340.

82. A somewhat earlier copy of the sonata, P 621 (c.1800), also refers to Fredersdorf. See NBA VI/3, KB, p. 22-23. Michael Gabriel Fredersdorf (1708-58), an amateur flute player, was the valet, private secretary, and personal confidante of Frederick the Great, as well as his flute partner (NBA VI/3, KB, p. 24).

83. See Eppstein 1972, pp. 14-15, 18-19. [Actually, the Sonata in E minor for Violin and Continuo, BWV 1023, mentioned earlier (n. 14a) is best described as a sonata da camera, as well.]

84. *Ibid.*

85. *Ibid.,* p. 19. See also "Bach the Progressive" [Chapter 2, this volume].

86. The letters were in answer to two letters written by J. S. Bach from Berlin. Both of Sebastian's letters are lost. See *Bach-Dokumente II,* No. 489 (pp. 391-92); *Bach Dokumente I,* No. 45a,b (p. 112); and BR, pp. 168-69.

87. See Becker 1955, col. 956.

88. *Bach-Dokumente II,* No. 554 (pp. 434-35), and BR, p. 176.

89. Wolff 1971, pp. 401-03.

90. Eppstein 1972, p. 19.

91. See Becker 1955, col. 956.

92. Quantz-Reilly 1966, p. xxii.

93. Could it be, for example, that Bach went to Berlin at the beginning of 1744 to attend the wedding of Emanuel and met one or another of his son's musical colleagues, including Fredersdorf, on that occasion? We are particularly ill-informed about Bach's activities and movements in the early 1740s. For example: with the exception of a number of receipts and routine letters of recommendation, no letters—in the proper sense of the term—survive in his hand from the period from July 1741 to July 1748. See *Kalendarium,* especially pp. 51-56.

94. This view is eloquently propounded throughout Eppstein 1966. See, in particular, pp. 32-33. [The complex matter of Bach's attitude towards idiomatic treatment of the instrumental medium is pursued further in "Organ or 'Klavier'?", Chapter 16, this volume.]

[94a. In light of the findings of Marissen 1985 and 1988 regarding the formal idiosyncrasies of BWV 1032 and the similar comments in Wolff 1985 regarding BWV 1030, I am even more inclined now to assume a Leipzig origin for the earliest forms of these works. See n. 68 and the discussion of BWV 1032 vis-à-vis BWV 29, p. 219.]

95. The "new chronology" and the *Neue Bach-Ausgabe,* of course, epitomize this.

96. As a symbol for the former the three volumes of *Bach-Dokumente* may serve admirably; Eppstein's monograph on the sonatas for melody instrument

and obbligato keyboard (Eppstein 1966), mentioned frequently in the course of this study, serves just as well as a symbol for the latter.

The Compositions for Solo Flute: Notes to the Postscript

1. Congress 1964, vol. 1, p. 97: "Des weiteren ist es für uns nicht so wichtig, wie gut Mozart geschrieben hat, sondern wir müssen uns vergegenwärtigen, wie 'schlecht' er hat schreiben können. Sein unteres Niveau—davon haben wir bisher kaum eine Kenntnis."

2. Plath 1964, p. 54.

13. "AUTHENTIC" PERFORMANCE

*The occasion and focus of this essay was the release of the first two volumes of Johann Sebastian Bach, *The Complete Cantatas.* Volume 1: Cantata Nos. 1–4 (Telefunken SKW 1); Volume 2: Cantata Nos. 5–8 (Telefunken SKW 2). Performers: Paul Esswood, alto; Kurt Equiluz, tenor; Max van Egmond, bass. Nos. 1–6: The Vienna Choir Boys, The Chorus Viennensis, The Vienna Concentus Musicus, conductor Nikolaus Harnoncourt. Nos. 7–8: The King's College Choir, The Leonhardt Consort, conductor Gustave Leonhardt.

1. Mendel 1952, p. 673.

[1a. The Rilling Series, encompassing all the authentic church cantatas from BWV 1 through BWV 200 (plus the Easter Oratorio, BWV 249), was completed in 1985. It is now distributed on the Laudate label (a production of the Hänssler Publishing Co., Stuttgart).]

2. Lang 1972.

[2a. In the more than fifteen years since this review was written there has been a veritable flood of articles dealing with virtually every aspect of the "authenticity movement." Among the most thoughtful and fundamental, surely, are Dreyfus 1983, Kerman 1985 (Chapter 6: "The Historical Performance Movement"), and Taruskin et al. 1984.]

3. The most sensational example to date in fact has been provided by the B-minor Mass. See Dadelsen 1959.

4. Harnoncourt nowhere maintains in the accompanying notes for the cantata recordings that he has personally compared the sources, and it is hard to believe that a heroic undertaking of the kind is contemplated for the series. There should have been some indication, though, of the editions used or the editorial policy followed.

5. Compare, for example, in Movement 1, mm. 14–17, the inconsistent slurring of the imitative figure with the different but equally inconsistent slurring of the same passage in mm. 128–30; or in Movement 2, the placement of slurs within the sequential passage, mm. 5–6, 7–8, or between m. 60 and the analogous m. 92. Note also the lack of trills in Movement 1, mm. 21 (Oboe I), 67 (Soprano), 122 (Soprano), 124 (all vocal parts); the lack

of dynamics in Movement 3, mm. 26, 31, 42; the treatment of dynamics in the string parts of Movement 5, mm. 7–11, 17 and 26, 19–21.

[5a. It has been proposed, however, that the pervasive inconsistency with respect to articulation and other performance indications that is a hallmark of eighteenth-century sources is in fact a true reflection not only of the actual, but also of the desired performance practice of the time. See Pont 1979.]

6. A cautious suggestion to that effect was put forth in Gilmore 1972, p. 74.

7. NBA I/15 was published in 1967; Rilling's performance of Cantata No. 75 was recorded during June/July 1970 (*Die Bach Kantate,* Claudius Verlag München, CLV 71901). The recording of Cantata No. 166, on the other hand, conducted by Helmut Barbe (Vanguard, SRV 244 SD), is based on the NBA edition and includes the reconstructed violin obbligato part.

8. Lang 1972, p. 121.

9. Kolneder 1967.

10. The soprano has no solo function in Cantata Nos. 2 or 7 and appears in Cantata Nos. 5 and 8 as a soloist in secco recitatives (BWV 5/6 and 8/5). There is a brief, presumably solo, role for the soprano in the chorale recitative BWV 3/2. Of the three appearances of the soprano in duet movements (BWV 3/5, 4/3, 4/7), one—BWV 4/3—is to intone the *cantus firmus.*

11. See W. Neumann 1938.

12. Mendel 1955, especially pp. 471ff. [In an extensive revision and expansion of that study, Mendel considers the arguments that have been advanced for a′ = 421 as the pitch norm with regard to Bach but in the end reaffirms his original finding. See Mendel 1978, especially p. 79. A more recent and important challenge to Mendel's views appears in Haynes 1985.]

13. See his program notes for the Brandenburg Concertos (Telefunken SAWT 9459/60) and for the St. John Passion (Telefunken SKH 19).

14. The notes for the B-minor Mass (Telefunken SKH 20).

15. Similarly, there can be little doubt that horn players in the eighteenth century were able to blend the natural and stopped notes to a much greater degree than Harnoncourt's players can. D. F. Tovey refers to Brahms as having justified his insistence on a valveless Waldhorn in the Horn Trio with the explanation that (in Tovey's words) "if the player were not compelled to blend his open notes with his closed ones, he would never learn to blend his tone in chamber music at all." (See Tovey 1959, p. 248.) Harnoncourt's description, and use, of a transposition hole on the baroque trumpet to remove the discrepancy between natural and chromatic notes (program notes for the Brandenburg Concertos) testify to the concern at the time for consistency and evenness of tone color. (My guess is that this blending of tone color on the natural horn was accomplished by tuning the instrument somewhat high and then stopping *all* the notes to a greater or lesser extent.) Finally, J. J. Quantz's emphasis on a clear, round flute tone and its "necessary similarity to the human voice," [and,] moreover, his description of the "innate defect" of the flute in regard to the intonation of chromatic notes for which the

player was obliged to compensate, lead to the same conclusion. (See Quantz-Reilly 1966, pp. 50 and 58.)

16. A five-string instrument (tuned C G d a e′), slightly larger than a viola, held on the arm, and presumably played by Bach's Leipzig violinist. [Specifically, by Georg Gottfried Wagner. Drüner 1987 is the most recent and extensive study of this instrument.]

17. See Sachs 1908, and Plate 6 in Bonanni 1723.

[17a. The most comprehensive and systematic discussion of this issue appears in MacCracken 1984.]

[17b. This "fact" has been forcefully challenged by Laurence Dreyfus, who argues that the harpsichord frequently (if not, indeed, normally) participated along with the organ in realizing the continuo part in Bach's own performances of his cantatas. See Dreyfus 1987; also Schulze 1987.]

18. The two surviving original continuo parts, one transposed down a tone and containing figures (thus intended for organ) and the other untransposed and without figures, are both simply headed "Continuo."

19. In this connection see the passage from Niedt 1721 reproduced and translated in Arthur Mendel's introduction to his vocal score edition of Bach's St. John Passion, p. vii.

[20. Dreyfus 1987 is precisely the study called for here. See also the review by Peter Williams (1988).]

21. The accompanying record notes would be a fitting place for this. It is unfortunate that in the program notes for the cantata albums Harnoncourt does not continue to set forth his views on specific problems of baroque performance practice (e.g., ensemble size, tempo, articulation, acoustics) as he had done for his earlier Bach recordings. The literature for the cantata albums includes, in addition to the libretti and BG scores, a brief history of the cantata genre (repeated identically so far in each album) and interpretations of the individual cantatas abridged from Dürr 1971, a general statement by Harnoncourt of his approach, and the statistical particulars for each cantata. [Later volumes in the series, however, have frequently included informative discussions of one or the other of these problems.]

[21a. Whether Bach's chorus, however, actually consisted of no more than a solo quartet, as proposed by Joshua Rifkin, seems quite unlikely. See Rifkin 1982a, 1983, Marshall 1983, and, especially, Wagner 1986.]

22. In other respects as well—the vivid, "naturalistic" declamation, the reedy, organ-like timbre of the sustained strings in accompagnato settings—the recitatives provide perhaps the most consistently successful feature in the entire cantata series.

23. Only the opening allabreve chorus of BWV 2, taken at ca. $\mathbb{C}$ $\downarrow$ = 88, seems to me uncomfortably fast—by just about the same amount, in fact, that the tempo exceeds the outer limit of the traditional *tempo ordinario*, derived from the normal pulse beat, of 60–80 per minute. Some timings follow now for the sake of comparison:

Recording	Total Time
BWV 1	
Fritz Lehmann, cond. (Archive ARC 3063)	25'09"
Harnoncourt	25'12"
BWV 4	
Fritz Lehmann, cond. (Archive ARC 3063)	24'10"
Wilhelm Ehmann, cond. (Vanguard SRV 225)	21'04"
Harnoncourt	19'49"
BWV 8	
Karl Richter, cond. (Archive ARC 3145)	23'56"
Leonhardt	18'45"

24. Reproduced in Mendel's introduction to his edition of the St. John Passion, p. xxix. [The handwriting is actually that of Christian Friedrich Penzel and dates from ca.1770. See NBA I/5, KB, p. 182. On Penzel, see also pp. 204, 208.]

25. F. Neumann 1964, 1965a, 1965b, 1965c. [These and other provocative articles by Neumann have been reprinted in F. Neumann 1982. See also his exhaustive study of ornamentation (F. Neumann 1978).]

26. F. Neumann 1965c, p. 343.

27. See the program notes for the Orchestral Suites or the B-minor Mass.

28. Lang 1972, pp. 124–25.

[28a. It would seem that the *messa di voce* was applied only to long notes, in relatively slow movements, and even then not invariably or indiscriminately. See Robison 1982, especially pp. 6 and 11.]

29. It must also be reported that the review copies of the Telefunken cantata albums, particularly Volume I, had rather poor record surfaces, considerable surface noise, and a shrill sound quality owing perhaps to an under-recorded bass. There have been rumors to the effect that the first pressings of new Telefunken releases are often defective.

14. "Editore Traditore"

1. Dadelsen 1978.

2. *Ibid.,* p. 104.

3. Of the slurs contained on f. 1ʳ of the autograph score only those in the following staves seem to be original: Stave 3 (Violino I): mm. 1–2; Stave 4 (Violino II): m. 4 (part of a correction); Stave 6 (Continuo): mm. 3–4. All the slurs in the two oboe staves (Staves 1 and 2, 7 and 8) are later additions.

4. Analogous slurs appear in m. 1 (Oboes I and II), in mm. 26, 44, 98 (Violino I; in m. 26 both Violini I and II). A complete tabulation appears in NBA I/19, KB.

5. The evidence for this is presented in NBA I/19, KB.

6. It should be noted that the four-note slur is also found in the principal sources of the parody of the movement, the *Kyrie* from the G-minor Mass, BWV 235: SPK P 15 and SPK P 18. See also NBA II/2, p. 129ff.

7. More precisely: the additional slurs in the autograph (there are approximately 85–90 such slurs in the manuscript) correspond either to (1) the newly added slurs in the Hering parts or to (2) unaltered—original—slurs in the Hering parts. In addition to the five-note figure in the main theme of Movement 1, previously discussed, the first category also includes a slur over the two cadential sixteenth-notes in m. 21 of Movement 4 (Violino I and II). To the second category belong (among others): in Movement 1 the slur over the two eighth-notes in the second measure of the opening oboe motif (in both oboe parts) and in corresponding passages; in Movement 3 the two-note slurs in the continuo; in Movement 4 the slurs in mm. 3, 4, and 7 of the main theme (and in corresponding passages).

8. The sources transmitting the C. P. E. Bach version are: (1) an organ part from C. P. E. Bach's circle; (2) C. P. E. Bach's autograph score of his arrangement of the sixth movement (now bound together with the J. S. Bach autograph score); (3) a score, copied ca.1820–30, once belonging to Felix Mendelssohn; (4) a score, copied in 1829, from the estate of Gustav Wilhelm Teschner (a leading Berlin voice teacher and former pupil of Carl Friedrich Zelter); and (5) an edition, prepared by Adolph Bernhard Marx, published by Simrock (Bonn, 1830).

9. As a result the bass arioso, "Verachtest du"—Movement 4 in the original version—is now the third movement. For the new fourth movement Philipp Emanuel provided the final four-part chorale setting—i.e., Movement 7— with one of the earlier strophes of the same hymn.

10. Since the Schwencke score (which may or may not be literally a "19th-century" source) contains only Movement 1 in any event, it may be discounted here.

11. Most likely these sources derive from a score, now lost, that itself was prepared from the (equally lost) original parts of Cantata No. 102—after they had been revised by C. P. E. Bach. That lost score may have been a C. P. E. Bach autograph. A complete discussion of the source transmission for Cantata No. 102 appears in NBA I/19, KB.

12. Besides using Movement 1 as the model for the *Kyrie* of the G-minor Mass, Bach reworked Movements 3 and 5 of the cantata as the "Qui tollis" and "Quoniam" movements, respectively, of the Mass in F, BWV 233.

13. On the Rudorff collection see Reich 1974.

14. See the Postscript to this essay.

15. The major stations in the history of the exposé are contained in Neufeldt 1912, Prieger 1913, and Calvocoressi 1914.

16. Neufeldt 1912, p. 342–43.

17. Prieger 1913, p. 276.

18. See *Hofmeisters Jahresverzeichnis der Deutschen Musikalien und Musikschriften* 9(1880–85): 547, 10(1886–91): 642; 11(1892–97): 722.

19. Kretzschmar 1899, p. xlvii.

20. Dadelsen 1963b, col. 1194.

21. Rust does not mention our control—the Schwencke score—in his tabulation of the sources. Under normal circumstances we would conclude that he did not know of its existence or at least did not examine it. The score, however, was surely in the Königliche Bibliothek (now the Deutsche Staatsbibliothek) at the time: its shelf number, P 98, immediately follows that of the autograph, P 97, and, like the autograph, it was formerly in the possession of Georg Poelchau.

22. For example, in the autograph score of Cantata No. 105, *Herr, gehe nicht ins Gericht*, P 99, and, once again, a Hering copy—the score SPK P 48/4. (See Chapter 8, this volume, n. 21.) The question arises as to the extent of the presence of posthumous slurrings, articulation marks, and other entries in the original Bach manuscripts and early copies. One suspects that they are considerably more extensive than has hitherto been reported.

23. The original parts, belonging to the Thomasschule, are housed in the Stadtarchiv, Leipzig.

24. Both oboe parts and the principal continuo part are mainly in the hand of Bach's principal Leipzig copyist, Johann Andreas Kuhnau (1703–?). A second copyist, identified in Dürr 1957/76 as "Anonymous Ia," entered the final chorale. The duplicate continuo part was copied by Dürr's "Anonymous Vo." (See NBA I/19, KB.) It is not impossible that the duplicate continuo part was only prepared after 1750. See NBA I/18, KB, p. 155.

15. TEMPO AND DYNAMICS

[a. *Bach-Dokumente III*, No. 803 (pp. 289–90); BR, p. 279.]

1. See the facsimile edition and NBA V/5.

2. There are in fact two sets of thoroughbass rules in the Clavier-Büchlein, both apparently dating from the early 1740s: the first entered in the hand of Johann Christoph Friedrich Bach, the second—and more elaborate—by Anna Magdalena. See *Bach-Dokumente I*, No. 183 (pp. 252–54).

3. See Walther 1732; also Eggebrecht 1957, especially p. 13. It is not surprising that Walther's *Lexicon* proves to be a most reliable guide to Bach's use and understanding of musical terminology. Both men, after all, shared very much the same musical tradition. Not only were they cousins who lived at the same time in the same town for close to a decade (1708–17), but they were clearly in close musical contact as well. Bach in fact later acted as the Leipzig sales representative for Walther's dictionary (*Bach-Dokumente II*, No. 260 [p. 191]).

4. The table preserves Bach's usual orthography. Alternative spellings have been placed in parentheses; editorial resolutions of abbreviations in square brackets.

5. Walther 1732, p. 479, which defines *più piano* as "wie ein zweytes *Echo*, so dass es als noch weit entlegener denn als *piano* klinge" ("like a second echo, so that it sounds as if much farther away than piano").

6. Walther, *ibid.*, p. 479, reports further that the abbreviation for *pianissimo*

was *ppp*: "gleichsam das dritte *Echo,* welches lässt, als wenn die Stimme oder der Instrument-Klang in die Lufft zergienge" ("a third echo which lets the sound of the voice or instrument seem to fade into the air"). Bach apparently never used the abbreviation *ppp.*

7. The autograph score of BWV 131 is in private possession. [See the facsimile edition, Marshall 1985, p. 16.]

8. SPK P 60.

9. See the movement in NBA II/5, as well as the facsimile reproduced in the KB, p. 231.

10. P 234.

11. The earliest source of BWV 106 is Christian Friedrich Penzel's score copy SPK P 1018, dated 1768. The earliest use of the term *pianissimo* preserved in an autograph score is found in the Köthen cantata *Durchlauchtster Leopold,* BWV 173a, (P 42), the precise date of which is uncertain. See NBA I/35, KB, pp. 132–33, [and Chapter 12, this volume, n. 47.]

12. Heinrich Besseler has argued that such *Ausdrucksdynamik* constituted one of Bach's major stylistic innovations: see Besseler 1955a, especially pp. 25, 39.

13. See, for example, the echo effects in the organ Prelude in E flat, BWV 552 (*Clavier-Übung III,* mm. 34–40, as well as those in the "Echo" movement of the French Overture, BWV 831 (*Clavier-Übung II.*).

14. The argument has been put forth, quite persuasively, that there could hardly have been much if any room for discretion with regard to the choice of dynamics in the keyboard and organ works beyond the initial establishment of the registration. See Bodky 1960, p. 34, regarding the keyboard compositions, and Stauffer 1981 regarding the organ compositions. (Stauffer suggests that Bach's free organ compositions should almost invariably be performed *pro organo pleno.*) It should be observed, however, that there is also an almost complete absence of dynamic marks in the fair-copy autograph (SPK P 967) of the Sonatas and Partitas for Unaccompanied Violin—again with the exception of echo effects in the final movement of the A-minor sonata, BWV 1003/4, and the Preludio of the E-major partita, BWV 1006/1. This would seem to confirm, after all, that the lack of dynamic markings in Bach's solo compositions reflects at least to some significant degree the composer's desire to grant the solo performer maximum artistic flexibility in this respect.

15. The autograph scores, especially the composing scores of the early Leipzig period, generally have few if any dynamic markings.

16. The only original source for BWV 63 is the set of performing parts, SPK St 9. The oboe part for the duet movement is autograph. See NBA I/2, KB, p. 11.

17. The sole source is the original set of parts, St 68. The dynamics in the instrumental parts were entered by Bach.

18. The autograph score, P 25, reads *m.f.;* the autograph continuo part, SPK St 110, reads *mezo forte.*

19. The dynamic markings appear only in the parts, not the autograph score. See NBA II/5, KB, p. 164.

20. The autograph Violino I part reads *Largo è un poco piano;* the equally autograph Violino II and Viola parts *Largo è poco piano.* See the facsimile edition of the original parts.

21. Cantata No. 165 survives only in a nonautograph, but original score dating from Bach's Leipzig period. The manuscript is part of the Amalienbibliothek and is now housed in the Deutsche Staatsbibliothek under the shelf number 105. Since the source is in a copyist's hand, the question arises as to whether the *piano piano* indication is completely authentic. It is conceivable, after all, that the copyist misconstrued his source—perhaps an autograph, perhaps containing at this point an abbreviation like *pi p* or even *pp.* The NBA score, in any case, prints *pp,* although the critical report describes the source situation. See NBA I/15, p. 12, and NBA I/15, KB, p. 22.

22. The autograph score is SPK P 330. This dating for the transcription has been suggested by Hans-Joachim Schulze; see Schulze 1978a, p. 89.

23. The date is suggested in the foreword of the facsimile edition of the *Orgel-Büchlein,* p. 18.

24. See the facsimile edition of the autograph score.

25. The number could be raised to forty-seven by including *a tempo* and *a batutta* [sic]. *A tempo* is typically found in the continuo parts of recitative movements at the beginning of an arioso section—i.e., at the moment when the static recitative bass line is activated. It also occurs in accompanied recitatives in which the instrumental accompaniment develops motivic figures. The term appears for the first time during the Weimar Period (in Cantata Nos. 21 and 185) and clearly has the meaning "in strict (that is, measured) time." (Walther's definition for *a tempo*—"nach dem Tact" ["according to the measure"]—confirms this.) This of course implies conversely that the recitative was normally performed in a rather free, unmeasured rhythm in order to achieve a flexible, naturalistic declamation of the text. *A batutta,* which so far has been found only in the motivically accompanied recitative "Ja freilich will in uns das Fleisch und Blut" from the St. Matthew Passion, is synonymous with *a tempo.* Bach's use of the term *tempo,* incidentally, as revealed by the headings *Tempo di Borea* (BWV 1002/7), *Tempo di Minuetta* [sic] (BWV 829/5, BWV 173a/4), *Tempo di Gavotta* (BWV 830/6), and *al Tempo di Giga* (BWV 988/7: an autograph addition), signified just that: tempo, speed. Walther 1732, (p. 598) explains, under *Tempo di Gavotta,* "man eine mit gedachten Worten bezeichnete Pièce, ob sie gleich keines von ihnen würcklich ist, dennoch noch dem *mouvement* derselben zu *execut*iren habe" ("one executes a piece so designated, even if it is not really one of them [i.e., such a dance], nonetheless according to the *Mouvement* of the same"). And under *Mouvement* (p. 426) we read: "die Beschaffenheit des Tacts, ob er nemlich langsam oder geschwinde sey" ("the character of the measure, i.e., whether it is slow or fast").

26. The first appearance of both *Aria* and *Recit* in the Bach sources is in the autograph score (P 42) of the "Hunting" Cantata *Was mir behagt,* BWV 208, composed February 1713—that is, if one disregards the "Aria di Postiglione" from the 1704 *Capriccio on the Absence of His Most Beloved Brother,* BWV 992.

27. The sources:

BWV	Manuscript Source	Date	Reference in NBA KB
1067	St 154 (copy)	ca. 1738	VII/1, p. 10
61	P 45 (autograph)	December 1714	I/1, p. 9
809	SPK P 1072 (copy)	ca. 1724/25	V/7, p. 20
995	Brussels, Bibl. Royale, Fétis MS II.4085 (autograph)	ca. 1727/31	V/10, p. 109
818a	SPK P 804 (copy)	ca. 1730–40	V/8, pp. 37, 47; V/7, pp. 25–26

28. Walther 1732, pp. 290, 361.

29. I am indebted for this observation to David M. Powers, a graduate student at the University of Chicago. The only exception so far is the aria "Wie freudig ist mein Herz" from Cantata No. 199. The *allegro* marking for this aria may have been called forth by the 12/8 meter in order to insure a more vigorous tempo than would perhaps otherwise by implied by the signature.

30. The inevitable exceptions are the C-major Sonata *à 2 Clav. et Pedal*, BWV 529; the G Major Sonata for Violin and Obbligato Harpsichord, BWV 1019; the Fourth Brandenburg Concerto, BWV 1049; and the B-minor Praeludium (*WTC II*), BWV 893.

[30a. *Bach-Dokumente III*, No. 666 (p. 87); BR, p. 222.]

31. Walther 1732, pp. 9, 355, 35, 27, 630, 496. Walther's reference to the evenness of execution under *andante* is quite pertinent for Bach, who often prescribes the term in passages characterized by unbroken "walking" motion in one or more parts, usually the bass (for example, the B-minor Prelude, BWV 869 (*WTC I*), or the Sinfonia of the C-minor Partita, BWV 826, at m. 8), most typically at arioso passages in recitatives where the continuo breaks into regular eighth-note motion (e.g., the fourth and sixth movements of Cantata No. 63).

[31a. See Plate 6, p. 86 of this volume.]

32. See the facsimile editions of the autograph score and the original parts.

33. See the facsimile edition.

34. For the datings see NBA VI/3, KB, p. 48 (for BWV 1039) and Eppstein 1966, p. 22 (for BWV 1027).

35. Mattheson 1739, p. 89; English translation in Harriss 1981, p. 219.

36. Walther's definition of *con discretione* appears on p. 211 of the *Lexicon* (Walther 1732). On p. 408 he describes *moderato* thus: "mit Bescheidenheit, d.i. nicht zu geschwinde auch nicht gar zu langsam" ("with discretion, i.e., not too quick but also not at all too slow").

37. For example BWV 527/2 (*Adagio è dolce*), BWV 1030/2 and 1032/2 (*Largo e*

dolce). The heading of the first movement of BWV 1015, however, reads simply *dolce.*

38. For example BWV 1019/3 (*Cantabile ma un poco Adagio*) and BWV 769/3 (*cantabile* alone).

39. See the facsimile of the libretto in W. Neumann 1974, p. 385.

40. BWV 1024 is not included in NBA VI/1, although the reasons for its elimination are not stated in the critical report.

41. Whereas the heading of the movement in the autograph score and in the solo parts reads *Affettuoso,* the indication in the *tacet* but likewise autograph ripieno parts for this movement reads *Adagio tacet. Affettuoso,* then, appears in the Bach sources rather like *dolce,* i.e., in association with both *adagio* and *larghetto.*

42. See for example BWV 596/2 (*Pleno Grave*), BWV 182/1 and BWV 826/1 (*Grave Adagio*), and BWV 1003/1 (*Grave* alone).

16. ORGAN OR "KLAVIER"?

1. Apel 1972, p. 3. See also Caldwell 1980, p. 11

2. See *Bach-Dokumente III,* No. 666 (p. 86); also BR, p. 221.

3. BR, p. 345.

4. See Heinz Lohmann's edition of Bach's organ works.

5. The following is the complete list of "appropriated" works in Lohmann's edition, in order of their appearance: vol. 2: BWV 900, 947, 894; vol. 3: BWV 910–916, 904, 944, 918–19, 961, 992, 993, 963, 820, 833, 989; vol. 4: BWV 899, 901, 902, 895, 943, 946, 952, 953, 948, 945, 956, 962, 949, 950, 947, 958, 951, 1079/1, 1079/5, 950a, 951a; vol. 5: BWV 984, 974, 978, 592a, 973, 985, 986, 917.

6. Bach reserves the French term, reasonably enough, for compositions in French style—overtures and suites.

7. It would be most interesting, but beyond the scope of this paper, to know whether they are mentioned explicitly in any practical sources of keyboard music of the late seventeenth or early eighteenth century.

8. See *Bach-Dokumente II,* No. 628 (p. 504); and BR, p. 197.

9. As in Dürr 1978, p. 76.

10. BR, p. 193; *Bach-Dokumente II,* No. 627 (p. 492).

11. Adlung 1768, vol. 2, pp. 158–62.

12. See Ripin 1980a and Ripin 1980b.

13. See BR, p. 311.

14. *Bach-Dokumente III,* No. 666 (p. 86); and BR, p. 221; see also Williams 1980, vol. 1, 8–9.

15. See NBA IV/5–6, KB, p. 131.

16. See Stauffer 1980, p. 2.

17. See the description of the *Möllersche Handschrift* in NBA IV/5–6, KB, pp. 100–103.

18. See BR, p. 193.

19. *Ibid.,* p. 311.

20. *Ibid.,* p. 311n.

21. Ripin 1980b.

[21a. Kerala J. Snyder makes the same point with regard to Buxtehude's *manualiter* compositions. She refers, in addition, to a toccata by Scheidemann and a chorale setting by Tunder that are explicitly marked *manualiter* and also contain *Rückpositiv* and *Oberwerck* indications. See Snyder 1987, p. 228.]

22. See May 1974.

23. The only other use of the *manualiter* indication that I have discovered so far is in the heading of the Fugue in A on a Theme of Albinoni, BWV 950. The heading in SPK P 595, copied by Johannes Ringk, reads "Fuga. ex A. Dur. Manualiter." [In this connection it is worth noting that a *Toccata manualiter* in G by Buxtehude, BuxWV 164, survives in a manuscript penned by one of Bach's Weimar copyists. (See Kobayashi 1978, p. 59, where this fact is interpreted as evidence that the work was part of Bach's performing repertoire in Weimar.)]

24. Summarized in NBA IV/5–6, KB, pp. 183–86.

[24a. See Stinson 1985b, p. 40.]

25. Dürr 1978, p. 79.

26. *Ibid.,* especially pp. 79–82.

27. See Schulze 1984, pp. 45–50.

28. See Keller 1950, p. 66; also Schulze 1984, p. 47.

29. Keller 1950, pp. 66–67.

[29a. The work's chromaticism does not argue against its having been written for the organ. Harald Vogel mentions that "the move away from mean-tone . . . temperament to the well-tempered system" was more advanced in Central Germany than in North Germany" (see Vogel 1986, p. 38.) But many of Buxtehude's harmonically most adventurous compositions, too—most notably the *Praeludium* in F♯ minor, BuxWV 146—clearly exceed the mean-tone system. Snyder suggests that they were composed soon after a major retuning of the organs of the Marienkirche in Lübeck in 1683, a tuning she argues was probably in accordance with Andreas Werckmeister's so-called "first correct temperament," described in his *Orgel-Probe* of 1681. Could J. S. Bach's chromatic Toccata in F♯ minor have been composed in conscious emulation of Buxtehude's harmonically extravagant *Praeludium* in the same key? The notion is particularly attractive since Buxtehude's composition is transmitted by a member of the Bach circle. (See Snyder 1987, pp. 84–85, 254–55, 317–18.)]

30. See Schulze 1984, especially p. 163.

31. Thus the title page in the Kellner manuscript, P 286. There are similar headings in other sources. See Stauffer 1980, p. 227.

32. See *ibid.,* pp. 228–29.

33. See NBA IV/5–6, KB, p. 404.

34. See Zietz 1969, p. 213.

35. See NBA I/35, KB, pp. 39–43.

36. Stauffer 1980, p. 108.

37. See Williams 1980, vol. 1, p. 127; and especially Oppel 1906.

38. See NBA IV/5–6, KB, p. 128.

[38a. The frequent presence of sustained bass notes—i.e., "pedal points"— in a number of *manualiter* compositions suggests that the term, strictly speaking, indicates only the absence of an *obbligato* pedal part. Pedal points, as well as the lowest notes of unusually wide-spaced chords in the "left-hand" part, (cf. BWV 911, m. 22) could clearly be taken on a pedal board, if one were present.]

39. The Concerto in E Flat, BWV 597, is now considered spurious. See Keller 1937, p. 66.

40. See Krause 1964, p. 10.

41. See NBA IV/5–6, KB, p. 199.

[42. Hans-Joachim Schulze has shown that while the title page is in the hand of Bach's godson, Johann Ernst Bach (1722–77), the manuscript itself was copied—probably between ca.1715 and ca.1730—by Johann Ernst's father (and J. S. Bach's cousin), Johann Bernhard Bach (1676–1749). See Schulze 1978b, pp. 20–22.]

43. The headings here, like those for BWV 972–82 in P 280, indicate at most the tonality of the concerto along with an attribution to J. S. Bach. See NBA V/5, KB, pp. 30–33.

44. See Lohmann's edition of Bach's organ works, vol. 5, Preface.

45. See NBA IV/5–6, KB, p. 62.

46. See Schulze 1984, pp. 154–63.

47. See the document, dated April 10, 1713, quoted in Schulze 1984, pp. 156–57.

48. See Max Seiffert's edition of Johann Gottfried Walther's organ works.

49. Dürr 1978, p. 80.

50. See *Bach-Dokumente II*, No. 434 (p. 335); also Williams 1980, vol. 1, pp. 321–22.

51. Part II is particularly modest in its range demands. See Dürr 1978, p. 83.

52. *Ibid.*, pp. 77–78.

53. See the critical notes in the *Wiener Urtext Edition*, edited by Walther Dehnhard, p. xi.

54. See Dürr 1978, pp. 80–83.

55. *Ibid.*, p. 83.

56. Published in vol. 3 of the Lohmann edition. The heading in P 804, in J. P. Kellner's hand, reads "Fantasia in A mol pro Cembalo." See NBA V/5, KB, p. 29.

57. See Keller 1950, pp. 67–68.

58. See the pertinent passages in BR, pp. 218 and 304.

Musical Editions and Facsimiles

BG. *Johann Sebastian Bach's Werke*. Complete edition of the Bach-Gesellschaft. 46 volumes. Leipzig: Breitkopf & Härtel, 1851-1900. Reprint edition. Ann Arbor. J. W. Edwards, 1947

NBA. *Johann Sebastian Bach. Neue Ausgabe sämtlicher Werke.* Edited by the Johann Sebastian-Bach-Institut, Göttingen, and the Bach-Archiv, Leipzig. Kassel: Bärenreiter and Leipzig: Deutscher Verlag für Musik, 1954–.

Albinoni, Tomaso. *Magnificat.* Edited by Felix Schröder. (Eulenburg No. 1074.) Zurich: Edition Eulenburg, 1968.

Bach, Johann Sebastian. *Aria mit 30 Veränderungen.* Edited by Ralph Kirkpatrick. New York: G. Schirmer, 1938.

———. *Brandenburgische Konzerte.* Facsimile edition of the autograph score with commentary by Peter Wackernagel. Leipzig: Edition Peters, [1960].

———. *Brandenburgisches Konzert Nr. 5, D-Dur.* BWV 1050. Facsimile edition of the Original Parts, edited by Hans-Joachim Schulze. Leipzig: Edition Peters, 1975.

———. *Brief an den Jugendfreund Georg Erdmann vom 28. Oktober 1730.* Facsimile edition, edited and with a commentary by Nathan Notowicz. (*Faksimile-Reihe Bachscher Werke und Schriftstücke,* 3.) Leipzig: Deutscher Verlag für Musik, n.d.

———. *Clavierbüchlein vor Wilhelm Friedemann Bach.* Facsimile edition, edited and with a preface by Ralph Kirkpatrick. New Haven: Yale University Press, 1959.

———. *Clavier-Übung.* Facsimile edition of the Original Edition with a commentary by Christoph Wolff. 4 volumes. (*Musikwissenschaftliche Studienbibliothek Peters.*) Leipzig: Edition Peters, 1984.

———. *Der Geist hilft unser' Schwachheit auf.* BWV 226. Facsimile edition with a commentary by Konrad Ameln. Kassel: Bärenreiter, 1964.

———. *Fantasia per il cembalo.* BWV 906. Facsimile edition with an introduction by Robert L. Marshall. Leipzig: Neue Bachgesellschaft, 1976.

———. *Fantasie und Fuge C-moll für Cembalo.* BWV 906. Facsimile edition of the Autograph in the Sächsische Landesbibliothek, Dresden, with a commentary by Hans-Joachim Schulze. Leipzig: Zentralantiquariat der Deutschen Demokratischen Republik, 1984.

———. *Fantasien, Präludien und Fugen.* Edited by Georg von Dadelsen and Klaus Rönnau. Munich: G. Henle, 1969–70.

———. *Gott ist mein König.* BWV 71. Mühlhäuser Ratswechselkantate 1708. Facsimile edition of the autograph score and of the original printed libretto with a preface by Werner Neumann. (*Faksimile-Reihe Bachscher Werke und Schriftstücke,* 9.) Leipzig: Deutscher Verlag für Musik, 1970.

———. *Herr, gehe nicht ins Gericht.* BWV 105. Facsimile edition of the autograph score, edited by Robert L. Marshall. Leipzig: Zentralantiquariat der Deutschen Demokratischen Republik and Neuhausen-Stuttgart: Hänssler, 1983.

———. *Herr, gehe nicht ins Gericht.* BWV 105. With a foreword by Arnold Schering. (Eulenburg No. 1040.) Zurich: Edition Eulenburg, 1936.

———. *Herr, gehe nicht ins Gericht.* BWV 105. Full score and vocal score edited by Adolf Bernhard Marx. Bonn: Simrock, 1830.

———. *Herr, gehe nicht ins Gericht.* BWV 105. Vocal score arranged by Günther Raphael. (Breitkopf edition, No. 6372.) Leipzig: Breitkopf & Härtel, 1931.

———. *Hochzeitsquodlibet 1707: ein Fragment.* BWV 524. Facsimile edition, edited and with a preface by Werner Neumann. (*Faksimile-Reihe-Bachscher Werke und Schriftstücke,* 12.) Leipzig: Deutscher Verlag für Musik, 1973.

———. *Konzert c-Moll für zwei Cembali und Streichorchester, BWV 1062. Sonate A-Dur für Flöte und Cembalo, BWV 1032.* Facsimile, edited by Hans-Joachim Schulze. (*Faksimile-Reihe Bachscher Werke und Schriftstücke,* 15.) Leipzig: Deutscher Verlag für Musik, 1979.

———. *Kurtzer, iedoch höchstnöthiger Entwurff einer wohlbestallten Kirchen Music; nebst einigen unvorgreiflichen Bedencken von dem Verfall derselben. Leipzig, den 23. August 1730.* Facsimile edition, edited and with a preface by Werner Neumann. (*Faksimile-Reihe Bachscher Werke und Schriftstücke,* 1.) Leipzig: Deutscher Verlag für Musik, n.d.

———. *Magnificat.* BWV 243. Facsimile edition of the autograph score, edited by Hans-Joachim Schulze. (*Faksimile-Reihe Bachscher Werke und Schriftstücke,* 21.) Leipzig: Deutscher Verlag für Musik, 1985.

———. *Magnificat.* BWV 243. D-major version. Edited and with a foreword by Hans-Joachim Schulze. (Peters No. 9850.) Leipzig: Edition Peters, 1979.

———. *Messe in H-moll.* BWV 232. Facsimile reproduction of the autograph with a commentary, edited by Alfred Dürr. Kassel: Bärenreiter, 1965.

———. *Messe in H-moll.* BWV 232. Facsimile edition of the Original Set of Parts in the Sächsische Landesbibliothek, Dresden, with a commentary by Hans-Joachim Schulze. Leipzig: Zentralantiquariat der Deutschen Demokratischen Republik, 1983.

———. *Orgelbüchlein.* Facsimile edition of the autograph score, edited and with a preface by Heinz-Harald Löhlein. (*Documenta musicologica. Zweite Reihe,* 11.) Leipzig, 1981.

———. *The Passion According to St. John.* BWV 245. Vocal Score, edited and with an Introduction by Arthur Mendel. New York: G. Schirmer, 1951.

———. *Sämtliche Orgelwerke.* Edited by Heinz Lohmann. 10 volumes. Wiesbaden: Breitkopf & Härtel, 1968–79.

———. *6 Sonaten für Violine und Cembalo.* Edited by Bernhard Stockmann and Hans-Christian Müller. (Wiener Urtext Edition.) 2 volumes. Vienna: Schott/Universal Edition, 1973).

———. *Sonata a Cembalo obligato e Travers. solo.* BWV 1030. Edited with an After-word by Werner Neumann. (*Faksimile-Reihe Bachscher Werke und Schriftstücke,* 4) Leipzig: Deutscher Verlag für Musik, n.d.

———. *Tilge, Höchster, meine Sünden.* Edited by Diethard Hellmann. (*Die Kantate,* 151.) Stuttgart-Hohenheim: Hänssler, 1963.

———. *Weihnachts-Oratorium.* BWV 248. Facsimile reproduction of the autograph with a commentary, edited by Alfred Dürr. Kassel: Bärenreiter, 1960.

———. *Das Wohltemperierte Clavier I.* Edited by Walther Dehnhard. (Wiener Urtext Edition.) Vienna: Schott/Universal Edition, 1977.

———. *Das Wohltemperierte Clavier II.* Facsimile of the autograph manuscript in the British Library *Add. MS. 35021,* with an introduction by Don Franklin and Stephen Daw. (*British Library Music Facsimiles,* 1.) London: The British Library, 1980.

Pisendel, Johann. *Sonate für Violine allein ohne Bass.* Edited by Günter Hausswald. (Hortus Musicus, 91.) Kassel: Bärenreiter, 1952.

Scarlatti, Domenico. *Domenico Scarlatti: Complete Keyboard Works in Facsimile from the Manuscript and Printed Sources.* Edited by Ralph Kirkpatrick. 18 volumes. New York: Johnson Reprint, 1972.

Walther, Johann Gottfried. *Gesammelte Werke für Orgel.* Edited by Max Seiffert. (*Denkmäler deutscher Tonkunst,* 26/27.) Leipzig: Breitkopf & Härtel, 1906.

Literature

Adlung, Jakob. *Musica mechanica Organoedi.* 2 volumes. Berlin, 1768. Facsimile reprint, edited by Christhard Mahrenholz. (*Documenta Musicologica. Erste Reihe,* 18.) Kassel: Bärenreiter, 1961.

Albrecht, Otto E. "Adventures and Discoveries of a Manuscript Hunter." *The Musical Quarterly* 31(1945): 492–503.

Apel, Willi. *The History of Keyboard Music to 1700.* Translated and revised by Hans Tischler. Bloomington: Indiana University Press, 1972.

Bach-Dokumente I: Schriftstücke von der Hand Johann Sebastian Bachs. Edited by Werner Neumann and Hans-Joachim Schulze. Kassel: Bärenreiter, 1963.

Bach-Dokumente II: Fremdschriftliche und gedruckte Dokumente zur Lebensgeschichte Johann Sebastian Bachs 1685–1750. Edited by Werner Neumann and Hans-Joachim Schulze. Kassel: Bärenreiter, 1969.

Bach-Dokumente III: Dokumente zum Nachwirken Johann Sebastian Bachs. Edited by Hans-Joachim Schulze. Kassel: Bärenreiter, 1972.

Barth, Karl. *Wolfgang Amadeus Mozart.* Zurich: Theologischer Verlag, 1956.

Becker, Heinz. "Friedrich II." In *Die Musik in Geschichte und Gegenwart,* IV, cols. 955–62. Kassel: Bärenreiter, 1955.

Besseler, Heinrich. "Bach als Wegbereiter." *Archiv für Musikwissenschaft* 12(1955a): 1–39.

———. "Zur Chronologie der Konzerte Joh. Seb. Bachs." In *Festschrift Max Schneider zum achtzigsten Geburtstage,* edited by Walther Vetter, 115–28. Leipzig: Deutscher Verlag für Musik, 1955b.

Blankenburg, Walter, ed. *Johann Sebastian Bach.* (*Wege der Forschung,* 170.) Darmstadt: Wissenschaftliche Buchgesellschaft, 1970.

Blume, Friedrich. "Bach, Johann Sebastian." In *Die Musik in Geschichte und Gegenwart*, I, cols. 962–1047. Kassel: Bärenreiter, 1949–51.

———. *Classic and Romantic Music.* New York: Norton, 1970.

Bodky, Erwin. *The Interpretation of Bach's Keyboard Works.* Cambridge: Harvard University Press, 1960.

Bonanni, Filippo. *Gabinetto Armonico.* Rome, 1723. Published under the title, *Antique Musical Instruments and Their Players.* Introduction and captions by Frank L1. Harrison and Joan Rimmer. New York: Dover, 1964.

Boyd, Malcolm. *Domenico Scarlatti: Master of Music.* New York: Schirmer Books, 1987.

Brainard, Paul. "Bach's Parody Procedure and the Saint Matthew Passion." *Journal of the American Musicological Society* 22(1969): 241–60.

Breckoff, Werner. "Zur Entstehungsgeschichte des zweiten Wohltemperierten Klaviers von Johann Sebastian Bach." Ph.D. dissertation, University of Tübingen, 1965.

Breig, Werner. "Bach's Violinkonzert d-Moll. Studien zu seiner Gestalt und seiner Entstehungsgeschichte." *Bach-Jahrbuch 1976:* 7–34.

Brokaw, James A. "Recent Research on the Sources and Genesis of Bach's *Well-Tempered Clavier*, Book II." *Bach* 16(1985): 17–35.

Bukofzer, Manfred. *Music in the Baroque Era.* New York: Norton, 1947.

Caldwell, John. "Keyboard Music." In *The New Grove Dictionary of Music and Musicians*, X, 11. London: Macmillan, 1980.

Calvocoressi, Dimitri. "Friedrich Rust, His Editors and his Critics." *The Musical Times* 55(1914): 14–16.

Cammarota, Robert M. "The Sources of the Christmas Interpolations in J. S. Bach's Magnificat in E-flat Major (BWV 243a)." *Current Musicology* 36(1983): 79–99.

Cannon, Beekman Cox. *Johann Mattheson: Spectator in Music.* New Haven: Yale University Press, 1947.

Casals, Pablo and Albert E. Kahn. *Joys and Sorrows, Reflections by Pablo Casals as Told to Albert Kahn.* New York: Simon and Schuster, 1970.

Castellani, Marcello. "Il 'Solo pour la flûte traversière' di J. S. Bach: Cöthen o Lipsia?" *Il flauto dolce* 13 (1985): 15–21.

Chafe, Eric. "J. S. Bach's *St. Matthew Passion:* Aspects of Planning, Structure and Chronology." *Journal of the American Musicological Society* 36(1982): 49–114.

Cone, Edward T. "Bach's Unfinished Fugue in C Minor." In *Studies in Renaissance and Baroque Music in Honor of Arthur Mendel*, edited by Robert L. Marshall, 149–55. Kassel: Bärenreiter and Hackensack: Joseph Boonin, 1974.

Congress, International Musicological Society. "Bach Problems." In *International Musicological Society: Report of the Eighth Congress New York 1961*, edited by Jan LaRue. *Volume 2—Reports*, 127–31. Kassel: Bärenreiter, 1962.

———. "Der gegenwärtige Stand der Mozartforschung." In *Internationale Gesellschaft für Musikwissenschaft: Bericht über den neunten internationalen Kongress Salzburg 1964*, edited by Franz Giegling. *Band II: Protokolle von den Symposia und Round Tables*, 88–97. Kassel: Bärenreiter, 1966.

Cox, Howard H., ed. *The Calov Bible of J. S. Bach.* Ann Arbor: UMI Research Press, 1985.

Crist, Stephen A. "Aria Forms in the Vocal Works of J. S. Bach, 1714–24." Ph.D. dissertation, Brandeis University, 1988.

von Dadelsen, Georg. *Bemerkungen zur Handschrift Johann Sebastian Bachs, seiner Familie und seines Kreises.* (*Tübinger Bach-Studien,* 1.) Trossingen: Hohner, 1957.

————. *Beiträge zur Chronologie der Werke Johann Sebastian Bachs.* (*Tübinger Bach-Studien,* 4/5.) Trossingen: Hohner, 1958.

————. "Friedrich Smends Ausgabe der h-Moll Messe von J. S. Bach." *Die Musikforschung* 12(1959): 315–34.

————. "Zur Entstehung des Bachschen Orgelbüchleins." In *Festschrift Friedrich Blume zum 70. Geburtstag,* edited by Anna Amalie Abert and Wilhelm Pfannkuch, 74–79. Kassel: Bärenreiter, 1963a.

————. "Wilhelm Rust." *Die Musik in Geschichte und Gegenwart,* XI, col. 1193–94. Kassel: Bärenreiter, 1963b.

————. "Die Crux der Nebensache: Editorische und praktische Bemerkungen zu Bachs Artikulation." *Bach-Jahrbuch 1978:* 95–112.

David, Hans T. *J. S. Bach's "Musical Offering:" History, Interpretation, and Analysis.* New York: G. Schirmer, 1945.

David, Hans T. and Arthur Mendel. *The Bach Reader: A Life of Johann Sebastian Bach in Letters and Documents.* Revised edition. New York: Norton, 1966.

Deutsch, Otto Erich. *Handel, A Documentary Biography.* New York: Norton, 1955.

Downes, Edward O. D. "The Operas of Johann Christian Bach as a Reflection of the Dominant Trends in *opera seria,* 1750–1780." Ph.D. dissertation, Harvard University, 1958.

————. "The Neapolitan Tradition in Opera." In *International Musicological Society: Report of the Eighth Congress New York 1961,* edited by Jan LaRue. I, 277–84. Kassel: Bärenreiter, 1961.

Dreyfus, Laurence. "Early Music Defended Against its Devotees: A Theory of Historical Performance in the Twentieth Century." *The Musical Quarterly* 59(1983): 297–322.

————. *Bach's Basso Continuo Group: Studies in the Performance of His Vocal Works.* Cambridge: Harvard University Press, 1987.

Drüner, Ulrich. "Violoncello piccolo und Viola pomposa bei Johann Sebastian Bach: Zu Fragen von Identität und Spielweise dieser Instrumente." *Bach-Jahrbuch 1987:* 85–112.

Dürr, Alfred. *Studien über die frühen Kantaten J. S. Bachs.* (*Bach-Studien,* 4.) Leipzig: Breitkopf & Härtel, 1951.

————. "Zur Chronologie der Leipziger Vokalwerke J. S. Bachs." *Bach-Jahrbuch 1957:* 5–162. Second revised edition: *Musikwissenschaftliche Arbeiten,* 26. Kessel: Bärenreiter, 1976.

————. "'Ich bin ein Pilgrim auf der Welt,' eine verschollene Kantate J. S. Bachs." *Die Musikforschung* 11(1958): 422–27.

————. "Penzel, Christian Friedrich." In *Die Musik in Geschichte und Gegenwart,* X, cols. 1021–22. Kassel: Bärenreiter, 1962.

————. "Neues über Bachs Pergolesi-Bearbeitung." *Bach-Jahrbuch 1968:* (1968a) 89–100.

————. Review of *Studien über J. S. Bachs Sonaten für ein Melodieinstrument und obligates Cembalo,* by Hans Eppstein. *Die Musikforschung* 21(1968b): 332–40.

————. "Zur Chronologie der Handschrift Johann Christoph Altnickols und Johann Friedrich Agricolas." *Bach-Jahrbuch 1970:* 44–65.

————. *Die Kantaten von Johann Sebastian Bach.* 2 volumes. Kassel: Bärenreiter, 1971.

————, ed. *Bach, Sonate C-dur für Flöte und Basso Continuo BWV 1033, Sonate Es-dur, g-moll für Flöte und obligates Cembalo BWV 1031, 1020 überliefert als Werke Johann Sebastian Bachs.* Kassel: Bärenreiter, 1975.

————. *Studien über die frühen Kantaten Johann Sebastian Bachs.* 2nd edition. Wiesbaden: Breitkopf & Härtel, 1977.

————. "Tastenumfang und Chronologie in Bachs Klavierwerken." In *Festschrift Georg von Dadelsen zum 60. Geburtstag,* edited by Thomas Kohlhase and Volker Scherliess, 73–88. Neuhausen-Stuttgart: Hänssler, 1978.

Eggebrecht, Hans-Heinrich. "Walthers Musikalisches Lexikon in seinen terminologischen Partien." *Acta Musicologica* 29(1957): 10–27.

Eller, Rudolph. "Vivaldi–Dresden–Bach." *Beiträge zur Musikwissenschaft* 3(1961): 31–48. Reprinted in *Johann Sebastian Bach,* edited by Walter Blankenburg, 466–92. (*Wege der Forschung,* 170.) Darmstadt: Wissenschaftliche Buchgesellschaft, 1970.

Emery, Walter. "The Compass of Bach's Organs as Evidence of the Date of His Works." *The Organ* 32(October 1952): 92–100.

————. "Goldberg: Information Wanted." *The Musical Times* 104(1963a): 788–89.

————. "The Goldberg Engraver." *The Musical Times* 104(1963b): 875

————. "Some Speculations on the Development of Bach's Organ Style." *The Musical Times* 107(1966): 596–603.

————. "Bach, Johann Sebastian." In *Encyclopaedia Britannica,* 14th edition, II, 962–89. Chicago: Encyclopaedia Britannica, 1970.

———— and Robert L. Marshall. "Bach, Johann Sebastian." In *Encyclopaedia Britannica,* 15th edition, II, 556–61. Chicago: Encyclopaedia Britannica, 1974.

Eppstein, Hans. "Zur Problematik von J. S. Bachs Sonate für Violine und Cembalo G-Dur (BWV 1019)." *Archiv für Musikwissenschaft* 21(1964): 217–42.

————. *Studien über J. S. Bachs Sonaten für ein Melodieinstrument und obligates Cembalo.* (*Acta universitatis Upsaliensis. Studia musicologica Upsaliensia. Nova series,* 2.) Uppsala: [University of Uppsala], 1966.

————. "Grundzüge in J. S. Bachs Sonatenschaffen." *Bach-Jahrbuch 1969*: 5–30.

————. "Über J. S. Bachs Flötensonaten mit Generalbass." *Bach-Jahrbuch 1972*: 12–23.

————. "Chronologieprobleme in Johann Sebastian Bachs Suiten für Soloinstrument." *Bach-Jahrbuch 1976*: 35–57.

————. "Zur Problematik von Johann Sebastian Bachs Flötensonaten." *Bach-Jahrbuch 1981*: 77–90.

Feldmann, Fritz. "Chr. Gottlob Wecker, ein Schüler Bachs als schlesischer Kantor." *Bach-Jahrbuch 1934*: 89–100.

Flade, Ernst. *Gottfried Silbermann.* Leipzig: Breitkopf & Härtel, 1953.

Forkel, Johann Nikolaus. *Über Johann Sebastian Bachs Leben, Kunst und Kunstwerke.* Leipzig, 1802. Facsimile reprint. Frankfurt am Main: H. L. Grahl, 1950.

Fürstenau, Moritz. *Zur Geschichte der Musik und des Theaters am Hofe zu Dresden.* 2 volumes. Dresden, 1861. Facsimile reprint. Leipzig: Edition Peters, 1971.

————. "Ein bisher noch unbekanntes Autograph von Joh. Seb. Bach." *Monatshefte für Musikgeschichte* 8(1876): 110–11.

Geck, Martin. "J. S. Bachs Weihnachts-Magnificat und sein Traditionszusammenhang." *Musik und Kirche* 31(1961): 257–66.

————. "Gattungstraditionen und Altersschichten in den Brandenburgischen Konzerten." *Die Musikforschung* 23(1970): 139–52.

Geiringer, Karl. *Johann Sebastian Bach: The Culmination of an Era*. New York: Oxford University Press, 1966.

Gerber, Rudolf. *Der Operntypus Johann Adolf Hasses und seine textlichen Grundlagen*. Leipzig: Kistner & Siegel, 1925.

Gilmore, Clifford F. Review of the first two volumes of Johann Sebastian Bach, *The Complete Cantatas*. (Telefunken SKW 1, 2). *High Fidelity*, 22/3 (March 1972): 73–74.

Härtwig, Dieter. "Buffardin, Pierre Gabriel." In *Die Musik in Geschichte und Gegenwart*, XV, cols. 1183–84. Kassel: Bärenreiter, 1973.

Harriss, Ernest Charles. *Johann Mattheson's 'Der vollkommene Capellmeister:' A Revised Translation with Critical Commentary*. Ann Arbor: UMI Research Press, 1981.

Haynes, Bruce. "Johann Sebastian Bach's Pitch Standards: The Woodwind Perspective." *Journal of the American Musical Instrument Society* 11(1985): 55–114.

Heinichen, Johann David. *Der General-Bass in der Composition*. Dresden, 1728. Facsimile reprint. Hildesheim: Georg Olms, 1969.

Heller, Karl. *Die deutsche Überlieferung der Instrumentalwerke Vivaldis*. (*Beiträge zur musikwissenschaftlichen Forschung in der DDR*, 2.) Leipzig: Deutscher Verlag für Musik, 1971.

Herz, Gerhard. "BWV 131: Bach's First Cantata." In *Studies in Eighteenth-Century Music: A Tribute to Karl Geiringer on his Seventieth Birthday*, edited by H. C. Robbins Landon and Roger E. Chapman, 272–91. London: Allen and Unwin, 1970.

———. "Toward a New Image of Bach (Part II)." *Bach: The Quarterly Journal of the Riemenschneider Bach Institute* 2(1971): 7–28.

———, ed. *Bach Cantata No. 140*. (*Norton Critical Scores*.) New York: Norton, 1972.

———. "Der lombardische Rhythmus im 'Domine Deus' der h-moll-Messe J. S. Bachs." *Bach-Jahrbuch 1974*: 90–97.

———. *Bach-Quellen in Amerika / Bach Sources in America*. (Neue Bach-Gesellschaft, Internationale Vereinigung Sitz Leipzig.) Kassel: Bärenreiter, 1984.

Hlawiczka, Karol. "Zur Polonaise g-moll (BWV Anh. 119) aus dem 2. Notenbüchlein für Anna Magdalena Bach." *Bach-Jahrbuch 1961*: 58–60.

———. "Die Herkunft der Polonaise-Melodie aus der Ouvertüre h-moll (BWV 1067)." *Bach-Jahrbuch 1966*: 99–101.

Hoffman-Erbrecht, Lothar. "Johann Sebastian und Carl Philipp Emanuel Bachs Nürnberger Verleger." In *Die Nürnberger Musikverleger und die Familie Bach: Materialien zu einer Ausstellung des 48. Bach-Fests der Neuen Bach-Gesellschaft*, 5–10. Nuremberg: Neue Bachgesellschaft, 1973.

Högg, Margarete. *Die Gesangskunst der Faustina Hasse und das Sängerinnenwesen ihrer Zeit in Deutschland*. Königsbrück, 1931.

Holton, Gerald. Review of *Einstein. The Life and Times*, by Ronald W. Clark. *The New York Times Book Review*, 5 September 1971.

Jung, Hans Rudolf. "Pisendel, Johann Georg." In *Die Musik in Geschichte und Gegenwart*, X, cols. 1300–02. Kassel: Bärenreiter, 1962.

Kalendarium zur Lebensgeschichte Johann Sebastian Bachs. Edited by the Bach-Archiv Leipzig. Leipzig: Bach-Archiv, 1970.

Kast, Paul. *Die Bach-Handschriften der Berliner Staatsbibliothek*. (*Tübinger Bach-Studien*, 2/3.) Trossingen: Hohner, 1958.

Keller, Hermann. "Unechte Orgelwerke Bachs." *Bach-Jahrbuch 1937*: 59–82.

––––––. *Die Klavierwerke Bachs*. Leipzig: Edition Peters, 1950.

––––––. *Das Wohltemperierte Klavier von Johann Sebastian Bach: Werk und Wiedergabe*. Kassel: Bärenreiter, 1965.

Kerman, Joseph. *Contemplating Music: Challenges to Musicology*. Cambridge: Harvard University Press, 1985.

Kilian, Dietrich. "Studie über Bachs Fantasie und Fuge c-moll." In *Hans Albrecht in Memoriam: Gedenkschrift mit Beiträgen von Freunden und Schülern*, edited by Wilfried Brennecke and Hans Hasse, 127–35. Kassel: Bärenreiter, 1962.

Kinsky, Georg. *Die Originalausgaben der Werke Johann Sebastian Bachs*. Vienna: Herbert Reichner, 1937.

Kirkpatrick, Ralph. *Domenico Scarlatti*. Princeton: Princeton University Press, 1953.

Kobayashi, Yoshitake. "Franz Hauser und seine Bachhandschriftensammlung." Ph.D. dissertation, University of Göttingen, 1973.

––––––. "Neuerkenntnisse zu einigen Bach-Quellen an Hand schriftkundlicher Unterschungen." *Bach-Jahrbuch 1978*: 43–60.

––––––. "Zur Chronologie der Spätwerke Johann Sebastian Bachs: Kompositions- und Afführungstätigkeit von 1736 bis 1750." *Bach-Jahrbuch 1988*: 7–72.

Kolneder, Walter. "Besetzung und Satzstil: Zu Johann Sebastian Bachs Violinkonzerten." In *Festschrift für Walter Wiora zum 30. Dezember 1966*, edited by Ludwig Finscher and Christoph-Hellmut Mahling, 329–34. Kassel: Bärenreiter, 1967.

König, Ernst. "Die Hofkapelle des Fürsten Leopold zu Anhalt-Köthen." *Bach-Jahrbuch 1959*: 160–67.

Krause, Peter. *Handschriften der Werke Johann Sebastian Bachs in der Musikbibliothek der Stadt Leipzig*. Leipzig: Musikbibliothek der Stadt Leipzig, 1964.

Kretzschmar, Hermann. "Die Bach-Gesellschaft. Bericht über ihre Thätigkeit." BG 46: xv–lxvi.

Lang, Paul Henry, ed. *The Creative World of Mozart*. New York: Norton, 1963.

––––––. "Editorial." *The Musical Quarterly* 58(1972): 117–27.

Lowinsky, Edward E. "On Mozart's Rhythm." *The Musical Quarterly* 42(1956): 162–86.

MacCracken, Thomas G. "Die Verwendung der Blechblasinstrumente bei J. S. Bach unter besonderer Berücksichtigung der Tromba da tirarsi." *Bach-Jahrbuch 1984*: 59–89.

Marissen, Michael. "A Trio in C major for recorder, violin and continuo by J. S. Bach?" *Early Music* 13(1985): 384–90.

––––––. "A Critical Reappraisal of J. S. Bach's A-major Flute Sonata." *The Journal of Musicology* 6(1988): 367–86.

Marshall, Robert L. Review of Johann Sebastian Bach, *Mass in B minor*, BWV 232: Facsimile reproduction of the autograph with a commentary, edited by Alfred Dürr. In *Notes* 23(1967): 828–30.

––––––. *The Compositional Process of J. S. Bach: A Study of the Autograph Scores of the Vocal Works*. (Princeton Studies in Music, 4.), 2 volumes. Princeton: Princeton University Press, 1972.

––––––. "Bach's Chorus: a Reply to Joshua Rifkin." *The Musical Times* 124(1983): 19–22.

––––––, ed. *Johann Sebastian Bach: Cantata Autographs in American Collections*. (Music in Facsimile, 2.) New York: Garland, 1985.

Matteson, Johann. *Das Neu-Eröffnete Orchestre*. Hamburg: Benjamin Schillers Wittwe, 1713.

———. *Der vollkommene Kapellmeister*. Hamburg, 1739. Facsimile reprint. Edited by Margarete Reimann. (Documenta musicologica. Erste Reihe, 5.) Kassel: Bärenreiter, 1954.

May, Ernest. "J. G. Walther and the Lost Weimar Autographs of Bach's Organ Works." In *Studies in Renaissance and Baroque Music in Honor of Arthur Mendel*, edited by Robert L. Marshall, 264–82. Kassel: Bärenreiter and Hackensack: Joseph Boonin, 1974.

McAll, May DeForest. *Melodic Index to the Works of Johann Sebastian Bach*. New York: C. F. Peters, 1962.

Mendel, Arthur. Review of various recordings of works by Heinrich Schütz and J. S. Bach. *The Musical Quarterly* 38(1952): 673–79.

———. "On the Pitches in Use in Bach's Time." *The Musical Quarterly* 41(1955): 332–54, 466–80.

———. "A Note on Proportional Relationships in Bach Tempi." *The Musical Times* 100(1959): 683–85.

———. "Recent Developments in Bach Chronology." *The Musical Quarterly* 46(1960a): 283–300.

———. "Bach Tempi: A Rebuttal." *The Musical Times* 101(1960b): 251.

———. "Evidence and Explanation." In *International Musicological Society: Report of the Eighth Congress New York 1961*, edited by Jan LaRue. *Volume 2—Reports*, 3–18. Kassel: Bärenreiter, 1961.

———. "Pitch in Western Music Since 1500: A Re-examination." *Acta Musicologica* 50(1978): 1–93.

Meyer, Ulrich. "Musikalisch-rhetorische Figuren in J. S. Bachs Magnificat." *Musik und Kirche* 43(1973): 172–81.

Miesner, Heinrich. "Philipp Emanuel Bachs musikalischer Nachlass." *Bach-Jahrbuch 1939*: 81–112.

Neufeldt, Ernst. "Der Fall Rust." *Die Musik* 12/6 (December 1912): 339–44.

Neumann, Frederick. "Misconceptions About the French Trill in the 17th and 18th Centuries." *The Musical Quarterly* 50(1964): 188–206.

———. "A New Look at Bach's Ornamentation." *Music and Letters* 46(1965a): 4–15, 126–33.

———. "La note pointée et la soi-distant 'manière française.'" *Revue de Musicologie* 51(1965b): 66–92.

———. "The French *Inégales*, Quantz, and Bach." *Journal of the American Musicological Society* 18(1965c): 313–58.

———. *Ornamentation in Baroque and Post-Baroque Music: With Special Emphasis on J. S. Bach*. Princeton: Princeton University Press, 1978.

———. *Essays in Performance Practice*. Ann Arbor: UMI Research Press, 1982.

———. "Bach: Progressive or Conservative and the Authorship of the Goldberg Aria." *The Musical Quarterly* 71(1985): 281–94.

Neumann, Werner. *J. S. Bachs Chorfuge: Ein Beitrag zur Kompositionstechnik Bachs*. (*Bach-Studien*, 3.) Leipzig: Breitkopf & Härtel, 1938. Reprint: 1953.

———, ed. *Johann Sebastian Bach. Sämtliche Kantatentexte*. Leipzig: Breitkopf & Härtel, 1956.

———. "Das 'Bachische Collegium musicum.'" *Bach-Jahrbuch 1960*: 1–27.

———. "Einige neue Quellen zu Bachs Herausgabe eigener und zum Mitvertrieb fremder Werke." In *Musa–Mens–Musici: Im Gedenken an Walther Vetter*, 165-68. Leipzig: Deutscher Verlag für Musik, 1969.

———, ed. *Sämtliche von Johann Sebastian Bach vertonte Texte*. Leipzig: Deutscher Verlag für Musik, 1974.

Newman, William S. *The Sonata in the Classic Era*. Chapel Hill, NC: University of North Carolina Press, 1963.

———. *The Sonata in the Baroque Era*. Chapel Hill, NC: University of North Carolina Press, 1966.

Niedt, Friedrich Erhardt. *Musicalische Handleitung zur Variation des Generalbasses*. 2nd edition. Hamburg, 1721. Facsimile reprint. (*Bibliotheca organologica*, 32.) Buren: Frits Knuf, 1976.

Noack, Elisabeth. "Georg Christian Lehms, ein Textdichter Johann Sebastian Bachs." *Bach-Jahrbuch 1970*: 7-18.

Oppel, Reinhard. "Die grosse A-moll-Fuge für Orgel und ihre Vorlage." *Bach-Jahrbuch 1906*: 74-78.

Platen, Emil. "Untersuchungen zur Struktur der chorischen Choralbearbeitung Johann Sebastian Bachs." Ph.D. dissertation, University of Bonn, 1959.

———. "Eine Pergolesi-Bearbeitung Bachs." *Bach-Jahrbuch 1961*: 35-51.

Plath, Wolfgang. "Der gegenwärtige Stand der Mozart-Forschung." In *Internationale Gesellschaft für Musikwissenschaft: Bericht über den neunten internationalen Kongress Salzburg 1964*, edited by Franz Giegling. I, 47-55. Kassel: Bärenreiter, 1964.

Pont, Graham. "A Revolution in the Science and Practice of Music." *Musicology* 5(1979): 1-66.

Prieger, Erich. "Rustiana." *Die Musik* 12/11 (March 1913): 269-77.

Quantz, Johann Joachim. "Herrn Johann Joachim Quantzens Lebenslauf, von ihm selbst entworfen." In Friedrich Wilhelm Marpurg, *Historisch-Kritische Beyträge zur Aufnahme der Musik I*: 197-250. Berlin, 1755. Reprint. Hildesheim: Georg Olms, 1970.

Quantz, Johann Joachim. *On Playing the Flute*. Translated by Edward R. Reilly. New York: Free Press, 1966.

Ratner, Leonard G. "Harmonic Aspects of Classical Form." *Journal of the American Musicological Society* 2(1949): 158-68.

———. "Eighteenth-Century Theories of Musical Period Structure." *The Musical Quarterly* 42(1956): 439-54.

Reich, Nancy B. "The Rudorff Collection." *Notes* 31(1974): 247-61.

Richter, Bernhard Friedrich. "Der Nekrolog auf Seb. Bach vom Jahre 1754. Neudruck." *Bach-Jahrbuch 1920*: 11-29.

Riemann, Hugo. "Spontane Phantasietätigkeit und verstandesmässige Arbeit in der tonkünstlerischen Produktion." *Jahrbuch der Musikbibliothek Peters für 1909*, 16(1910): 33-46.

Rifkin, Joshua. "The Chronology of Bach's Saint Matthew Passion." *The Musical Quarterly* 61(1975): 360-87.

———. "Bach's Chorus: A Preliminary Report." *The Musical Times* 123(1982a): 747-51.

———. "The B-minor Mass and its Performance." Liner notes for the recording, Nonesuch 79036. Los Angeles, 1982b.

———. "Bach's Chorus: A Response to Robert Marshall." *The Musical Times* 124(1983): 161-62.

Ripin, Edwin M. "Pedal Clavichord." In *The New Grove Dictionary of Music and Musicians,* X, 327. London: Macmillan, 1980a.

————. "Pedal Harpsichord." In *The New Grove Dictionary of Music and Musicians,* X, 327. London: Macmillan, 1980b.

Robison, John O. "The *messa di voce* as an Instrumental Ornament in the Seventeenth and Eighteenth Centuries." *The Music Review* 43(1982): 1–14.

Rose, Bernard. "Some Further Observations on the Performance of Purcell's Music." *The Musical Times* 100(1959): 385–86.

————. "A Further Note on Bach Tempi." *The Musical Times* 101(1960): 107–08.

Rose, Gloria. "Father and Son: Attributions to J. S. Bach by C. P. E. Bach." In *Studies in Eighteenth-Century Music: A Tribute to Karl Geiringer on his Seventieth Birthday,* edited by H. C. Robbins Landon and Roger E. Chapman, 364–69. London: Allen and Unwin, 1970.

Rosen, Charles. *The Classical Style.* New York: Norton, 1971.

Sachs, Curt. "Bachs 'Tromba da tirarsi.'" *Bach-Jahrbuch 1908:* 141–43.

Schenker, Heinrich. *Der freie Satz.* Edited by Oswald Jonas. Revised edition. Vienna: Universal Edition, 1956.

Schering, Arnold. *Die Musikgeschichte Leipzigs. Band II: Von 1650 bis 1723.* Leipzig: Kistner & Siegel, 1926.

————. *Johann Sebastian Bachs Leipziger Kirchenmusik: Studien und Wege zu ihrer Erkenntnis. (Veröffentlichungen der Neuen Bachgesellschaft Vereinsjahr 36,?.)* Leipzig: Breitkopf & Härtel, 1936.

————. *Johann Sebastian Bach und das Musikleben Leipzigs im 18. Jahrhundert. (Die Musikgeschichte Leipzigs, Band III: Von 1723 bis 1800.)* Leipzig: Kistner & Siegel, 1941.

Schmieder, Wolfgang. *Musikerhandschriften in drei Jahrhunderten.* Leipzig: Breitkopf & Härtel, 1939.

————. *Thematisch-systematisches Verzeichnis der musikalischen Werke von Johann Sebastian Bach. Bach-Werke-Verzeichnis (BWV).* Leipzig: Breitkopf & Härtel, 1950.

————. "Bemerkungen zur Bachquellenforschung." In *Bericht über die Wissenschaftliche Bachtagung der Gesellschaft für Musikforschung, Leipzig 23. bis 26. Juli 1950,* edited by Walther Vetter and Ernst Hermann Meyer, 219–30. Leipzig: C. F. Peters, 1951.

Schmitz, Arnold. *Die Bildlichkeit der wortgebundenen Musik Johann Sebastian Bachs. (Neue Studien zur Musikwissenschaft.)* Mainz: B. Schott's Söhne, 1950.

Schulze, Hans-Joachim. "Wer intavolierte Johann Sebastian Bachs Lautenkompositionen?" *Die Musikforschung* 19(1966): 32–39.

————. "Die Bachüberlieferung: Plädoyer für ein notwendiges Buch." *Beiträge zur Musikwissenschaft* 17(1975): 45–57.

————. "Johann Sebastian Bachs Konzertbearbeitungen nach Vivaldi und anderen—Studien- oder Auftragswerke?" *Deutsches Jahrbuch der Musikwissenschaft für 1973-1977,* 18(1978a): 80–100.

————. "'Das Stück in Goldpapier.' Ermittlungen zu einigen Bach-Abschriften des frühen 18. Jahrhunderts." *Bach-Jahrbuch 1978b:* 19–42.

————. "Ein 'Dresdner Menuett' im zweiten Klavierbüchlein der Anna Magdalena Bach. Nebst Hinweisen zur Überlieferung einiger Kammermusikwerke Bachs." *Bach-Jahrbuch 1979:* 45–64.

————. *Studien zur Bach-Überlieferung im 18. Jahrhundert.* Leipzig: Edition Peters, 1984.

————. "Zur Frage des Doppelaccompagnements (Orgel und Cembalo) in Kirchenmusikaufführungen der Bach-Zeit." *Bach-Jahrbuch 1987:* 173–74.

Schünemann, Georg. "Bachs Verbesserungen und Entwürfe." *Bach-Jahrbuch 1935:* 1–32.

————. *Musikerhandschriften von Bach bis Schumann.* Berlin: Atlantis, 1936.

Schweitzer, Albert. *J. S. Bach.* Translated by Ernest Newman. London: Breitkopf & Härtel, 1911.

Seiffert, Max. "Die Sperontes-Lieder: 'Ich bin nun wie ich bin'—'Ihr Schönen höret an' und Seb. Bach." In *Festschrift Fritz Stein zum 60. Geburtstag,* 66–70. Braunschweig: Litolff, 1939.

Siegele, Ulrich. "Die musiktheoretische Lehre einer Bachschen Gigue." *Archiv für Musikforschung* 17(1960): 152–67.

————. *Kompositionsweise und Bearbeitungstechnik in der Instrumentalmusik Johann Sebastian Bachs. (Tübinger Beiträge zur Musikwissenschaft,* 3). Neuhausen-Stuttgart: Hänssler, 1975.

Smend, Friedrich. *Joh. Seb. Bach. Kirchen-Kantaten.* Heft 1–6. Berlin: Christlicher Zeitschriftenverlag, 1950.

Snyder, Kerala J. *Dieterich Buxtehude: Organist in Lübeck.* New York: Schirmer Books, 1987.

Spitta, Philipp. *Johann Sebastian Bach.* 2 volumes. Leipzig: Breitkopf & Härtel, 1873–80.

————. "Beethoveniana." In *Zur Musik: Sechzehn Aufsätze,* 177–95. Berlin, 1892. Reprint. Hildesheim: Georg Olms, 1976.

Staehelin, Martin. "Orchester." In *Handwörterbuch der Musikalischen Terminologie.* Wiesbaden: Franz Steiner, 1981.

Stauffer, George B. *The Organ Preludes of Johann Sebastian Bach. (Studies in Musicology,* 27.) Ann Arbor: UMI Research Press, 1980.

————. "Über Bachs Orgelregistrierpraxis." *Bach-Jahrbuch 1981:* 91–105.

Stiller, Günther. *Johann Sebastian Bach und das Leipziger gottesdienstliche Leben seiner Zeit.* Kassel: Bärenreiter, 1970.

Stinson, Russell. "Bach's Earliest Autograph." *The Musical Quarterly* 71(1985a): 235–63.

————. "The Bach Manuscripts of Johann Peter Kellner and his Circle." Ph.D. dissertation, University of Chicago, 1985b.

Strunk, Oliver. *Source Readings in Music History.* New York: Norton, 1950.

Talbot, Michael. "Albinoni, Tomaso Giovanni." In *The New Grove Dictionary of Music and Musicians,* I, 216–20. London: Macmillan, 1980.

Taruskin, Richard et al. "The Limits of Authenticity: A Discussion." (Contributions by Richard Taruskin, Daniel Leech-Wilkinson, Nicholas Temperley, and Robert Winter), *Early Music* 12(1984): 3–25.

Terry, Charles Sanford. *Joh. Seb. Bach Cantata Texts Sacred and Secular.* London, 1925. Reprint edition. London: Holland Press, 1964.

————. *Bach: The Magnificat, Lutheran Masses and Motets.* London, 1929. Reprint edition. New York: Johnson Reprint, 1972.

————. *Bach's Orchestra.* London: Oxford University Press, 1932.

Tovey, Donald Francis. *Essays in Musical Analysis: Chamber Music.* London: Oxford University Press, 1944.

————. "Brahms Chamber Music." In *The Main Stream of Music and Other Essays*, 220-70. Cleveland: World Publishing, 1959.

Trautmann, Christoph. "Ex libris Bachianis: eine Kantate Johann Sebastian Bachs im Spiegel seiner Bibliothek." *Internationale Ausstellung zum 44. Deutschen Bachfest der Neuen Bachgesellschaft . . . Heidelberg 1969.* Zurich, 1969.

Tunger, Albrecht. "Johann Sebastian Bachs Einlagesätze zum Magnificat: Beobachtungen und Überlegungen zu ihrer Herkunft." In *Bachstunden: Festschrift für Helmut Walcha zum 70. Geburtstag,* edited by Walther Dehnhard and Gottlob Ritter, 22-35. Frankfurt: Evangelischer Presseverband, 1978.

Turnow, Hans. "Mattheson, Johann." In *Die Musik in Geschichte und Gegenwart*, VIII, cols. 1795-1815). Kassel: Bärenreiter, 1960.

Vogel, Harald. "North German Organ Building of the Late Seventeenth Century: Registration and Tuning." In *J. S. Bach as Organist: His Instruments, Music, and Performance Practices,* edited by George Stauffer and Ernest May, 31-40. Bloomington: Indiana University Press, 1986.

Wagner, Günther. "Die Chorbesetzung bei J. S. Bach und ihre Vorgeschichte: Anmerkungen zur 'hinlänglichen' Besetzung im 17. und 18. Jahrhundert." *Archiv für Musikwissenschaft* 43(1986): 278-304.

Walther, Johann Gottfried. *Musikalisches Lexikon.* Leipzig, 1732. Facsimile reprint, edited by Richart Schaal. (*Documenta musicologica. Erste Reihe, 3.*) Kassel: Bärenreiter, 1953.

Williams, Peter. *The Organ Music of Johann Sebastian Bach.* 3 volumes. New York: Cambridge University Press, 1980-84.

————. Review of Laurence Dreyfus, *Bach's Basso Continuo Group.* In *Journal of the American Musicological Society* 41 (1988): 349-55.

Wolff, Christoph. "Zur musikalischen Vorgeschichte des Kyrie aus Johann Sebastian Bachs Messe in H-moll." In *Festschrift Bruno Stäblein zum 70. Geburtstag,* edited by Martin Ruhnke, 316-26. Kassel: Bärenreiter, 1967.

————. *Der stile antico in der Musik Johann Sebastian Bachs: Studien zu Bachs Spätwerk.* (*Beihefte zum Archiv für Musikwissenschaft, 6.*) Wiesbaden: Franz Steiner, 1968.

————. "Ordnungsprinzipien in den Originaldrucken Bachscher Werke." In *Bach-Interpretationen,* edited by Martin Geck, 144-67. Göttingen: Vandenhoeck & Ruprecht, 1969.

————. "New Research on Bach's *Musical Offering*." *The Musical Quarterly* 57(1971): 379-408.

————. "Zur Chronologie und Kompositionsgeschichte von Bachs Kunst der Fuge." *Beiträge zur Musikwissenschaft* 25(1983): 130-43.

————. *Johann Sebastian Bachs Klavierübung: Kommentar zur Faksimile-Ausgabe.* Leipzig: Edition Peters, 1984.

————. "Bach's Leipzig Chamber Music." *Early Music* 13(1985): 165-75.

Wotquenne, Alfred. *Thematisches Verzeichnis der Werke von Carl Philipp Emanuel Bach.* Leipzig: Breitkopf & Härtel, 1905.

Zietz, Hermann. *Quellenkritische Untersuchungen an den Bach Handschriften P 801, 802, und 803.* (*Hamburger Beiträge zur Musikwissenschaft, 1.*) Hamburg: Karl Dieter Wagner, 1969.

Indexes

Index to Cited Works of Bach

NOTE: All page references beginning with p. 295 are to the endnotes

Principal Compositions and Collections

Individual Compositions (in BWV Order)

General Index

NOTE: All page references beginning with page 295 are to the endnotes. An * preceding a manuscript or BWV number signifies that the source is partially or entirely autograph.